Frameworks for Sustainable Development Goals to Manage Economic, Social, and Environmental Shocks and Disasters

Cristina Raluca Gh. Popescu
University of Bucharest, Romania & The Bucharest University of Economic Studies, Romania

IGI Global
PUBLISHER of TIMELY KNOWLEDGE

A volume in the Practice, Progress, and Proficiency in Sustainability (PPPS) Book Series

Published in the United States of America by
IGI Global
Engineering Science Reference (an imprint of IGI Global)
701 E. Chocolate Avenue
Hershey PA, USA 17033
Tel: 717-533-8845
Fax: 717-533-8661
E-mail: cust@igi-global.com
Web site: http://www.igi-global.com

Library of Congress Cataloging-in-Publication Data

Names: Popescu, Cristina Raluca Gh., 1983- editor.
Title: Frameworks for sustainable development goals to manage economic, social, and environmental shocks and disasters / Cristina Raluca Gh. Popescu, editor.
Description: Hershey, PA : Engineering Science Reference, [2023] | Includes bibliographical references and index. | Summary: "This book provides valuable insight of today's context concerning the creation of an international successful framework for Sustainable Development Goals (SDGs) that requires managing the economic, social and environmental shocks and disasters in the Post-COVID-19 Era"-- Provided by publisher.
Identifiers: LCCN 2022027236 (print) | LCCN 2022027237 (ebook) | ISBN 9781668467503 (hardcover) | ISBN 9781668467510 (paperback) | ISBN 9781668467527 (ebook)
Subjects: LCSH: Sustainable development--International cooperation. | Disasters--Economic aspects. | Crises--Economic aspects.
Classification: LCC HC79.E5 F6953 2022 (print) | LCC HC79.E5 (ebook) | DDC 338.9/27--dc23/eng/20220629
LC record available at https://lccn.loc.gov/2022027236
LC ebook record available at https://lccn.loc.gov/2022027237

This book is published in the IGI Global book series Practice, Progress, and Proficiency in Sustainability (PPPS) (ISSN: 2330-3271; eISSN: 2330-328X)

British Cataloguing in Publication Data
A Cataloguing in Publication record for this book is available from the British Library.

For electronic access to this publication, please contact: eresources@igi-global.com.

Practice, Progress, and Proficiency in Sustainability (PPPS) Book Series

Ayman Batisha
International Sustainability Institute, Egypt

ISSN:2330-3271
EISSN:2330-328X

Mission

In a world where traditional business practices are reconsidered and economic activity is performed in a global context, new areas of economic developments are recognized as the key enablers of wealth and income production. This knowledge of information technologies provides infrastructures, systems, and services towards sustainable development.

The **Practices, Progress, and Proficiency in Sustainability (PPPS) Book Series** focuses on the local and global challenges, business opportunities, and societal needs surrounding international collaboration and sustainable development of technology. This series brings together academics, researchers, entrepreneurs, policy makers and government officers aiming to contribute to the progress and proficiency in sustainability.

Coverage

- Socio-Economic
- Intellectual Capital
- Green Technology
- ICT and knowledge for development
- Global Business
- E-Development
- Sustainable Development
- Technological learning
- Environmental informatics
- Eco-Innovation

IGI Global is currently accepting manuscripts for publication within this series. To submit a proposal for a volume in this series, please contact our Acquisition Editors at Acquisitions@igi-global.com or visit: http://www.igi-global.com/publish/.

The Practice, Progress, and Proficiency in Sustainability (PPPS) Book Series (ISSN 2330-3271) is published by IGI Global, 701 E. Chocolate Avenue, Hershey, PA 17033-1240, USA, www.igi-global.com. This series is composed of titles available for purchase individually; each title is edited to be contextually exclusive from any other title within the series. For pricing and ordering information please visit http://www.igi-global.com/book-series/practice-progress-proficiency-sustainability/73810. Postmaster: Send all address changes to above address.

Titles in this Series

For a list of additional titles in this series, please visit: http://www.igi-global.com/book-series/practice-progress-proficiency-sustainability/73810

Climatic and Environmental Significance of Wetlands Case Studies from Eurasia and North Africa
Abdelkrim Ben Salem (Mohammed V University, Morocco) Laila Rhazi (Mohammed V University, Morocco) and Ahmed Karmaoui (University of Moulay Ismail, Morocco & Southern Center of Culture and Science, Morocco)
Engineering Science Reference • copyright 2022 • 310pp • H/C (ISBN: 9781799892892) • US $250.00 (our price)

Eco-Friendly and Agile Energy Strategies and Policy Development
Mir Sayed Shah Danish (University of the Ryukyus, Japan) and Tomonobu Senjyu (University of the Ryukyus, Japan)
Engineering Science Reference • copyright 2022 • 335pp • H/C (ISBN: 9781799895022) • US $240.00 (our price)

Handbook of Research on Global Institutional Roles for Inclusive Development
Neeta Baporikar (Namibia University of Science and Technology, Namibia & University of Pune, India)
Information Science Reference • copyright 2022 • 398pp • H/C (ISBN: 9781668424483) • US $270.00 (our price)

Analyzing Sustainability in Peripheral, Ultra-Peripheral, and Low-Density Regions
Rui Alexandre Castanho (WSB University, Poland)
Engineering Science Reference • copyright 2022 • 300pp • H/C (ISBN: 9781668445488) • US $240.00 (our price)

Handbook of Research on Building Inclusive Global Knowledge Societies for Sustainable Development
Cristina Raluca Gh. Popescu (University of Bucharest, Romania & The Bucharest University of Economic Studies, Romania)
Information Science Reference • copyright 2022 • 405pp • H/C (ISBN: 9781668451090) • US $295.00 (our price)

Handbook of Research on Principles and Practices for Orchards Management
Waleed Fouad Abobatta (Horticulture Research Institute, Agriculture Research Center, Egypt) Ahmed Farag (Central Laboratory for Agricultural Climate, Agriculture Research Center, Egypt) and Mohamed Abdel-Raheem (National Research Center, Egypt)
Engineering Science Reference • copyright 2022 • 400pp • H/C (ISBN: 9781668424230) • US $295.00 (our price)

Handbook of Research on Algae as a Sustainable Solution for Food, Energy, and the Environment
Mostafa M. El-Sheekh (Tanta University, Egypt) Norhayati Abdullah (Universiti Teknologi Malaysia, Malaysia) and Imran Ahmad (Universiti Teknologi Malaysia, Malaysia)
Engineering Science Reference • copyright 2022 • 795pp • H/C (ISBN: 9781668424384) • US $325.00 (our price)

IGI Global
PUBLISHER of TIMELY KNOWLEDGE

701 East Chocolate Avenue, Hershey, PA 17033, USA
Tel: 717-533-8845 x100 • Fax: 717-533-8661
E-Mail: cust@igi-global.com • www.igi-global.com

Dedication

The editor would like to heartily and to warmly dedicate this book entitled *Frameworks for Sustainable Development Goals to Manage Economic, Social, and Environmental Shocks and Disasters*, published by IGI Global – International Academic Publisher, to all the leaders, the politicians, the specialists, the researchers, the scholars, the entrepreneurs, and the managers who dedicated both their time and their work to supporting the great success of achieving the Sustainable Development Goals (SDGs) which are believed to support the most powerful and the most expected global partnership that targets peace and prosperity at a universal level.

In this matter, the editor would like to point out that the 2030 Agenda for Sustainable Development, adopted by all United Nations Member States in 2015, has irreversible implications upon all our lives and has irrevocable connections with all the surrounding domains that have existed so far on Planet Earth, which positions the success of the Sustainable Development Goals (SDGs) on top of the priorities that currently are due to be encountered at an international level. According to the United Nations (UN) Economic and Social Council, the most recent documentation (which belongs to the year 2022) on the Progress towards the Sustainable Development Goals (SDGs), which is due to be published as a Report of the Secretary-General and currently may be found under the form of a draft (as work in progress), starts with an earthshattering introduction, as follows: "As the world enters the third year of the COVID-19 crisis, the catastrophic effects on people's lives and livelihoods and on global efforts to realize the Sustainable Development Goals is now beyond dispute. (…) the present report shows that years, or even decades, of development progress have been halted or reversed. As of end of 2021, more than 5.4 million people worldwide had died directly due to COVID-19 with estimates suggesting that excess deaths were nearly 15 million. Global health systems were overwhelmed, and many essential health services were disrupted, posing major health threats and undermining years of progress fighting other deadly diseases. Furthermore, an additional 75 million to 95 million people will live in extreme poverty in 2022 compared to pre-pandemic level. Billions of children significantly missed out on schooling and over 100 million more children fell below the minimum reading proficiency level and other areas of academic learning. This generation of children could lose a combined total of $17 trillion in lifetime earnings in present value. Women have also been disproportionately affected by the socioeconomic fallout of the pandemic, struggling with lost jobs, increased burdens of unpaid care work and domestic violence." (the first two points of the "Introduction" section that is part of the United Nations (UN) Economic and Social Council, the most recent documentation (which belongs to the year 2022) on the Progress towards the Sustainable Development Goals (SDGs), which is due to be published as a Report of the Secretary-General. https://sdgs.un.org/goals and https://sustainabledevelopment.un.org/content/documents/29858SG_SDG_Progress_Report_2022.pdf).

Based on the aforementioned most recent statistical data, the editor would like to take this opportunity to express a great concern and a tremendous worry for the future of the present generations as well as for the fate that the next generations will embrace, since the global economy seems to be still affected by the impact of the new COVID-19 variants on our society. In continuation to these unexpected situations that have led to a troubled state of mind for the editor, the editor has to turn the attention to some other information emphasized by the United Nations (UN) Economic and Social Council, in the most recent documentation (which belongs to the year 2022) on the Progress towards the Sustainable Development Goals (SDGs), which is due to be published as a Report of the Secretary-General and currently may be found under the form of a draft (as work in progress), which mentions that "the world is also witnessing the highest number of violent conflicts since 1945, with approximately 2 billion people living in conflict-affected countries by the end of 2020" (the fourth point of the "Introduction" section that is part of the United Nations (UN) Economic and Social Council, the most recent documentation (which belongs to the year 2022) on the Progress towards the Sustainable Development Goals (SDGs), which is due to be published as a Report of the Secretary-General. https://sdgs.un.org/goals and https://sustainabledevelopment.un.org/content/documents/29858SG_SDG_Progress_Report_2022.pdf).

As a consequence, the editor would like to wholeheartedly and to vigorously dedicate this book entitled "Frameworks for Sustainable Development Goals to Manage Economic, Social, and Environmental Shocks and Disasters", published by IGI Global – International Academic Publisher, to all the individuals and to all the organizations that have turned their attention and their lives to bringing joy to people, to helping our Planet, and to generating and to increasing prosperity for us all. It seems that these days, by finding undeniable solutions for better lives for all and by being eager to transform our world – as promoted so enthusiastically and so zealously by the 2030 Agenda for Sustainable Development (SD), we will be able to find ourselves one step ahead on the road of promoting "universal peace" and "larger freedom" (United Nations (UN), Department of Economic and Social Affairs, Sustainable Development, Transforming our world: the 2030 Agenda for Sustainable Development, https://sdgs.un.org/2030agenda).

In the same line with the aforementioned aspects, the editor would like to joyfully dedicate this book entitled "Frameworks for Sustainable Development Goals to Manage Economic, Social, and Environmental Shocks and Disasters", published by IGI Global – International Academic Publisher, to Professor Dr. Arturo Luque González, from Universidad Técnica de Manabí, Ecuador and Observatorio Euromediterráneo de Espacio Público y Democracia URJC, Spain. Dr. Arturo Luque González is full professor at the Technical University of Manabí, Ecuador, and member of Euro-Mediterranean Observatory on Public Policies and Democratic Quality at the University King Juan Carlos (Spain). He holds a Ph.D. in Social Sciences and Law and a Master of two years about Labor Relations. He supervises several doctoral theses (Ph.D.) in Córdoba (Spain) and in the Basque Country (GEZKI Institute) like a director and co-director. It has 74 indexed articles and his latest publications includes topics about corporate social (Ir) responsibility (How corporate social (ir)responsibility in the textile sector is defined, and its impact on ethical sustainability: An analysis of 133 concepts), transnational companies (The transnational textile companies relationship with environment: a Delphi analysis approach) and their relations with ethics (Corruption in the transnational textile industry: an exception or the rule?), social economy and cooperative system like economic alternative (Socially responsible public management: case spinning development in Ecuador), media analysis and social conflicts (Analysis of the indigenous uprising of Ecuador, 2019). The editor would like to bring to the attention Professor Dr. Arturo Luque González dedication towards the "2030 Agenda for Sustainable Development", adopted by all United Nations Member States in 2015, and the importance of his scientific works on the 17 Sustainable Development Goals (SDGs) – among other relevant and noteworthy topics that Professor Dr. Arturo Luque González chose to analyze over the years. Among the most recent studies belonging to Professor Dr. Arturo Luque González (as single author or as coauthor), could be mentioned the following ones, which are represented by book chapters published with IGI Global – International Academic Publisher, namely: "Implications and Asymmetries of the Knowledge Society: An Analysis of 82 Constructs" (https://doi.org/10.4018/978-1-6684-3374-4.ch008); "Fallacies of Consumerism: An Analysis of Its Impact and Depth in Today's Society" (https://doi.org/10.4018/978-1-6684-2523-7.ch004); "Public Policies, Traffic Light Signpost Labeling, and Their Implications: The Case of Ecuador" (https://doi.org/10.4018/978-1-6684-3380-5.ch009); "Analysis of the Increase in Femicide Following Its Classification as a Crime in the Digital World" (https://doi.org/10.4018/978-1-7998-9187-1.ch008); "Legendary, Life-Changing, and Memorable Benefits of Digitalization to Restart the Economy: Impact of COVID-19 on Global Economic Environment for Sustainable Development" (https://doi.org/10.4018/978-1-6684-5109-0.ch008); "Importance and Implications of Influential, Powerful, and Remarkable Economic Policy Mix: Pre-Pandemic and Post-Pandemic Challenges in Building Inclusive Global Knowledge Societies" (https://doi.org/10.4018/978-1-6684-5113-7.ch003); "The Social and Solidarity Economics, Public Policies, and Non-Monetary Economic Practices: The Case of Associative Firms in Loja, Ecuador" (https://doi.org/10.4018/978-1-7998-7689-2.ch012); "Women Victims of Economic Violence: An Analysis of the Associative Sector Through Santa Marta Women's Association, Manabí, Ecuador" (https://doi.org/10.4018/978-1-6684-5113-7.ch002); "Analysis of Labor Reform During COVID-19: The Case of Ecuador" (https://doi.org/10.4018/978-1-6684-5113-7.ch001); "Academic Migration From Scientist Networks in the Global Environment: A Case Study" (https://doi.org/10.4018/978-1-7998-9542-8.ch016); "Sensationalism vs. Information During COVID-19 in Ecuador: A Framing Theory-Based View" (https://doi.org/10.4018/978-1-7998-7164-4.ch012); and "Analysis of the Concept of Femicide: A Study of 102 Concepts" (https://doi.org/10.4018/978-1-7998-9187-1.ch003).

All in all, the editor would like to take this opportunity to dedicate this book entitled "Frameworks for Sustainable Development Goals to Manage Economic, Social, and Environmental Shocks and Disasters", published by IGI Global – International Academic Publisher, to all the IGI Global team members as a sign of deep appreciation for the dedication that they have shown during the entire editing and publication process, for the heart and soul that they have displayed during the procedures that such a complex scientific project requires, and for the genuine desire to be part of the movement that promotes and that supports the Sustainable Development Goals (SDGs), by trying to show the importance of reaching a universal balance for the three dimensions of Sustainable Development, namely: the economic dimension, the social dimension, and the environmental dimension.

Let us all take – on the one hand, the necessary steps in bringing our constructive and our positive contribution in those areas and in those situations that seem to be of critical importance for humanity and the Planet, and let us all reflect – on the other hand, on the manner in which we can genuinely and truly support the needs of the present and of the future generations, thus supporting equilibrium, life, love, harmony with nature, health, progress, prosperity, success, sustainable development, sustainability, and well-being!

Editorial Advisory Board

List of Reviews

Table of Contents

Detailed Table of Contents

The accentuated digital transformation and the unprecedented worldwide collaboration, as results of the COVID-19 pandemic changes and the COVID-19 crisis challenges, have generated noteworthy concerns in terms of individuals' health and well-being in the light of the development of vaccines and in the attempt to understand better vaccination willingness. The case of vaccination willingness has been addressed in the powerful context generated by the influence of the Sustainable Development Goals, with a preeminent accent on health and well-being, while emphasizing that the pandemic has accentuated the inequalities between people in terms of vaccine distribution and has irreversibly transformed the approach of the society in terms of decision-making in matters related to health, society, and economy. The economic growth and the economy recovery of all countries have proven highly dependent on the success of the COVID-19 vaccines and the fiscal and the monetary support programs.

Corporate social responsibility (CSR) represents the voluntary commitment of companies to behave appropriately, fairly, and responsibly with the environment in which they operate. It refers to a business approach that takes into account economic, environmental, and social issues in a balanced, holistic, and long-term manner for the benefit of current and future stakeholders. Thus, since the introduction of the concept, more managers are including social and environmental objectives in their decision-making process. The aim of CSR is therefore to seek the well-being of society and the environment through business activities. However, when did the term come into being, how has the term evolved since its foundation, and how has the concept of CSR evolved over time? Through a narrative review of the literature, the research addresses these research questions to bring clarity to the field of study.

There is currently an economic metamorphosis underway that involves myriad (mis)development processes. At the same time, processes of inequality are emerging, imbued with their own historical context. This study evaluated the eco-social program known as Good Living (Buen Vivir, Sumak Kawsay) in Ecuador as a tool for change for the most vulnerable sectors that are intrinsically connected to their culture and customs. The study also examined the parallel processes of inequality and the excessive protection of private interests that favor a new world order driven by the maximization of profit. With this objective, the current state of the processes associated with Good Living in the Ecuadorian province of Orellana was analyzed through interviews with relevant local representatives of institutional life. The results highlight the abandonment of the processes of the solidarity and social economy and the resurgence, both by action and omission, of an extractivist model far removed from the principles of compassion, inclusion, and social participation.

The current worldwide pandemic due to COVID-19 confronts all industries with considerable economic challenges. This text analyses the subject of organizational risks from the perspective of the board of directors. It argues that compliance is a necessary condition, however not sufficient, for an effective risk governance. It suggests that prudence is something that should be nurtured and promoted at the level of organizational governance. Organizations being complex systems, a holistic framework should be used in approaching risk governance. Risk approaches have been particularly influenced by regulation focusing on financial risks, while there are many additional types of risks, potentially more damaging for organisations. The role of the board of directors has undergone a long evolution from merely "ceremonial" to its current "progressive" form. This chapter argues on a more prudential action by those responsible for corporate governance beyond a normativism approach.

Sustainable business is suffering an increasing demand by part of different stakeholders, especially those in the end of the value chain. One way to accomplish it is through a business longevity assessment model. If companies last in a sustainable way that is also recognizable, they will create value not only from an economic perspective but also from a social one. In this chapter, the authors expose the reasons why migrating from the main profit maximization goal to pursuing business longevity (survival in an adequate manner) may help to enhance sustainable development both inside and outside the organization, as well as some action proposals to achieve it.

Youth unemployment is a rising concern for many countries across the world. The gap between youth and adult is even wider in Sub-Saharan Africa than the world average. There might be several reasons to explain, yet this chapter focuses on one controversial potential reason: immigration. This continent has experienced considerable migration flows and one could expect that immigration worsens labour market conditions for native youth. Uganda as one of the Sub-Saharan countries is investigated to see if immigrants have a significant impact on unemployment probability of young Ugandans using cross-sectional census data for the years of 1991, 2002, and 2014. Data set was drawn from IPUMS-International. Findings indicate that regional share of immigrants does not have a significant large effect on unemployment probability of youth in Uganda. A further investigation showed that higher share of immigrants in a given region lowers the probability of being not in the labour force across specifications. This means immigrants do not push native youth out of the labour force in the Uganda case.

Using primary and secondary data, this case study analyzes the issue KORFEZ must face during the COVID-19 pandemic and demonstrates how KORFEZ may deal with its lack of digital marketing-related initiatives and digital communication weaknesses throughout the pandemic. It highlights the need of making judgments while considering all promotional instruments in marketing, including digital ones, and provides a real-world example that can be addressed from both an academic and a practical standpoint. The teaching case's subject field is marketing, specifically marketing communication. The teaching case may be utilized at the undergraduate and MBA levels. Successful students will be able to improve their theoretical knowledge of strengths and weaknesses analysis, critique elements of the promotional mix in integrated marketing communication, critique a digital marketing strategy, and learn how to lead unusual situations such as a pandemic in terms of marketing-related issues after completing this case study.

Green innovation (GI) represents the voluntary commitment of companies to develop new environmentally friendly products and/or processes. This type of innovation represents a new business paradigm in which social, environmental, and societal issues are taken into consideration in a balanced way, satisfying the different types of demands of the organizations' stakeholders. GI is therefore a long-term commitment to balancing the economic needs of the organization and the environmental and social demands of customers. Given the relevance of the topic, this chapter aims to answer the following research questions: What are the characteristics that make up the concept of GI? Has there been any terminological evolution? and Under what theoretical approaches has the concept been addressed? Through a narrative review of the literature, the research addresses these research questions in order to bring clarity to the field of study, thus serving as a reference study for both neophyte and experienced researchers in the field.

Foreword

The Global Indicator Framework for the Sustainable Development Goals (SDGs) and the targets of the 2030 Agenda for Sustainable Development (SD) – in the novel and universally treasured vision highlighted over the years by the United Nations (UN) – have had on the one hand, far-reaching implications for all the individuals worldwide and have attracted, on the other hand, major successes for our planet. However, these successes have been achieved particularly when ensuring a better life for the present and the future generations was understood appropriately and in situations in which correct and constructive measures were taken. Accordingly, building an inclusive and a robust society for all people has clearly represented a tremendous challenge. For instance, it necessitates finding viable solutions capable of ending poverty in all its forms, ending hunger, achieving food security, improving nutrition, and promoting sustainable agriculture. Likewise, there is increased pressure on specialists to find solutions that promote healthy lives and well-being for people across all ages, which at its roots, involve discovering innovative and powerful programs that substantially increase health financing activities. These objectives are also expected to foster inclusive and equitable quality education and promote life-long learning opportunities for all, because the level of education in a society reflects its ability to cope with daily challenges and identify and develop solutions that generate progress for all. Along the same lines, our society seeks to achieve gender equality, empower all women and girls, and end all forms of discrimination against them.

Now more than ever before, the COVID-19 pandemic as well as the associated COVID-19 crisis have exacerbated the need to support health, well-being, and life-long actions towards good forms and decent standards of living, such as availability and sustainable management of water and sanitation for all. The pressure on the planet's resources has raised alarm over the last few decades, which has ultimately led to the need to find alternative resources, and ensure access to affordable, reliable, sustainable and modern energy, while also finding the necessary means to promote inclusive and sustainable economic growth, full and productive employment, and decent work for all.

In line with these bold and crucial aims, the post-COVID-19 Era has brought to light the need for humanity to focus to a greater extent and more intensely on the well-being of individuals and on the health of our planet, rather than on obtaining economic growth and economic productivity. In this way, the importance of key factors such as the sustainable per capita economic growth, development-oriented policies, job creation, entrepreneurship, creativity, innovation, full and productive employment, and decent work for all people, has grown considerably in our society in these last months and years.

In this context, this book titled *Frameworks for Sustainable Development Goals to Manage Economic, Social, and Environmental Shocks and Disasters*, published by IGI Global, represents a vital scientific resource for academics, leaders, scientists, researchers, students, Ph.D. scholars, and postdoctoral students, since it brings to attention particular solutions that are most likely to help reduce inequality within and among countries, especially in new demographic, economic, financial, and social contexts created by the COVID-19 pandemic and the COVID-19 crisis. Thus, through the dedication and hard work of its book chapter authors, this book answers numerous questions:

- In what ways do the actions and activities supported by the SDGs have the capacity to make cities and human settlements inclusive, safe, resilient, and sustainable?
- In what manner do the actions and activities supported by the SDGs have the capability to ensure sustainable consumption and production patterns?
- What are the best solutions that specialists worldwide ought to focus on in order for countries to take urgent action to combat climate change and its impacts?
- What are the most reliable actions capable of helping specialists all around the globe conserve and sustainably use the oceans, seas, and marine resources for sustainable development?
- How can humanity protect, restore, and promote the sustainable use of terrestrial ecosystems, sustainably manage forests, combat desertification, halt and reverse land degradation, and halt biodiversity loss?
- What will our society look like if it commits vigorously to promoting peaceful and inclusive societies for sustainable development, providing access to justice for all, and building effective, accountable, and inclusive institutions at all levels?
- What is the key for a bright and successful future for all via strengthening of the means of implementation and revitalizing Global Partnership for Sustainable Development?

As an expert in the field, I am excited that the present book published by IGI Global, sheds light on the most important problems confronting our society and offers thoughtful solutions that can move us forward on the SDGs as envisioned by the UN Agenda. As such, it will help academics, leaders, scientists, researchers, students, Ph.D. scholars, and postdoctoral students better cope with the repercussions of the COVID-19 pandemic and the COVID-19 crisis and offer insight into current best practices that may serve us well in the post-COVID-19 Era.

I am pleased to highlight the thoughtful contributions of the authors of the book chapters, the considerable effort of the Editorial Advisory Board members, and the noteworthy dedication of the Editorial Review Board members, which have enabled this scientific project to come to life.

Most of all, I heartily congratulate the editor, Professor Dr. Cristina Raluca Gh. Popescu, from the University of Bucharest, Bucharest, Romania, and The Bucharest University of Economic Studies, Bucharest, Romania, on this important undertaking.

Finally, I congratulate the IGI Global team members for their hard work in preparing and publishing the "Frameworks for Sustainable Development Goals to Manage Economic, Social, and Environmental Shocks and Disasters", knowing that the UN SDGs have constantly attracted specialists' attention over time as well as leaders' and researchers' desire to address the environmental, economic, financial, managerial, political, demographic, and socio-cultural aspects of sustainability principles.

I hope that the process of reading this volume will transform the way in which you envision people, partnership, peace, planet and prosperity, and inspire you to think more deeply about your own approach to economic growth, environmental balance and social progress in today's world.

Meg A. Warren

Department of Management, College of Business and Economics, Western Washington University, Bellingham, USA

***Meg A. Warren** is an Associate Professor of Management at Western Washington University, USA. She is a researcher, author, keynote speaker, and psychologist with expertise in positive psychological approaches to equity, diversity and inclusion in institutions, and cultural factors affecting well-being. Her award-winning research uses a positive psychology approach to study how individuals from relatively privileged groups can serve as allies to marginalized outgroups. She is the lead editor of two books, Scientific Advances in Positive Psychology (2017), and Toward a Positive Psychology of Relationships: New Directions in Theory and Research (2018) and has published her work in over 50 peer-reviewed journals, book chapters, and reports and in over 175 news media and popular media outlets. She has held prestigious leadership positions such as the Founding President of the Work & Organizations Division of the International Positive Psychology Association, Co-Founder of the Western Positive Psychology Association, and Co-Editor of the International Journal of Wellbeing. To access publications, media, white papers, and other resources on her work, please visit www.megwarren.com. ORCID ID: 0000-0002-7462-3580.*

Preface

It ought to be emphasized that the "2030 Agenda for Sustainable Development (SD)", adopted by all United Nations Member States in 2015, focuses on the achievement of the 17 Sustainable Development Goals (SDGs) that revolve around key concepts, such as: Well-Being, Happiness, Strong Health, Peace, Prosperity, People, Planet Earth, Global Partnership(s), Ending Poverty, Education, Diminishing Inequality, Economic Growth, and finding solutions to support Climate Change. Moreover, according to specialists worldwide, the 17 Sustainable Development Goals (SDGs) were built on decades of work by countries and the United Nations (UN), including the United Nations (UN) Department of Economic and Social Affairs. Furthermore, according to the SDG Progress Report (2022) – Advanced Unedited Version – which highlights the "Progress towards the Sustainable Development Goals", under the form of the "Report of the Secretary-General", the following important aspects are highlighted, as follows: "As the world enters the third year of the COVID-19 crisis, the catastrophic effects on people's lives and livelihoods and on global efforts to realize the Sustainable Development Goals is now beyond dispute. Despite continued data gaps at national and sub-national levels, the present report shows that years, or even decades, of development progress have been halted or reversed. As of end of 2021, more than 5.4 million people worldwide had died directly due to COVID-19 with estimates suggesting that excess deaths were nearly 15 million. Global health systems were overwhelmed, and many essential health services were disrupted, posing major health threats and undermining years of progress fighting other deadly diseases. Furthermore, an additional 75 million to 95 million people will live in extreme poverty in 2022 compared to pre-pandemic level. (…) In 2021, the global economy started to rebound, with the global output expanding by 5.5%. However, new COVID-19 variants and continued vaccine inequity, together with rising inflation, major supply-chain disruptions, policy uncertainties, and unsustainable debt in developing countries, caused the global economy to slow down again at the end of 2021. 4. The world is also witnessing the highest number of violent conflicts since 1945, with approximately 2 billion people living in conflict-affected countries by the end of 2020. Refugees were at the highest absolute number on record in 2021 and forced displacement has continued to occur and even grow. These numbers will only increase with the war in Ukraine creating one of the largest refugee crises of modern time. (…) To get the SDGs back on track and to keep the 1.5-degree goal alive, we need to capitalize on the opportunity afforded by the recovery to adopt low-carbon, resilient and inclusive development pathways that will reduce carbon emissions, conserve natural resources, transform our food systems, create better jobs and advance the transition to a greener, more inclusive and just economy" (SDG Progress Report (2022), Advanced Unedited Version, pp. 2-3, points no. 1, 2, 3, 4, and 8, part of the "Progress towards the Sustainable Development Goals", the "Report of the Secretary-General").

Based on the aspects displayed in the lines above, there are numerous questions that come to mind and that need immediate attention and that require immediate answers (SDG Progress Report (2022), Advanced Unedited Version, pp. 2-3, points no. 1, 2, 3, 4, and 8, part of the "Progress towards the Sustainable Development Goals", the "Report of the Secretary-General"):

- Which are the best frameworks for Sustainable Development Goals (SDGs) capable to manage economic, social, and environmental shocks and disasters?
- In what manner can the effects of the COVID-19 crisis be limited by the frameworks for Sustainable Development Goals (SDGs) capable to manage economic, social, and environmental shocks and disasters?
- Are the global efforts to realize the Sustainable Development Goals (SDGs) enough or should specialists and organizations struggle to find and to implement new frameworks for Sustainable Development Goals (SDGs) capable to manage economic, social, and environmental shocks and disasters?
- In what manner can "the global economy" be helped "to rebound" under the conditions in which the new COVID-19 variants continue to create economic and social disparities, there are still "vaccine inequity" problems, "rising inflation", "major supply-chain disruptions", "policy uncertainties", and "unsustainable debt in developing countries"?
- Will the current high "number of violent conflicts" worldwide have the power to turn away all the efforts done so far to promote and to support the achievement of the Sustainable Development Goals (SDGs), or will the new frameworks for Sustainable Development Goals (SDGs) be capable to manage economic, social, and environmental shocks and disasters?

The main objective of this reference book entitled *Frameworks for Sustainable Development Goals to Manage Economic, Social, and Environmental Shocks and Disasters*, published by IGI Global – International Academic Publisher – is to provide valuable insight of today's context concerning the creation of an international successful framework for Sustainable Development Goals (SDGs) that requires managing the economic, social and environmental shocks and disasters in the Post-COVID-19 Era; ensuring healthy lives and promote well-being for all at all ages in the Post-COVID-19 Era; and promoting sustained, inclusive and sustainable economic growth in the Post-COVID-19 Era.

This book aims at providing an updated view of the newest trends, novel practices and latest tendencies concerning the benefits, advantages, opportunities, and challenges that building an international successful framework for Sustainable Development Goals (SDGs) implicates in terms of: (a) managing the economic, social and environmental shocks and disasters in the Post-COVID-19 Era; (b) ensuring healthy lives and promote well-being for all at all ages in the Post-COVID-19 Era; (c) promoting sustained, inclusive and sustainable economic growth in the Post-COVID-19 Era.

The target audience is represented by academics, scientists, researchers, students, PhD scholars, and Post - doctoral students.

The main objective of this reference book is to provide a platform for sharing researchers' and professionals' most recent ideas, findings and works concerning the creation of an international successful framework for Sustainable Development Goals (SDGs) implicates in terms of: (a) managing the economic, social and environmental shocks and disasters in the Post-COVID-19 Era; (b) ensuring healthy lives and promote well-being for all at all ages in the Post-COVID-19 Era; (c) promoting sustained, inclusive and sustainable economic growth in the Post-COVID-19 Era. In this context, researchers and professionals submitted their contributions in form of original research papers, case studies or essays, in particular on the following topics (but not limited to the following topics) highlighted below. It should also be stated that interdisciplinary and cross section contributions were welcomed as long as they fell in the area specific to the theme of this current book.

- Competency-Based Education
- Constructing Modern Knowledge
- COVID-19 Domains
- Entrepreneurship and Greening Economy
- Entrepreneurship Measuring Indicators
- Entrepreneurial Finance
- Environmental sustainability and justice
- Financial security and safety
- Food security
- Future Energy Scenarios, with Focus on Smart Energy Markets
- Health Education And Awareness
- Intellectual Capital, Sustainability And Resilience
- International Entrepreneurship
- Intelligence
- New And Sustainable Agribusiness Management Models
- Pandemic-Related Domains
- Resiliency
- Risk Assessments For Coronavirus Threats
- Smart Cities
- Stability
- Sustainable Conservation Management
- Sustainable Development In Business Reporting
- Sustainable Entrepreneurship
- Sustainable Entrepreneurship Skills And Competences
- Sustainable Human Resource Development
- Sustainable Rural Community Development
- Global Entrepreneurship
- Social Entrepreneurship
- Corporate Social Responsibility
- Creativity
- Creating An Inclusive And Competitive Entrepreneurship
- Information Technology
- Innovation
- Innovative Business Models
- Intellectual Capital
- Leadership
- Knowledge Management
- Organizational Performance
- Responsible Innovation, Performance and Excellence for A Sustainable Future

- Responsible Consumption And Production
- Social Responsibility
- Sustainable Entrepreneurial Ecosystems
- Sustainable Energy, with Responsible Consumption and Production
- Sustainability Practices
- Sustainable Society, with Responsible Consumption and Production
- Technologies and Policies For a Sustainable Society
- Technological and Social Innovation For Sustainable Business
- Innovative Applications of Artificial Intelligence in Business and Management
- Artificial Intelligence for Business and Management in the Big Data Era
- Artificial Intelligence in Value Creation for Business and Management
- Artificial Intelligence in Business and Management: A Modern Approach
- Artificial Intelligence in Business and Management: A New Synthesis
- Applications of Artificial Intelligence in Business and Management
- Artificial Intelligence Techniques in Business and Management
- Foundations of Artificial Intelligence in Business and Management
- Artificial Intelligence in Business and Management: An Exploration
- The Impact of Artificial Intelligence on Business and Management
- Understanding Artificial Intelligence in Business and Management
- The Use of Artificial Intelligence in Business and Management
- Artificial Intelligence and the power to influence the future
- Business Excellence and Innovation
- Circular Economies
- Cybernetics

The keywords that are specific to this book entitled "Frameworks for Sustainable Development Goals to Manage Economic, Social, and Environmental Shocks and Disasters", published by IGI Global – International Academic Publisher – are the following ones:

- Sustainable Development Goals (SDGs)
- COVID-19
- The Post-COVID-19 Era
- Knowledge
- Human Resources
- Traditional Knowledge
- International Cooperation
- Sustained, Inclusive and Sustainable Economic Growth
- Development-Oriented Policies
- Productive Activities
- Decent Job Creation
- Entrepreneurship
- Creativity and Innovation
- Innovation
- Green Innovation

- Green Process Innovation
- Green Product Innovation
- Global Economic Environment
- Growth of Micro-, Small- And Medium-Sized Enterprises
- Financial Services
- Sustainable Consumption and Production
- Health
- Healthy Lives
- Well-Being for All at All Ages
- Social Protection Systems
- International Poverty
- Mobilization of Resources
- Mental Health
- Gender Equality
- Enhanced Development Cooperation
- Climate-Related Extreme Events
- Sustainable Management of Water
- Wastewater Treatment, Recycling and Reuse Technologies
- Vaccination Willingness
- Business
- Business Policy
- Intangible Assets
- Intellectual Capital
- Digitalization
- Restart the Economy
- Sustainability
- Intention-Behavior Gap
- Motivation-Behavior Gap
- Green Purchasing Inconsistency
- Environmental Sustainability
- Pro-Environmental Behavior
- United Nations Environment Program
- Sustainable Travel
- Ecological Conservation
- Institutional Analysis
- Literature Analysis
- Environmental-Friendly Policy
- Ecotourism Development Trends
- Stakeholder
- Survival
- Success
- Failure
- Entrepreneurship
- Firms

- Organizations
- Companies
- Management
- Economy
- Human Rights
- United Nations
- Rights
- Development
- Economy
- Good Living
- Market
- Solidarity
- Integrated Marketing Communication
- Digital Marketing
- B2B Companies
- Corporate Social Responsibility
- Historical Evolution
- Narrative Literature Review
- Immigration
- Youth Unemployment
- Risk Governance
- Risk Typologies
- Compliance
- Systems Thinking
- Economic Model
- Pandemic Scenario
- Waste Energy
- Environmental Liability
- Interdisciplinary
- Risk Analysis
- Industrial Projects
- Environmental Governance
- Social Governance

ORGANIZATION OF THE BOOK

The book is organized into 13 chapters. A brief description of each of the chapters may be found below, as it results based on the authors' own statements:

Chapter 1 highlights the aspects concerning coping with COVID-19 while focusing on Good Health and Well-Being, emphasizing the case of Vaccination Willingness. This chapter presents a novel and highly challenging perspective on coping with COVID-19 while focusing on Good Health and Well-Being, emphasizing the case of Vaccination Willingness, in times in which our society confronts itself with numerous changes, challenges, opportunities, and threats which may be even considered far different than the ones encountered in the past. The authors have mentioned the fact that nowadays, the accentuated digital transformation and the unprecedented worldwide collaboration – as results of the COVID-19 pandemic changes and the COVID-19 crisis challenges, have generated noteworthy concerns in terms of individuals' Health and Well-Being, in the light of the development of vaccines and in the attempt to understand better Vaccination Willingness. Moreover, the authors have stressed the fact that the case of Vaccination Willingness has been addressed in the powerful context generated by the influence of the Sustainable Development Goals (SDGs), with a preeminent accent on Health and Well-Being, while emphasizing that the pandemic has accentuated the inequalities between people in terms of vaccine distribution and has irreversibly transformed the approach of the society in terms of decision-making in matters related to Health, Society and Economy. Furthermore, it is the authors' powerful belief that the economic growth and the economy recovery of all countries have proven highly dependent on the success of the COVID-19 vaccines and the fiscal and the monetary support programs. The keywords that are due to be subject of analysis in this current book chapter are the following ones, namely: Health, Well-Being, Vaccination Willingness, Knowledge, Human Resources, Innovation, Sustainable Development Goals, Global Economic Environment, and COVID-19.

Chapter 2 presents Corporate Social Responsibility (CSR) under the form of a narrative literature review. The authors mentioned the fact that Corporate Social Responsibility (CSR) represents the voluntary commitment of companies to behave appropriately, fairly and responsibly with the environment in which they operate. Moreover, the authors mentioned that it refers to a business approach that takes into account economic, environmental and social issues in a balanced, holistic and long-term manner, for the benefit of current and future stakeholders. Thus, according to the authors, since the introduction of the concept, more and more managers are including social and environmental objectives in their decision-making process. Furthermore, the authors have brought to the attention their opinion according to which the aim of CSR is therefore to seek the well-being of society and the environment through business activities. However, the authors have asked themselves when did the term come into being, how has the term evolved since its foundation, and how has the concept of CSR evolved over time? The authors have noted that through a narrative review of the literature, the research addresses these research questions to bring clarity to the field of study. The keywords used by the authors are the following ones: Corporate Social Responsibility, sustainability, historical evolution, and narrative literature review.

Chapter 3 targets the delicate and highly valuable subject of Market Economy and Good Living, while emphasizing the case of the obstacles to its Achievement in Orellana, Ecuador. This is an important book chapter, in which the authors have dedicated their attention and their focus to the importance of the Market Economy and the aspects that surround the concept of "Good Living", while presenting as a case study the obstacles to its Achievement in Orellana, Ecuador. In this matter, the authors have noted that there is currently an economic metamorphosis underway that involves a myriad of (mis)development processes. Also, the authors have mentioned that, at the same time, processes of inequality are emerging, imbued with their own historical context. Based on the authors' comments, presentation, and notes, this study evaluated the eco-social program known as "Good Living" ("Buen Vivir", "Sumak Kawsay") in Ecuador as a tool for change for the most vulnerable sectors that are intrinsically connected to their culture and customs. What is more, according to the authors, the study also examined the parallel processes of inequality and the excessive protection of private interests that favor a new world order driven by the maximization of profit. Furthermore, with this objective, the current state of the processes associated with "Good Living" in the Ecuadorian province of Orellana was analyzed through interviews with relevant local representatives of institutional life. The results presented by the authors have the power to highlight the abandonment of the processes of the solidarity and social economy and the resurgence, both by action and omission, of an extractivist model far removed from the principles of compassion, inclusion and social participation. In terms of keywords, the authors have displayed the following main concepts, namely: rights, development, economy, Good Living, Ecuador, market, Solidarity, and Sustainability.

Chapter 4 presents the topic of Risk Governance and the need for a multidisciplinary approach. The authors have noted the fact that the current worldwide pandemic due to COVID-19 confronts all industries with considerable economic challenges. In addition, the authors have mentioned that this text analyses the subject of organizational risks, from the perspective of the board of directors, which argues that compliance is a necessary condition, however not sufficient, for effective risk governance. In continuation, the authors have mentioned that their work suggests that prudence is something that should be nurtured and promoted at the level of organizational governance. Moreover, the authors have stressed the fact that being organizations complex systems, a holistic framework should be used in approaching risk governance. Also, the authors have drawn the attention to the fact that risk approaches have been particularly influenced by regulation focusing on financial risks, while there are many additional types of risks, potentially more damaging for organizations. Furthermore, the authors have mentioned that the role of the board of directors has undergone a long evolution from merely "ceremonial" to its current "progressive" form. Thus, according to the authors, this chapter argues on a more prudential action by those responsible for corporate governance, beyond a normativism approach. The keywords brought to the attention by the authors are the following ones: risk governance, risk typologies, compliance, business policy, and systems thinking.

Chapter 5 presents the topic of pursuing business longevity, while highlighting the ways to enhance Sustainable Development. The authors have noted the fact that sustainable business is suffering an increasing demand by part of different stakeholders, especially those in the end of the value chain. In this matter, the authors have mentioned that one way to accomplish it is through a business longevity assessment model. Also, the authors have pointed out the fact that if companies last in a sustainable way that is also recognizable, they will create value not only from an economic perspective but also from a social one. In this chapter, the authors have exposed the reasons why migrating from the main profit maximization goal to pursuing business longevity (it is, survival in an adequate manner) may help to enhance sustainable development both inside and outside the organization, as well as some action proposals to achieve it. The keywords brought to light by the authors are the following ones: survival, success, failure, entrepreneurship, firms, organizations, companies, management, economy, human rights, and United Nations.

Chapter 6 displays the topic of immigration and unemployment nexus, a micro level investigation of Ugandan youth. The authors have pointed out that youth unemployment is a rising concern for many countries across the world. Also, the authors have mentioned that the gap between youth and adult is even wider in Sub-Saharan Africa than the world average. In continuation, the authors have stressed that there might be several reasons to explain, yet, this chapter focuses on one controversial potential reason: immigration. Based on the authors work, it has been noted that this continent has experienced considerable migration flows and one could expect that immigration worsens labor market conditions for native youth. Thus, the authors have showed that Uganda as one of Sub-Saharan countries is investigated to see if immigrants have a significant impact on unemployment probability of young Ugandans using cross-sectional census data for the years of 1991, 2002, and 2014. Data set was drawn from IPUMS-International (2021). Based on the findings presented by the authors, it can be mentioned that these findings indicate that regional share of immigrants does not have a significant large effect on unemployment probability of youth in Uganda. Also, according to the authors, a further investigation showed that higher share of immigrants in a given region lowers the probability of being not in the labor force across specifications; this means immigrants do not push native youth out of labor force in Uganda case. In terms of keywords, the following key concepts were brought to the attention: immigration, youth unemployment, census data, Uganda, Sub-Saharan, and IPUMS-International Data.

Chapter 7 presents the subject of the Pandemic and learning the way of continuous communication with customers. The authors noted that using primary and secondary data, this case study analyzes the issue KORFEZ must face during the COVID-19 pandemic and demonstrates how KORFEZ may deal with its lack of digital marketing-related initiatives and digital communication weaknesses throughout the pandemic. Also, the authors stressed that it highlights the need of making judgments while considering all promotional instruments in marketing, including digital ones, and provides a real-world example that can be addressed from both an academic and a practical standpoint. The authors have brought to the attention the fact that the teaching case's subject field is marketing, specifically marketing communication; and the teaching case may be utilized at the undergraduate and MBA levels. Also, the authors have displayed the fact that successful students will be able to improve their theoretical knowledge of strengths and weaknesses analysis, critique elements of the promotional mix in integrated marketing communication, critique a digital marketing strategy, and learn how to lead unusual situations such as a pandemic in terms of marketing-related issues after completing this case study. In terms of keywords, the following important concepts can be mentioned: integrated marketing communication, digital marketing, and B2B Companies.

Chapter 8 presents a very hot and novel topic, represented by current high-powered challenges and high-reaching reforms, while centering on the perspective of moving to a New Economic Model Based on Green Energy, Digitalization, and Shock Resistance. The book chapter presents the authors opinion according to which nowadays, knowledge has the miraculous power to advance the United Nations Sustainable Development Goals (SDGs) at an international level, with the notable help provided by courageous reforms due to promote a New Economic Model based on quality, green energy, digitalization, and shock resistance. Also, according to the authors, it has been mentioned the fact that Environmental Sustainability relies on collaboration in achieving the SDGs and on communication in making the SDGs a way of living. Hence, the authors have prompted the fact that the unforgettable challenges brought in today's society by the COVID-19 pandemic and the COVID-19 crisis posed even a greater pressure than before to achieve a better and more sustainable future for all, thus placing on pivotal positions the answers for the following questions: "What steps are due to be taken for ensuring Affordable and Clean Energy?"; "What role do Sustainable Cities and Communities play in people's lives?"; "What does Climate Action involve in terms of the partnerships for the Global Goals?"; and "What does digitalization implicates in terms of supporting long term positive economic, social and environmental links in the Post-COVID-19 Era?" The keywords that have the immeasurable power to stress the importance of this current scientific work are the following ones, namely: business, knowledge, Human Resources (HR), innovation, Intangible Assets (IA), Intellectual Capital (IC), Sustainable Development Goals (SDGs), digitalization, global economic environment, restart the economy, and COVID-19.

Chapter 9 presents the topic of application of sustainable projects in the paper industry in Rio de Janeiro. Based on the authors' notes, this analyzes the environmental, social, and governance (ESG) risk management practices currently used in sustainable projects in the paper industry in the state of Rio de Janeiro. Also, based on the authors' comments, this is exploratory research, in which a case study was carried out, supported by structured interviews with 17 specialists, who work in the main paper industries in Rio de Janeiro. According to the authors, the results indicate that the approaches of preliminary risk analysis, failure mode analysis, and WHAT –IF (WI) are the main practices used by the consulted managers. The authors have mentioned that these practices are incomplete, in the search for convergence of objectives and expansion of the life cycle of products and processes, as they comprise industrial processes in a fragmented way, without systematically covering the entire life cycle of products or the socio-environmental interests of the community. Hence, according to the authors, critical points for sustainable industrial projects were also pointed out as the possibility of a power outage in the global economy and society's lack of adaptability to the ongoing structural changes. The keywords brought under analysis by the authors are: risk analysis, industrial projects; environmental governance; social governance; sustainability; ESG; and paper industry.

Chapter 10 presents the case of waste management analysis for energy generation, an interdisciplinary study. The authors mentioned that currently, sustainable means of production and consumption are insufficient to meet the Sustainable Development Goals, requiring high awareness from managers of organizations and consumers. The authors have stressed that the production of urban solid waste, climate change, the emission of greenhouse gases, as well as energy demands are complex problems that require solutions from various branches of knowledge, including in the "POST COVID ERA". The authors have emphasized that considering the challenges of urban solid waste management and energy recovery technology, it is important to reflect on the level of understanding of municipal managers, in addition to observing the economic, social and environmental impacts of the pandemic. Also, the authors have commented that through a structured literature review, the study highlights multiple perspectives that can understand and seek alternatives for socio-environmental liabilities. The keywords mentioned as having a great importance to the authors are the following ones: economic model, pandemic scenario, waste energy, environmental liability, and interdisciplinary

Chapter 11 seeks finding an answer the following question: "Are there sustainable development trends in Chinese ecotourism policies?" The authors have mentioned the fact that defined as a type of tourism uniting conservation, communities and sustainable travel, ecotourism is becoming increasingly important. Also, based on the authors notes, for governments, developing guidance for the industry which helps address the potential conflicts between ecological conservation and economic development is of utmost importance. Thus, the authors have stressed that the changes of government policies in tourism have significantly driven the ecotourism development in China. However, the authors have mentioned that most of current research findings on ecotourism paid insufficient attention on the significance of the interlinked relationships among policies & research studies and the trends inside them. Also, the authors have presented that Implementing research methods including literature analysis and institutional analysis, this paper aims to examine these dynamic relationships from the regulators' perspective. Hence, according to the authors' comments, this chapter contributes to the field by demonstrating a sustainable development trend of Chinese ecotourism driven by the unique institutional settings with Chinese characteristics and analyzing the potential implications for various stakeholders due to the rising standards of ecotourism. The keywords brought to the attention by the authors are: sustainable travel, ecological conservation, institutional analysis, CiteSpace, literature analysis, environmental-friendly policy, ecotourism development trends, and stakeholder.

Chapter 12 presents the subject of understanding the attitude-behavior gap in the context of Green Consumption Behavior. Based on the authors' comments, the purpose of this chapter is to delineate the attitude-behavior gap phenomenon as it relates to green consumption behavior, an important component of environmental sustainability considerations. The authors have pointed out that, after a brief introduction to the topic, a number of possible explanations for the gap are reviewed. According to the authors, some of the viable steps to overcome the associated problems - in light of various actions that can be taken by governments/public policy makers, environmental non-governmental organizations, the business sector, and individual consumers - are considered in the discussion section. Suggestions for future research and some concluding remarks follow, which, altogether, try to shed some light on the issue and hence encourage consumers, be more involved -rather than just concerned- with the environmental betterment of the planet. The keywords of great importance to the authors were: intention-behavior gap, motivation-behavior gap, green purchasing inconsistency, environmental sustainability, pro-environmental behavior, UNDP, United Nations Environment Program, and SDG 12.

Chapter 13 presents the topic of Green Innovation, while balancing economic efficiency with environmental protection. According to the authors, Green Innovation (GI) represents the voluntary commitment of companies to develop new environmentally friendly products and/or processes. Also, based on the authors' comments, this type of innovation represents a new business paradigm in which social, environmental and societal issues are taken into consideration in a balanced way, satisfying the different types of demands of the organizations' stakeholders. The authors have stressed that GI is therefore a long-term commitment to balancing the economic needs of the organization and the environmental and social demands of customers. Also, according to the authors, given the relevance of the topic, this chapter aims to answer the following research questions: what are the characteristics that make up the concept of GI, has there been any terminological evolution, and under what theoretical approaches has the concept been addressed? The authors have stressed, also, that through a narrative review of the literature, the research addresses these research questions in order to bring clarity to the field of study, thus serving as a reference study for both neophyte and experienced researchers in the field. The keywords presented as decisive for this current research are: Green Innovation, green process innovation, green product innovation, and Sustainability.

Cristina Raluca Gh. Popescu
University of Bucharest, Romania & The Bucharest University of Economic Studies, Romania

REFERENCES

SDG Progress Report. (2022). *Advanced Unedited Version. Progress towards the Sustainable Development Goal: Report of the Secretary-General.* https://digitallibrary.un.org/record/1627573. https://digitallibrary.un.org/record/3930067

United Nations (UN). (2022). *Department of Economic and Social Affairs. Sustainable Development. The 2030 Agenda for Sustainable Development. Transforming our world: the 2030 Agenda for Sustainable Development.* https://sdgs.un.org/goals

Acknowledgment

On this special occasion, the editor would like to draw the attention to the groundbreaking studies that belong to the Indian economist and the 1998 Nobel Prize in Economic Sciences winner Amartya Sen (born November 3, 1933, in Santiniketan, India), who expressed a great concern towards the development and the evolution of our society and who made a powerful contribution to the welfare economics and the social choice theory. According to this great professor and this illustrious scientist, even though sustainability does not represent a new subject for these days analysis and for today's discussions, it has the immense and the immeasurable power to move individuals lives and to shed a new light on the manner in which the natural world that people inhabit should be constantly taken care of for the benefit of humankind and for the general good of all.

In the same line with the aforementioned bold ideas, the editor would like to emphasize the depth found in the ideas promoted by the well-known American environmentalist, entrepreneur, author, economist, and activist Paul Gerard Hawken (born February 8, 1946, in San Mateo, California, U.S.), who highlighted the fragility of our Planet, the power that sustainability can offer to individuals willing to work together with the nature, to successfully align with the natural forces among us, and to support life, equilibrium, and stability for all.

In this general context, the book suggestively entitled "Frameworks for Sustainable Development Goals to Manage Economic, Social, and Environmental Shocks and Disasters", published by IGI Global, comes to support the marvels that the natural beauty embodies, the strength that the quality of life promotes, and the will the natural forces possess, which are meant to promote environmental sustainability, economic stability, resilient political choices, and social cohesion, in a world expected to become more responsible and more centered on ensuring sustainable development for the present generations and the future generations.

Besides all these, the Secretary-General of the United Nations, Portuguese politician and diplomat António Manuel de Oliveira Guterres (born April 30, 1949, in Santos-o-Velho, Lisboan, Portugal) has prompted on numerous occasions so far the fact that humanity faces these days "a triple planetary crisis", which leads to the urgent involvement of all individuals in generating and in participating in changing actions and preservation activities, which do not require any heroic attempts or any grand gestures; the solution resides in putting an end to "our senseless and suicidal war against nature" and making a priority for all individuals to "protect and nurture our planet, that is our only home" (Secretary-General António Guterres addresses the opening of the Stockholm+50 summit in Sweden, United Nations (UN), UNEP, https://www.un.org/sg/en).

In this particular context, the Sustainable Development Goals (SDGs) – assiduously and vigorously promoted by the 2030 Agenda for Sustainable Development (SD), may bring to our thoughts the astonishing ideas and the core shaking beliefs of the Indian lawyer, politician, social activist, and writer Mahatma Gandhi, byname of Mohandas Karamchand Gandhi (born October 2, 1869, in Porbandar, India – died January 30, 1948, in Delhi, India), who stated in his attempt to touch our souls and to open our eyes that: "Earth provides enough to satisfy every man's need, but not every man's greed" (quoted in Ernst Friedrich Schumacher, "Small is Beautiful", United States Environmental Protection Agency (EPA), Quotations about the Environment, https://www.epa.gov/history/quotations-about-environment).

The editor would like to express a tremendous gratitude to the reputed specialist that was so kind and so dedicated in preparing the "Foreword" section of the book on the "Frameworks for Sustainable Development Goals to Manage Economic, Social, and Environmental Shocks and Disasters", published by IGI Global, namely: Dr. Meg Warren – Associate Professor of Management at Western Washington University, USA.

All in all, the editor would like to express the deepest appreciation, the greatest consideration, and the warmest thoughts to all the IGI Global team members for being so committed, devoted, and enthusiastic in all the stages that were an integrating part of the editing process of the book on the "Frameworks for Sustainable Development Goals to Manage Economic, Social, and Environmental Shocks and Disasters", published by IGI Global.

The effort and the passion that made this research project come to life will forever support sustainability in the world and the people's commitment towards the creation of a healthy society in which ordinary actions and situations will have the magical strength needed in order to generate extraordinary circumstances to do good actions now and in the future.

Cristina Raluca Gh. Popescu
University of Bucharest, Romania & The Bucharest University of Economic Studies, Romania

Chapter 1
Coping With COVID-19 While Focusing on Good Health and Well-Being:
Vaccination Willingness

Esra Karapınar Kocağ
https://orcid.org/0000-0002-2239-0519
Gümüşhane University, Turkey

Cristina Raluca Gh. Popescu
https://orcid.org/0000-0002-5876-0550
University of Bucharest, Romania & The Bucharest University of Economic Studies, Romania

ABSTRACT

The accentuated digital transformation and the unprecedented worldwide collaboration, as results of the COVID-19 pandemic changes and the COVID-19 crisis challenges, have generated noteworthy concerns in terms of individuals' health and well-being in the light of the development of vaccines and in the attempt to understand better vaccination willingness. The case of vaccination willingness has been addressed in the powerful context generated by the influence of the Sustainable Development Goals, with a preeminent accent on health and well-being, while emphasizing that the pandemic has accentuated the inequalities between people in terms of vaccine distribution and has irreversibly transformed the approach of the society in terms of decision-making in matters related to health, society, and economy. The economic growth and the economy recovery of all countries have proven highly dependent on the success of the COVID-19 vaccines and the fiscal and the monetary support programs.

INTRODUCTION

Nowadays, specialists worldwide are becoming more and more acquainted with the changes, disruptions, and implications of the COVID-19 pandemic in the society. In the same line, leaders all around

DOI: 10.4018/978-1-6684-6750-3.ch001

the globe are becoming more and more aware of the challenges, commitments, and opportunities that the COVID-19 crisis has brought in terms of health, diplomacy, world peace, and international cooperation.

The Sustainable Development Goals (SDGs) which are regarded as crucial according to the United Nations Development Program (UNDP), have mainly centered on 17 targets or objectives due to ensure a better and a more sustainable future for the generations due to come (United Nations (UN), 2015). On the list of these 17 decisive goals can be found the "Good Health and Well-Being" objective, which represents the third target according to the United Nations Agenda presented in the year 2015 (United Nations (UN), 2015). Even though, over time, specialists have managed to find different cures for several threatening and dangerous diseases, which made life expectancy increase over the years in a dramatically manner, there are numerous threats on individuals health and well-being. The rhythm of life and people's expectations have severely changed in the last decades, which placed stress and pollutions on one of the top positions in terms of life threatening day to day circumstances. Going further with our analysis, it ought to be noted that pollution and rapid environmental degradation lead inevitably to severe health deterioration and alteration. In this matter, the COVID-19 pandemic came as a warning of what might the future bring in a more aggressive manner and in different circumstances, in terms of time and place. The 2030 Agenda part of the United Nations Development Program focuses on the importance of "good health" as well as on the power of ecosystems sustainability, in an attempt to show the complexity that resides between sustainable development, strong health, and well-being. There are overpowering connections that may be encountered at all levels between the environment, individuals' health, and the evolution of life on Planet Earth.

Besides all these, it should be highlighted that the COVID-19 pandemic as well as the COVID-19 crisis have generated serious disruptions in the process of accomplishing the United Nations (UN) third objective centered on "Good Health and Well-Being", since the economic and social inequalities have been dangerously widened, while the spread of this new form of virus led to climate and environmental destabilization, and alarming increases in the rate of poverty. In this matter, it can be noticed that building good health for all remains a priority for the 2030 Agenda part of the United Nations Development Program (UNDP) and a bold desiderate for the present and the future generations.

In this pressing matter, the researchers and the specialists all around the Globe are trying to find viable ways in which people could manage to cope with COVID-19 while focusing on good health and well-being, showing a great interest in analyzing and in understanding the vaccination willingness – since the vaccines have proven of substantial help in saving lives and in keeping the number of the infected individuals at lower levels.

There are several key aspects that this scientific book chapter intends to highlight, given the particular attention that this theme has drawn at present moment, as follows in the lines below:

Step 1: This book chapter centers on addressing the importance of good health and well-being in a society that calls for immediate action in terms of reaffirming the Sustainable Development Goals (SDGs) as well as their importance for the entire humanity.

Step 2: In the same line, this book chapter focuses on finding solutions capable to enable individuals to cope with COVID-19 while focusing on good health and well-being, while analyzing vaccination willingness, while displaying an analysis on the publicly available microdata from the World Bank's COVID-19 High Frequency Phone Survey of Households (2021-Round 4).

Step 3: In like manner, this book chapter tackles the COVID-19 pandemic changes as well as the COVID-19 crisis challenges on today's society, while striving to find solutions for the Post-COVID-19 Era sustainable development, sustainable economic growth, and good and strong health for all.

In addition, it needs to be stressed that the general structure of this book chapter revolves around the following main sections, namely: the introduction, in which the authors have shown the importance of the theme chosen for their analysis and have created the right connections between the topic addressed and the significant importance of the Sustainable Development Goals (SDGs) for the society and its evolution; the background, in which the authors have presented the general framework addressed in this given context as well as the key concepts that require a particular attention in order to have more reasons to value good and strong health, people's well-being and powerful mental health, vaccination willingness in times in which individuals' both mental and physical state of mind are seriously challenged, knowledge, human resources, innovation, Sustainable Development Goals (SDGs) with a deep accent on health and well-being, and the global economic environment under the influence of the COVID-19; the data and methodology, in which the authors have utilized for their analysis publicly available microdata from the World Bank's COVID-19 High Frequency Phone Survey of Households (2021-Round 4), in order to discover people's vaccination willingness, thus hoping to establish different connections and different patterns capable to shed a new light on how things are due to look like in the Post-COVID-19 Era; the discussion and synthesis of results, in which the authors have emphasized their most significant discoveries based on the data analyzed, centering on variable such as vaccination willingness, employed, job changed, job lost, money lending, online shopping, food insecurity, financial threat, feeling about pandemic, income, and region; the solutions and recommendations, in which the authors have presented some of the main challenges, changes, and opportunities that the COVID-19 crisis has brought, while referring mainly to the role of health and well-being in a society profoundly affected by the shockwave launched by the COVID-19 pandemic; the future research directions, in which the authors have chosen to discuss what will their new ventures be in terms of novel analysis and valuable contributions that they intend to bring to light on the short and medium term; the conclusion, in which the authors have stated which are their main contributions and which are their believes in terms of the evolution of the COVID-19 pandemic and of the COVID-19 crisis, in order to address a more secure future for individuals and the environment in the Post-COVID-19 Era; the references, in which the authors have displayed some of the most relevant works on the theme chosen, willing to expend their research, in the near future, in order to bring more knowledge and more substance in the works due to come; and the key terms and the definitions, in which the authors have turned their attention to the most valuable concepts that are part of the analyzed theme, offering explanations and presenting examples in order to show in a profound way the significance of the subject under debate.

BACKGROUND

These days, specialists believe that the Sustainable Development Goals (SDGs) represent "a core principle of the Treaty on European Union and a priority objective for the Union's internal and external policies", and the power that the sustainable development of our Planet resides at the very core of human well-being and environmental health (European Commission (EC), 2022a). According to the European Commission (EC), the United Nations' Agenda for the year 2030 "is crucial to strengthen resilience and prepare the world for future shocks", while sustainability needs to be enhanced with the aid of the new growth strategies due to focus on "a fair, inclusive and prosperous society, with a modern, knowledge-driven, resource-efficient and competitive economy where there are no net emissions of greenhouse gases in 2050, and which protects, conserves and enhances the EU's natural capital, and protects the health and well-being of citizens from environment-related risks" (European Commission (EC), 2022b). A major priority on the European Commission's agenda is represented by the "environmental degradation (...) influences on human health", especially in the context in which "competitive sustainability has always been at the heart of Europe's social market economy and should remain its guiding principle for the future" (European Commission (EC), 2019, p.3).

The COVID-19 pandemic has irreversibly affected "environmental sustainability, productivity gains, fairness and macro-economic stability", which represented the four dimensions of a healthy, inclusive and robust economic policy, turning the immediate focus on changing the order of the priorities and on shifting the attention on individuals' health and well-being (European Commission (EC), 2019, p.3). In this way, the necessity of creating a new paradigm has come to light, which led to the idea that the transformations due to be expected in terms of individuals' health and well-being "are prerequisite for success and should complete our framework", thus positioning "health and the planet at the center stage of economic policy" (European Commission (EC), 2019, pp.3-4). In continuation, a prominent framework was created by specialists willing to comply with the new social, economic, financial, and political expectations, in order to be part of "an economy that works for people and planet", focusing on the strong belief according to which "to succeed, costs and benefits need to be balanced in the short and long term", based on the idea that "the green transition will also create new jobs and greater well-being, for example in the form of healthier working and living environments" (European Commission (EC), 2019, p.4).

The European consensus on development has positioned "health and social protection systems" at the very core of an inclusive, robust, and resilient economic policy, stating that the COVID-19 pandemic as well as the COVID-19 crisis have shown the importance of an appropriate budget for the health systems of nations worldwide, as follows: (a) "Budget support can enable the development of broad social protection policies and the strengthening of health and social protection systems"; and, in the same light, (b) "The COVID-19 global public health emergency has demonstrated in particular the need for effective social protection systems, which are crucial in safe-guarding the poor and vulnerable when a crisis hits", since "for years, EU budget support has been instrumental in tackling disparities in health (SDG 3), which has increased the resilience of health systems and prepared countries to respond better to the pandemic" (United Nations (UN), 2022).

According to the United Nations (UN) document entitled "The Sustainable Development Goals Report 2021", a notable accent has been placed on vaccination in order to support life and to foster a healthier future for all, as follows: "A global vaccination plan, designed and implemented by the countries that can produce vaccines today or will be able to do so if properly supported, is an urgent first step in that direction" (United Nations (UN), 2021, p.2). Likewise, António Guterres – the Secretary-General of the United Nations, mentioned that the COVID-19 pandemic as well as the COVID-19 crisis "challenges are immense, but there are also reasons for hope", stressing the fact that "the COVID-19 crisis demonstrated inspiring community resilience, highlighted the Herculean work by essential workers in myriad fields and facilitated the rapid expansion of social protection, the acceleration of digital transformation and unprecedented worldwide collaboration on the development of vaccines", which led to the belief that "a brighter future is possible", thus the present generations need to take advantage of the opportunities that the crisis brought in order "to transform our world, deliver on the 2030 Agenda and keep our promise to current and future generations" (United Nations (UN), 2021, p.2).

As highlighted in the "The Sustainable Development Goals Report 2021", COVID-19 has sadly created a lot of disruptions in the society by "amplifying health inequalities" (United Nations (UN), 2021, p.32). For instance, in this regard, the figures obtained for the year 2020 have displayed the worrying situation at a global level, highlighting the fact that the COVID-19 crisis and the COVID-19 pandemic affected the lives of the most vulnerable categories of population, namely "the elderly, the poor, refugees and migrants, and a broad range of vulnerable groups due to their specific health and socioeconomic circumstances, poor living conditions and lack of access to high-quality public health care" (United Nations (UN), 2021, p.32).

However, it was extremely fortunate that, due to innovation in the medical sector – vigorously promoted and actively supported in terms of financial programs, the creation and the development of the vaccines against COVID-19 was made possible almost in record time; also, the effort done in this matter at a universal level led leaders worldwide to the undeniable conclusion that "the COVID-19 pandemic has demonstrated that no institution or individual alone can address the economic, environmental, social and technological challenges" (World Economic Forum, 2021).

The Council of Europe (CE) brought to the attention the importance of the third target included in the Sustainable Development Goals (SDGs), namely ensuring healthy lives and promoting well-being for all at all ages by linking health and well-being to the preservation of human race and the "human dignity" obligation that the institutions have, as follows: "human dignity is the fundamental value and indeed the core of positive European human rights law – whether under the European Social Charter or under the European Convention of Human Rights - and health care is a prerequisite for the preservation of human dignity" (Council of Europe (CE), 2022).

Individuals' well-being is of essence in the Post-COVID-19 Era, while environmental health is a matter of great concern for all, since the targets are represented by the preservation of the current resources, in order to offer a better future for all, the discovery of new resources, in order to provide alternatives to the ones the resources that are limited and in danger of disappearing, and the discovery of new and more reliable meanings for people's existence, in order to justify the constant efforts done to support life, to preserve the natural habitats, to maintain the ecosystems, and to accomplish an equilibrium between acting sustainably and developing responsibly (Popescu, 2021; Popescu, 2022).

Data and Methodology

This chapter utilizes publicly available microdata from the World Bank's COVID-19 High Frequency Phone Survey of Households (2021-Round 4). There are 5 rounds of this survey; however, all of them do not contain the same questions. A particular question that was used in this chapter was only included in Round 4. Hence, this chapter will utilize only Round 4 in empirical investigation. Survey aimed to evaluate how households were affected by COVID-19, and it covers 3,945 households in total.

The dependent variable is based on a survey question asking whether the respondent would be willing to get vaccinated with an approved vaccine to prevent coronavirus at no cost. There are three answer categories that are 1-Yes; 2-No; and 3-Depends on which vaccines. As part of the aim of this chapter, only "Yes" and "No" answers were considered and observations (61 observations) who reported their preference would depend on the type of vaccine was dropped. Additionally, those who do not know or refuse the question among the independent variables were also dropped. Eventually, empirical part of this chapter relies on 3,805 observations. The number of observations in the analysis may vary across specifications.

Summary statistics of the variables used in the empirical investigation is presented in Table 1 below. With respect to the dependent variable, survey respondents are mostly seen to be willing to get vaccinated. Only about 13 per cent of them reported they wouldn't be willing to get vaccinated.

A wide range of independent variables that are likely to influence individuals' behavior to prevent COVID-19 are included in the model. Participants were asked whether they worked in the last week (Employed: Yes; No); whether their main job is same (Job changed: Yes; No); whether they know someone who lost his/her job since February 2020 (Job lost: Yes; No); whether they lend money since February 2020 (Money lending: Yes; No); whether they bought products online (Online shopping: Yes; No); whether any household member went without eating for a whole day (Food insecurity: Yes; No); how much their household finance threaten by coronavirus (Financial threat: A substantial threat; A moderate threat; Not much of a threat; Not a threat at all); how they feel about pandemic (Feeling about pandemic: More optimistic; Same; Less optimistic); how their income changed (Income: Increase; Same; Decrease). It should be noted that regions of Vietnam were also included to consider regional variation.

Table 1. Summary statistics of the variables used in the empirical investigation

Variable	Survey question	Obs.	Mean	Std. Dev.	Min	Max	Frequency	Percent
Vaccination willingness	If an approved vaccine to prevent COVID-19 was to become available at no cost, would you agree to be vaccinated?							
Yes	(Base)	3805	0.873062	0.332948	0	1	3,322	87.31
No		3805	0.126938	0.332948	0	1	483	12.69
Employed	In the last 7 days, did you do any work to generate income, even if only for one hour?							
Yes	(Base)	3805	0.830486	0.375254	0	1	3,160	83.05
No		3805	0.169514	0.375254	0	1	645	16.95
Job changed	Is your main job the same job you were doing in September?							
Yes	(Base)	3405	0.939794	0.237902	0	1	3,200	93.98
No		3405	0.060206	0.237902	0	1	205	6.02
Job lost	Do you know someone who lost their job since Feb 2020							
Yes	(Base)	3805	0.36636	0.481873	0	1	1,394	36.64
No		3805	0.63364	0.481873	0	1	2,411	63.36
Money lending	Did you lend money to someone since Feb 2020?							
Yes	(Base)	3805	0.071748	0.258104	0	1	273	7.17
No		3805	0.928252	0.258104	0	1	3,532	92.83
Online shopping	Did you buy products using an online platform e.g. website, mobile app before Feb 2020?							
Yes	(Base)	3805	0.223916	0.416921	0	1	852	22.39
No		3805	0.776084	0.416921	0	1	2,953	77.61
Food insecurity	You, or any other adult in your household, went without eating for a whole day?							
Yes	(Base)	3805	0.022339	0.147803	0	1	85	2.23
No		3805	0.977661	0.147803	0	1	3,720	97.77
Financial threat	How much of a threat would you say the coronavirus outbreak is to your household's finances?							
A substantial threat	(Base)	3805	0.52615	0.499381	0	1	2,002	52.61
A moderate threat		3805	0.217346	0.412494	0	1	827	21.73

Continued on following page

Table 1. Continued

Variable	Survey question	Obs.	Mean	Std. Dev.	Min	Max	Frequency	Percent
Not much of a threat		3805	0.12431	0.329978	0	1	473	12.43
Not a threat at all		3805	0.132195	0.338747	0	1	503	13.22
Feeling about pandemic	How do you feel about the pandemic now compared to September							
More optimistic	(Base)	3805	0.643364	0.479069	0	1	2,448	64.34
Same		3805	0.19159	0.393604	0	1	729	19.16
Less optimistic		3805	0.165046	0.371271	0	1	628	16.5
Income	How is your household's income this month compared to this time last year?							
Increase	(Base)	3805	0.088042	0.283393	0	1	335	8.8
Same		3805	0.443101	0.496817	0	1	1,686	44.31
Decrease		3805	0.468857	0.499095	0	1	1,784	46.89
Region	Six geographic regions of Vietnam							
Red River Delta	(Base)	3805	0.204468	0.403365	0	1	778	20.45
Midlands and Northern Mountainous Areas		3805	0.276216	0.447184	0	1	1,051	27.62
Northern and Coastal Central Region		3805	0.202891	0.402205	0	1	772	20.29
Central Highlands		3805	0.075953	0.264957	0	1	289	7.6
South eastern Area		3805	0.09067	0.287177	0	1	345	9.07
Mekong Delta		3805	0.149803	0.356925	0	1	570	14.98

Source: The authors, based on the references highlighted in this book chapter

Table 2. Pairwise correlations

Variables	Vaccination willingness	Employed	Job changed	Job lost	Money lending	Online shopping	Food insecurity	Financial threat	Feeling about pandemic	Income	Region
Vaccination willingness	1										
Employed	0.036**	1									
Job changed	0.032*	0.076***	1								
Job lost	0.050***	-0.033**	-0.027*	1							
Money lending	0.001	0.059***	-0.008	0.080***	1						
Online shopping	0	0.097***	0.01	0.054***	0.172***	1					
Food insecurity	0.01	-0.036**	-0.005	0.040**	-0.015	-0.030*	1				
Financial threat	0.063***	0.025	-0.025	0.216***	0.009	0.039**	0.038**	1			
Feeling about pandemic	-0.012	0.060***	0.011	-0.036**	0.026*	0.036**	-0.053***	-0.059***	1		
Income	-0.038**	0.016	0.018	-0.165***	0.02	0.024	0.003	-0.242***	0.084***	1	
Region	0.059***	-0.021	-0.004	0.019	0.047***	0.01	-0.029*	0.064***	0.101***	0.002	1

*** $p<0.01$, ** $p<0.05$, * $p<0.1$

Source: The authors, based on the references highlighted in this book chapter

Pairwise correlations were also checked to have an idea on the relationships between variables of interest and results are presented in Table 2. It should be noted that they do not refer a robust relationship. Correlations range from -1 to +1 and correlation coefficient of -1 or +1 means a perfect correlation. This is a useful tool to detect highly correlated variables that would cause multicollinearity problem. More clearly, independent variables must be independent. Otherwise, it may give rise to unreliable estimation results. As seen in Table 2, independent variables used in this empirical investigation do not seem to have high correlations between each other. Therefore, it can be said that this chapter is not likely to suffer multicollinearity problem.

In terms of methodological preference, this chapter utilizes probit model because of the fact that the dependent variable investigated here is a binary variable that can take values 0 and 1 for each observation. The interpretation of the estimation results of the probit model is not straightforward. To interpret these results, calculation of marginal effects is commonly used. Marginal effects show the change in probability independent variable increases by one unit. Therefore, following the probit estimation, marginal effects were calculated to make the interpretation of the coefficients of explanatory variables. As seen from the descriptive statistics in Table 1, all of the explanatory variables are dummy categorical variables. Hence, in the interpretation of the categorical explanatory variable, the change refers to a change from 0 (i.e., reference/base category) to 1.

With regards to weighting strategy, population weight that is provided in the survey was used. Goodness of fit was measured through Pseudo R^2. This is slightly different than standard R^2 as in an OLS regression. Getting an R^2 value close to 1 is almost impossible for the binominal response variables. Pseudo- R^2, hence, is used as a useful measure.

DISCUSSION AND SYNTHESIS OF RESULTS

This section presents empirical findings of the probit model that investigates the determinants of vaccination willingness of individuals. Table 2 shows results of probit model. The first column of the table presents the original coefficients obtained from probit specification, while the second column presents calculated marginal effects that help to interpret findings in a meaningful way.

Apart from the original specification, rural and urban sub-specification was also estimated to see whether results change based on the rural and urban locations of the country. Rural area may not access information and facilities as much as urban area. Besides, work and living conditions in urban may bring more risk on those who live in urban areas. Therefore, attitudes of these people towards vaccination may differ. Accordingly, column 3 and 4 show original probit coefficients and calculated marginal effects for urban Vietnam, respectively. Columns 5 and 6, on the other hand show results for rural Vietnam.

Table 3. Estimation results of the probit model with marginal effects

Variables	Original	Margins	Urban-Original	Urban-Margins	Rural-Original	Rural-Margins
Employed (Base: Yes)						
No	-0.094	-0.020	-0.309	-0.076	0.016	0.003
	(0.171)	(0.037)	(0.308)	(0.084)	(0.202)	(0.037)
Job changed (Base: Yes)						
No	-0.228	-0.051	-0.411	-0.104	-0.210	-0.044
	(0.159)	(0.039)	(0.290)	(0.084)	(0.195)	(0.045)
Job lost (Base: Yes)						
No	-0.236***	-0.045***	-0.198	-0.042	-0.265**	-0.048**
	(0.088)	(0.017)	(0.156)	(0.033)	(0.110)	(0.019)
Money lending (Base: Yes)						
No	0.026	0.005	0.161	0.037	-0.103	-0.018
	(0.154)	(0.031)	(0.235)	(0.057)	(0.203)	(0.035)
Online shopping (Base: Yes)						
No	0.037	0.007	-0.198	-0.042	0.148	0.029
	(0.099)	(0.020)	(0.155)	(0.031)	(0.124)	(0.026)
Food insecurity (Base: Yes)						
No	0.099	0.021	0.500	0.133	-0.144	-0.025
	(0.316)	(0.070)	(0.519)	(0.162)	(0.301)	(0.048)
Financial threat (Base: A substantial threat)						
A moderate threat	-0.016	-0.003	0.173	0.035	-0.111	-0.020
	(0.110)	(0.021)	(0.185)	(0.037)	(0.134)	(0.025)

Continued on following page

Table 3. Continued

Variables	Original	Margins	Urban-Original	Urban-Margins	Rural-Original	Rural-Margins
Not much of a threat	0.015	0.003	0.209	0.042	-0.106	-0.019
	(0.129)	(0.024)	(0.226)	(0.043)	(0.155)	(0.029)
Not a threat at all	-0.420***	-0.099***	-0.501**	-0.138**	-0.410***	-0.088**
	(0.126)	(0.033)	(0.222)	(0.068)	(0.154)	(0.037)
Feeling about pandemic (Base: More optimistic)						
Same	-0.312***	-0.071***	-0.331*	-0.084*	-0.319***	-0.067**
	(0.101)	(0.025)	(0.178)	(0.048)	(0.119)	(0.027)
Less optimistic	0.151	0.027	0.339*	0.062*	0.060	0.010
	(0.118)	(0.020)	(0.196)	(0.032)	(0.144)	(0.024)
Income (Base: Increase)						
Same	-0.133	-0.025	-0.239	-0.047	-0.069	-0.013
	(0.151)	(0.027)	(0.279)	(0.051)	(0.175)	(0.032)
Decrease	-0.097	-0.018	-0.216	-0.042	-0.038	-0.007
	(0.151)	(0.027)	(0.277)	(0.050)	(0.174)	(0.031)
Region (Base: Red River Delta)						
Midlands and Northern Mountainous Areas	0.243**	0.046*	0.037	0.007	0.269*	0.050*
	(0.124)	(0.024)	(0.244)	(0.049)	(0.143)	(0.028)
Northern and Coastal Central Region	0.208*	0.040*	-0.010	-0.002	0.290*	0.054*
	(0.124)	(0.024)	(0.212)	(0.044)	(0.149)	(0.028)
Central Highlands	0.458***	0.076***	0.147	0.028	0.659***	0.098***
	(0.163)	(0.026)	(0.261)	(0.049)	(0.206)	(0.028)
South Eastern Area	-0.145	-0.034	-0.202	-0.046	-0.064	-0.014
	(0.141)	(0.033)	(0.213)	(0.048)	(0.191)	(0.043)
Mekong Delta	-0.047	-0.010	0.024	0.005	-0.063	-0.014
	(0.132)	(0.029)	(0.253)	(0.051)	(0.153)	(0.034)
Constant	1.317***		0.979		1.599***	
	(0.384)		(0.635)		(0.399)	
Observations	3,405	3,405	908	908	2,497	2,497
Pseudo-R2	0.0487		0.0764		0.0526	
Robust standard errors in parentheses *** p<0.01, ** p<0.05, * p<0.1						

Source: The authors, based on the references highlighted in this book chapter

From original results, one can have an idea on the significance and sign of the relationship with the dependent variable. However, only marginal effects can give a more precise idea on the size of the impact. As seen, job lost variable has a negative and statistically significant (at 1 per cent level) impact on vaccination willingness. More precisely, those who do not know someone lost his/her job since February 2020 are less likely to be willing to get vaccinated by 4.5 percentage points. It is negative but not statistically significant for Urban. However, the rural specification shows that this significant negative relationship driven by this sub group of the sample. This might be due to the fact that rural regions are mostly characterized by agricultural production and undocumented labor. In comparison with the urban life, these parts of the country are less likely to suffer considerable job loss. This may cause to underestimate the effects of coronavirus, and ending up with an unwillingness to get vaccinated.

Another statistically significant impact is found in the financial threat variable. Those who think coronavirus is not a threat at all in household finances is less likely to get vaccinated than those who think pandemic is a substantial threat to household finance. The impact is larger for urban sub group than the rural one. That means individuals who are not financially affected by this outbreak are not willing to get vaccinated.

Furthermore, individual feeling about the pandemic also shows some significant impact on this willingness. Those who feel the same compared to September are less likely to be willing to get vaccinated than those who are more optimistic. The magnitude of the impact is larger for urban subgroup though it is only marginally significant. On the contrary, for the urban sub group, those who feel less optimistic are more likely to be willing to get vaccinated than those who are more optimistic though it is statistically significant only at 10 percent significance level. Yet, it still provides an important insight that people who are more concerned about coronavirus seem to be more willing to take necessary measures.

It should also be noted that there is regional differences on this preference. Considering Red River Delta region as a reference, Midlands and Northern Mountainous Areas, Northern and Coastal Central Region, and Central Highlands are more likely to be willing. However, South Eastern Area and Mekong Delta are less likely to be willing to get vaccinated, although this is not statistically significant.

SOLUTIONS AND RECOMMENDATIONS

The solutions and recommendations that the authors of this book chapter focused on in order to show the manner in which the society these days copes with COVID-19 while focusing on good health and well-being as well as the existing status of vaccination willingness among individuals at a global level are believed to be essential prerequisites in the Post-COVID-19 Era.

Step 1: The first step that the authors believe is crucial for the future of our society is reaffirming the need to accomplish the Sustainable Development Goals (SDGs) as well as the need to accentuate the role and the importance of health and well-being for all individuals. In this matter, the chapter has discussed the implications of populations' inequalities all around the Globe, and has presented the position of the Council of Europe (CE) which prioritizes people's health and well-being according to the European Social Charter and the European Convention on Human Rights. In this matter, a good solution would be to promote knowledge and to foster innovation, in order to be able to show a deeper and a greater concern for the population. In continuation, the health system should receive more funds in order to avoid health risks and to exclude discriminatory practices.

Step 2: The second step that the authors believe is vital for enabling today's society to find the way out of the COVID-19 crisis is by valuing the results related with vaccination willingness based on the publicly available microdata from the World Bank's COVID-19 High Frequency Phone Survey of Households (2021-Round 4) and by understanding the links between the Sustainable Development Goals (SDGs), health and well-being, in order to create a better world for all individuals.

Step 3: The third step that the authors believe is pivotal in order to be able to cope with the COVID-19 is represented by accentuating solidarity among individuals and among countries, since the COVID-19 implications might be regarded also as an opportunity for humankind that cannot be missed under these given circumstances.

FUTURE RESEARCH DIRECTIONS

When analyzing the issues surrounding the topic related to coping with COVID-19 while focusing on good health and well-being as well as the existing status of vaccination willingness there are several future directions that ought to be considered.

First of all, a possible future research direction could be represented by a complex analysis regarding the manner in which our economies and societies might be fundamentally reorganized in order to value more the chances missed and the opportunities offered especially as a result of the vaccines that were able to save lives and the climate challenges that threatens the balance in the society.

Second of all, another possible future research direction might be represented by a thorough analysis of the manner in which the COVID-19 pandemic and the COVID-19 crisis have managed to put the Sustainable Development Goals (SDGs) in the center of attention, by reaffirming the importance of these international targets, but with not too much progress registered for the last two years in a row (as displayed by the data highlighted in this book chapter). Current cross-sectional investigation may not represent a robust relationship. However, new available data sets that cover more waves and more detailed survey questions asked into more individuals in the future may help to explore vaccination willingness behavior in a clearer way.

CONCLUSION

The pre-pandemic and post-pandemic challenges in building inclusive global knowledge societies have been strongly connected by specialists with the aspects brought on by the COVID-19 pandemic and the COVID-19 crisis. It has been noted that the COVID-19 created numerous disruptions in our society, which led the authors to the belief that the general framework containing the Sustainable Development Goals (SDGs) needs to be readjusted and reaffirmed in order to cope in a better and in a more constructive manner with the changes and the challenges that our society are facing.

Also, this book chapter is highly important in terms of research analysis since it basis its results on a complex analysis of the publicly available microdata from the World Bank's COVID-19 High Frequency Phone Survey of Households (2021-Round 4). The variables used in the empirical investigation are the following ones: vaccination willingness; employed; job changed; job lost; money lending; online shopping; food insecurity; financial threat; feeling about pandemic; income; and region. It has been shown that from the original results, one can have an idea on the significance and sign of the relationship with the dependent variable and nevertheless, only marginal effects can give a more precise idea on the size of the impact.

ACKNOWLEDGMENT

This research received no specific grant from any funding agency in the public, commercial, or not-for-profit sectors.

REFERENCES

Council of Europe (CE). (2022). *Goal 3 Ensure healthy lives and promote well-being for all at all ages.* https://www.coe.int/en/web/un-agenda-2030/goal-3

European Commission (EC). (2019). *Communication From The Commission To The European Parliament, The Council, The European Central Bank, The European Economic And Social Committee, The Committee Of The Regions And The European Investment Bank. Annual Sustainable Growth Strategy 2020.* https://eur-lex.europa.eu/legal-content/EN/TXT/?qid=1578392227719&uri=CELEX%3A52019DC0650

European Commission (EC). (2022a). *Sustainable Development Goals.* https://ec.europa.eu/info/strategy/international-strategies/sustainable-development-goals_en

European Commission (EC). (2022b). *EU holistic approach to sustainable development.* https://ec.europa.eu/info/strategy/international-strategies/sustainable-development-goals/eu-holistic-approach-sustainable-development_en

Popescu, C. R. (2021). Impact of Innovative Capital on the Global Performance of the European Union: Implications on Sustainability Assessment. In C. Popescu (Ed.), *Handbook of Research on Novel Practices and Current Successes in Achieving the Sustainable Development Goals* (pp. 90–124). IGI Global. doi:10.4018/978-1-7998-8426-2.ch005

Popescu, C. R. (2022). Mindfulness at Work, a Sound Business Investment: Focusing on the Employee Well-Being While Increasing Creativity and Innovation. In C. Popescu (Ed.), *Handbook of Research on Changing Dynamics in Responsible and Sustainable Business in the Post-COVID-19 Era* (pp. 1–34). IGI Global. doi:10.4018/978-1-6684-2523-7.ch001

Sustainable Development Solutions Network (SDSN). A Global Imitative for the United Nations (UN). (n.d.). *The 2022 Sustainable Development Report (SDR): From Crisis to Sustainable Development, the SDGs as Roadmap to 2030 and Beyond.* https://www.sdgindex.org/reports/sustainable-development-report-2022/

Sustainable Development Solutions Network (SDSN). (n.d.). *A Global Imitative for the United Nations (UN).* https://www.unsdsn.org/

United Nations (UN). (2015). *What are the Sustainable Development Goals?* https://www.undp.org/sustainable-development-goals

United Nations (UN). (2021). *The Sustainable Development Goals Report 2021*. https://unstats.un.org/sdgs/report/2021/The-Sustainable-Development-Goals-Report-2021.pdf

United Nations (UN). (2022). *SDG-contracts – EU budget support to partner countries to meet their financing needs*. European Commission (Intergovernmental organization). https://sdgs.un.org/partnerships/sdg-contracts-eu-budget-support-partner-countries-meet-their-financing-needs

World Bank (WB). (2021). *Vietnam COVID-19 High Frequency Phone Survey of Households (HFPS-R4) 2021, Round 4*. Ref. VNM_2021_HFPS_v01_M. www.microdata.worldbank.org

World Economic Forum. (2021). *The Davos Agenda*. https://www.weforum.org/events/the-davos-agenda-2021

World Health Organization (WHO). (2022a). *Coronavirus Disease (COVID-19). Overview*. https://www.who.int/health-topics/coronavirus#tab=tab_1

World Health Organization (WHO). (2022b). *Coronavirus disease (COVID-19): Vaccines*. https://www.who.int/news-room/questions-and-answers/item/coronavirus-disease-(COVID-19)-vaccines

KEY TERMS AND DEFINITIONS

Coronavirus Disease (COVID-19): According to the World Health Organization (WHO) this form of disease, known as Coronavirus Disease (COVID-19), represents an infectious disease that has been caused by the SARS-CoV-2 virus and which is characterized by "mild to moderate respiratory illness" that individuals experience; based on specialists findings, this form of disease might be contracted by individuals at any age and depending on the case, individuals might develop less aggressive or more aggressive forms (WHO, 2022a).

Good Health and Well-Being: This represents the third objective or target stipulated by the UN Sustainable Development Goals (SDGs), which positions individuals' state of being, at both at physical and at mental level, on the top of the priorities; even though life expectancy has increased over time due to the tremendous medical progress in finding solutions for some of the major causes of illnesses and death, our Planet is continuously threatened by irresponsible actions and activities that have overbearing implications on people's lives, health, and well-being; in essence, the 2030 Agenda clearly suggests that sustainable development (SD) and good health are interconnected and go hand-in-hand, depending one on the other (UN, 2015).

Health and Sustainability: These days, the Sustainable Development Goals (SDGs) have successfully managed to place individuals' health and the Planet's sustainable development needs and desires as top priorities in terms of all actions and all activities that ought to be taken at an international level, thus ensuring a better and a more secure for all the generations to come; in continuation, health and sustainability have the power to promote robust, inclusive and sustainable economic growth, in a world that calls for sustainable business and sustainable finance.

Sustainable Development (SD): Is being defined by specialists worldwide as a particular, most needed and most desired form of development that focuses on sustainability in a way that enables today's society to take into consideration the needs of the present generations without altering the future of the next generations, by also finding solutions to ensure the best possible life conditions to the next generations that will soon inhabit our Planet Earth.

Sustainable Development Goals (SDGs): The Sustainable Development Goals (SDGs) are known, also, at an international level, as the Global Goals, being part of the United Nations (UN) Agenda which has led to their adoption in the year 2015; due to their overwhelming and overpowering importance in our society, the 17 goals that were included by the UN on their Agenda have required, over time, immediate attention and a high level of responsibility from all the involved parties, in order to be able to learn how to manage better and more constructively economic, social, and environmental shocks and disasters, such as the COVID-19 pandemic and the COVID-19 crisis (UN, 2015).

Sustainable Development Solutions (SDS): The 2022 Sustainable Development Report (SDR) entitled "From Crisis to Sustainable Development, the SDGs as Roadmap to 2030 and Beyond", published on the 2nd of June 2022, states that "peace, diplomacy, and international cooperation are fundamental conditions for the world to progress", and, in the same manner, stresses the fact that for two years in a row the world has not registered any new process in terms of reaching the UN proposed Sustainable Development Goals (SDGs) (SDSN, 2022).

Vaccines for Coronavirus Disease (COVID-19): The World Health Organization (WHO) published on the 17th of May 2022 an updated list of vaccines for Coronavirus Disease (COVID-19) which includes nine validated for use types by WHO (given Emergency Use Listing), stating the specialists' strong belief that by being part of the vaccination process individuals could save their own lives as well as the lives of others, due to the fact that "COVID-19 vaccines provide strong protection against serious illness, hospitalization and death" (WHO, 2022b).

Chapter 2
Corporate Social Responsibility: A Narrative Literature Review

Bartolomé Marco-Lajara
https://orcid.org/0000-0001-8811-9118
University of Alicante, Spain

Patrocinio Zaragoza-Sáez
University of Alicante, Spain

Javier Martínez Falcó
https://orcid.org/0000-0001-9004-5816
University of Alicante, Spain

Luis A. Millan-Tudela
https://orcid.org/0000-0003-3669-9960
University of Alicante, Spain

ABSTRACT

Corporate social responsibility (CSR) represents the voluntary commitment of companies to behave appropriately, fairly, and responsibly with the environment in which they operate. It refers to a business approach that takes into account economic, environmental, and social issues in a balanced, holistic, and long-term manner for the benefit of current and future stakeholders. Thus, since the introduction of the concept, more managers are including social and environmental objectives in their decision-making process. The aim of CSR is therefore to seek the well-being of society and the environment through business activities. However, when did the term come into being, how has the term evolved since its foundation, and how has the concept of CSR evolved over time? Through a narrative review of the literature, the research addresses these research questions to bring clarity to the field of study.

DOI: 10.4018/978-1-6684-6750-3.ch002

INTRODUCTION

This research exposes the main proposals in the academic literature to address the study of Corporate Social Responsibility (CSR) in organizations. Through the review carried out, the study shows the importance of social and environmental issues for companies, as well as the intensification of their study and relevance in recent decades.

CSR is essentially a concept whereby companies voluntarily decide to contribute to a better society and a cleaner environment. It is based on the idea that the overall performance of a company should be evaluated in terms of its combined contribution to the economic prosperity, environmental quality and social well-being of the society in which it operates (Rhou & Singal, 2020). It aims to seek excellence in the company, paying special attention to people and their working conditions, as well as to the quality of its production processes with the incorporation of the three facets of sustainable development: economic, social and environmental, which favors the consolidation of the company, promotes its economic success and allies its future projection (Velte, 2021).

The debate, therefore, focuses on the degree of involvement of the company with its own shareholders, with its workers, with its customers, with its suppliers and with the community in which it operates. This allows concepts such as sustainable development, continuous improvement of health and safety conditions in the workplace or the company's civic responsibility to be placed at the center of the discussion (Agudelo et al., 2019). The successive financial scandals, the economic crisis and the food crises that have impacted European society have led to a crisis in corporate credibility. Society is increasingly demanding more information on the activities of companies at all levels, as well as on the impact of their activities on the environment (Malik, 2015) . We are undoubtedly in a period of change in production systems. Until relatively recently, businesses were driven by fierce competition and an excessive ambition to increase their market capitalization, which has led, in some cases, to undesirable accounting, environmental and social practices that have brought several companies to the brink of bankruptcy and, consequently, jeopardized the money invested by shareholders. At present, however, organizations have become aware of the need to broaden their objectives beyond traditional economic issues (Pour et al., 2014).

Thus, since the introduction of the CSR concept, more and more managers are including social and environmental objectives in their decision-making process (Bansal, 2005). CSR represents the voluntary commitment of companies to behave appropriately, fairly and responsibly with the environment in which they operate. The concept also refers to a business approach that takes into account economic, environmental and social issues in a balanced, holistic and long-term manner, for the benefit of current and future stakeholders. The aim of CSR is therefore to seek the well-being of society and the environment through business activities. However, when did the term come into being, how has the term evolved since its foundation, and how has the concept of CSR evolved over time? The research addresses these research questions to bring clarity to the field of study.

In order to achieve the proposed research objectives, the research is structured as follows. After this brief introduction, section two presents the methodology developed for the narrative literature review. Section three presents the results of the research in two sections: firstly, the historical evolution of CSR and, secondly, the conceptualization and the different characteristics of the term. Section four presents the conclusions drawn from the study and, finally, section five shows the limitations and future lines of research.

METHODOLOGY

In the present research, a narrative literature review is conducted with the purpose of analyzing the historical evolution and conceptualization of CSR. The literature review is considered a detailed study that aims to gather information on a given topic through the analysis of published literature (Oliver, 2012).

The aim of the narrative review of the literature is to synthesize the fragmented knowledge of previous research on CSR. The research, therefore, presents a descriptive scope, given that there are no hypotheses to be contrasted, but rather the information collected is described and given meaning. Furthermore, the present review follows more flexible and less restrictive procedures than systematic reviews (Ferrari, 2015). Therefore, the present review does not intend to generalize the results obtained to the population (Tranfield et al., 2003), but to offer an interpretation of the literature that allows for a better understanding of the field of study of CSR. To conduct the literature review, the phases proposed by Wee and Banister (2016) were followed, which are: topic selection, source selection and reading, and topic writing. First, the selected topic is the historical evolution of CSR. Second, manuals, readings, books, books, chapters and articles focused on the evolution and conceptualization of CSR were included for the research, excluding colloquium reports, seminars, doctoral dissertations and working papers. The time period of the publications covers the period from the beginnings of the concept of CSR in the 1950s to the present day, given that the aim of the research is to analyze the historical evolution and conceptualization of the discipline of CSR. Likewise, the Scopus and Web of Science databases were used to select the publications, as they are prestigious databases that contain articles published in high-impact journals, which ensures that the information obtained is accurate and of high value, legitimizing reliable results. A total of 65 academic papers were reviewed and read in depth, this being the scientific production that allowed us to reflect on the historical evolution of CSR as well as its conceptual evolution. Thirdly, once the article and sources had been selected and the publications had been read, the bibliographic review was drafted.

RESULTS

Historical Evolution of CSR

Today's prevailing belief that companies should take responsibility for the society and the territory in which they operate is not new, as such convictions can be found several centuries ago (Carroll, 2008). However, it was not until the 1950s that the identification of the social responsibilities that organizations should have was first addressed in the academic literature, which is understood as the birth of the modern construct of CSR.

The post-World War II period is seen as a time of adaptation and changing attitudes towards the CSR debate, as well as a period characterized by few corporate actions that went beyond philanthropic activities (Carroll, 2008). The change in attitude towards corporate behavior came from the author Bowen (1953), who believed that the large corporations of the time concentrated a great deal of power, as their actions had a great impact on society. Consequently, according to this author, it was necessary to change the decision-making process of organizations to include considerations of the impact of their activities on society. Following Bowen's (1953) contribution, other authors addressed business behavior and its effect on the social context of the time. For example, in the book *Corporation Giving in a Free Society*,

Eells (1956) argues that the large corporations of the time were not living up to their social responsibility. Similarly, in *A Moral Philosophy for Management*, Selekman (1959) explores the evolution of corporate moral responsibility as a response to the labor expectations of the time.

During the 1960s, academic contributions sought to respond to the problems and desires of the new society that was flourishing. In this regard, Davis (1960) argued that the social, economic and political changes of the time put added pressure on businessmen to re-examine their role in society and their social responsibility. He argued that organizations needed to take responsibility for the environment in which they operated, highlighting the positive relationship of social responsibility to the economic profitability of business (Davis, 1960; Carroll, 1999). Other influential authors of the time such as Frederick (1960), McGuire (1963) or Walton (1967) defended the same claims.

It is important to note that, although most authors began to take a position in favor of CSR, there were others who were skeptical of the concept. In particular Friedman (1962) considered that companies should limit themselves to profit maximization. Friedman (1970) elaborated on his position in the article. The social responsibility of business is to increase its profits, in which he considers CSR activities to be an inappropriate use of company resources as they result, according to the author, in an unjustified waste of money for the general social interest. In Friedman's (1962) words, "few trends could so thoroughly undermine the very foundations of our free society as the acceptance by businessmen of a social responsibility other than to make as much money for their shareholders as possible" (p. 1).

The 1970s saw the creation of some of the most relevant companies in terms of social responsibility, such as the Body Shop, founded in 1976 in the United Kingdom, and Ben and Jerry's, founded in 1978 in the United States. Whether in response to new social expectations, a new regulatory framework or their competitive strategies, the companies described above were two notable examples of organizations that began to formalize and integrate policies that addressed the social and public issues of an era characterized, according to Carroll (2015, p. 88), by "corporate social responsibility management". This led to the term CSR becoming increasingly popular, resulting in its indistinct use in various contexts (Votaw, 1973; Sethi, 1975).

The ambiguous use of the term CSR during the 1970s created uncertainty about its definition. In order to address this problem, in the late 1970s, Carroll (1979) proposed the first unified definition of CSR, defining it as the set of "economic, legal, ethical and discretionary expectations that society has of organizations at a given point in time" (p. 500). Although Carroll's (1979) approach to CSR corresponded to the debate on corporate behavior at the time, its relevance lies in the fact that his definition built on the work of other scholars to provide a clear and concise conceptualization that could be applicable in any context, unlike previous definitions (Frederick, 1960; Friedman, 1962; McGuire, 1963; Walton, 1967; Davis, 1973). Another relevant contribution of Carroll's (1979) conceptualization is that it does not consider ecological and social objectives as mutually exclusive trade-offs, but as an integral part of the business framework of social responsibility (Lee, 2008).

During the 1980s, the Reagan and Thatcher administrations introduced a new liberal doctrine characterized by reduced fiscal pressures on corporations (Feldstein, 2013; Wankel, 2008). As the role of governments in regulating corporate behavior was reduced, managers had to respond to different interest groups that continued to expect companies to meet the social expectations of the time. In particular, the reduction of the regulatory framework led scholars to consider business ethics and the operationalization of CSR as an appropriate response to various stakeholders involved in the organization, such as shareholders, employees and consumers (Carroll, 2008; Wankel, 2008). Social concerns were also on the rise during the decade, as seen through a series of events reflecting the international community's approach to sustainable development and, to some extent, to corporate behavior. The most relevant of these were: the creation of the European Commission's Directorate-General for Environment (1981), the creation of the World Commission on Environment and Development chaired by Norwegian Prime Minister GroHarlem Brundtland (1983), the Chernobyl nuclear disaster (1986), the publication of the Brundtland Commission's report Our Common Future (1987) defining sustainable development, the creation of the United Nations and the establishment of the European Commission, the adoption by the United Nations of the Montreal Protocol (1987) and the creation of the Intergovernmental Panel on Climate Change (1988).

Although these events were not directly related to CSR and therefore did not directly influence the evolution of the concept, they reflect a growing awareness of the international community for environmental protection and sustainable development. Indeed, for Carroll (2008), society's most relevant concerns and expectations about corporate behavior during the 1980s revolved around "environmental pollution, employment discrimination, consumer abuses, employee health and safety, quality of working life, deterioration of urban life, and questionable/abusive practices of multinational corporations" (p. 36).

The 1990s were no exception to the growing interest in CSR and, indeed, it was during this decade that the concept gained appeal as a result of the international focus on sustainable development at the time along with the globalization process that was taking place (Agudelo et al., 2019). As Carroll (2015) argues, during the 1990s the globalization process increased the operations of multinational corporations in countries with weak regulatory frameworks. For these global corporations, the incorporation of CSR represented a series of new opportunities that were accompanied by global competition, increased reputational risk due to increased global visibility, as well as conflicting pressures, demands and expectations from home and host countries (Carroll, 2015).

Many multinational companies understood that being socially responsible could balance the challenges and opportunities of the globalization process they were experiencing. As a result, the institutionalization of CSR became stronger (Carroll, 2015). The most notable example of its institutionalization was the founding in 1992 of the Business for Social Responsibility (BSR) association, which initially included 51 companies with the vision of becoming a "force for positive social change, a force that preserves and restores natural resources, ensures human dignity and justice, and operates transparently" (Business for Social Responsibility, 2000). Another key contribution to the debate on corporate behavior was the concept of the Triple Bottom Line (TBL), as it conceived for the first time a sustainability framework for balancing the social, environmental and economic impact of organizations (Elkington, 1998). The TBL concept became popular in the late 1990s as a comprehensive approach to achieve sustainability, being relevant in the CSR debate, since, under such an approach, companies should have a balanced social and environmental performance along with their economic objectives (Agudelo et al., 2019).

The globalization process of the 1990s increased the global reach of multinational companies, increasing their concern for competitiveness, reputation, global visibility and stakeholder network (Carroll, 2015). This led to the generation of new alternative theoretical perspectives to CSR, such as Stakeholder Theory (Freeman, 1994), corporate social performance (Swanson, 1995) and corporate citizenship (Carroll, 1998). The introduction of these new perspectives created uncertainty regarding the definition of CSR to the extent that the concept ended up having "unclear boundaries and debatable legitimacy" (Lantos, 2001, p. 1). In fact, in the late 1990s there was no globally accepted definition of CSR (Lantos, 2001).

The 2000s saw important contributions to the concept of CSR. In the early years of the 21st century, Smith (2001) argued that business policies had changed in response to the public interest, allowing for a positive impact on the environment in which organizations operated. This meant that the scope of social responsibility included a broader set of stakeholders, establishing a new definition of CSR. In the words of Smith (2001), CSR refers to "a company's obligations to its stakeholders, i.e. the people affected by business policies and practices. These obligations go beyond legal requirements and the company's duties to its shareholders. The fulfilment of these obligations aims to minimize any harm and maximize the long-term beneficial impact of the company on society" (p. 142).

Underlying the definition of CSR proposed by Smith (2001) was the idea that such socially responsible practices should be part of the strategic perspective of organizations in order to meet their long-term obligations. Similarly, Lantos (2001) asserted that during the 21st century, society would demand that companies include social issues in their strategies. In fact, Lantos (2001) drew on Smith's (2001) definition to include strategic considerations in his own definition of CSR, concluding that "CSR implied the obligation arising from the implicit social contract between business and society to meet the needs and wants of society over the long term, optimizing the positive effects and minimizing the negative effects of their actions on society" (p. 9). Furthermore, Lantos (2001) explained that CSR could become a strategic activity when it was part of the company's management plans to generate profits, as companies engaged in activities that could be understood as socially responsible only if they translated into economic benefits. On the other hand, Freeman (2001) and Friedman & Miles (2002) made further contributions to Stakeholder Theory in the early 2000s, reinforcing the belief that companies should be managed for the benefit of a broader set of stakeholders. Thus, while Freeman (2001) argued that firms had responsibilities to suppliers, consumers, employees, shareholders and the local community, Friedman & Miles (2002) argued that the relationship between firms and their stakeholders was dynamic, having different levels of influence on the firm. Thus, Freeman (2001) and Friedman & Miles (2002) contributed to the evolution of CSR by reinforcing the belief that companies were accountable to an increasingly broad set of stakeholders.

Van Marrewijk (2003) introduced the concept of Corporate Sustainability (CS) as a new perspective for understanding CSR. Van Marrewijk (2003) explained this new approach as a strategic response to new business challenges which, he argued, were the result of the evolving roles and responsibilities of each sector in society. For Van Marrewijk (2003), companies responded to their challenges by adopting different levels of integration of CSR into the company structure. The holistic interpretation provided by Van Marrewijk (2003) implied the full integration of CSR under the sustainability approach, understanding that companies had a new role within society and, consequently, had to make strategic decisions to adapt to the environment, transforming CSR "from a minimal commitment to become a strategic necessity" (Werther & Chandler, 2005, p. 319).

Later, Porter & Kramer (2006) argued that firms could gain competitive advantage through the creation of shared value. This term was conceived by these authors as a necessary step in the evolution of firms, defining it as the "operational policies and practices that enhance a firm's competitiveness and at the same time improve the economic and social conditions of the communities in which it operates" (p. 2). For Porter & Kramer (2006), a company should look inward to determine the social impact of its value chain and identify the positive and negative effect of its activities on society, focusing on those of greatest strategic value. The company then had to focus externally to understand the influence of its social context on its productivity and the execution of its business strategy. In this way, the work of these authors provided a new understanding of CSR by representing a way to maximize the interdependence between business and society through a strategic approach rather than a narrow focus on a set of objectives.

While not directly contributing to the concept of CSR, Porter & Kramer (2011) called for a shift in business strategies to focus on the generation of shared value as a primary objective. This new theoretical approach was embodied in what Trapp (2012) called the third generation of CSR, which he defined as the moment when companies reflect their concern for social and global issues in their activities, even when some of these concerns may not be directly linked to their core business. In the mid-2010s, Carroll (2015) revisited his work on CSR to complement his 1999 and 2010 literature review (Carroll, 1999; Carroll & Shabana, 2010) by analyzing the competing and complementary concepts that have become part of the modern business vocabulary. Carroll (2015) reviewed the concepts of stakeholder engagement and management, business ethics, corporate citizenship, CS and shared value creation, concluding that they were all interrelated and overlapping with the concept of CSR. In particular, Carroll (2015) points out that all these concepts have been incorporated into CSR and, as a consequence, CSR has to be taken as a reference point and centerpiece of the socially responsible business movement.

In addition, 2015 saw the launch of the United Nations 2030 Agenda for Sustainable Development, articulated under seventeen Sustainable Development Goals (SDGs), which represents a "shared vision of humanity and a social contract between world leaders and people" (Ban, 2015). Although the SDGs do not represent any obligations for the private sector, countries that adopt them must create specific policies and regulations that translate into pressures for companies to implement new business practices or improve their current practices (Agudelo et al., 2019; Marco-Lajara et al., 2022a). This is particularly relevant given that the Sustainable Development Goals (SDGs) cover a wide range of areas, from climate change to eradicating poverty and hunger, as well as promoting innovation and sustainable consumption. Thus, since their emergence, the academic literature has tended to address the application of CSR and its impact on specific SDG performance areas (Chuang & Huang, 2016; Benites-Lazaro & Mello-Théry, 2017; Kao et al., 2018).

Definition and Characteristics of CSR

Since the 1950s, various definitions of CSR have been put forward by academics as well as national and international institutions. Table 1 shows a selection of the most prominent definitions over the last seven decades, identifying which dimension of CSR each definition focuses on.

Table 1. Definitions of CSR

Author	Definition	Dimensions
Bowen (1953, p. 6)	"The obligation of business people to follow those policies, make those decisions, or pursue those courses of action that are desirable in terms of the goals and values of our society."	Social
Davis (1960, p. 70)	"Decisions and actions taken by employers for reasons, at least partially, beyond the economic or technical interests of the company."	Social
Frederick (1960, p. 60)	"It means that entrepreneurs must oversee the operation of an economic system that meets the expectations of the public. This means, in turn, that the means of economic production must be employed in such a way that production and distribution improve overall socio-economic welfare."	Social, Economic
McGuire (1963, p. 144)	"It assumes that a company not only has economic and legal obligations, but also has certain responsibilities to society that go beyond economic and legal obligations."	Social

Continued on following page

Table 1. Continued

Author	Definition	Dimensions
Davis & Blomstrom (1966, p. 12)	"Social responsibility refers to a person's obligation to consider the effects of his or her decisions and actions on the social system as a whole. Entrepreneurs apply Social Responsibility when they consider the needs and interests of third parties that may be affected by the actions of the business. In doing so, they look beyond the economic and technical interests of the company."	Social
Walton (1967, p. 18)	"CSR recognizes the depth of relationships between business and society and realizes that these relationships must be taken into account by senior management as business and related groups pursue their respective objectives."	Social
Manne & Wallich (1972, p. 40)	"The company is, to some extent, a free agent to implement its CSR. When the company has social objectives imposed by law, the company does not exercise responsibility when it implements them."	Social
Eilbert & Parket (1973, p. 7)	"Perhaps the best way to understand social responsibility is to think of it as good neighborliness. The concept encompasses two phases. On the one hand, it means not doing things that spoil the neighborhood. On the other, it should be expressed as the voluntary acceptance of an obligation to help solve neighborhood problems. Businesses have an active role to play in solving social problems such as racial discrimination, pollution, transport or urban decay."	Social, Environmental
Eells & Walton (1974, p. 247)	"It represents a concern for the needs and goals of society, which go beyond the purely economic. Since the business system as it exists today can only survive with the effective functioning of a free society, CSR represents a general concern with the role of business in supporting and improving the social order".	Social
Sethi (1975, p. 62)	"It involves taking corporate behavior to the level where it is congruent with the prevailing social norms, values and performance expectations of society."	Social
Fitch (1976, p. 38)	"The serious attempt to solve social problems caused in whole or in part by business."	Social
Carroll (1979, p. 500)	"It encompasses the economic, legal, ethical and discretionary expectations that society has of companies at a given point in time."	Social, Economic
Jones (1980, p. 60)	"The idea that companies have an obligation to the groups that make up society, beyond shareholders and beyond what is established by law and contract. Two facets of this definition are critical. First, that the obligation must be voluntarily adopted; behavior influenced by the coercive forces of law or union contracts is not voluntary. Second, the obligation extends beyond the duty to shareholders to other social groups such as customers, employees, suppliers and surrounding communities."	Social
Hopkins (1998)	CSR is concerned with dealing with the company's stakeholders in an ethical or socially responsible manner. Stakeholders exist both inside and outside the company. Therefore, socially responsible behavior will enhance the human development of stakeholders both inside and outside the company.	Social
Carroll (1999, p. 43)	"A socially responsible company must generate profit, comply with the law, be ethical and be a good corporate citizen."	Social, Economic
Khoury, Rostami & Turnbull (1999)	CSR is the company's overall relationship with all its stakeholders. These include customers, employees, communities, owners/investors, government, suppliers and competitors. Elements of social responsibility include community investment, employee relations, job creation and retention, environmental protection and financial performance.	Social, Economic, Environmental
Business for Social Responsibility (2000)	Making business decisions linked to ethical values, compliance with legal requirements and respect for people, communities and the environment.	Social Economic
Comisión Europea (2001, p. 7)	"The voluntary integration, by companies, of social and environmental concerns into their business operations and their relations with their stakeholders."	Social, Environmental

Continued on following page

Table 1. Continued

Author	Definition	Dimensions
Marsden (2001)	CSR refers to the basic behavior of companies and their responsibility for their overall impact on the societies in which they operate. CSR is not an optional extra or an act of philanthropy. A socially responsible company is one that runs a profitable business that considers all the positive and negative environmental, social and economic effects it has on society.	Social, Economic, Environmental
Mohr et al. (2001, p. 47)	"The company's commitment to minimize or eliminate any detrimental effects and to maximize its beneficial impact on society in the long term."	Social
Van Marrewijk (2003)	In general, CS and CSR refer to corporate activities, voluntary by definition, that demonstrate the inclusion of social and environmental concerns in business operations and stakeholder interactions.	Social, Economic, Environmental
Cuesta & Valor (2003, p. 7)	"The set of obligations and commitments, legal and ethical, national and international, with stakeholders, which are derived from the impacts that the activity and operations of organizations produce in the social, labor, environmental and human rights spheres. Therefore, CSR affects the very management of organizations, both in their productive and commercial activities and in their relations with stakeholders."	Social, Economic, Environmental
Smith (2003, p. 2)	"The company's obligations to society or, more specifically, to its stakeholders."	Social
Hopkins (2004, p. 1)	"It refers to treating the company's stakeholders in an ethical or responsible manner. Ethical or responsible treatment of its stakeholders means acting in a way that is accepted by society. Social includes economic responsibility. There are stakeholders internal and external to the company - the environment is a stakeholder. The aim of corporate social responsibility in its broadest sense is to create ever higher standards of living, while preserving the profitability of the company, for people inside and outside the company."	Social, Economic, Environmental
Maignan & Ferrell (2004)	"It designates the duty to meet or improve stakeholder standards by defining desirable business behaviors."	Social
García-Marzá (2004, p. 187)	"It defines the set of actions, decisions and policies that make up the company's response to the demands and requirements of its corresponding interest groups."	Social
McWilliams, Siegel & Wright (2006)	A situation in which a company goes beyond the requirements imposed on it and includes in its activities actions that create a social good.	Social
Waldman et al. (2006, p. 824)	"Actions by the company that meet the needs or objectives of an identifiable stakeholder group, or a broader social group (...) Actions that go beyond the immediate legal requirements of the company. Shareholders or other owners are included as constituting a stakeholder group relevant to CSR, along with broader stakeholders."	Social
Foro de Expertos sobre RSE (2007, p. 7)	"It is, in addition to strict compliance with current legal obligations, the voluntary integration in its governance and management, in its strategy, policies and procedures, of the social, labor, environmental and human rights concerns that arise from the relationship and transparent dialogue with its stakeholders, thus taking responsibility for the consequences and impacts that derive from its actions."	Social, Environmental
Kotler & Lee (2007)	The company's commitment to enhancing the well-being of society through independent business practices and the use of company resources.	Social
Carroll (2008)	CSR refers to companies' commitments to pursue strategies, make decisions or follow lines of activity that are in line with society's values and expectations.	Social

Continued on following page

Table 1. Continued

Author	Definition	Dimensions
Castillo (2009, p. 226)	"It is a fundamental component of the organization and involves concern for ethics, people, community and the environment, within the context of the company's operations and decision-making process. It encompasses all the actions and policies that are part of a corporation's normal operations, and includes an internal dimension, focused on employee relations and management practices, and an external dimension, directed at the environment and the commitment to contribute to the economic and social development of the community. Its practice generates a series of connections or linkages that lead to relationships and thus interactions and dialogue between the company and all its stakeholders."	Social, Economic, Environmental
Cuervo (2009, p. 51)	"It implies that companies voluntarily incorporate social and environmental criteria into economic activities and stakeholder relations."	Social, Environmental
Ismail (2009)	The concept that business organizations consider the public interest by taking responsibility for the impact of their activities on customers, suppliers, employees, shareholders, communities and other stakeholders, as well as the environment.	Social, Environmental
Hediger (2010)	Programs in which companies not only seek to increase their profits, but also contribute to the well-being of stakeholders.	Social
Comisión Europea (2011, p. 6)	"The responsibility of business for its impact on society. To fully embrace their social responsibility, companies should implement, in close collaboration with stakeholders, a process to integrate social, environmental and ethical concerns, respect for human rights and consumer concerns into their business operations and core strategy."	Social, Environmental
Aguinis & Glavas (2012)	Context-specific organizational actions and policies that consider stakeholder expectations and the triple bottom line (economic, social and environmental).	Social, Economic, Environmental
Fontaine (2013)	The ongoing commitment of companies to behave appropriately, fairly and responsibly and to contribute to economic development by improving the lives of workers and their families, as well as the local community and society as a whole.	Social, Economic
Observatorio de RSC (2014, p. 5)	"It involves mandatory compliance with national and international social, labor, environmental and human rights legislation, as well as any other voluntary action that the company wishes to undertake to improve the quality of life of its employees, the communities in which it operates and society as a whole."	Social, Environmental
Sheehy (2015, p. 639).	"A socio-political movement that generates private self-regulatory initiatives, incorporating public and private international law standards that seek to ameliorate and mitigate social harms and promote the public good by industry organizations."	Social
Sarkar & Searcy (2016)	CSR implies that companies should voluntarily assume their social responsibility to be ethical in all their activities and consider the impact of their actions on their stakeholders, while contributing to global sustainability.	Social, Economic, Environmental
Monfort & Villagra (2016)	It is a strategy aligned with the company's corporate values to share with the environment.	Social
Ayala del Pino (2021, p. 7)	"CSR is, in addition to strict compliance with legal obligations, the voluntary integration of CSR concerns into its governance and management, strategy, policies and procedures. legal obligations, the voluntary integration into its governance and management, strategy, policies and procedures of the social, labor, environmental and human rights concerns that arise from the relationship and social, labor, environmental and human rights concerns that arise from the relationship and transparent dialogue with its stakeholders, thus taking responsibility for the consequences and impacts of its actions."	Social, Economic, Environmental

Source: own elaboration

As can be seen, there is no consensus on the definition of CSR, since, from the 1950s to the present day, various authors and definitions have contributed to defining the concept. However, there are a number of characteristics that recur in the definitions that have been proposed.

Firstly, authors such as Eilbert & Parket (1973), Jones (1980), Van Marrewijk (2003), Cuervo (2009), the CSR Observatory (2014) and Sarkar & Searcy (2016) argue that CSR is voluntary for companies. Its conception as a voluntary practice is closely linked to the idea of going beyond strict compliance with legal requirements put forward by Waldam et al. (2006) and the Expert Forum on Corporate Social Responsibility (2007). Davis (1973, p. 313) clearly reflects this idea when he states that "social responsibility begins where the law ends". Similarly, in the words of Manne & Wallich (1972, p. 40) "when the company has social objectives imposed by law, the company does not exercise its responsibility when it implements them".

Likewise, while Walton (1967), Van Marrewijk (2003), Hopkins (2004), Castillo (2009), Cuervo (2009) and the European Commission (2011) highlight the close relationship that the company must maintain with its stakeholders, David & Blosmstrom (1966) and Waldman et al. (2006) focus on satisfying the needs and expectations of the different stakeholders. Along the same lines, Jones (1980), Cuesta & Valor (2003), Smith (2003), García-Marzá (2004) and Corredera & González (2011) conceive CSR practices as a commitment and obligation that the company has towards its stakeholders. On the other hand, other authors highlight in their definitions those actions that transcend the economic interests of the organization (Davis, 1960; Davis & Bomstrom, 1966; Eells & Walton, 1974), since the underlying idea is to integrate social and environmental concerns in the activities carried out by the organization (European Commission, 2001; Cuesta & Valor, 2003; Van Marrewijk, 2003; Ismail, 2009; Corredera & González; 2011; Aguinis & Glavas, 2012; Observatorio de RSC, 2014).

The responsibility of organizations to mitigate the negative externalities generated by their activity is another common denominator when defining CSR (Fitch, 1976; Mohr et al., 2001; Cuesta and Valor, 2003; Expert Forum on Corporate Social Responsibility, 2007; European Commission, 2011; CSR Observatory, 2014). As Eilbert & Parket (1973, p. 7) point out very clearly, organizations "should not do things that spoil the neighborhood". By way of conclusion, Table 2 sets out the main characteristics of the term CSR derived from the definitions analyzed.

Table 2. Main characteristics of CSR

There is no standardized definition of CSR
Voluntary practice
Management of negative externalities
Stakeholder orientation
Alignment of social, environmental and economic responsibilities
Beyond philanthropy

Source: own elaboration

CONCLUSION

The present research is of great relevance both for scholars experienced in the field of CSR and for those who are beginning to study it, since it provides new knowledge through the collection and understanding of fragmented knowledge on the subject.

The results of the study show that it was not until the 1950s that the identification of the social responsibilities that organizations should have was first addressed in the academic literature, which is understood to be the birth of the modern construct of CSR. During the 1960s, academic contributions sought to respond to the problems and desires of the new society that was flourishing. A number of academics argued that the social, economic and political changes occurring at the time represented added pressure for businessmen to reexamine their role in society and their social responsibility.

The 1970s saw the creation of some of the most relevant companies in terms of social responsibility, which began to formalize and integrate policies that addressed the social and public issues of the era. This led to the term CSR becoming increasingly popular, giving rise to its indistinct use in various contexts. During the 1980s, the Reagan and Thatcher administrations introduced a new liberal doctrine characterized by the reduction of fiscal pressures on corporations. Thus, as the role of governments in regulating corporate behavior was reduced, managers had to respond to different interest groups that continued to expect companies to meet the social expectations of the time. In particular, the reduction of the regulatory framework led scholars to consider business ethics and the operationalization of CSR as an appropriate response to the various stakeholders involved in the organization, such as shareholders, employees and consumers. In addition, during the decade, social concerns were on the rise, as seen through a series of events that reflect the international community's approach to sustainable development and, to a certain extent, to corporate behavior.

The 1990s were no exception to the growing interest in CSR and, in fact, it was during this decade that the concept gained appeal as a result of the international focus on sustainable development at the time together with the process of globalization that was taking place. Indeed, during that decade the globalization process increased the operations of multinational corporations in countries with weak regulatory frameworks. For these global corporations, the incorporation of CSR represented a series of new opportunities that were accompanied by global competition, increased reputational risk due to increased global visibility, as well as conflicting pressures, demands and expectations from home and host countries. The 2000s saw important contributions to the concept of CSR. The scientific output of the time argued that business policies had changed in response to the public interest, making it possible to generate a positive impact on the environment in which organizations operated. This meant that the scope of social responsibility included a broader set of stakeholders.

In the mid-2010s, Carroll (2015) revisited his work on CSR to complement his 1999 and 2010 literature review by analyzing the competing and complementary concepts that have become part of the modern business vocabulary. Carroll (2015) reviewed the concepts of stakeholder engagement and management, business ethics, corporate citizenship, CS and shared value creation, concluding that they were all interrelated and overlapping with the concept of CSR, noting that all of these concepts had been incorporated into CSR and, as a consequence, such term is to be taken as a reference point and centerpiece of the socially responsible business movement. Additionally, 2015 saw the launch of the 2030 Agenda by the United Nations for Sustainable Development, articulated under seventeen SDGs (Marco-Lajara et al., 2021a; Marco-Lajara et al., 2021b; Marco-Lajara et al., 2022a; Marco-Lajara et al., 2022b, Marco-Lajara et al., 2022c, Marco-Lajara et al., 2022d).Thus, although the SDGs do not represent any obligation for the private sector, the countries that adopt them must create specific policies and regulations that translate into pressures for companies to implement new business practices or improve their current practices. This is especially relevant considering that the SDGs cover a wide range of areas, from climate change to the eradication of poverty and hunger, as well as the promotion of innovation and sustainable consumption. Thus, since their emergence, academic publications have tended to address the application of CSR and its impact on specific areas of SDG performance.

Based on a review of the literature on the concept of CSR, it is possible to state that: (1) there is no standardized definition of CSR, with the consequent problems that this entails, (2) it is a voluntary practice, (3) it implies the management of negative externalities, (4) it involves orienting practices to meet the needs of different stakeholders, (3) practices must align social, environmental and economic responsibilities, and (4) they must go beyond philanthropy.

LIMITATIONS AND FUTURE LINES OF RESEARCH

Despite the important contributions of the study, it is important to note that the research suffers from certain limitations. The fundamental limitation of the study is of a methodological nature, given that in narrative reviews the subjective criterion of the authors prevails and the data found in the different publications are not quantitatively synthesized. In order to overcome these limitations of narrative reviews, a systematic review of the evolution of CSR over time is planned as a future line of research with the aim of increasing the reproducibility of research and increasing the validity of the results obtained.

REFERENCES

Agudelo, M., Jóhannsdóttir, L., & Davídsdóttir, B. (2019). A literature review of the history and evolution of corporate social responsibility. *International Journal of Corporate Social Responsibility*, *4*(1), 1–23. doi:10.118640991-018-0039-y

Aguinis, H., & Glavas, A. (2012). What we know and don't know about corporate social responsibility: A review and research agenda. *Journal of Management*, *38*(4), 932–968. doi:10.1177/0149206311436079

Ayala del Pino, C. (2021). La responsabilidad social corporativa: Concepto, ámbito de aplicación, grupos de interés y objetivos. *Anuario Jurídico y Económico Escurialense*, *54*(54), 173–198. doi:10.54571/ajee.462

Ban, K. (2015). *Launch of new sustainable development agenda to guide development actions for the next 15 years.* Disponible en: https://sustainabledevelopment. un.org/?page=view&nr=1021&type=230&menu=2059

Bansal, P. (2005). Evolving sustainably: A longitudinal study of corporate sustainable development. *Strategic Management Journal*, *26*(3), 197–218. doi:10.1002mj.441

Benites-Lazaro, L., & Mello-Théry, N. (2017). CSR as a legitimatizing tool in carbon market: Evidence from Latin America's clean development mechanism. *Journal of Cleaner Production*, *149*, 218–226. doi:10.1016/j.jclepro.2017.02.095

Bowen, H. (1953). *Social responsibilities of the businessman*. University of Iowa Press.

Business for Social Responsibility. (2000). *Introduction to Corporate Social Responsibility*. Disponible en: http://www.khbo.be/~lodew/Cursussen/4eingenieurCL/The%20Global%20Business%20Responsibility%20Resource%20Center.doc

Carroll, A. (1991). The Pyramid of CSR: Toward the Moral Management of Organizational Stakeholders. *Business Horizons*, *34*(4), 39–48. doi:10.1016/0007-6813(91)90005-G

Carroll, A. (1998). The four faces of corporate citizenship. *Business and Society Review*, *100*(1), 1–7. doi:10.1111/0045-3609.00008

Carroll, A. (1999). Corporate social responsibility. *Business & Society*, *38*(3), 268–295. doi:10.1177/000765039903800303

Carroll, A. (2008). A history of corporate social responsibility: concepts and practices. In A. M. Andrew Crane, D. Matten, J. Moon, & D. Siegel (Eds.), *The Oxford handbook of corporate social responsibility* (pp. 19–46). Oxford University Press.

Carroll, A. (2015). Corporate social responsibility: The centerpiece of competing and complementary frameworks. *Organizational Dynamics*, *44*(2), 87–96. doi:10.1016/j.orgdyn.2015.02.002

Carroll, A., & Shabana, K. (2010). The business case for corporate social responsibility: A review of concepts, research and practice. *International Journal of Management Reviews*, *12*(1), 85–105. doi:10.1111/j.1468-2370.2009.00275.x

Carroll, A. B. (1979). A three-dimensional conceptual model of corporate performance. *Academy of Management Review*, *4*(4), 497–505. doi:10.2307/257850

Castillo, A. (2009). *Relaciones Públicas. Teoría e historia*. Editorial UOC.

Chuang, S., & Huang, S. (2016). The effect of environmental corporate social responsibility on environmental performance and business competitiveness: The mediation of green information technology capital. *Journal of Business Ethics*, *150*(4), 991–1009. doi:10.100710551-016-3167-x

Comisión Europea. (2001). *Libro Verde de la Comisión Europea para Fomentar un Marco Europeo para la Responsabilidad Social de las Empresas*.

Comisión Europea. (2011). Estrategia renovada de la UE para 2011-2014 sobre la responsabilidad social de las empresas. Brussels.

Cuervo, A. (2009). Corporate social responsibility, corporate governance and stakeholders (Corporate social responsibility, corporate governance and stakeholders.). In *Responsabilidad social: una reflexión global sobre la RSE* (pp. 51–61). Pretince Hall.

Cuesta, M., & Valor, C. (2003). Responsabilidad social de la empresa: concepto, medición y desarrollo en España (Corporate social responsibility: concept, measurement and development in Spain). *Boletín Económico De ICE. Información Comercial Española*, *2755*, 7–20.

Davis, K. (1960). Can business afford to ignore social responsibilities? *California Management Review*, *2*(3), 70–76. doi:10.2307/41166246

Davis, K. (1973). The case for and against business assumption of social responsibilities. *Academy of Management Journal*, *16*(2), 312–322.

Davis, K., & Blomstrom, R. (1966). *Business and its environment*. McGraw-Hill.

Eells, R. (1956). *Corporation giving in a free society*. Harper.

Eells, R., & Walton, C. (1974). Conceptual Foundations of Business. Richard D. Irwin.

Eilbert, H., & Parket, I. R. (1973). The current status of corporate social responsibility. *Business Horizons*, *16*, 5–14.

Elkington, J. (1998). Partnerships from cannibals with forks: The triple bottom line of 21st-century business. *Environmental Quality Management*, *8*(1), 37–51. doi:10.1002/tqem.3310080106

Feldstein, M. (2013). *The Reagan-Thatcher revolution*. Disponible en: https://www.dw.com/en/the-reagan-thatcher-revolution/a-16732731

Ferrari, R. (2015). Writing narrative style literature reviews. *Medical Writing*, *24*(4), 230–235. doi:10.1179/2047480615Z.000000000329

Fitch, H. (1976). Achieving corporate social responsibility. *Academy of Management Review*, *1*(1), 38–46. doi:10.5465/amr.1976.4408754

Fontaine, M. (2013). Corporate social responsibility and sustainability: The new bottom line? *International Journal of Business and Social Science*, *4*(4), 1–10.

Foro de Expertos en Responsabilidad Social de las Empresas. (2007). *Informe del foro de expertos en responsabilidad social de las empresas* [Report of the forum of experts in corporate social responsibility]. Constituido el 17 de marzo de 2005 por iniciativa del Ministerio de Trabajo y Asuntos Sociales [Established on March 17, 2005 at the initiative of the Ministry of Labor and Social Affairs].

Frederick, W. (1960). The growing concern over business responsibility. *California Management Review*, *2*(4), 54–61. doi:10.2307/41165405

Freeman, R. (2001). A stakeholder theory of the modern corporation. *Perspectives in Business Ethics*, *3*, 144.

Friedman, A., & Miles, S. (2002). Developing stakeholder theory. *Journal of Management Studies*, *39*(1), 1–21. doi:10.1111/1467-6486.00280

Friedman, M. (1962). *Capitalism and freedom*. University of Chicago Press.

Friedman, M. (1970). The social responsibility of business is to increase its profits. *The New York Times Magazine*.

García-Marzá, D. (2004). *Ética empresarial. Del diálogo a la confianza [Business ethics. From dialogue to trust]*. Trotta.

Hediger, W. (2010). Welfare and capital-theoretic foundations of corporate social responsibility and corporate sustainability. *Journal of Socio-Economics*, *39*(4), 518–526. doi:10.1016/j.socec.2010.02.001

Hopkins, M. (1998). *The Planetary Bargain: Corporate Social Responsibility Comes of Age*. Macmillan.

Hopkins, M. (2004). *The Planetary Bargain. Corporate Social Responsibility Matters*. Routledge.

Ismail, M. (2009). Corporate social responsibility and its role in community development: An international perspective. *Journal of International Social Research*, *2*(9), 1–12.

Jones, T. (1980). Corporate social responsibility revisited, redefined. *California Management Review*, *22*(3), 59–67. doi:10.2307/41164877

Kao, E., Yeh, C., Wang, L., & Fung, H. (2018). The relationship between CSR and performance: Evidence in China. *Pacific-Basin Finance Journal*, *51*, 155–170. doi:10.1016/j.pacfin.2018.04.006

Khoury, G., Rostami, J., & Turnbull, J. (1999). *Corporate Social Responsibility: Turning Words into Action*. Conference Board of Canada.

Kotler, P., & Lee, N. (2007). *Corporate Social Responsibility: doing the most good for your company and your case*. John Wiley & Sons.

Lantos, G. (2001). The boundaries of strategic corporate social responsibility. *Journal of Consumer Marketing*, *18*(7), 595–632. doi:10.1108/07363760110410281

Lee, M. (2008). A review of the theories of corporate social responsibility: Its evolutionary path and the road ahead. *International Journal of Management Reviews*, *10*(1), 53–73. doi:10.1111/j.1468-2370.2007.00226.x

Maignan, I., & Ferrell, O. (2004). Corporate social responsibility and marketing: An integrative framework. *Journal of the Academy of Marketing Science*, *32*(1), 3–19. doi:10.1177/0092070303258971

Malik, M. (2015). Value-enhancing capabilities of CSR: A brief review of contemporary literature. *Journal of Business Ethics*, *127*(2), 419–438. doi:10.100710551-014-2051-9

Manne, H., & Wallich, H. (1972). *The Modern Corporation and Social Responsibility*. American Enterprise Institute for Public Policy Research.

Marco-Lajara, B., Seva-Larrosa, P., Martínez-Falcó, J., & Sánchez-García, E. (2021b). How Has COVID-19 Affected The Spanish Wine Industry? An Exploratory Analysis. *Natural Volatiles & Essential Oils Journal*, *8*(6), 2722–2731.

Marco-Lajara, B., Seva-Larrosa, P., Ruiz-Fernández, L., & Martínez-Falcó, J. (2021a). The Effect of COVID-19 on the Spanish Wine Industry. In *Impact of Global Issues on International Trade* (pp. 211–232). IGI Global. doi:10.4018/978-1-7998-8314-2.ch012

Marco-Lajara, B., Zaragoza-Saez, P., Falcó, J. M., & Millan-Tudela, L. A. (2022b). Analysing the Relationship Between Green Intellectual Capital and the Achievement of the Sustainable Development Goals. In *Handbook of Research on Building Inclusive Global Knowledge Societies for Sustainable Development* (pp. 111–129). IGI Global. doi:10.4018/978-1-6684-5109-0.ch005

Marco-Lajara, B., Zaragoza-Sáez, P., Martínez-Falcó, J., & Sánchez-García, E. (2022d). El capital intelectual verde como hoja de ruta para la sostenibilidad: El caso de bodegas Luzón. GeoGraphos. *Revista Digital para Estudiantes de Geografía y Ciencias Sociales*, *13*(147), 137–146.

Marco-Lajara, B., Zaragoza-Saez, P., Falcó, J. M., & Sánchez-García, E. (2022c). COVID-19 and Wine Tourism: A Story of Heartbreak. In Handbook of Research on SDGs for Economic Development, Social Development, and Environmental Protection (pp. 90-112). IGI Global.

Marco-Lajara, B., Zaragoza-Sáez, P., Martínez-Falcó, J., & Sánchez-García, E. (2022a). Green Intellectual Capital in the Spanish Wine Industry. In Innovative Economic, Social, and Environmental Practices for Progressing Future Sustainability (pp. 102-120). IGI Global. doi:10.4018/978-1-7998-9590-9.ch006

Marsden, C. (2001). *The Role of Public Authorities in Corporate Social Responsibility*. http://www.alter.be/socialresponsibility/ people/marchri/en/displayPerson

McGuire, J. (1963). *Business and society*. McGraw-Hill.

McWilliams, A., Siegel, D., & Wright, P. (2006). Corporate social responsibility: Strategic implications. *Journal of Management Studies*, *43*(1), 1–18. doi:10.1111/j.1467-6486.2006.00580.x

Mohr, L., Webb, D., & Harris, K. (2001). Do consumers expect companies to be socially responsible? The impact of corporate social responsibility on buying behavior. *The Journal of Consumer Affairs*, *35*(1), 45–72. doi:10.1111/j.1745-6606.2001.tb00102.x

Monfort, A., & Villagra, N. (2016). Corporate Social Responsibility and Corporate Foundations in Building Responsible Brands. *El Profesional de la Información*, *25*(5), 767–777. doi:10.3145/epi.2016.sep.07

Observatorio de RSC. (2014). *Introducción a la Responsabilidad Social Corporativa [Introduction to Corporate Social Responsibility]*. Observatorio de RSC.

Oliver, P. (2012). *Succeeding with your literature review. A handbook for students*. McGraw-Hill, Open University Press.

Porter, M., & Kramer, M. (2006). Strategy & Society. *Harvard Business Review*, *84*(12), 1–16. PMID:17183795

Pour, B. S., Nazari, K., & Emami, M. (2014). Corporate social responsibility: A literature review. *African Journal of Business Management*, *8*(7), 228–234. doi:10.5897/AJBM12.106

Rhou, Y., & Singal, M. (2020). A review of the business case for CSR in the hospitality industry. *International Journal of Hospitality Management*, *84*, 102330. doi:10.1016/j.ijhm.2019.102330

Sarkar, S., & Searcy, C. (2016). Zeitgeist or chameleon? A quantitative analysis of CSR definitions. *Journal of Cleaner Production*, *135*, 1423–1435. doi:10.1016/j.jclepro.2016.06.157

Selekman, B. (1959). *A moral philosophy for management*. McGraw-Hill.

Sethi, S. (1975). Dimensions of corporate social performance: An analytical framework. *California Management Review*, *17*(3), 58–64. doi:10.2307/41162149

Sheehy, B. (2015). Defining CSR: Problems and solutions. *Journal of Business Ethics*, *131*(3), 625–648. doi:10.100710551-014-2281-x

Smith, N. (2001). Changes in corporate practices in response to public interest advocacy and actions. Handbook of Marketing and Society.

Smith, N. (2003). Corporate social responsibility: Whether or how? *California Management Review*, *45*(4), 52–76. doi:10.2307/41166188

Swanson, D. (1995). Addressing a theoretical problem by reorienting the corporate social performance model. *Academy of Management Review*, *20*(1), 43–64. doi:10.2307/258886

Tranfield, D., Denyer, D., & Smart, P. (2003). Towards a methodology for developing evidence-informed management knowledge by means of systematic review. *British Journal of Management*, *14*(3), 207–222. doi:10.1111/1467-8551.00375

Trapp, N. (2012). Corporation as climate ambassador: Transcending business sector boundaries in a Swedish CSR campaign. *Public Relations Review*, *38*(3), 458–465. doi:10.1016/j.pubrev.2012.03.004

Van Marrewijk, M. (2003). Concepts and definitions of CSR and corporate sustainability: Between agency and communion. *Journal of Business Ethics*, *44*(2), 95–105. doi:10.1023/A:1023331212247

Velte, P. (2021). Meta-analyses on corporate social responsibility (CSR): a literature review. *Management Review Quarterly*, 1-49.

Votaw, D. (1973). Genius becomes rare: A comment on the doctrine of social responsibility Pt. II. *California Management Review*, *15*(3), 5–19. doi:10.2307/41164435

Waldman, D., Luque, M., Washburn, N., & House, R. (2006). Cultural and leadership predictors of corporate social responsibility values of top management: A GLOBE study of 15 countries. *Journal of International Business Studies*, *37*(6), 823–837. doi:10.1057/palgrave.jibs.8400230

Walton, C. (1967). *Corporate social responsibilities*. Wadsworth Publishing Company.

Wankel, C. (2008). *21st century management: A reference handbook*. SAGE Publications. doi:10.4135/9781412954006

Wee, B. V., & Banister, D. (2016). How to write a literature review paper? *Transport Reviews*, *36*(2), 278–288. doi:10.1080/01441647.2015.1065456

Werther, W. Jr, & Chandler, D. (2005). Strategic corporate social responsibility as global brand insurance. *Business Horizons*, *48*(4), 317–324. doi:10.1016/j.bushor.2004.11.009

ADDITIONAL READING

Abreu, J., & Badii, M. (2007). Análisis del concepto de responsabilidad social empresarial [Analysis of the corporate social responsibility concept]. *Mexico: Daena: International Journal of Good Conscience*, *2*(1), 54-70.

Leonard, D., & McAdam, R. (2003). Corporate social responsibility. *Quality Progress*, *36*(10), 27.

Lindgreen, A., & Swaen, V. (2010). Corporate social responsibility. *International Journal of Management Reviews*, *12*(1), 1–7. doi:10.1111/j.1468-2370.2009.00277.x

Matten, D., & Moon, J. (2004). Corporate social responsibility. *Journal of Business Ethics*, *54*(4), 323–337.

KEY TERMS AND DEFINITIONS

Corporate Social Responsibility: It is the responsibility that each organization has with the environment in which it operates and with the society of which it is a part.

Corporate Sustainability: A business management approach that seeks to generate organizational value, as it generates societal value.

Sustainability: It refers to the balance of a species with the resources of its environment.

Sustainable Development Goals: There are 17 interconnected global goals designed to be a blueprint for achieving a better and more sustainable future for all.

Chapter 3
Market Economy and Good Living:
Obstacles to Its Achievement in Orellana, Ecuador

Arturo Luque González
https://orcid.org/0000-0002-4872-891X
Universidad Tecnica de Manabí, Ecuador & Observatorio Euromediterráneo de Espacio Público y Democracia URJC, Spain

Leonor Karina Guamán
Universidad Técnica de Manabí, Ecuador & Observatorio Euromediterráneo de Espacio Público y Democracia URJC, Ecuador

Cristina Raluca Gh. Popescu
https://orcid.org/0000-0002-5876-0550
University of Bucharest, Romania & The Bucharest University of Economic Studies, Romania

ABSTRACT

There is currently an economic metamorphosis underway that involves myriad (mis)development processes. At the same time, processes of inequality are emerging, imbued with their own historical context. This study evaluated the eco-social program known as Good Living (Buen Vivir, Sumak Kawsay) in Ecuador as a tool for change for the most vulnerable sectors that are intrinsically connected to their culture and customs. The study also examined the parallel processes of inequality and the excessive protection of private interests that favor a new world order driven by the maximization of profit. With this objective, the current state of the processes associated with Good Living in the Ecuadorian province of Orellana was analyzed through interviews with relevant local representatives of institutional life. The results highlight the abandonment of the processes of the solidarity and social economy and the resurgence, both by action and omission, of an extractivist model far removed from the principles of compassion, inclusion, and social participation.

DOI: 10.4018/978-1-6684-6750-3.ch003

1. INTRODUCTION

The market economy has become an autonomous system in which decisions are remotely directed toward the goal of the maximization of profit within a framework of poorly enforced and tailor-made legislation. This makes it often difficult to know what is being produced (components, origin), under which conditions (job insecurity, social dumping), what the present and future consequences of the production are, and what proportion of the resulting profits are subject to processes of tax avoidance and evasion. This systemic reality, though a relatively recent phenomenon, plays a formative role in contemporary societies, making them more complex (Cesaratto, 2020).

The origins of neoliberal theory are diffuse but generally coalesced in 1947 when, in addition to the promulgation of the Universal Declaration of Human Rights, the Mont Pelerin Society was created, whose founding members include two outstanding neoliberal theorists, Friedrich Hayek and Milton Friedman. The Society provided a forum for discussion of post-war problems. One side advocated the coverage of social rights and the deployment of an inclusive economic model while the other saw the encroachment of the welfare state as a totalitarian threat to market freedom. Ultimately, the latter group succeeded in stripping away greater social coverage to reveal their philosophy of capital, albeit with a friendly face. This new philosophy was to use the family unit as the means to colonize new spaces, establishing a role for women that appeared equal, but in fact remained clearly chauvinist, and drawing on concepts of voluntariness and false empowerment, with religion as a central element of cohesion. This was, in short, the establishment of a new social order tailored to economic interests (Whyte, 2019). The paradigm brought with it corruption, incipient eco-social complexes and the unequal distribution of wealth and power in post-war organizations such as the UN. Once neoliberalism had managed to divest itself of its commitments, there remained two more spaces to secure. First was the protection of investments by minimizing risks through a process of transferal to weak countries or governments eager to attract foreign money. This was carried out through tools of high economic precision, artificial intelligence and legal and economic engineering, such as free trade and investment agreements established through pseudo-tribunals of arbitrage in which a corporation can be both "judge" and attorney at the same time. The second area was the justification of environmental predation through an unsustainable model of life. As Stratford observes, "reining in rentier power is a pre-condition for imposing tough limits on resource use without social damage, and tough limits on resource use and waste emissions are a precondition for reining in rent extraction without environmental damage" (Stratford, 2020). This approach allows new growth alternatives to be promoted on the one hand while economic, social and environmental problems emerge on the other. The constant crises caused by this hegemonic system generate complex situations of impoverishment and exclusion that affect a large proportion of the population, who are unable to satisfy their basic needs, and that impact nature and all its interdependent elements. In fact, there is a systemic relationship between nature and economy on the one hand, and on the other between economy and environmental deterioration (Naredo, 2010; González de Molina, 2014; Haberl et al., 2016; Alier, 2021). The situation is exemplified by the expert panel of the IPCC (Intergovernmental Panel on Climate Change of the United Nations) composed of 270 scientists from 67 countries, who, after reviewing more than 34,000 research articles, concluded that human-induced global warming compromises "human well-being and planetary health" and that "the scope and magnitude of the impacts are greater than estimated" being immersed in a global process of "unsustainable development". Some of the damage is already irreversible, such as the loss of certain species (in 47% of the 976 species examined, extinction is associated with the increase in temperature) and much more is bordering on becoming irreversible.

The report itself points out that "the global hotspots of high human vulnerability are particularly found in West, Central and East Africa, South Asia, Central and South America, small island developing states and the Arctic" and that such a situation can be quantified: "between 2010 and 2020, human mortality from floods, droughts and storms was 15 times higher in highly vulnerable regions, compared to regions with very low vulnerability". Additionally, climate change drives humanitarian crises and forced displacement contributing to violent conflicts in some countries (IPCC, 2022). According to González and Ramiro (2022),

In addition to the environmental dimension of the company's impacts, which have to do with the pollution and destruction of ecosystems, there are impacts in at least three other dimensions: at the economic level, with the destruction of the local economic fabric and the difficulty of access to common goods; in the political sphere, with the criminalization and repression of social activists and the defenders of human rights; and in the socio-cultural dimension, affecting the ways of life and rights of indigenous peoples. After observing the expansion of monoculture forest plantations in lands inhabited by indigenous communities, the ethnic axis crosses the entire analysis of the socio-ecological impacts generated.

Social and economic gaps are increasingly widening, wealth is concentrated in fewer power groups while the system continues to guarantee human rights to those who can pay for them while violating those of people who, due to their meagre spending capacity, cannot meet the expectations of capital. The latter are relegated to the level of second-class citizens and societies, subordinates within the system (Solano & Muntuberria Lazarini, 2009; Hernández Zubizarreta & Ramiro, 2016).

This economy of the few is known as "the free market" and it pervades everyday society because it has become a way of life from which it is difficult to detach oneself. According to Hernández Zubizarreta & Ramiro (2022),

At the institutional level, debates focus on the discussion of laws and regulations. But in this legal dispute all that is at stake, basically, is a matter of political will, to put it in classical terms of relations of strength. Normative asymmetry has been considered, not without grounds, the basis of neoliberal globalization: facing the strength of the legal armor built to shield the "rights" of large corporations is the extreme fragility of the mechanisms for the control of their obligations. To put it another way: while transnational private businesses are continuously re-regulated, deregulation of the protection of fundamental rights continues apace.

Ecuador has various mechanisms of intervention and the state favors the imposition of certain limits to the way the economy functions. According to the Constitution (National Constituent Assembly 2008), article 281, section 1 seeks a transformation of small and medium-sized production units of the community and social and solidarity economy within the agri-food and fishing sectors. Additionally, article 310 specifically refers to the public financial sector as having as its purpose the sustainable, efficient, accessible and equitable provision of financial services whereby loans and credit will be oriented preferentially to increase the productivity and competitiveness of less favored groups of the productive sectors included within the national development plan and in order to promote their active inclusion in the economy.

Provisions such as these indicate a clear intention of the Ecuadorian state to intervene in the economy. This research seeks to establish the extent of this intention and clarify the objectives of the state at the provincial level (Orellana) and to derive inferences at the national scale through the study of related elements. This situation opens up other scenarios and complex disputes, such as inequalities in economic movements, which, based on their recognition, visibility and achievements, contribute to the construction of alternatives in order to provide solutions for the benefit of collective well-being (Solano & Muntuberria Lazarini, 2009; Luque, 2022). The neoliberal economic model has failed at the global level: While it has improved the general standard of living it has often contributed little or nothing to development or, indeed, has led to undesirable developments when the model is imposed from above, from central governments, transnational corporations and dominant elites of the capitalist system (Iza & Heredia, 2011). This has given rise to alternatives, such as the concept of good living (buen vivir, or *sumak kawsay),* which, as an economic concept, has its origin in a different worldview, one that breaks with the central ideas of the current economy. It is certainly a concept still in development although, to an extent, it is as old as human culture itself. The *Alli Káusai* (full life) is concerned with more than the mere satisfaction of needs and access to services and goods and, therefore, it cannot be understood as a concept analogous to development, rather, *sumak kawsay* (good living) refers to certain attitudes and ideas that allow themselves to be expressed through various dimensions (Altmann, 2016).

Similarly, there are wide differences between the welfare state and good living (Quadagno, 1987). Good living is a new policy paradigm, but the origins of its conceptualization derive from the traditional Andean world view; meanwhile, the welfare state is related to Western economic reasoning. Despite containing some common elements, these two concepts have marked differences in their definition of living collectively. Good living is largely preventive in nature, manifested through its respect for solidarity between the people and local commerce and through its promotion of the non-accumulation of capital. This is in accordance with traditions of the peoples of the Andean region. In contrast, the Western welfare state is a palliative measure and is based on developmental policies; it is also part of an increasingly racist and neoliberal discourse that seeks retrenchment in spending and implements a society of first- and second-class citizens, defined in terms of their acquisitive power. In fact, the welfare state has established its own legal and social scaffolding in response to economic exhaustion. The model of continuous growth and the consequent marginalization from mainstream society of large sections of the public is not questioned, rather, it helps to sustain the contradiction of a Keynesian-Fordist capital economy that seeks to keep producing what a significant part of the population cannot buy and to focus efforts on inherently unsustainable goods and services. The result is a two-fold punishment of the poor. It is in this context that states eager for investment and votes in elections are pressured by industrial lobbies to, in effect, recast citizens as consumers (Luque, 2021). On the other hand, the concept of good living does not replace the state with the market; instead, the market must seek to establish a harmonious relationship with the public and to form interdependent connections with elements present in the natural environment, a quality that otherwise would be unlikely to develop.

In recent history, a number of instances of great economic impact related to social problems have emerged. Germany experienced this in its overcoming of internal divisions after the reunification process of 1989 (Resico, 2011). Other countries, especially those that were more stagnant, chose to implement policies at the outset of the market economy (Passet, 2012). In the case of Ecuador, monetary policy does not seem to be compatible with the mission that the economy seeks to exercise within financial institutions outside of state control. In the nineteenth century, private banks were able to issue their own money, but, as a result of the crisis of the early twentieth century, this was replaced by the monopoly of control of the central bank, justified as a means to control inflation (Garrison, 1996). This emerged as a long-term tendency, yet it failed to offer new models of social, political, cultural and technological development by ignoring the influence exerted by economic interest groups on the political class and public decision-making processes in the institutions of liberal democratic states (Luque, 2018). Organized business action in the market economy has predominated in the theoretical constructions that have been put forward by studies in this field (Crespo, 2019). At present, the preponderant role of the economy in the labor market represents an imperfect situation due to processes of standardization and asymmetric competition. The normalization of this situation depends on innumerable factors that both help and hinder the productive sector (Laval & Dardot, 2017; Battisti, Marcuello, & Messias, 2020) .

2. BACKGROUND AND CURRENT REALITY

The origins of the economy can be discerned in the oldest and most productive civilizations of human history. The economy arose de facto almost at the same time as human culture itself, being derived from basic needs and the capacity for understanding and negotiation. Humans at first used barter as the method of exchange and, although a simplistic system, it was able to cover, partially or totally, the subsistence of families. Barter then gave way to commerce and the sale of products in exchange for economic remuneration (Humphrey & Hugh-Jones, 1992). The term economy was used for the first time in Hellenistic civilization although the concept was applied in a different way: Ancient Greeks considered that the economy was synonymous with the administration of an entire family by the head of the household (Glotz, 2013; University of San Martín de Porres, 2017). Plato considered that economics could be understood from different points of view: both as a family system and as a discipline that requires the study of the administration and organization of the entire economic system in terms of monetary value (Shell, 1993).

According to Capdevielle (1993), in the late nineteenth century, neoclassical economists radically transformed the classical "view" of economic science. Economics ceased to be a social science dedicated to the study of human relations based on the production and distribution of commodities and became a science that studies the way in which scarce productive resources for the production of different goods and services are used and financed by transnational speculative processes. Justice has always played a transcendental role throughout economic history since the economy is often a tool for personal profit due to its inappropriate use and the interconnected elements that pivot around vested interests. At the same time, the economy is concerned with social processes, developing their purposes within the labor and productive market.

In Ecuador, the processes of *sumak kawsay*, good living, bring together elements at the global level with the objectives and priorities of the needs of social groups in accordance with their economic status (Silva Portero, 2008). This is a principle that encompasses every individual without distinction and exclusion. Table nº1, Good living, sets out the most relevant articles of the Constitution of Ecuador related to *sumak kawsay*.

Table 1. Good living

Legal Text	*Year*	*Article*	*Content*
Constitution of Ecuador	2008	Art. 3 section 5.	Plan for national development, eradicate poverty, promote sustainable development and the equitable redistribution of resources and wealth to access good living.
		Art. 14.-	The right of the population to live in a healthy and ecologically balanced environment is recognized, which guarantees sustainability and good living, *Sumak Kawsay*.
		Art. 26.-	Education is a people's right throughout their lives and an inescapable and inexcusable duty of the state. It is a priority area of public policy and state investment, a guarantee of equality and social inclusion and an indispensable condition for good living. Individuals, families and society have the right and responsibility to participate in the educational process.
		Art. 32.	Health is a right guaranteed by the state, the fulfillment of which is linked to the exercise of other rights, including the right to water, food, education, physical exercise, work, social security, healthy environments and others that sustain good living.
		Art. 74.	Individuals, communities, peoples and nationalities have the right to benefit from the environment and the natural wealth that allows them to Live Well.
		Art 83 section 7.	Promote the common good and put the general interest before the private interest, in accordance with good living.
		Art. 85 section 1.	Public policies and the provision of public goods and services will be oriented toward making good living and all rights effective, and will be formulated based on the principle of solidarity.
		Art. 275.-	The regime of development is an organized, sustainable and dynamic set of economic, political, socio-cultural and environmental systems, which guarantee the fulfillment of good living, *sumak kawsay*.
		Art. 387 section 2.	Promote the generation and production of knowledge, encourage scientific and technological research, and enhance ancestral knowledge, in order to contribute to the fulfillment of good living, *sumak kawsay*.

Source: compiled by the author from the Constitution of Ecuador, 2008.

From this basis, the relationship between the market economy and good living may be identified, which raises different questions concerning their coexistence and the nature of this relationship: What are the most outstanding difficulties that prevent these two paradigms from moving forward together? Which states participate in the market economy at the international level? What are the objectives of good living at all levels of society? In which countries can we find good living being practiced?

The market economy and good living are two elements of common sense that drive new ideologies in the socio-political and economic field at the global level. The term good living does not have a specific origin, but obviously it has arisen, to a greater or lesser extent, alongside the improvement of life in society. In parallel, the processes of good living constitute a new social dimension based on common welfare; not only does it represent an alternative to capitalism, but it also distances itself from socialism and even from progressivism. It comprehends only policies that are far removed from the traditional projects of the left, and is part of a left without complexes and with the capacity to introduce disruptive measures, even at the risk of losing many of our current comforts. This is a feminist, ecological and inclusive left, one not merely concerned with production and the maximization of capital, but having as a driving force the promotion and deployment of human rights. According to Ramírez, (2008, p. 387), good living is conceptualized through:

the satisfaction of needs, the achievement of a dignified quality of life and death, the wish to love and be loved, and the healthy flourishing of all, in peace and harmony with nature and the indefinite prolongation of human cultures. Good living implies having free time for contemplation and emancipation, and that the freedoms, opportunities, capacities and real potentialities of individuals are expanded and flourish so that they allow the simultaneous achievement of what society, the regions, the various collective identities and each person—seen as a universal and individual human being— value as a desirable life objective (both materially and subjectively, and without leading to the predomination of one or the other). Our concept of good living obliges us to reconstruct the public sphere in order for us to recognize, understand and value one another—as different but equal—so that the possibility of reciprocity and mutual recognition may prosper and thus enable self-fulfillment and the construction of a shared social future.

It is also a response to the limitations, dysfunctions and contradictions of the current developmental model by decisively incorporating values demanded by society, such as ethics, conservation and environmental respect, and increasingly a desire to limit the tendency of growth. Specifically, outstanding examples of good living concern: 1) living in areas free of pollution or at least at levels compatible with natural life in which its impact is minimized; 2) being able to feel a part of a system that is made up of each individual contribution and that provides security and collective protection; 3) having access to basic necessities such as water, electricity, education and transport, and more recently, the Internet; 4) complying with labor legislation and establishing mechanisms for redress and real protections (e.g. a binding labor inspectorate with executive powers); 5) having free time to devote to family, leisure or any type of activity that generates personal and spiritual satisfaction; 6) being part of collective participation in the political dimension and feeling that individual views are taken into account.

Good living, *sumak kawsay*, cannot function on the basis of working and consuming, or working to perhaps retire and have a pension. There is no unified definition that takes into account the differences and existing needs arising from other types of non-Western values, that is, cultural aspects such as traditions, knowledge, relationships, together with other logical spaces such as spiritual or physical elements. Well-being must take precedence over a mercantile voracity that is a travesty of modernity, and be allowed to give room to non-productive, physical or logical concepts such as time spent on leisure or quality free time. The traditional market economy and its excesses drive the need for good living (Dávalos, 2008) and the desire to put life at the service of interdependent elements such as nature and the cosmos, which become the determining elements of society, over and above the maximization of profit (Luque, 2017).

Good living requires the redefinition of classic concepts of the traditionalist economy such as development processes and progress in well-being and social inclusion. It shares a direct relationship with the practices of a social economic system, or what is known as socio-economy, in which its contribution both benefits and revalues the individual from the economic perspective and dynamizes and enhances the creativity of work. From the political perspective, it generates a convergence of thought that ensures the dignity of life for all and, from the environmental angle; it leads to the recognition of the rights of nature (Maldonado, Bastidas Aráuz, & Durán Pinos, 2017; Luque & Álvarez, 2021).

This study focuses on the province of Orellana in Ecuador, a region of abundant wealth derived from the local economic processes on the one hand and the activity of extractivism (mainly oil) on the other. It is one of the youngest provinces of the Ecuadorian state and is part of the Amazonian region. It is internationally considered an ecological and ethnological jewel due to its many ancestral cultures that also protect the natural environment. These peoples are fundamental to the concept of *sumak kaw-*

say and the Constitutional criteria that guarantee the rights of the most vulnerable and disconnected (National Secretariat of Planning and Development, 2015). This study is based on the legal framework existing within the province of Orellana, Ecuador and its participation in the provision of the economic framework or social welfare. It also tests hypotheses about the problems and consequences of these elements within different areas of analysis: i) economic valuations, together with the risks involved in determining the stability related to supply and demand in goods and services; ii) the coexistence of peoples and nationalities that make up part of the province of Orellana in relation to the development of rights, freedoms and capacities for transforming the economy; iii) the certainty that good living and the preponderant economy both condition the current social and economic reality in Ecuador, based on its taxonomy of inconsistencies.

The market economy and the Sustainable Development Goals (SDGs) taken together have the immense power to offer and to ensure new and inclusive market opportunities which will ultimately lead to novel market value for individuals, especially in a society that strives to accomplish long term economic growth in key economic areas (Popescu *et al.*, 2015a). Besides all these, the development of the market economy strongly relates to sustainability, since sustainable development (SD) affects in a positive and in a constructive manner the economy, offering valuable market opportunities that will promote, in time, the economic, social, and environmental balance (Popescu *et al.*, 2015b).

2.1 Development of the Market Economy in the Province of Orellana

The province of Orellana has four cantons: Francisco de Orellana, Loreto, Joya de los Sachas and Aguarico, each composed of various parishes, Alejandro Labaka, Dayuma, El Dorado, El Edén, García Moreno, Ines Arango, La Belleza, Nuevo Paraiso, San Jose de Guayusa, San Luis de Armenia and Taracea. It is situated on the border with Colombia and Peru, leading to considerable movement of people, especially as it is a territory of great natural wealth (Arregui, 2020). Orellana has both urban and rural areas in which significant economic progress is evident in the technification of agribusiness and the consolidation of the local population. With the growth of production and the increase in productivity, land is no longer regarded as a mere reserve of value as it was in earlier times. In recent years, there has been an increase in the raising of livestock, leading to significant changes in economic terms (Koiffmann, 2019). However, Orellana is one of the least populated provinces in Ecuador, according to the National Institute of Statistics and Censuses (2021), with a total of 136,396 citizens of which 64,266 are women and 72,130 men. The province includes three surviving indigenous nationalities, Kichwa, Waorani and Shuar, considered the most representative of the Ecuadorian Amazon peoples due to their defence of their ancestral practices (Program Development and Cultural Diversity for Poverty Reduction and Social Inclusion, 2004). Part of the native population of the Amazon region holds extensive lands in common that have been managed collectively since colonial times (Luque, Bengoetxea & Ordoñez, 2021). These are extensive kinship groups that possess thousands of hectares acquired in many cases through purchases from the Spanish Crown or from various republican governments represented by their indigenous authorities in the Republican era. Domestic groups have governed these lands for centuries, enjoying relative political autonomy and their links to the capital market through the commercialization of local resources have distant origins (Álvarez, 2017).

Based on these foundations, Orellana channels its commercial and economic productivity with neighboring provinces, in particular Napo and Sucumbíos. Orellana is considered one of the main economic and financial centers of the Ecuadorian Amazon thanks to its petroleum resources (Secretariat of Hydrocarbons, 2022). The Amazon region contains abundant oil fields and a powerful oil industry that has supported the Ecuadorian state both economically and politically since the 1970s, which is why Orellana is one of the nation's main sources of income. Other industries that operate in Orellana are timber and agriculture (fishing, agrarian farming and poultry farming being the most important) (EpJafeta, 2019; Orellana, 2022). Tourism, both foreign and domestic is also an important source of income and Orellana takes advantage of its products, riches, cultures, places and even gastronomy as an instrument of economy and even communities far from the urban areas draw considerable numbers of visitors. There are products from the area as well as medicinal plants and ancestral traditions; local attractions include Amarun Yaya—face painting as a symbol that represent nature—the guayusa water drink, the practice of ancestral games, hiking and the Amazonian cooking style known as *maito* (Ministry of Tourism, 2020).

2.2 General Aspects Related to the Political, Legal and Judicial Model in Ecuador

The national economy has suffered countless stagnations and declines arising from various socio-political and historical contexts, which has caused people to only value objectives of a productive nature. This economic perspective is encapsulated in article 1 of the Organic Law of the Social and Solidarity Economy, defining itself as a form of economic organization in which its members come together to produce, exchange, market, finance, and consume goods and services that allow them to satisfy their needs and generate income (Coral, 2018). On the other hand, the great development that this economic model represents demonstrates that the most vulnerable sectors can benefit from their culture or customs, hence the need to promote living conditions by jealously caring for and protecting local inhabitants and communities. It should be noted that the role played by supply and demand is decisive in terms of the level of production and is prioritized by the global economic organization that relates countries and people that arose after the Second War and ushered in a new economic model.

In 2008, mainly in the port city of Guayaquil, there were political tensions, renewed confrontations and demonstrations of adhesion to and rejection of the Government of the then president, Rafael Correa. In this context, the Constituent Assembly progressed in the conceptual development of Constitutional issues, generating a dialogue with citizens by convening various stakeholders in different regions through the forums organized by the constituent committees (Muñoz, 2008). From this basis, a new political and legal model emerged, which reflected the Ecuadorian context of that time, as well as its historical claim to dignity for its people. To better understand this transition, Table nº2, A historical timeline of Ecuador, summarizes the most notable developments from 2008 to the present and comments on whether each represents a progressive or retrograde step. Many of these regulations and laws are still current within the Constitution, such as Article 1, which states that Ecuador is a Constitutional state of rights, and social, democratic, sovereign, independent, unitary, intercultural, pluri-national and secular justice. It is organized in the form of a republic and governed in a decentralized manner. Sovereignty lies with the people, whose will is the basis of authority, which is exercised through the organs of public power and the forms of direct participation provided for in the Constitution.

Table 2. A historical timeline of Ecuador

Event	Year	Legal, judicial or political progress or setback
The Constitution of the Republic is created	2008	Established greater organization within the economic, political and legal system, generating certainty at the social level.
National Development Plan	2008	Created by the National Secretariat of Planning in order to generate a pluri-national and multicultural context.
High level of crisis and unemployment	2009	The Ecuadorian public experienced a large-scale social crisis and great economic impact.
Political crisis	2010	Protests against existing wage laws and demanding labor rights.
Constitutional Referendum	2011	Justice reforms in terms of the content of laws and regulations.
Declaration of Guayaquil	2012	Signed by UNASUR with the intention of demanding diplomatic inviolability.
Presidential elections	2013	Promotion of new ideologies and opportunities for Ecuadorian society.
Telecommunications Law	2014	Regulation of the range of inter and extra-social communication between various territories.
Demonstrations and transfers due to Constitutional changes	2015	Not eliminated, but it stagnated and gave added value to the social sphere.
Ecuador and the European Union sign the Free Trade Agreement	2016	Promising commercial and productive expansion.
The "Lifetime" plan	2017	Extended inclusion to all people with disabilities by offering help and benefits according to economic and social status.
Trade agreement with the European Free Trade Association	2018	Extension of supply and demand on the sale of products, thereby generating greater income.
Constitutional Court rules in favor of equal marriage	2019	Right to equal opportunities and greater freedom of choice.
Organic Law on Aquaculture and Fisheries	2020	Guaranteed the right to nature and its protection.
Guillermo Lasso becomes president of Ecuador	2021	New judicial, legal and political model that ensured guaranteed human rights.
Source: compiled by the author.		

2.2 Organization and Social Structure of good living in the Province of Orellana

The criteria of good living established by the Constitution of Ecuador reflects in detail the historical transformation that has occurred in different contexts and the analysis of major social, cultural and political changes set out along a clear timeline. The study of the case of the province or Orellana deepens this analysis through a process of reinterpretation of the indigenous origins of this region based on a long historical tradition of criticisms and questioning. This is made more interesting by the inclusion of other conceptions, normally marginalized from conventional discourse and practices that have their origin in and are typical of ancestral peoples and nationalities (Acosta, 2015). According to Ruíz et al. (2015):

in recent years in Latin America, particularly in the Andean area, good living has emerged as a current of thought that, by incorporating the ethical principles and ancestral knowledge of our native peoples and critical postulates of development models, has become a radical means of questioning hegemonic ways of life and a topic of debate and universal concern, especially following its embodiment in the Ecuadorian and Bolivian Constitutions.

The province of Orellana is a rich example of the concept of good living within Ecuador since its main means of ancestral identification is present in all the communities and cultures that play a great role in Ecuadorian society, such as those outlined in Table n°1. The Constitution supports these eco-social ideologies by promoting development and collective coexistence in the most remote and unprotected areas.

2.3 Main Limitations and Impediments to the Development of the Economy and Good Living

Economic freedom interferes with all other freedoms (Garcia, 2019) and the dismantling of the public sphere leads to its exhaustion (Polanyi & MacIver, 1944). Among the most common limitations of the economy and good living is the existence of processes of normative asymmetry and the lack of a clear, peaceful coexistence between the different existing interests (Guzmán, 2015). As an example, within the influence of the economy, there are issues such as citizen insecurity, political uncertainty, the increase in prices of inputs and raw materials and general inflationary pressures, the lack of a universal basic income, weakness in the internal market and instrumentalized fiscal policy, all of which are based on the premise of unlimited growth yet are developed within a reality in which the resources of the planet are manifestly finite (Luque & Casado, 2020a; García-Albán, González-Astudillo & Vera-Avellán, 2021). As far as the current economy is concerned, a low level of production, distribution and consumption of products can seriously affect the economy of any country that follows this model, leading to the destabilization of the monetary equilibrium. The economy of Ecuador is rooted in small producers who are in constant commercial demand, and whose products are exported, generating benefits for the entire community. Good living reflects the application of the current laws and is affected when these are not complied with by the government, to the extent of causing social disorder.

3. METHODOLOGY

The processes of good living are multidimensional, which makes their study complex, especially when considering their many imbrications and interrelations. This research was based on descriptive-analytical study of the existing situation, presented through space and time, taking the specific case of the province of Orellana, Ecuador. The relevant phenomena were observed and recorded in their natural state, without introducing modifications. The research was guided by the questions: What is it? How is it managed? Where does it occur? When does it occur? How many individuals or cases are observed? At the analytical level (explanatory, relational, stochastic, correlational, etc.), the study looked for the association or correlation between the different possible existing variables without establishing causal relationships and by inferring probabilistic relationships (Rojas, 2015; Lopera, Ramírez, Zuluaga, & Ortíz, 2010).

The primary research tool took the form of unstructured interviews, based around six questions (see Appendix I) to active members of institutional and/or moral life in the province of Orellana. Specifically, these were the parish priest of Loreto canton (Angle Alvarado), the technician of the Parish Government of Huiruno (José Gaviria), the deputy mayor of the Loreto canton (José Morocho) and the mayor of the Loreto canton (René Grefa). The questions were guided by observations of the processes of good living in the region, as well as drawing on other studies in the published literature (Gudynas & Acosta, 2011; Galiano-Maritan & Tamayo-Santana, 2018). Different methodologies were used in the treatment of the data obtained, such as description, analysis, reflection, explanation and other tools that necessarily made use of personal reasoning based on the informative or historical background. The resulting analysis was intended to help guide solutions to future problems related to the economy of good living and its functioning in society. Indeed, the informative and descriptive data gathered stand out for their ability to anticipate consequences or developments in the long or short term.

It should be noted that the results of this type of analysis depend on the continuity of study. In fact, a classification can be made by sectors, be they social, productive, cultural, political, religious, scientific, and philosophical or leisure, framed by the constant changes within the object of study, in this case Orellana, Ecuador. This is also the case of studies concerned with international politics, in which it is possible to identify new opportunities for citizens regarding economic or ancestral conditions, determined by the study carried out on the historical politico-social patterns. In this way, vulnerable groups can be identified, useful approaches to planning can be developed, and the demand for certain services within society can be determined. In summary, descriptive-analytical research can visualize long-term objectives based on a previous inquiry that help to optimize and stabilize certain characteristics within the social sphere.

4. ANALYSIS AND DISCUSSION

The historical political changes in Ecuador, after two hundred years of Constitutionalism, have been substantial (Alberdi, 2011). At present, these changes are imbued with processes of globalization, which has modified the way the most basic needs are covered and related to at the local level, and has strongly influenced the political structure at the international level. It is within this framework that the processes of good living in Ecuador are implemented and deployed, and their interrelation must necessarily be understood through both external factors (treaties, agreements, etc.) and internal factors (political parties, citizenship, capital). At the same time, the effect of the processes of speculation and political ideology must be taken into account. There are certain similarities in the characteristics of the legal regulations and Constitutional protections relating to good living, but the focus comes from different angles since some are more guarantors of rights than others, some more eco-social, and others prioritize areas outside of the predominant model influenced by specific concerns of the public (Luque & Casado, 2020b).

This study shows that the economy has undergone divergence in all areas; in part, due to the implicit moral decay that emerges from a maximization of continuous profit, but also leading to sequelae for the market, such as recession within the productive matrix and marked economic instability. The results obtained help to identify areas of confusion regarding the most idyllic forecasts of good living processes, as well as to highlight the most neglected sectors, showing that there could be better positioning and development in different sectors. With regard to legality, the visibility good living within the community lends it an implicit legitimacy. This visibility is not a dimension of power that originates in the intimate space of personal relationships, but rather is cultivated and mediatized in the public sphere (Dalmau, 2018). This study contemplates the analogy between good living and the economy within the context of the Ecuadorian Amazon where the importance of the social sphere and adequate preparation for the promotion of the social economy is evident. At the same time, the analysis of the relationship between good living, or *sumak kawsay,* and the economy highlights the limited importance that aspects such as values, ethical competences, or simply the way of understanding and transmitting the functioning of the economy have in the financial system. According to Larrouy (2022), "big banking demands fewer obligations to make the ecological transition and not have to act as a 'climate policeman'". In other words, necropolitics becomes the norm and not the exception in this unscrupulous process of the accumulation of capital. Based on these observations, a series of recommendations may be made to contribute to promoting and energizing the formation of the appropriate use of legal norms regarding the economy linked to good living (Flores, Guzmán, & Barroso, 2015).

The interviews conducted with representatives of local institutional life revealed some notable insights. Ángel Alvarado, Parish Priest of Loreto canton, defined the processes of good living as a full and harmonious life in which the ecological system plays a fundamental developmental role, one in which it is included and applied in all social areas. He recognizes that the oil sector is an important source of revenue for the government and helps sustain the entire country, but the processes of extractivism have consequences for the Amazon region, such as environmentally devasting oil spills. Currently, interests tend to be more personal than collective, which agrees with the observations made by González & Ramiro (2022), who note that in certain companies, "financial capacity, proximity to governments and the ability to lobby for regulatory changes and tax incentives have been essential factors for the expansion of the company in the country." The economy that underpins the country must sustain all its sectors based on principles of equality, justice and equity. However, Father Alvarado relates centralism with politics and blames it for the neglect in the most remote and unprotected sectors of Ecuador, especially for its effect on education. In fact, the challenge of education in the Amazon region should be set as a priority since the deficiencies and failings are many and significant. Furthermore, communication with some communities is limited because of a lack of access roads; since all communities of Amazonian Ecuador sustain their economy through agriculture, this limitation has serious consequences for production. These problems largely explain the lack of progress at the national level and lead Father Alvarado to conclude that "those who are benefited are foreigners with their vision and education." It is worth noting that, in contrast to the failings of the state, church missions have for many years made access roads between different communities in the Amazon and provided education to many indigenous people. In the same way, he points out that a barrier that limits good living is the selfishness of the many and the application of centralism for the benefit of the few. Corruption at all political levels has been growing and expanding to such an extent that the Amazon is now affected by it.

The development of both good living and the economy is promoted through community and social policy. In the view of José Gaviria, representative of the Ávila Huiruno Parish, the processes of good living and its influence on the communities and parishes promote social organization for the benefit of an entire people. With regard to the centralized economy, the parish yearns to promote it through tourism projects that will benefit many rural sectors. He believes that the economy and Good Living go hand in hand since the ventures that have been implemented in the parish were aimed at the public. In addition, he pointed out that one of the greatest weaknesses of good living in the parish is the lack of basic services such as clean water and electricity to all communities. Meanwhile, the deputy mayor of Loreto, José Morocho, points out that the processes of good living and the economy are two areas that require special care. The Loreto canton has one oil-producing parish, but this is dominated by foreigners who are the main beneficiaries of this development. He states that the profits of oil production are not directed to within the canton; on the contrary, they are destined elsewhere, even outside the country. Despite these limitations, there are other sources of income such as agriculture and livestock although the pandemic led to a decline in this sector to a subsistence level.

Among the greatest barriers to the functioning of good living is the political dimension. The mayor of Loreto canton, Rene Grefa, states that the processes of good living influence the development of the functions exercised by the economy in society while claiming that coexistence is synonymous with the social economy. He contends that it is a mistake for the state and society in general to depend excessively on non-renewable resources since they will come to an end and alternatives should be in place. He also laments the centralism of both the public and private sectors and urges both to join forces to work for the benefit of the human being.

One manifest weakness of good living is the regulatory process, which allows the preponderant economy to act as the regulatory system. The consensus of international policies in multilateral organizations such as the World Bank and the International Monetary Fund suggests the relative importance of efficient markets in developing countries (Ziegler, 2013). Because economic decisions have significant implications for the wealth of two of the pillars of the economy, the financial system and the government, the adoption of economic regulation generates regulatory certainty by turning an economic theory into financial and political dogma (Prieto & Tejedor, 2017). These two entities play a fundamental role worldwide since they control both the circulation of money and its origin, linked to the decisions and functions of the government. This creates a vicious circle that is only likely to worsen if no inclusive economic rules of the game are introduced. This study suggests that the term economics is currently being used erroneously and is confused with politics; unfortunately, two successive governments of Ecuador, those of Lenin Moreno and Guillermo Lasso, have aggravated the situation through neoliberal policy and a view of citizens as expendable elements, or even a necessary evil. Of course, for this to happen, the market needs to be complicit. In this case, politicians offer the social economy a catalogue of unfulfilled functions and the neglect to work for the benefit of society.

With regard to good living as described in the Constitution (*sumak kawsay*), it is defined as a resource as long as the Constitutional norms prevail. Good living is considered of great importance for Ecuador due to the continual extinction of many cultures and areas of national life. Over the last few decades, the intervention of man and his technology in the Amazon region have led to local peoples abandoning their roots, dialect and even traditional clothing. True modernity means maintaining traditions while achieving progress and there are a few who identify themselves as Amazonians and citizens of the megadiverse country that is Ecuador. For these, the more inclusive and protective laws of good living exist to reward their perseverance and ensure that their way of life is not eroded with the passage of time.

CONCLUSIONS

The transformations that have taken place both in the global economy and in the processes of good living constitute a complex and distorted trajectory and the evaluation of policies is challenging. Much of the economic activity in Ecuador during the period of good living has indirectly promoted extractivist processes and the unrestricted consumption of goods and services, relegating the processes of good living to a subordinate economy, in spite of its sound regulatory construction. In other words, the dominance of commodities is sustained. In the province of Orellana, in Ecuador in general, and indeed throughout South America, economies have sought to increase exports of raw materials as a solution to their crises. In fact, extractivist expansion has increased even more by incorporating the mining of minerals in high demand, such as lithium, and by implementing monoculture exploitation that is often transgenic or not suitable for specific ecosystems, such as balsa wood or corn. One of the great problems lies in the conception of the Andean world as relatively untouched and perfect, an image that is also projected by governments who, in fact, espouse neoliberal policies. Both sequelae and disparate benefits derive from this situation in the province of Orellana, where clear potential is evident at the same time as a lack of real implementation of the processes of good living. The sell-off of natural resources has turned much of the province into hollow facades with no real alternative activity, areas that permit constant environmental aggression in return for the remunerations of mining and hydrocarbon companies assisted by corruption.

One of the current dilemmas is to try to internationalize the processes of social economy derived from good living. The market economy depends on many factors, but will always be linked to international trade and the stock exchange while good living is a model that is not applied in all countries and is restricted to several Constitutions that apparently promote democracy and the respect for freedom, culture and the common good. Orellana is a highly productive province, sustained by abundant non-renewable natural resources but with limited scope in terms of social benefit. It would be prudent for society to intervene with more diligence to create strategic development plans for Orellana, promoting, among other things, tourism, and guaranteeing that its resources be exploited only as long as the derived profits are destined to elements of social welfare. The local inhabitants have not lost hope that the government will turn Orellana into a model province that, together with the whole Amazon region, may be considered the green lung of Ecuador.

REFERENCES

Acosta, A. (2015). El Buen Vivir como alternativa al desarrollo. Algunas reflexiones económicas y no tan económicas [Good Living as an alternative to development. Some economic and not so economic reflections]. *Politica y Sociedad*, *52*(2), 301–305. doi:10.5209/rev_POSO.2015.v52.n2.45203

Alberdi, O. (2011). La Separación de poderes en el Constitucionalismo Burgués [The separation of powers in bourgeois constitutionalism]. *Nómadas*, *32*(4), 32–45. doi:10.5209/rev_NOMA.2011.v32.n4.38083

Alier, J. M. (2021). *El ecologismo de los pobres: conflictos ambientales y lenguajes de valoración* [The environmentalism of the poor: environmental conflicts and languages of valuation]. Icaria.

Altmann, P. (2016). Buen Vivir como propuesta política integral: Dimensiones del Sumak Kawsay [Good Living as a comprehensive political proposal: Dimensions of Sumak Kawsay]. *Mundosplurales*, *3*(1), 57–60. doi:10.17141/mundosplurales.1.2016.2318

Álvarez, S. (2017). Territorio comunal en la costa de Ecuador: Buscando caminos de entendimiento entre el Buen Vivir y el principio de bien común [Communal territory on the coast of Ecuador: looking for paths of understanding between Good Living and the principle of the common good]. *Revista de Antropología Social*, *26*(2), 355–378. doi:10.5209/RASO.57610

Arregui, A. (2020). Conectando con la Amazonia transparente. El cuerpo afroindígena y la comunicación más allá de las élites [Connecting with the transparent Amazon. The Afro-indigenous body and communication beyond the elites]. *Journal of American Anthropology, 50*, 291-306. doi:10.5209/reaa.70442

Battisti, L., Marcuello, C., & Messias, J. (2020). Las perspectivas Latinoamericana y Europea de la Economía Solidaria [The Latin American and European perspectives of the Solidarity Economy]. *Revista de estudios cooperativos, 134*, 1-10. doi:10.5209/reve.69171

Capdevielle, M. (1993). *Economía de mercado y solidaridad* [Market economy and solidarity]. Política y Cultura.

Cesaratto, S. (2020). *Heterodox Challenges in Economics: Theoretical Issues and the Crisis of the Eurozone*. Springer Nature. doi:10.1007/978-3-030-54448-5

Coral, C. (2018). Emprendimiento indígena, ¿Una dimensión económica del Sumak? [Indigenous entrepreneurship, an economic dimension of Sumak? *Revesco: Revista de Estudios Cooperativos*, *129*, 123–141. doi:10.5209/REVE.62849

Crespo, G. G. (2019). La democracia del libre mercado. La intervención patronal en el sistema político de la transición [Free market democracy. Employer intervention in the political system of the transition]. *Centro de Estudios sobre Dictaduras y Democracias (CEDID)*, 299-300.

Dalmau, P. (2018). La reputación del notable. Escándalos y capital simbólico en la España Liberal [The reputation of the notable. Scandals and symbolic capital in Liberal Spain]. *Historia y Política*, *39*(39), 79–107. doi:10.18042/hp.39.04

Dávalos, P. (2008). Reflexiones sobre el sumak kawsay (buen vivir) y las teorías del desarrollo [Reflections on sumak kawsay (good living) and development theories]. *ALAI (Agencia Latino Americana Informaciones), Quito, Agosto 5*. Disponible en: http://alainet.org/ac-tive/25617

EpJafeta. (2019). *Orellana*. Retrieved from El Popular: https://www.elpopular.com.ec/orellana/

Flores, D., Guzmán, C., & Barroso, M. (2015). La formación en economía social. Análisis de la oferta universitaria de posgrado en España [Training in social economy. Analysis of the postgraduate university offer in Spain]. *Revesco*, *121*, 89–113. doi:10.5209/rev_REVE.2016.v121.49703

Galiano-Maritan, G., & Tamayo-Santana, G. (2018). Análisis constitucional de los derechos personalísimos y su relación con los derechos del buen vivir en la Constitución de Ecuador [Constitutional analysis of very personal rights and their relationship with the rights of good living in the Constitution of Ecuador]. *Revista de Derecho Privado*, (34), 123–156. doi:10.18601/01234366.n34.05

Garcia, G. (2019). La democracia del libre mercado. La intervención patronal en el sistema político de la transición [Free market democracy. Employer intervention in the political system of the transition]. *Historia y Política*, *42*(42), 297–330. doi:10.18042/hp.42.11

García-Albán, F., González-Astudillo, M., & Vera-Avellán, C. (2021). Good policy or good luck? Analyzing the effects of fiscal policy and oil revenue shocks in Ecuador. *Energy Economics*, *100*, 105321. doi:10.1016/j.eneco.2021.105321

Garrison, R. (1996). Central Banking, Free Banking, and Financial Crises. *The Review of Austrian Economics*, *9*(2), 109–112. doi:10.1007/BF01103332

Glotz, G. (2013). *Ancient Greece at work*. Routledge. doi:10.4324/9781315005348

González, E., & Ramiro, P. (2022). *Smurfit Kappa en Colombia: impactos socioecológicos y violaciones de derechos humanos*. Omal. Retrieved from https://omal.info/spip.php?article9737

González de Molina, M., & Toledo, V. M. (2014). *The Social Metabolism. A Socio-Ecological Theory of Historical Change*. Springer.

Gudynas, E., & Acosta, A. (2011). El buen vivir más allá del desarrollo [Good living beyond development]. *Revista Quehacer*, (181), 70–83.

Guzmán, M. (2015). *Del concepto a la medicion: Propuesta metodologica para medir el Buen Vivir en Ecuador* [From concept to measurement: Methodological proposal to measure Good Living in Ecuador]. Instituto Nacional de Estadisticas y Censos.

Haberl, H., Fischer-Kowalski, M., Krausmann, F., & Winiwarter, V. (2016). *Social Ecology. Society-Nature relations across Time and Space*. Springer.

Hernández Zubizarreta, J., & Ramiro, P. (2016). *Contra la lex mercatoria* [Against the lex mercatoria]. Ed. Icaria.

Hernández Zubizarreta, J., & Ramiro, P. (2022). *Declaración universal de los derechos del poder corporativo* [Universal declaration of the rights of corporate power]. Ctxt. Retrieved from https://ctxt.es/es/20220501/Firmas/39628/poder-corporativo-derechos-humanos-necropolitica-derecho-internacional.htm

Humphrey, C., & Hugh-Jones, S. (Eds.). (1992). *Barter, exchange and value: an anthropological approach*. Cambridge University Press. doi:10.1017/CBO9780511607677

IPCC. (2022). AR6 Synthesis Report. Ginebra: ONU. Retrieved from https://www.ipcc.ch/report/sixth-assessment-report-cycle/

Iza, M., & Heredia, D. (2011). *Sumak Kawsay? Los derechos humanos al agua y al trabajo en la provincia de Orellana* [Sumak kawsay? The human rights to water and work in the province of Orellana]. INREDH.

Koiffmann, B. (2019). Geopolítica de la Amazonía [Geopolitics of the Amazon]. *Revista de estudios sobre espacio y poder, 10*(1), 135-151. Doi: doi:10.5209/GEOP.63836

Larrouy, D. (2022). *La gran banca pide menos obligaciones para la transición ecológica y no tener que ejercer como "policía del clima"* [The banking sector asks for fewer obligations for the ecological transition and not having to act as "climate police"]. Retrieved from https://www.eldiario.es/economia/gran-banca-pide-obligaciones-transicion-ecologica-no-ejercer-policia-clima_1_8983575.html

Laval, C., & Dardot, P. (2017). *La pesadilla que no se acaba nunca: El neoliberalismo contra la democracia* [The nightmare that never ends: Neoliberalism against democracy]. 360º Claves contemporáneas.

Lopera, J., Ramírez, C., Zuluaga, M., & Ortíz, J. (2010). El Método Analítico como método natural [The analytical method as a natural method]. *Nómadas*, *1*, 25–30. doi:10.5209/NOMA.27128

Luque, A. (2017). Promoción del hiperconsumo textil transnacional: la moda y el exceso como leit motiv [Promotion of transnational textile hyperconsumption: fashion and excess as leitmotiv]. *Revista Chasqui, 134*, 83-104. doi:10.16921/chasqui.v0i134.3016

Luque, A. (2018). Transnational Systemic Corruption: Exceptionality or Norm? *Revista Empresa y Humanismo*, *21*(2), 123–184. doi:10.15581/015.XXI.2.123-184

Luque, A. (2021). Fallacies of Consumerism: An Analysis of Its Impact and Depth in Today's Society. In Handbook of Research on Changing Dynamics in Responsible and Sustainable Business in the Post-COVID-19 Era. IGI Global. doi:10.4018/978-1-6684-2523-7.ch004

Luque, A. (2022). Analysis of the concept of informal economy through 102 definitions: Legality or necessity. *Open Research Europe*, *2022*, 1–134. doi:10.12688/openreseurope.13990.2

Luque, A., & Álvarez, J. (2021). How the social and solidarity economy is defined: an analysis of 100 concepts. In P. Baisotti & H. López (Eds.), The Social and Solidarity Economy in Latin America. The development of the common good (pp. 1-47). Cambridge Scholars Publishing.

Luque, A., Bengoetxea, A., & Ordoñez, J. L. (2021) The Social and Solidarity Economics, Public Policies, and Non-Monetary Economic Practices: The Case of Associative Firms in Loja, Ecuador. In Handbook of Research on Emerging Business Models and the New World Economic Order. IGI Global. doi:10.4018/978-1-7998-7689-2.ch012

Luque & Casado. (2020a). Procesos de Covid-19 en Ecuador: cuando la distopía se convierte en realidad [Covid-19 processes in Ecuador: when dystopia becomes reality"]. Revista Venezolana de Gerencia, 25(92), 1271-1281. Doi: doi:10.37960/rvg.v25i92

Luque & Casado. (2020b). Public Strategy and Eco-Social Engagement in Latin American States: An Analysis of Complex Networks Arising from Their Constitutions. *MDPI Sustainability, 12*(20), 1-29. doi:10.3390/su12208558

Maldonado, W. P., Bastidas Aráuz, M., & Durán Pinos, A. (2017). Propuesta metodológica de evaluacion del balance social en asociaciones de economía popular solidaria del Ecuador [Methodological proposal for the evaluation of the social balance in associations of popular solidarity economy of Ecuador]. *CIRIEC-España, Revista de Economía Pública. Social y Cooperativa, 90*(90), 123–157. doi:10.7203/CIRIEC-E.90.9240

Ministry of Tourism. (2020). *Orellana un destino para conocer la cultura amazónica* [Orellana a destination to learn about the Amazonian culture]. Retrieved from https://www.turismo.gob.ec/orellana-un-destino-para-conocer-la-cultura-amazonica/

Muñoz, F. (2008). El debate de la nueva Constitución [The debate on the new Constitution]. *La Tendencia. Revista de analisis politico, 16*, 7-8. Doi: doi:10.4067/S0718-52002018000200527

Naredo, J. M. (2010). *Raíces económicas del deterioro ecológico y social* [Economic roots of ecological and social deterioration]. Siglo XXI de España Editores.

National Constituent Assembly. (2008). *Constitución de la Republica del Ecuador* [Constitution of the Republic of Ecuador]. https://www.asambleanacional.gob.ec/sites/default/files/documents/old/constitucion_de_bolsillo.pdf

National Institute of Statistics and Censuses. (2021). *INEC*. Retrieved from Demografia: https://www.ecuadorencifras.gob.ec/censo-de-poblacion-y-vivienda/

National Institute of Statistics and Censuses. (2021). *Estadísticas - Diciembre 2021*. Retrieved from https://www.ecuadorencifras.gob.ec/estadisticas-diciembre-2021/

National Secretariat of Planning and Development. (2015). *Provincias de Pichincha, Napo y Orellana. Quito* [Pichincha, Napo and Orellana provinces. Quito]. Senplades.

Orellana. (2022). *Gobierno de Orellana* [Government of Orellana]. Retrieved from https://www.orellana.gob.ec/es/canton/datos-del-canton.html

Passet, R. (2012). *Las grandes representaciones del mundo y la economía a lo largo de la historia: del universo mágico al torbellino creador* [The great representations of the world and the economy throughout history: from the magical universe to the creative whirlwind]. Clave Intelectual.

Peralta, B. I., & Roldán Monsalve, D. (2019). La importancia de la evaluación como paso previo a la implementación de una moneda complementaria. Un estudio de caso rural en Ecuador, la parroquia Sinincay [The importance of evaluation as a preliminary step to the implementation of a complementary currency. A rural case study in Ecuador, the Sinincay parish]. *CIRIEC-España, Revista de Economía Pública, Social y Cooperativa,* 283-284.

Polanyi, K., & MacIver, R. M. (1944). *The great transformation, 2*. Beacon press.

Popescu, C. R. G., Popescu, G. N., & Popescu, V. A. (2015a). Corporate Governance in Romania: Theories and Practices. In *Corporate Governance And Corporate Social Responsibility: Emerging Markets Focus* (pp. 375-401). World Scientific Publ. https://www.worldscientific.com/doi/abs/10.1142/9789814520386_0014 doi:10.1142/9789814520386_0014

Popescu, C. R. G., Popescu, V. A., & Popescu, G. N. (2015b). The Entrepreneur's Role In The Performance Growth Of The Financial Audit Activity In Romania. *Amfiteatru Economic, 17*(38), 228-246.

Prieto, W., & Tejedor, J. (2017). La ciencia económica en tiempos de crisis [Economic science in times of crisis. *Cenes, 38*(64), 47–78. doi:10.19053/01203053.v36.n64.2017.5937

Program Development and Cultural Diversity for Poverty Reduction and Social Inclusion. (2004). *Nacionalidades y Pueblos Indígenas, y Políticas Interculturales en Ecuador*. Manthra Editores.

Quadagno, J. (1987). Theories of the welfare state. *Annual Review of Sociology, 13*(1), 109–128. doi:10.1146/annurev.so.13.080187.000545

Ramírez, R. (2008). *Igualmente pobres, desigualmente ricos* [Equally poor, equally rich]. Ariel-PNUD.

Resico, M. (2011). *Introducción a la Economía de Mercado* [Introduction to the Market Economy]. Konrad Adanauer Stifung.

Rojas, C. (2015). Tipos de Investigación científica: Una simplificación de la complicada incoherente nomenclatura y clasificación [Scientific Research Types: A Simplification of Complicated Incoherent Nomenclature and Classification]. *Redvet, 16*, 6–9.

Ruíz, C., René, P., Fernández, G., Luz del Carmen, Lecuona, M., & Gómez, N. (2015). Elementos para el debate e interpretación del Buen Vivir/Sumak Kawsay [Elements for the debate and interpretation of Good Living/Sumak Kawsay]. *Contribuciones desde Coatepec*, 6-7.

Secretariat of Hydrocarbons. (2022). *Mapa de bloques petroleros* [Oil block map]. Retrieved from http://www.historico.secretariahidrocarburos.gob.ec/mapa-de-bloques-petroleros/

Shell, M. (1993). *The economy of literature*. JHU Press.

Silva Portero, C. (2008). *Qué es el buen vivir en la Constitución? Constitución del 2008 en el contexto andino: análisis de la doctrina y el derecho comparado* [What is good living in the Constitution? Constitution of 2008 in the Andean context: analysis of the doctrine and comparative law] (R. Á. Santamaría, Ed.). Ministerio de Justicia y Derechos Humanos.

Solano, H. C., & Muntuberria Lazarini, V. (2009). Procesos de construcción de otras alternativas: Desarrollo y planteamiento de la Economia Social Comunitaria en America Latina [Construction processes of other alternatives: development and approach of the Community Social Economy in Latin America]. *Ciriec, 52*, 301–305. doi:10.5209/rev_POSO.2015.v52.n2.45203

Stratford, B. (2020). The threat of rent extraction in a resource-constrained future. *Ecological Economics, 169*, 106524. doi:10.1016/j.ecolecon.2019.106524

Universidad de San Martín de Porres. (2017). *Manual de Introducción a la Economía* [Manual of Introduction to Economics]. Author.

Whyte, J. (2019). *The morals of the market: Human rights and the rise of neoliberalism*. Verso Books.

Ziegler, J. (2013). Destrucción Masiva: Geopolítica del hambre [Mass Destruction: Geopolitics of Hunger]. Barcelona: Booket (Península).

KEY TERMS AND DEFINITIONS

Cooperative: An autonomous association of persons united voluntarily to meet their common economic, social, and cultural needs and aspirations through a jointly owned and democratically controlled enterprise.

Economic Globalization: This is a phenomenon in expansion that causes profound changes on the world stage. It revolves around trade, the flow of investment, financial capital, division of labor and specialization. The concept is not limited only to economic variables since its effects extend to individuals, society to the state. Developing countries are experiencing stagnation in the face of their inability to cope with globalization, which is compounded by poor management of their financial markets, leading to an increase in the income inequality gap. Economic globalization brings with it the mobilization of goods and capital, reduces distance between borders and energizes international trade with some alterations to sovereignty.

Public Policy: This refers to decisions and actions that a government takes when addressing public or collective issues.

Resilience: Transformations within a complex system related to the capacity for self-organization while maintaining internal structure, together with the ability to create adaptive responses, generate knowledge, experience, and learning. Resilience and sustainability are directly related to changes within societies, economies, and the human system as a whole. The transformation of systems is inevitable since it allows systems to strengthen.

Social Economy: Encompasses a variety of businesses, organizations and different legal entities. They share the objective of systematically putting people first, producing a positive impact on local communities and pursuing a social cause.

Sumak Kawsay: Describes a way of doing things that is community-centric, ecologically balanced, and culturally sensitive.

Welfare State: A system the state and supranational organizations undertake to protect the health and well-being of its citizens, especially those in financial or social need, by means of grants, pensions, and other benefits.

APPENDIX

To deepen the topic investigated, the following interview was designed, organized on the basis of six questions:

1. Do you think that good living influences the quality of life of citizens? Why?
2. How do you reconcile with the coexistence of the oil sector and the local economy?
3. What are the main problems that arise in the centralized economy?
4. What factors constitute the biggest barriers to achieving good living?
5. How is the effectiveness of both the economy and good living promoted?
6. What are the greatest weaknesses in the processes of good living?

Chapter 4
Risk Governance:
The Need for a Multidisciplinary Approach

Pedro B. Agua
https://orcid.org/0000-0003-1886-9938
Portuguese Naval Academy, Portugal

Anacleto Correia
https://orcid.org/0000-0002-7248-4310
Portuguese Naval Academy, Portugal

ABSTRACT

The current worldwide pandemic due to COVID-19 confronts all industries with considerable economic challenges. This text analyses the subject of organizational risks from the perspective of the board of directors. It argues that compliance is a necessary condition, however not sufficient, for an effective risk governance. It suggests that prudence is something that should be nurtured and promoted at the level of organizational governance. Organizations being complex systems, a holistic framework should be used in approaching risk governance. Risk approaches have been particularly influenced by regulation focusing on financial risks, while there are many additional types of risks, potentially more damaging for organisations. The role of the board of directors has undergone a long evolution from merely "ceremonial" to its current "progressive" form. This chapter argues on a more prudential action by those responsible for corporate governance beyond a normativism approach.

1. INTRODUCTION

In 2014, CalPERS (California Public Employee's Retirement System) objected to the re-election of four board members of Duke Energy, a US based energy company, surprising the business world because institutional shareholders were unwilling to tolerate levity when it comes to risk governance. They opposed the re-election of four directors with responsibility for risk management, when their profiles did not show evidence of the minimum competence requirements on the subject (Ormazabal, 2016). Although this case took place in the United States of America, it was a warning to the fact that risk governance is

DOI: 10.4018/978-1-6684-6750-3.ch004

no longer an exclusive issue of executive management, but one in which shareholders are determined to hold the board accountable.

Not only is there increasing pressure on boards directors for a more careful supervision of organisational risks, but organisations need to coordinate for a more proactive involvement of boards in what risks concerns; among other matters generally left to the discretion of executive management. This highlights the need for a more critical and pragmatic analysis of risk governance beyond mere compliance.

The etymological origin of the term 'risk' suggests a semantics associated with 'being in danger'. For its part, the word 'governance', of older origin, was originally related to the art of directing or establishing the course of a ship. From the Latin *gubernare*, to set course or guide, or from the Greek *kybernan*, to direct or command a ship. Within the scope of this text, risk governance can be understood as the art and science, of driving a company towards the desired direction, keeping it away from potential dangers, however diverse they might be.

Although governance codes address the responsibility of board directors, it is a normative positioning. Other positions, as for instance the well-known north American *business judgment rule*, although legitimate at first sight, it may not contribute significantly to the effective governance of a company's risks, because it has the potential to act as a shield in protecting misbehaviour.

This means going beyond compliance, because the election and realisation of the company's future is a matter of initiative, not optimisation. In this way, the governing bodies must make the best use of their skills and knowledge in achieving their objectives, while being constrained by the need to carry out adequate governance of the multiple risks, some more strategic, with the potential to severely damage the company. To refer two well-known examples of strategic risks that are not financial in nature, but were quite harming, one can refer the Boeing case. The aerospace manufacturer which seems not to have managed adequately the product and engineering risks regarding some of its plane models, which after the collapse of some of their planes, ended up severely affecting the company´s reputation for safety, together with business performance costs.

Another example, related to the impact of the culture on risk, would be the case of the international oil company BP, which ended up having a cost of more than 62 billion U.S. dollars, related to the accident of the well *Makondo* on their *Deepwater Horizon* programme. This seems to derive from a pattern where the need to cut costs to ensure the expected "shareholder's return" has potentially led to a culture of lack of attention to maintenance and engineering risks, which in the oil industry may have enormous consequences for the environment and human life of those involved in oil fields operations (Lustgarten, 2012).

From these two examples it is clear that there are risks, perhaps greater than the strictly financial ones, which need attention, from the part of those ultimately responsible for corporate governance. It is equally visible that in the last decades events due to *force majeure* and *acts of God* are occurring more frequently and with an increasing devastating impact. However, when compared to the financial costs of disasters caused by human behaviour, they often fall short.

The aim of this text is to provide a critical and holistic view over the main strategic risks. Attention is drawn to the fact that in addition to financial risks, which have gained more attention and media coverage, and which are almost exclusively the ones targeted by regulatory efforts, there are many other risk typologies, potentially more strategic than strictly financial ones, to which attention must be paid in order to avoid governance 'blind spots'. By way of example, one can look into the way in which the present pandemic situation has surprised the overwhelming majority of companies, ill-prepared national health systems to respond to pandemics, or countries with ineffective economic strategies which are overdependent on one or a few sectors of economic activity, or because it has chosen the wrong sectors – the ones that are most exposed to the consequences of a pandemic and damaging economic externalities.

The current risk endeavour requires a growing dedication from individual board directors, which may foster a growing tendency for many of them to decline or resign from such roles, and make recruitment more difficult (Ormazabal, 2016).

Reality does not draw borders between fields of knowledge, and therefore risks know no borders. Hence the analysis done in this text is multidisciplinary in order to be comprehensive enough. Everything is divided for sake of analysis, must be re-integrated again, so that it makes sense. According to Sterman (2000), all models are wrong. All models are wrong in the sense that they are incomplete and partial representations of a reality much richer in detail and especially endowed with complexity resulting from the interconnection between the diverse variables representing the problem or system of interest. These decompositions for sake of analysis are procedures that help us deal with complexity, however, the risk body of knowledge is relatively young compared to other fields of knowledge. Partial approaches, whether originating from law, engineering or management, among others, are clearly insufficient because they are incomplete, which carries a risk in itself. Hence, this text argues on approaching the subject of risk governance in a pragmatic and multidisciplinary way, considering the board of directors as a 'progressive' one (Charan, 2005). Progressive boards place the focus on risk prevention, as opposed to crisis resolution.

In addition to this introduction and the conclusion, this text has six sections where a holistic model of the organization will be introduced, something which is useful in identifying and addressing risks. It is followed by one possible characterization of the current risk endeavour, together with some critical analysis on the limitations of mere compliance in the face of the great diversity of potential risks. It also addresses the role that culture, and ethics play in risk governance.

For a better critical analysis about corporate risk governance it is useful to have a reference framework to address the organization in a holistic way, something which is dealt with in the following section.

2. A HOLISTIC MODEL OF ORGANIZATIONS

The work of leaders is to act in order to achieve a future situation for the organization, better than the current one in relative terms. This requires, first, addressing the organization holistically to ensure that undesirable side effects are minimized. Among various possible approaches Christensen, Andrews & Bower (1978) created the initial roots of what can be considered a holistic organizational approach - Business Policy - originally consisting of three areas: (1) business strategy, (2) structure and, (3) incentive systems.

Subsequently, and departing from those former authors' work, Valero & Lucas (2018), developed the Business Policy Model (BPM), a conceptual framework of reference, which conceives the work of top management and directors as including four areas of governance, along with specific procedures. These four areas of governance are: (i) the Business; (ii) the Directing Structure; (iii) the Incentive Systems; and (iv) the Institutional Configuration. Distinguishing these four aspects is useful to preserve a wholistic approach to organizations (Calleja & Melé, 2017). Figure 1 illustrates this framework.

Figure 1. The organization as an open system, interrelating with its surroundings. Source: Água & Morgado (2020)

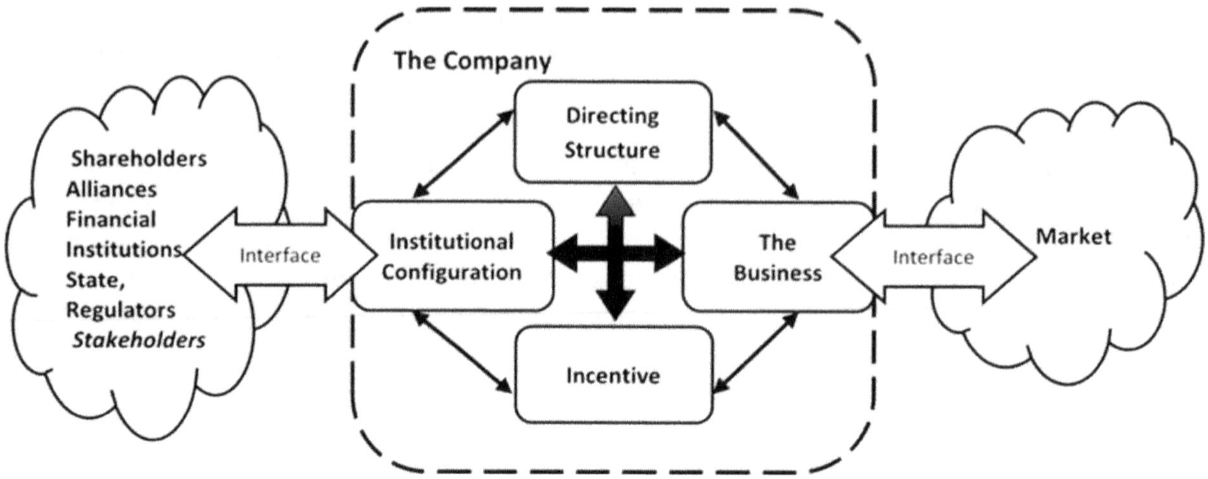

Choosing the business means deciding to carry out the particular content of activities or operations that, when harmoniously related, allow an optimal evolution of the organization's performance. Within the BPM, the 'Business' is something very specific and can refer to performance results, other than just profit. Bringing people together and getting them to work is one of the basic pillars of leadership. Therefore, creating a 'Directing Structure' means entrusting individuals with specific parts of what needs to be done to effectively move the organization into the future and in a sustainable way. By means of 'Incentive Systems' board directors and top management may seek procedures that help people carry out their work, ensuring professional commitment throughout the organization. Getting the people who integrate the organization to work professionally, suggesting new ideas through creativity and knowledge and promoting innovation, is one of the key tasks of a leader. These criteria shape the culture of organizational innovation and vice versa.

The final governing area referred as the 'Institutional Configuration', is critical for organizational sustainability, where the critical dimensions of Initiative, Finance and Power are at play, sometimes entailing considerable complex dynamics (Valero & Figueroa, 2011).

Those authors suggests that there is not necessarily a *de facto* separation between executive management and the corporate governance structure, but rather a continuum that integrates the two layers, as illustrated in Figure 2, representing a generic configuration where the managing director, (black circle), may be a common element of both layers.

Figure 2. The double pyramid
Source: Valero & Figueroa (2011)

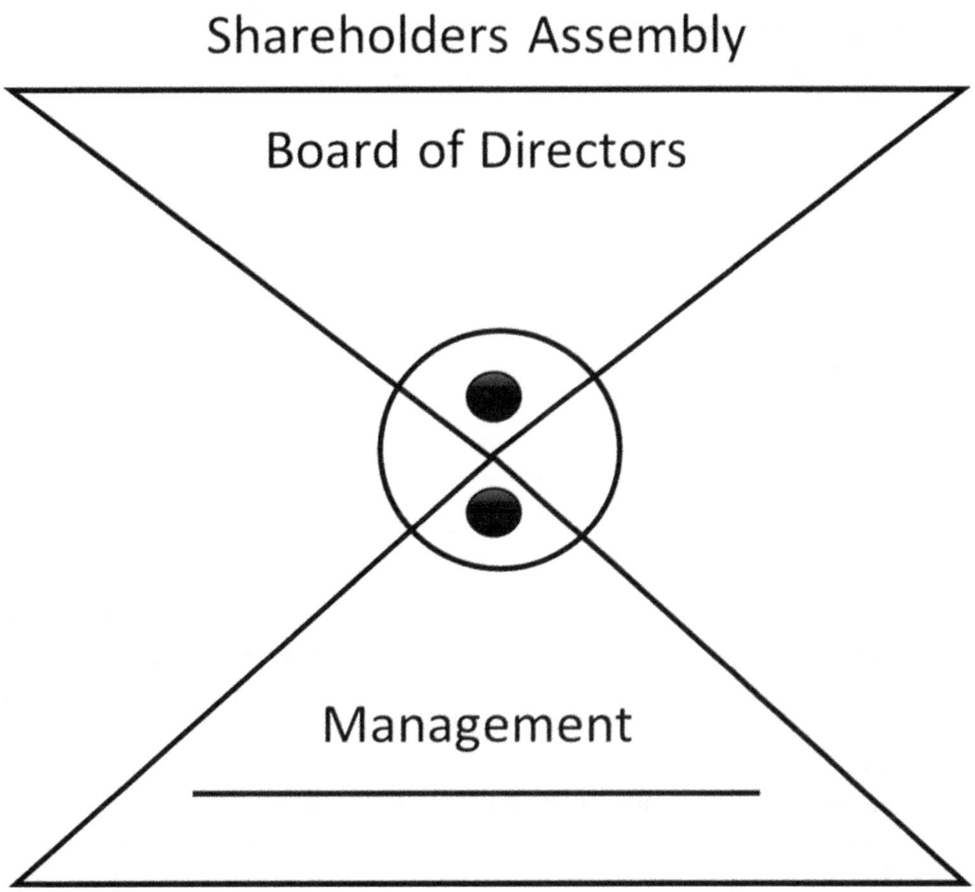

This model facilitates the identification, classification and framing of a multitude of potential risks that may potentially affect an organization.

3. THE CURRENT RISK ENDEAVOUR AND THE GROWING RESPONSIBILITY OF DIRECTORS

Among the main trends pointed out by Nueno (2016), which concern future boards of directors, are: (1) greater accountability, (2) fewer directors, (3) more rigorous requirements, (4) more transparency, (5) better prepared directors, (6) a greater role for specialised governance committees. Lorsch (2012) supports this trend and suggests increasing attention to risk governance issues.

For his part, Ormazabal (2016), argues that this growing demand and accountability upon directors, not restricted to risk governance, but to their role as responsible directors, may put some pressure over many directors who will tend to leave their jobs. This suggests that companies may face some shortage of suitable candidates for such roles, because at their stage of life they may be unwilling to take certain risks, even though insurance may generally be involved; or to spend the time and energy that today's board directors roles require from them on the subject of risk governance (Figure 3) [1]. Certain companies due to the nature of their business models or the markets in which they operate, may begin to experience difficulties in finding suitable directors, precisely because of the greater demands and effort required, as well as the risk perceived in personal terms by such professionals.

Figure 3. Consequences of the current corporate governance endeavour
Author's elaboration

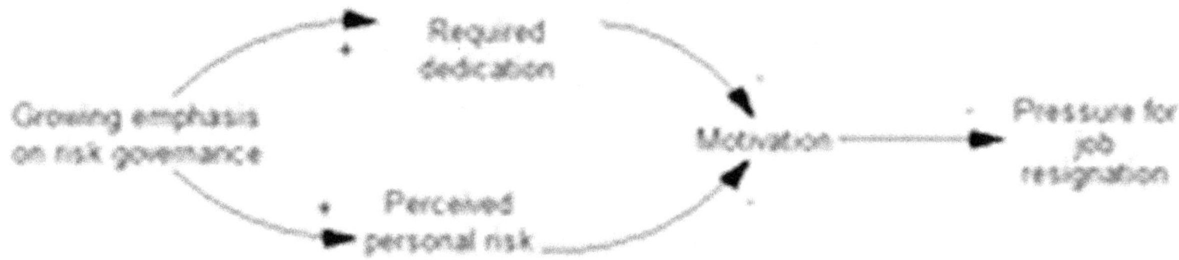

On the other hand, the existence of a *Chief Risk Officer*, who is directly answerable to the Board of Directors, namely to committees responsible for risk governance, is becoming common across several industries. Although sometimes uncomfortable for the managing director or CEO, the creation of this figure, can help the board of directors being more effective in what risk governance concerns, and seems indeed a best practice.

A business encompasses a compromise between benefits and the amount of risk taken (Figure 4a). However, the acceptance of too much risk has the potential to collapse the business at some times (Figure 4[REMOVED REF FIELD]b). Moreover, a potential call under the well-known business *judgment rule* may be just acts of self-defence in an argument to justify aggressive risk-taking decisions, with the potential to shield misbehaviour.

Figure 4a. Business should maintain a balance between risk and profit

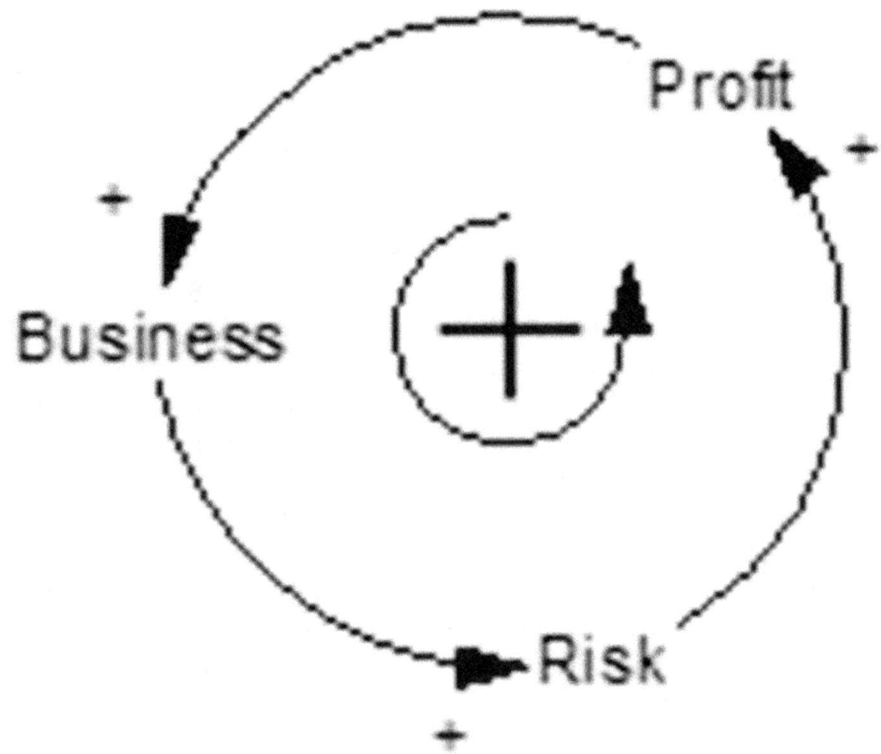

Figure 4b.
Author's elaboration

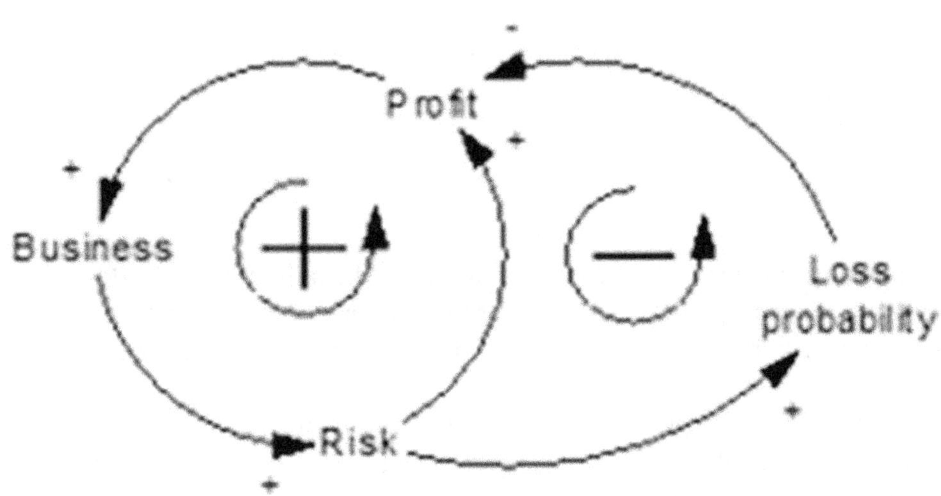

It is, therefore, in the context of this systemic interrelationship between cycles, one positive and the other negative, each of which will be dominant under certain conditions, in which the risks will materialize. Moreover, there has been a growing pressure globally for listed companies to disclose their remuneration policies, not for the sake of scrutiny of the amounts itself, but because the larger the variable part of such compensations the greater the tendency for such organisations' professionals to engage in more aggressive risk taking. By analysis the various variables of the previously mentioned business policy model, helps visualize the most critical areas in order to clarify the balance between profit and risk, as well as the design of better policies and company risk and governance codes of practice.

Various efforts have been made to understand and better manage risks. Ranging from the introduction of the ISO 31000 standard, to the spending of hundreds of millions on Enterprise Risk Management (ERM) systems, in some cases with results that fall short of expectations. ERM systems tend to cover each and every one of the identifiable risks in a company, generating an overwhelming amount of data, which ends up distracting those responsible for risk governance and management. Moreover, the introduction of ERM systems brought with it a false sense of safety, due to its mere existence within the organization.

Most of these systems treat risks as independent of each other, when this is not necessarily true. Interdependencies among distinct risk types may produce amplified and catastrophic effects when risks materialize (Bromiley & Rau, 2016). It is within this paradigm of the balance between risk and profit that risk governance has to be carried out, which when taking the events of recent years, has been demanding greater involvement and responsibility from board directors. Charan (2005), based mainly on the American context, provides a brief review of the stages through which the boards have evolved to the current concept of 'progressive' board (Figure 5).

Figure 5. Boards of directors' evolution
Adapted from Charan (2005)

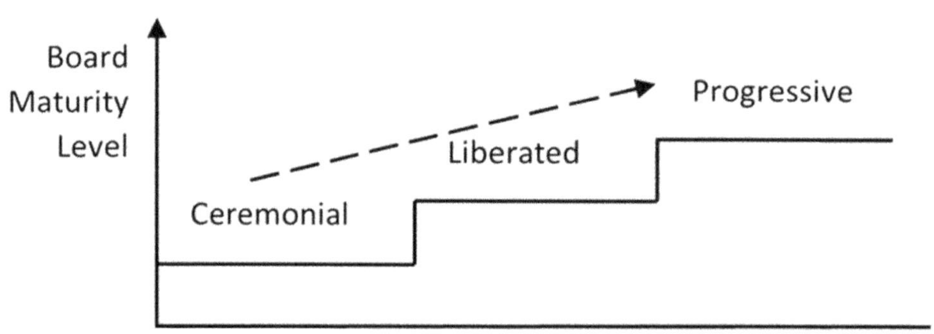

Charan defines a 'ceremonial' board as the typology in which little value is added and governance resembles more of a ceremony than an actual governing action of the board, which represents the possibility for maximum risk for a company. Various corporate governance scandals have their origin in this context.

Charan characterizes a 'liberated' board, as a board where there is more active debate and supervision, but still far from the paradigm where such board engages proactively with executive management, supporting it, and carrying out a more effective risk governance; a trend corroborated by other authors (Canals, 2014). This stage would correspond to the so-called 'progressive' board, where directors are not only there to ratify whatever executive management brings them, but are proactive in asking for information and, even visiting the organization's facilities and operations. Progressive boards ask the right questions to management and question their answers.

This whole new corporate governance context has the potential to make boards 'too' risk averse, which is a risk in itself, as such an attitude could hamper business initiatives - initiatives that are the engine of innovation and the guarantor of the sustainability of companies (Água & Correia, 2020).

4. COMPLIANCE – A NECESSARY CONDITION, HOWEVER NOT SUFFICIENT

Distinguishing between risk governance and risk management is a mere formalism. Just as the whole world constitutes a system, which is only divided into subsystems for sake of analysis in order for decision makers to deal with complexity and be able to discuss them. The same could be said regarding risks approaches. When addressing the subject of risks, regardless of the perspective being from the governance layer or from the executive management layer, when risks materialize, they will affect the entire organization, regardless. Parmalat, the scene of a scandalous governance case, where the *Preda Code* of corporate governance was supposedly being followed, is a classic example of how a passive compliance could have helped prevent the notorious outcome. However, mere compliance would not exempt it from falling into catastrophic outcomes due to risks incurred where dubious ethics, mismanagement judgment and wrong investment decisions were not prudentially considered at the level of risk governance (Tapies & Toninato, 2005). Risk governance is further affected by the fact that the risk body of knowledge is relatively immature when compared to other fields, such as law, engineering, or mathematics, and the aforementioned cognitive limitations of humans when it comes to estimates. Consider for instance the cases illustrated in Table 1.

Table 1. Humans have a limited ability to estimate outcomes

"Flying machines heavier than air is simply an impossibility".	Lord Kelvin, British mathematician, physicist, and president of the British Royal Society, 1895.
"With more than 50 foreign car brands already on sale here, the Japanese car industry will hardly affect the US car market".	*Business Week*, 2nd of August 1968.
"A severe depression like the one in 1920-21 is outside the range of probabilities".	The Harvard Economic Society, 16Th of November 1929.
"I think the world market will only have room for about five computers".	Thomas J. Watson, Chairman of IBM, 1943.
"There is no reason for an individual to have a computer at home".	Ken Olson, President of Digital Equipment Corporation, 1977.
"We don't like their musical style. Groups with guitarists will leave the market".	Decca Recording Co. executive dismissing the Beatles in 1962.
"No matter what happens, the United States Navy will never be caught off guard".	Frank Knox, Secretary of *US Navy*, 4Th of December 1941, just before the Japanese attack to Pearl Harbour.

Adapted from Cerf & Navasky (1984)

Several other examples, such as the invention of the digital camera, which was not given initial relevance by Kodak board of directors, are examples of boards that might have fall short from being "progressive", as per Charan (2005) terminology. These examples reinforce the idea that the subject of risk governance not only goes beyond the mere attention to compliance, but will benefit from multidisciplinary approaches where law, engineering and management knowledge, should cooperate more effectively if the objective is to achieve an effective risk governance. This line of thought is reinforced by with (Taleb, 2010) concept of "black swans" or unforeseen surprises, or Hubbard's criticism (2009) on the traditionally narrow approach to risk, not only within corporate governance, but in general. In addition, considering the works of Simon (1957), Schoemaker & Russo (1990), regarding human cognitive limitations, the scenario seems even more worrying when approaching risk governance in a conscious manner.

Having established the level of human proficiency in predicting, estimating, and dealing with risk scenarios - something central in dealing with risk governance - it is suggested that the subject will need to promote cooperation between multiple areas of knowledge, so that an effective risk governance can be achieved. However, most of the time, professionals from different fields of knowledge rarely work together to conceive, operationalize, and create policies related to the multitude of risk types that an organization may face. Such a culture of isolationism among knowledge fields constitutes a risk in itself, because it minimises the chances of uncovering 'blind angles'.

The tasks that boards of directors should address are essentially those tasks that determine the prosperity and sustainability of the business by accepting an 'adequate' level of risk. Corporate governance codes generally suggest some form of risk management system to be set up. But they typically address the subject quite superficially, as expressed by the following sentence: *Based on medium and long-term strategy. The company should establish a risk management and control system together with an internal audit system to anticipate and minimise the risks inherent in the activity carried out.* Although little progress has been made in specific terms regarding the 'how' to do it, such reference lines are deemed good practice, as it helps focus the debate within the board during the acceptance of strategic plans and when designing policies, considering the several applicable risk typologies. This suggests that organisations should systematically establish risk management system; and that they should, on an annual basis, re-assess the performance of such risk management system, while updating the organisation's risk map. These responsibilities should be interrelated with the design and establishment of the chosen strategy - how the organisation will achieve its objectives - which can be designed and defined jointly with the executive management, considering the double pyramid in Figure 2.

Since human organisations are systems, a comprehensive and holistic approach shall consider multiple risk-related domains. It is therefore desirable to adopt an analysis framework broad enough when looking into organisational risks. Such a model starts by identifying risks within a considerable taxonomic diversity. Authors such as Hubbard (2009) have been critical of risk management for its consistently failing to provide adequate responses when risks materialize, which in part, according to this author is due to the inability to identify risks and keep them visible – uncovering 'blind spots'.

For his part, Senge (1990) draws attention to the need to develop the ability for systems thinking in order to increase organizational learning and performance, which may include the subject of how risks are addressed. Dorner (1996) provides evidence of the consequences of the aforementioned cognitive limitations of humans, namely the common estimation errors concerning outcomes and the unfolding of plausible future events, and the *naïve* form with which the subject is usually dealt with. This author stresses the tendency to underestimate values or the probability of occurrence of certain events. For instance, Filkelstein, Whitehead & Campbell (2009) suggest that such a syndrome may have been behind the catastrophic results of hurricane *Katrina* that struck New Orleans a few years ago. The director in charge of managing the situation, a former Brigadier General accustomed to 'inaccurate' and 'exaggerated' initial reports, estimated the situation to be less serious than it actually was, and did not act in due time, even though he had information that allowed him to infer the consequences of the flooding that occurred, about three days before it happened.

It therefore appears that effective risk governance cannot rely just on compliance to regulations or codes of good practice. These codes are a necessary, however not a sufficient condition for effective risk governance. Starting with a 'taxonomy of species', that is to say, the identification of several strategic risks potentially affecting the company seems to be a good practice, as it allows a prompter identification of known risk typologies. Several methodologies exit to identify risk, from group processes to Future Scenarios theory. Former U.S. president Dwight Eisenhower suggested that 'plans are worthless, planning is everything'. Eisenhower suggested that the exercise of planning actions into the future, forces us to perform *pre-mortem* analyses, and contingency foresight, which will more easily uncover responses during the course of events, even if they are different than expected. The Royal Dutch Shell oil company was known for its use of scenario methodologies, which allegedly helped it respond to the oil crises of the 1970s.

Preventive mechanisms such as 'layers of defence', which have a position beyond normativism, are examples of good practices for effective risk governance in the context of organisations, but especially in non-financial organisations. In non-financial organizations there are comparatively more strategic risk categories, as shown in previous references to the Boeing aerospace manufacturer or the BP oil company. A systematic approach to risk governance therefore appears to be a wise first step, a line of thought supported by Malik (2012).

5. RISK GOVERNANCE BENEFITS FROM SYSTEMATIC APPROACHES

Using a systematic approach to risk governance is not only a necessary condition, but an essential one for their good governance. Those responsible for corporate governance, should take at least a systematic approach. Some governance codes frame risk governance in a similar way to the following text:

Based on its risk policy, the company shall establish a risk management system, identifying (i) the main risks to which it is subject in the development of its activity, (ii) the probability of their occurrence and their impact, (iii) the instruments and measures to be adopted with a view to mitigation, (iv) the monitoring procedures, aimed at monitoring them and (v) the procedure of monitoring, periodic evaluation and adjustment of the system.

An organization risk policy is closely associated with the concept of risk profile, specific to each organization, and should be considered as the steps of any risk governance process unfold. In practice it can be summarized in the following steps:

1. Plan the overall approach to corporate risk governance.
2. Identify potential risks by using appropriate techniques and considering a multitude of risk types.
3. Carry out or request a qualitative analysis of the identified risks.
4. Carry out or request a quantitative analysis of the identified risks.
5. Plan the response to identified risks.
6. Monitor and control, in close collaboration with executive management.

Several tools exist, which can help a better view of the risk scenarios. Generally, these tools, at the governance and top management levels, end up having graphical expression, such as the two-dimensional matrix that shows probability of occurrence versus the potential impact of the identified risks (Figure 6).

Figure 6. Typical risk matrix
Author's elaboration

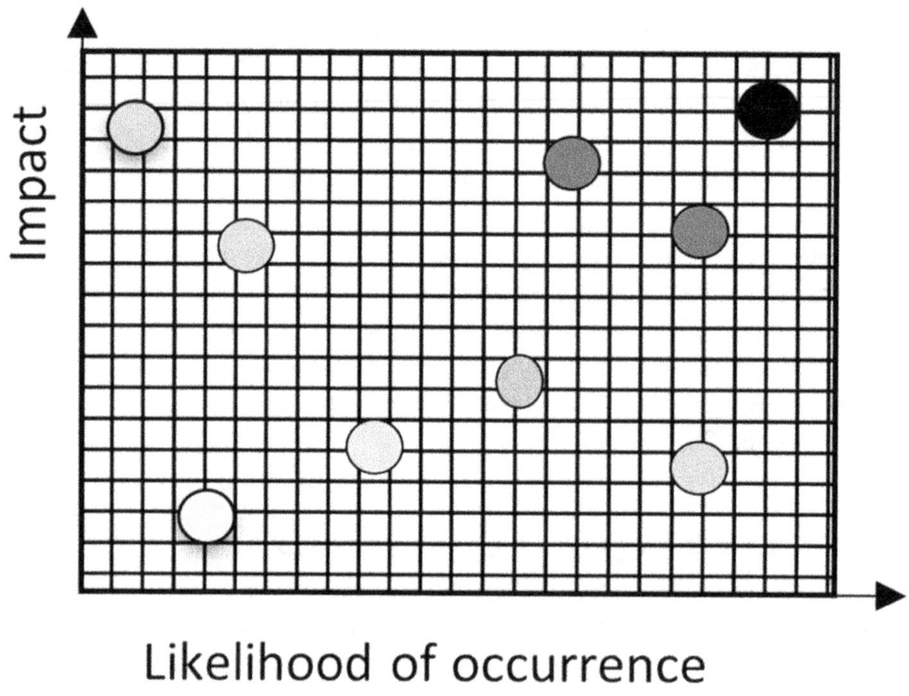

Although it is a simple representation of the broad risk picture, the risk matrix already allows a first orientation towards areas where to devote more attention and resources in what risk governance concerns. In this illustration, risks that are more likely to occur and have greater potential impact should benefit from more attention and resources than the other way around (e.g. risk in darker gray in the previous figure demand more attention). In the same fashion, risks of high potential impact, but low likelihood of occurrence (e.g. earthquakes), should be mapped, but it may be prudent not to devote many resources to them (e.g. light grey risks in the previous figure).

Naturally, the concept of uncertainty is inherent to risk, so the use of decision trees as a tool to deal with risk scenarios under uncertainty may be advisable. Those responsible for risk governance may request or ensure that the organization has competences in the use of these risk analysis tools, producing the respective analyses as requested by the board or risk subcommittees. With regard to risk response, those responsible for corporate governance generally have at their disposal the following options: (1) avoid the risk[2], (2) mitigate the risk[3], (3) transfer the risk[4], or (4) accept the risk[5]. But to realize an effective risk governance the first step is the identification of potential risks, and there is a considerable diversity of risk types to consider.

6. A CONSIDERABLE DIVERSITY OF RISKS

In addition to financial risks, there is a great diversity of risks, which can severely affect an organization. Although there has been a focus on the financial industry, perhaps because of the well-known problems of the recent past involving this industry and global financial crises, some authors have drawn attention to the multitude of risks, many of a non-financial nature, which may also affect the financial sector (Cerrone, 2019).

Other authors, with a broader approach, try to group risks into categories as a first step, in an attempt to better deal with them (Bromiley & Rau, 2016), Table 2.

Table 2. Broad categories of risk

Categories of Risks	Examples
Strategic risks	Industry and economics; political change; competitors; consumer preferences; market share; reputation; brand value; strategic focus; investor confidence
Operational risks	Customer satisfaction; product failure; supply chain; sourcing; concentration; outsourcing; political election cycles; disasters; process execution; procedures; environmental; contracts; regulation and legal; human resources; health and safety; integrity; authorities; leadership; culture; initiative and knowledge
Financial risks	Cash flow; liquidity; interest rates; exchange rates; credit capacity; credit concentration; accounting and budgeting; taxation and pricing; performance and portfolio measures; access to systems and infrastructure; systems availability; data relevance and integrity.

Adapted from Bromiley & Rau (2016)

To the multitude of risks listed in the previous table, one could add the following types:

- The risk of technological disruption and engineering (e.g., consortia in large projects)
- The risk inherent to the specific governance model (single layer or double layer)

Regardless of financial risks getting most of the attention, perhaps because they are (relatively) easier to quantify; or because it has benefited from the attention of many financial professionals, consultants and auditors; or simply by attracting attention in recent decades, the truth is that it is not the only serious risk that an organization may face, and perhaps not even the most serious. For instance, consider the issue of 'being trustable' in the context of the banking industry. Trust may dictate the fate of financial institutions by triggering vicious cause-and-effect chains, which in turn could negatively affect purely financial variables. Such trust can be decisive, for example, in triggering a "run into banks" in order take off savings or deposits, which in turn would further aggravate the situation, under a vicious and catastrophic reinforcing loop, as suggested by Figure 7.

Figure 7. Causal diagram relating trust and banks
Authors' elaboration

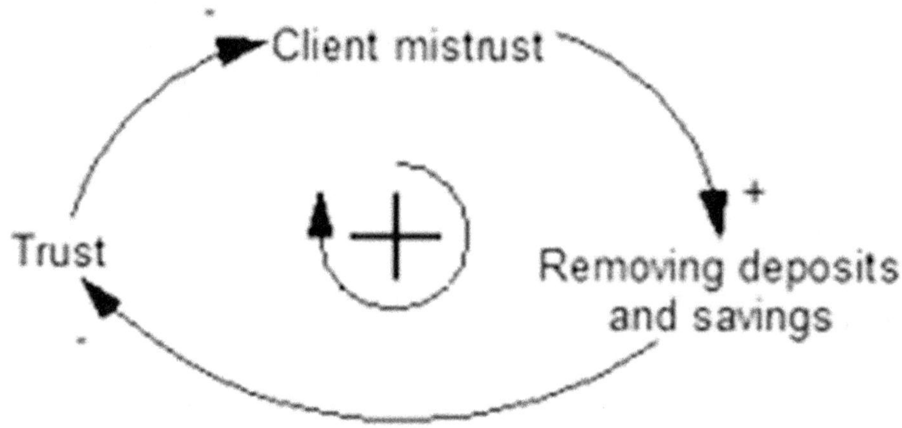

Another example of the danger of putting too much emphasis on the financial performance and where catastrophic effects of inadequate risk governance may be visible was the above-mentioned accident that affected BP in its *Deepwater Horizon* project in the Gulf of Mexico in 2010. A potentially overly aggressive attitude towards risk, aimed at serving financial indicators (sometimes short-term), might have been at the origin of a chain of events that led to the known outcome, which culminated with a fine of around US$62 billion for the company, in addition to the loss of several human lives and major environmental damage. When we place these figures into perspective, it would be wise to question whether in fact the focus should be essentially on financial results, whose associated risk is nothing more than an exercise in mathematics. Instead, technical, operational, reputation, among others, are *de facto* risks that could dictate the fate of an organization more severely than some short-term financial performance.

Given these examples, one may ask what risks should then be considered? Let us recall that it was necessary to reach into the eighteenth century for probability to become a systematic approach to uncertainty and risk. Authors such as Hubbard (2009) suggest that the way risk is approached by most organizations is superficial, rarely taking cause and effect into consideration, in favour of probabilistic techniques. Dorner (1996) goes in the same direction, providing examples of our inability to estimate outcomes of events that are distant in time and space. This may be related to the fact that systems thinking is not as developed and widespread ability as would be desirable, and most do not engage in understanding the underlying structures of systems, which are behind the observed problems.

Organizations are systems; systems that need governance. Natural systems have evolved over thousands of years and as such are in relatively steady states. Conversely, human made systems, including organizations, are comparatively young and whose governance laws (and policies) are more difficult to establish. In any case, a first step approach would be the identification of the relevant variables, i.e., the types of risk parameters to which attention should be focused. An exhaustive identification is very difficult to achieve, however it would be of reasonable benefit if the main types of risk could be identified.

The *Kashagan* oil project provides a good example, to identify in a single project a considerable range of different strategic risks with the potential to seriously affect the organisation - in this case a consortium of large oil companies – if any such risks materialize. The megaproject Kashagan, by its nature, illustrates the great diversity of risks that such an organisation can entail (Água & Morgado, 2020b). The Kashagan project in Kazakhstan is considered the most expensive oil project ever (Esty & Bitsch, 2013). Some estimates suggest that the final investment amounted to $116 billion, well beyond initial estimations. With investment amounts of this order of magnitude, as easily understandable, the risk takes a more serious shape if it materializes. For any variation in uncertainty affecting the related variables results in potential negative results of enormous dimensions. It is a project that has a governance structure integrating the various partners and the State of Kazakhstan, even if indirectly through the Ministry of Energy that owns the national oil company. Such a project exposes its governance structure to a diversity of strategic risks, far beyond the purely financial ones (Figure 8).

Figure 8. Diversity of identifiable risks within the Kashagan megaproject
Adapted from Esty & Bitsch (2013)

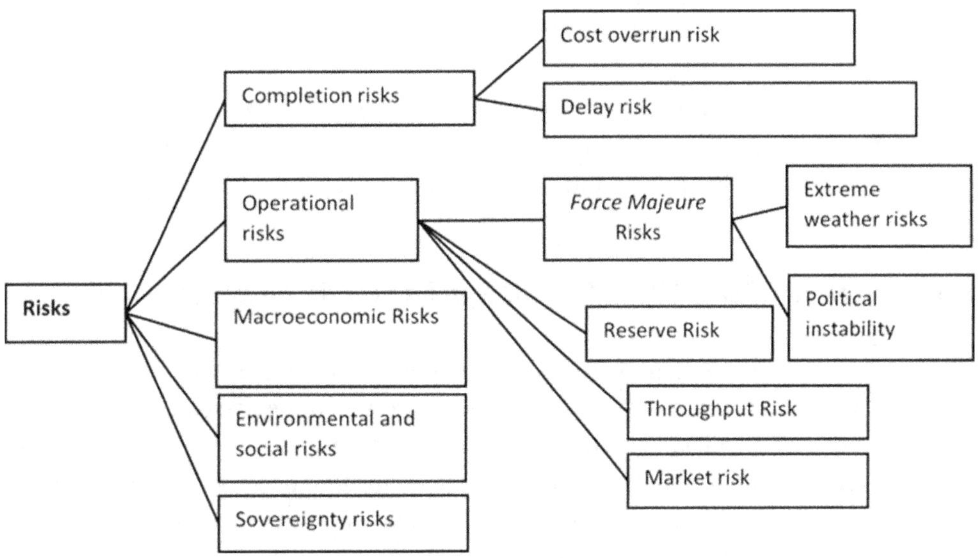

The board's focus should be on strategic risk management by being selective, instead of potentially trying to cover all the risks that an ERM system might suggest, with brings in the potential risk of "not being able to see the forest by focusing on so many trees" (Bromiley & Rau, 2016).

In this sense it is useful to relate the risks with each of the four areas of the business policy model, in order to identify how each organizational area would be affected and, by which risks:

- How does risk X affect the business area and is affected by it in turn? What is risk X relation to the corporate structure? Are there less resilient configurations when considering these risk types?
- What is the relationship between the company's incentive systems and specific risk types? We may recall the case of incentive systems that induce less ethical behaviour on employees towards customers, with a view to increasing such employees' appraisals within the organisation or even short-term performance bonus awards. How does the organization's culture affect some risks or is affected by then in turn?

- How does a given institutional configuration aggravate organizational risks, or specifically certain types of risks? Is the company´s financial structure robust enough or is there excessive leverage? How is the level of initiative and innovation - guarantor of sustainability and future competitiveness – across the company? And how does power affect some risk types or is affected by these in turn?

In order to generate similar questions, it is useful to have a holistic model of the organization, which makes it easier to identify risks, classify them and manage them, or sometimes just being aware of how they can potentially affect the organization's four dimensions: business, directing structure, incentive systems or institutional configuration.

The board of directors should have a systemic approach to risk governance, as not all risks are independent, and therefore may reinforce their effects and consequences. To this end, the training of directors on systems thinking, an area of knowledge that is not widely disseminated, either in law, management, and economics schools, together with many engineering curricula, would contribute positively. Systems thinking is not widespread as would be desirable and many of the great disasters throughout history have in this fact their origin (Dorner, 1996).

Valerdi & Rouse (2010) in his article *When systems thinking is not a natural Act*, suggest that human evolution has been based on immediate dealing with the superficial aspects of problems, something which prevents systems thinking and the understanding of the underlying structure of system.

7. ORGANISATIONAL CULTURE, ETHICS, AND RISK GOVERNANCE

Compliance is a necessary condition, however not sufficient, to conduct effective corporate governance, as illustrated by numerous corporate governance scandals in which the affected companies supposedly followed "good governance" codes, sometimes explicitly written in a company's mission statement. Compliance tries to ensure minimum standards, but it is ethics that aspires to maximum performance. This makes it necessary to take a critical look into the subject of culture and ethics, since a less careful attitude in this area can set in motion potentially risky situations, some with potential strategic impact for organizations. Drew, Kelley, & Kendrick (2006), suggest that there are five fundamental dimensions to the governance of strategic risks, the culture being one of them (Figure 1).

Figure 9. Five relevant variables in strategic risk governance
Adapted from Drew, Kelley, & Kendrick (2006)

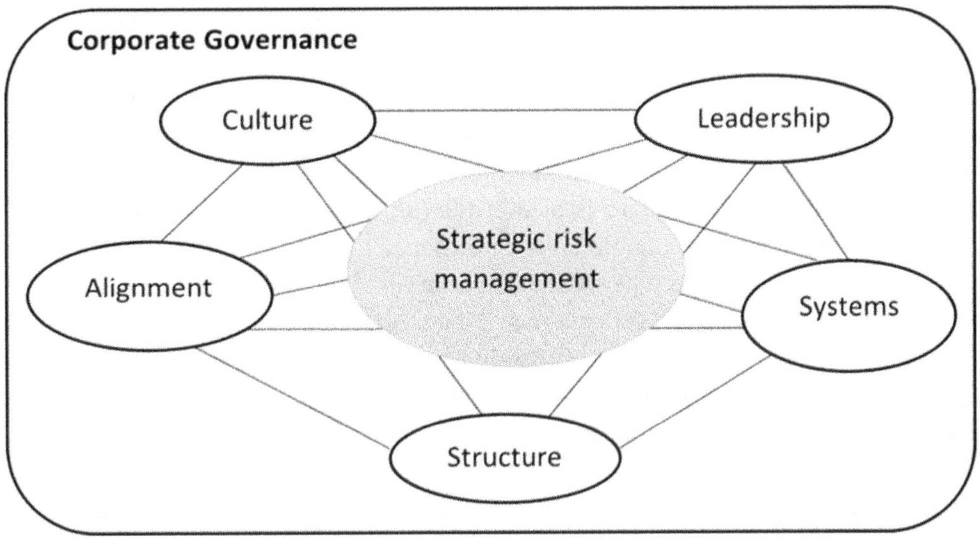

Culture is a critical dimension, and inseparable from ethics, as illustrated by various corporate governance scandals. Sometimes, even national culture introduces risk on its own. Ethics, on the other hand, requires a situational analysis, which may sometimes be unclear, especially without a strong ethical reference frame based on proper prudential knowledge (Calleja & Melé, 2017). Consider, for ins, the Royal Bank of Scotland (RBS) case and its excessive exposure to risk during the first decade of this century. Fred Goodwin, CEO of RBS during the years 2000 to 2008 initially performed exemplarily by driving the bank's inorganic growth through mergers and acquisitions, making RBS the world's largest bank for some time (BBC, 2012).

However, the overconfidence bias resulting from the success of so many acquisitions led to the accumulation of too much risk, visible in the wake of the 2008 financial crisis, which culminated in a bailout by the British Treasury (supported by taxpayers' revenues) of the order of £45.5 billion British pounds. It could be asked if Sir Fred Goodwin proceed ethically? Bearing in mind that it would be creating value for the bank, with all the externalities for the economy and the maintenance of thousands of jobs. Opinions differ on the conduct of the then RBS CEO. In the light of ethics, perhaps it should have given more weight to the risk that RBS was accumulating by the increasing risk exposure arising from the amounts of leverage practiced, which would leave it fragile.

The overconfidence constitutes a mental fallacy described in the literature, which translates itself into an overconfidence state of mind that can make us prone to take more risk in an unwise way, due to the previous successes one achieved. Moreover, if as suggested by Kahneman (2011), one is prone to risk in a situation of loss, then one can still further aggravate an already critical risky situation. Starting from this example, it is clear the role of ethics and the need for a clear awareness of "the value of values".

Organizations could promote more ethical cultures at all organizational levels. Fontrodona & Sanz (2015) suggest that the embedded cultures and values are one of the biggest problems when corporate governance scandals occur, arguing that the proactive establishment of "positive cultures" is a solution. Positive cultures ensure greater cross-cutting transparency across the organization, allowing for faster risk identification and management. Conversely, organizations where there is fear of addressing some issues, or where communication does not flow freely, are more likely to have 'blind angles' and miss the detection of risks, which once materialized can dictate the future of the organization.

Somehow related with culture at governance level is the role of the chairman of the board. The chairman can contribute to a better risk governance through effective and assertive leadership forcing the board to focus on the mentioned risks, together with the management of the dynamics within the meetings of the board of directors, and eliminating potential blind angles which may hide certain risks.

The role of the chairman of the board is also critical in different ways depending on the specific governance models - single layer or double layer governance models. Mandate & Devine (2020) draw attention to three contemporary cases where the accumulation of the functions of Chairman of the Board of Directors together with the role of CEO may have led to disastrous outcomes.

The chairman is also a key element in preventing the groupthink phenomenon[6], which generally entails a de-responsibility, sometimes not conscious, of those responsible, which is confirmed by Asaoka (2018) in a study on Japanese organisations, which involves a culture of no debate - a risk in itself. The chairman of a "progressive" board must therefore have a much more watchful and interventive role within a collegiate governance body, as opposed to the traditional "ceremonial" style.

8. CONCLUSION

The board of directors' main tasks are essentially those tasks that determine the prosperity and sustainability of the business. The Board may delegate authority into the CEO, but it cannot delegate its own accountability concerning the supervision of management actions, and this includes accountability for risk governance.

This text suggests that the excessive, and sometimes exclusive, focus on financial risks, as well as the normative approach with a focus on compliance, may be a somewhat limited approach. Although a necessary condition, it is not sufficient by itself in the wider context of risk governance. Compliance allows to comply with the minimum standards, but it is prudence and ethics that aspires to maximum performance, as evidenced by the multiple examples of bad corporate governance witnessed in recent decades, where many companies had information, codes of good governance practices, however they could not avoid the disastrous outcomes.

The reality of risk knows no organizational or knowledge boundaries, so the use of multiple models or approaches can lead to improved governance if the goal is to protect organizations. Hence, it is necessary to go beyond the focus on financial risks, to re-focus on any type of risk that may be considered strategic, i.e., the type of risk that can seriously damage an organization or cause it to collapse.

A classification of typologies of real risks with potential strategic impacts for organizations was carried out. Attention was drawn to the role of organizational culture and the importance that the "value of values" can have in minimizing certain types of risk, namely those that cross the line of ethics.

In conclusion, the normative approach, closely tied to the law school of thought, is a necessary condition, however not sufficient, for the effective governance of organizational risks. It is necessary to go beyond normativism, using prudence, for risk governance to improve.

REFERENCES

Água, P. B., & Correia, A. (2020). Innovation governance in practice: A business policy approach. *Corporate Board: Role. Duties and Composition*, *16*(2), 54–64.

Água, P. B., & Morgado, A. V. (2020a). Business Policy: A Systems Approach to Corporate Governing. In Dynamic Strategic Thinking for Improved Competitiveness and Performance (pp. 216-242). IGI Global. doi:10.4018/978-1-7998-4552-2.ch009

Água, P. B., & Morgado, A. V. (2020b). An essay on the business policy approach as applied to the governance of megaprojects. *The Journal of Modern Project Management*, *8*(2).

Asaoka, D. (2018). Collective intelligence or groupthink? Group decision making under the Japanese Companies Act. *Corporate Board: Role, Duties and Composition*, *14*(2), 27–37.

BBC. (2012). *Former RBS boss Fred Goodwin stripped of knighthood.* https://www.bbc.com/news/uk-politics-16821650

Bromiley, P., & Rau, D. (2016). Strategic risk management. A better way of managing major risks. *IESEInsight, 28.*

Calleja, R., & Melé, D. (2017). Valero's "Enterprise Politics": A model of humanistic management and corporate governance. *Journal of Management Development*, *36*(5), 644–659. doi:10.1108/JMD-12-2015-0187

Canals, J. (2014). Renewing the board's mission. 6 Items for the top of every board's agenda. *IESEInsight, 21.*

Cerf, C., & Navasky, V. (1984). *The Experts Speak.* Pantheon Books.

Cerrone, R. (2019). Risk management as increased corporate governance requirement in Italian banks and insurance companies. *Corporate Board: Role, Duties and Composition*, *15*(3), 58–69.

Charan, R. (2005). Boards that Deliver: Advancing Corporate Governance from Compliance to Competitive Advantage. Jossey-Bass Ed.

Christensen, C. R., Andrews, K. R., & Bower, J. L. (1978). Business Policy: Text and Cases (4th ed.). R. D. Irwin Ed.

Dorner, D. (1996). The Logic Of Failure: Recognizing And Avoiding Error. In *Complex Situations.* Metropolitan Books.

Drew, S. A., Kelley, P. C., & Kendrick, T. (2006). CLASS: Five elements of corporate governance to manage strategic risk. *Business Horizons*, *49*(2), 127–138. doi:10.1016/j.bushor.2005.07.001

Esty, B. C., Bitsch, F. (2013). *The Kashagan Production Sharing Agreement (PSA).* Harvard Business School Case Study 9-213-082.

Filkelstein, S., Whitehead, J., & Campbell, A. (2009). *Think Again: Why Good Leaders Make Bad Decisions and How to Keep it From Happening to You.* Harvard Business Review Press.

Fontrodona, J., & Sanz, P. (2015). The value of values. The keys to a positive business culture. *IESEInsight, 27.*

Forrester, J. W. (1968). *Principles of Systems.* Pegasus Communications.

Hubbard, D. W. (2009). *The failure of risk management. Why it's broken and how to fix it.* John Wiley & Sons, Inc.

Kahneman, D. (2011). Think fast and slow. New York: Farrar, Straus & Giroux Ed.

Lorsch, J. W. (2012). *The Future of Boards.* Harvard Business Review Press.

Lustgarten, A. (2012). *Run to Failure: BP and the Making of the Deepwater Horizon Disaster.* W. W. Norton & Company.

Malik, F. (2012). *The right corporate governance. Effective Top management for mastering complexity.* Campus Verlag.

Mandato, J, & Devine, W. (2020). Why the CEO shouldn't also be the board chair. *Harvard Business Review.*

Nueno, P. (2016). *The 2020 Board: The Future of Company Boards.* LID Publishing.

Ormazabal, G. (2016). Risk oversight: What every director should know. *IESEInsight, 28.*

Russo, J. E., & Schoemaker, P. J. H. (1990). Decision Traps. The Ten barriers To Brilliant Decision-Making and how to Overcome Them. New York: Fireside Ed.

Senge, P. (1990). *The fifth discipline.* Doubleday.

Simon, H. A. (1957). *Models of man, social and rational.* Wiley.

Sterman, J. (2000). *Business dynamics: Systems thinking and modeling for a complex world.* Irwin McGraw-Hill.

Taleb, N. (2010). *The black swan. The impact of the highly improbable.* Penguin Books.

Tapies, J., & Toninato, F. (2005). Milking Money out of Parmalat. IESE Business School Case Study IES119-PDF-ENG.

Valerdi, R., & Rouse, W. B. (2010). When systems thinking is not a natural act. *IEEE International Systems Conference*, 184-189.

Valero, A., & Figueroa, E. T. (2011). La empresa de negocios y la alta dirección: Procedimientos políticos de gobierno (3rd ed.). Pamplona: Eunsa.

Valero, A., & Lucas, J. L. (2018). Business Policy. Sevilla: San Telmo Eds.

By itself, a causal diagram does not show the detailed dynamics that emerges from the behaviour of a system. This is only possible using a simulator that can be built from a causal diagram using *System Dynamics*, a technique created in the late 50s at MIT to simulate complex systems (Forrester, 1961). However, although limited, the causal model can still provide useful information to help focus attention on key relationships. Sterman (2000) provides a good introduction to system dynamics and causal loop diagrams.

ADDITIONAL READING

Agyemang, O. S., Ansong, A., & Agyei-Mensah, B. K. (2019). *Corporate Governance Models and Applications in Developing Economies*. IGI Global. doi:10.4018/978-1-5225-9607-3

Bernstein, P. L. (1996). *Against the Gods. The Remarkable Story of Risk*. Wiley & Sons Inc.

Caldart, A. A., Ricart, J. E., & Carrera, A. A. (2020). *General Management in Latin America and Ibero-American Organizations. A Humanistic Perspective*. Routledge.

Fernández, A. L., & Mazza, C. (2014). *Boards Under Crisis. Board Action Under Pressure*. Palgrave Macmillan. doi:10.1057/9781137379221

Jennex, M. E. (2019). *Current Issues and Trends in Knowledge Management, Discovery, and Transfer*. IGI Global. doi:10.4018/978-1-7998-2189-2

Malik, F. (2011). *Corporate Policy and Governance*. Campus Verlag.

Malik, F. (2012). *The Right Corporate Governance*. Campus Verlag.

Strang, K. D., Korstanie, M. E., & Vajjhala, N. (2018). *Research, Practices, and Innovations in Global Risk and Contingency Management*. IGI Global. doi:10.4018/978-1-5225-4754-9

ENDNOTES

1. The basic grammar of causal loop diagrams is provided in Annex A. The systems thinking approach helps visualize risks that are not independent of each other, allowing for more elaborated risk scenarios than non-systemic approaches.
2. It means putting effort and resources so that either the probability of occurrence, or the impact, is nullified.
3. In practice it means putting effort and resources so that either the probability of occurrence, or the impact, are close to zero, but not zero.
4. The risk is transferred to third parties, e.g. by means of insurance.
5. Normally when a particular risk has minimal probability of occurrence or potential impact.
6. The term groupthink was introduced by Irving L. Janis in 1972 and refers to a psychological phenomenon in which people align themselves by consensus within a group. In many cases, people abandon their own personal beliefs and eventually adopt the opinion of the rest of the group.

APPENDIX - CAUSAL LOOP DIAGRAMME NOTATION

A Causal Loop Diagram (CLD) is a model of the important relationships between variables or system parameters. It is a tool used in systems thinking that has some virtues, namely:

- It's a simple way to represent ideas, which sometimes are still confusing at the beginning of any study of a problem or system.
- Supports a clear and effective communication with stakeholders about a model or study.

A causal relationship uses "+" and "-" signs to represent the type (or direction) of influence between two variables. For instance, a causal relationship between two variables A and B with a "+" sign means they change in the same direction (direct effect). That is, with everything else being equal, when A increases, B tends to increase or when A decreases, B tends to decrease. Conversely, a relationship with a "-" sign means a change in opposite direction (inverse effect). That is, with everything else being equal, when A increases, B tends to decrease and when A decreases, B tends to increase:

Figure 10. Labelled arrows combine into Causal Loop Diagrams

Combinations of these two types of relationships allow the drawing of causal diagrams as complex as needed (Senge, 1990). Particularly important are the feedback loops that may arise in the structure of a system, which potentially can be positive or negative as shown in the next figure.

Figure 11. Inner "+" or "- "signs show loop polarity

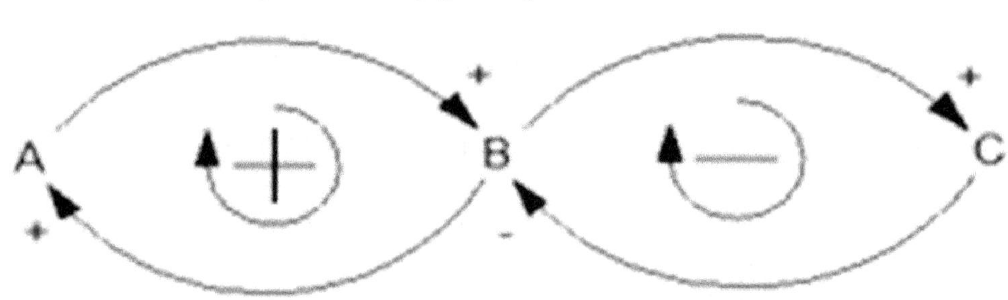

It is normal to represent the effect of A over B. However, this representation is incomplete, because the result of B is a new condition in the system which in turn may influence A. In a positive cycle (reinforcement cycle) there is either no negative influences or an even number of causal relationships with a "-" sign. In a negative cycle (balancing cycle) there is an odd number of causal relationships with a "-" sign.

Chapter 5
Pursuing Business Longevity: Ways to Enhance Sustainable Development

Luis A. Millan-Tudela
https://orcid.org/0000-0003-3669-9960
University of Alicante, Spain

Bartolomé Marco-Lajara
https://orcid.org/0000-0001-8811-9118
University of Alicante, Spain

Javier Martínez-Falcó
https://orcid.org/0000-0001-9004-5816
University of Alicante, Spain

Eduardo Sánchez-García
https://orcid.org/0000-0002-8524-4906
University of Alicante, Spain

ABSTRACT

Sustainable business is suffering an increasing demand by part of different stakeholders, especially those in the end of the value chain. One way to accomplish it is through a business longevity assessment model. If companies last in a sustainable way that is also recognizable, they will create value not only from an economic perspective but also from a social one. In this chapter, the authors expose the reasons why migrating from the main profit maximization goal to pursuing business longevity (survival in an adequate manner) may help to enhance sustainable development both inside and outside the organization, as well as some action proposals to achieve it.

DOI: 10.4018/978-1-6684-6750-3.ch005

INTRODUCTION

Sustainability can be defined as "meeting the needs of the present without compromising the ability of future generations to meet their own needs" (United Nations, 1987). Despite the shortness of the statement, a powerful spirit emerges from it: satisfying the needs in a way that resources can be regenerated at the same pace they are exploited and, consequently, ensuring that changes in the environment are minimum. Many examples can be given. Some of them may be ensuring reforestation in a certain rate to allow keeping ecosystems unaltered, planning land use to avoid deforestation, controlling polluting spills to rivers, seas, oceans and other water sources, or maximizing the most efficient energy generation technologies. However, the definition given by the UN goes beyond nature. Other goals that appear from it are the building of strong societies, eradication of corruption and guaranteeing a minimum living standard for every person (which includes, among others, access to healthcare infrastructures, decent wages and basic human rights). As it is shown, and despite only some examples have been given, all perspectives sustainability covers share one common feature: the need for standardization.

Many indicator systems and standards exist to do so. For example, GRI Standards, ISO 14000, Sustainable Development Goals (SDGs) and so on aim to establish a framework to assess and, consequently, strengthen sustainable activities in the different economic sectors. Despite the intentions followed, all those initiatives focus on controlling certain variables, but to not address the main problem, so the next question arises: "What is driving this kind of behavior among companies?" It is, why are some organizations developing practices that are so unsustainable that can even harm themselves?

In order to give an appropriate answer, a deep analysis needs to be done as a society. In this chapter, the authors take an overview, but further and much more intensive work needs to be done in this sense. Summing up, the answer would be the main goal pursued: profit maximization. When firms (and even non-private organizations) take this as the main variable and translate every single aspect they are involved into a monetary analysis (such as waste recovery processes), decisions get distorted and move away from sustainable practices.

Thus, the objectives pursued in this chapter can be summarized as follows:

- Highlight the way businesses have been made up to date.
- Expose the consequences profit maximization triggers.
- Show how a change from profit maximization to business longevity should help in achieving sustainable development for both companies and the environment.

BACKGROUND

Sustainability has been claimed in recent years as a topic to take into consideration in human lives, although it has been explored for decades. In the case of epidemics, people began to understand the effect of microbes (e.g. bacteria) in the XIX century, leading to some initiatives such as Chicago's sewing system (National Ocean Service, n.d.). The same source points out a report to the Royal Commission on River Pollution in 1897 that claimed the presence of "alkali works, copper works, sulfuric acid liquid, sulfate of iron from tin-plate works, and by slag, cinders and small coal" in the Tawe River (Wales). However, and going back to the United States of America (USA) as an example, water pollution continued indiscriminately until many events related to water discharges were broadly noticed (National Ocean Service, n.d.). This shows how awareness of the problem is crucial to take serious actions against it.

But the harm is not just limited to water. Air and soil can also be affected. Most of the times, damage occurs as a negligence (whether or not on purpose) by human actions. Giving more examples, this time in the case of soil, many different agents have endangered (or even destroyed) huge areas. Nuclear disasters as Chernobyl (1986) and Fukushima (2011), deforestation in the Amazon as a consequence of intensive agriculture and introduction of non-indigenous species in ecosystems (whether animals or plants), among others, endanger the environment in different ways. Moving to air, it is affected by polluting elements in form of gases such as carbon oxides (CO and CO_2), nitrogen oxides (NO_X) or sulfur dioxide (SO_2) or small particles (divided by its size and, thus, by harm caused, as PM_{10} and $PM_{2.5}$) among many others.

Pollution is a big problem related to sustainability, but not the only one (Marco-Lajara et al., 2022). Social inequalities have both persisted and been related all along history. For example, slavery was well recognized (and even accepted) in times of colonization. In spite of the current rejection by a broad part of the population, it is still present as an endemic disease in society. Privileges of some are achieved at the expense of others. As an example of this, the United Nations release an annual list of the called Human Development Index (HDI) (United Nations, 1990) that shows in a single measure the quality of inhabitants in different countries considering health, education and wealth. This index shows considerable differences between territories, as can be seen in Figure 1 made from the 2020 report (United Nations, 2020).

Figure 1. 2019 Human Development Index by countries
Source: United Nations, 2020

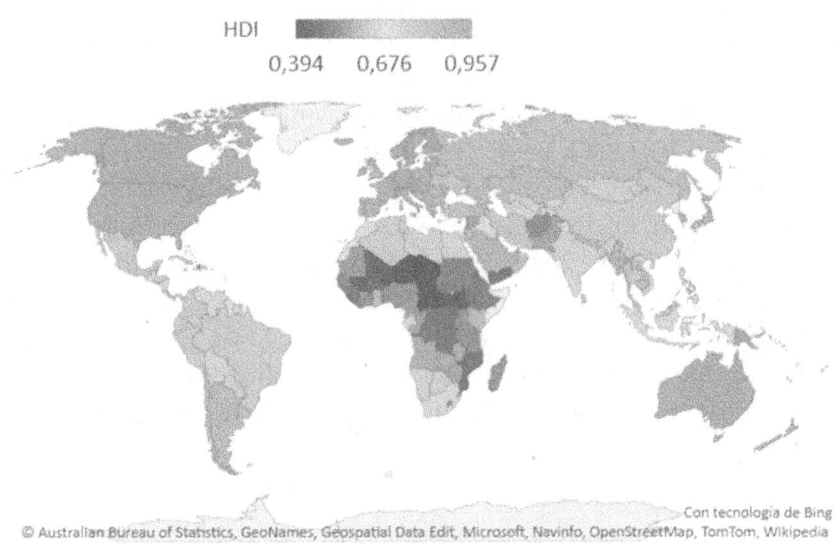

African, Asian and most Central and South American countries have lower HDI rates than European and North American territories. In this sense, labor exploitation and lack of freedom rights, proper healthcare systems and earnings are the main differences that put millions of people in a critical, unsustainable situation.

HDI shows the current status of the situation in aggregated terms. However, HDI does not show the problems that are present in the so called “high-developed countries”. Exposing those problems transcends the main purpose of this chapter, but a few examples can be given.

Going back to pollution to do so, CO_2 credit markets allow countries to exchange carbon dioxide emissions through trading, just as the Article 6 of the Paris Agreement allows (United Nations, 2015a) and the European Commission (n.d.) confirms. That is, countries can buy surplus emission rights to those who do not fully employ them due to the adoption of more efficient technologies or the lack of infrastructures to do so. Even though these initiatives may lead to some improvements, they do not focus on the main problem: the intensive use of resources (in this case, the energetic ones). By CO_2 credit trading, companies and governments can make profits from improvements in their productive systems. However, it also enhances those energy generation technologies that are more profitable but also more polluting. As a result, in aggregate terms, it seems an undesirable solution that has been applied for years.

Edmonds et al. (2020) propose a tax compensation for CO_2 caption, consuming and storage to reduce carbon dioxide levels in the atmosphere, which is indeed a more operative solution as it focus on the problem: resources (in this case, recovering CO_2 to be reintroduced in the market as a revalued product). However, as they hint, this solution (and, obviously, others that encouraged to sustainability) cannot affect business profits to convince companies for its adoption, what shows that the main variable (profit maximization) still remains above sustainability in society.

Knowing that lack of sustainability (in all its dimensions) is an anthropogenic problem, solutions as the one proposed can be provided. CO_2 credit markets have been highlighted, but there are subtle ways (at least in daily life) that are more extended and harm the environment in different ways. One of those examples is outsourcing. Outsourcing can be defined as the transfer of non-core functions of a company to another (Bilan et al., 2017). The key term is “non-core functions”, because if they are not crucial for business strategy by themselves, then outsourcing is made in order to cut costs down. To do so, those activities are reallocated in places where labor force is much cheaper, but the only way they achieve these reductions in costs is at the expense of workers.

One of the toughest ways of cost decreasing to assimilate is child labor, what has been a problem for centuries, having records of intellectuals like Adam Smith, Friedrich Engels or Karl Marx giving their vision about this issue (Edmonds, 2008). So long as wages do not reach the threshold for a decent living, children labor will remain where this condition is not met. One way to demonstrate child labor distribution by countries is through expected schooling years. The lower it is, the less time children remain in the education system and, thus, the sooner they begin working. Figure 2 shows the difference between national schooling years and world average for 2019 (United Nations, 2020).

Figure 2. 2019 differences in schooling years compared to world average
Source: United Nations, 2020

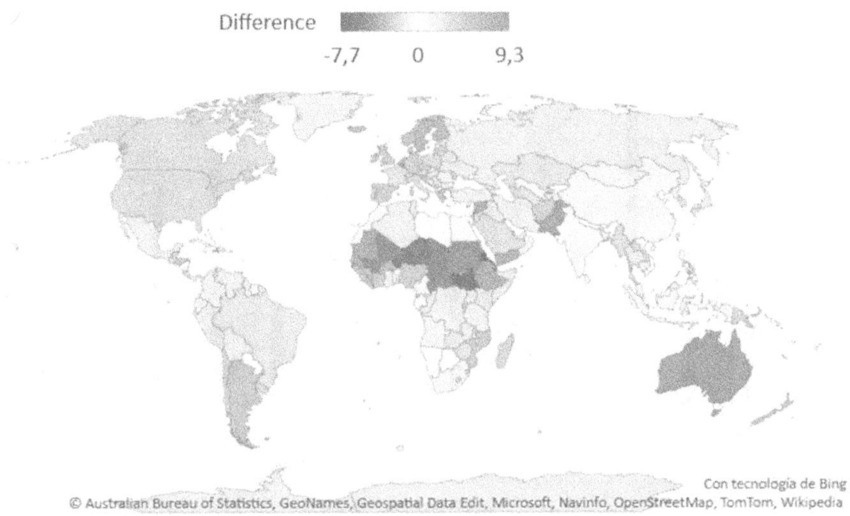

As can be seen, poorest countries also show the lowest schooling years as children leave the system in order to join work labor, depriving them from basic knowledges that would allow them to pursue better work conditions and, thus, condemning their future generations to the same problem. On the other side, wealthy countries also show the highest schooling years, proving that knowledge is a competitive advantage for countries to ensure wellbeing.

As can be inferred from the above statements, sustainability is a whole. When things go wrong, they usually go wrong in various aspects. In the case of developed countries, the main problem is not only related to pollution, as other patterns (such as mental disorders) emerge. A study conducted by Nishi et al. (2019) shows that twelve-month prevalence on common mental disorders is significative in current society, and especially present in USA and Europe, where 1 in 5 people suffer from them, as Figure 3 shows.

Figure 3. Twelve-month prevalence of common mental disorders
Source: Nishi et al., 2019

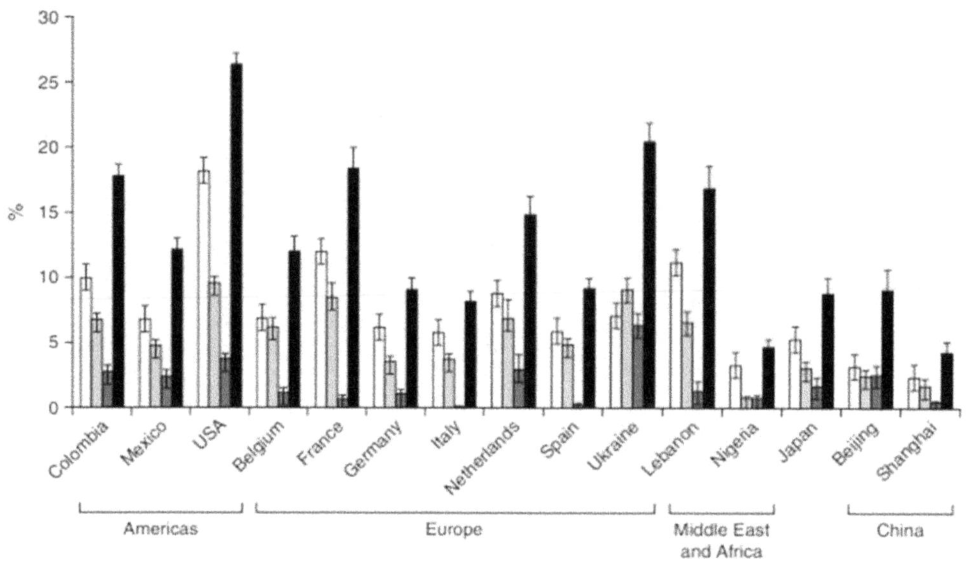

Summarizing, sustainability is currently threatened in its various perspectives. Pollution, inequalities and health are suffering, from a greater or lesser extent, an invisible prevalence that must be solved if society wants to reach sustainable development. As the 2030 Agenda states (United Nations, 2015b), among different actors to reach sustainability, private sector is found to be one of them. As the main goal from companies (in most cases) has been (and keeps being) profit maximization, this milestone has become such a preference that, whether or not on purpose, is currently threating humans' most basic need: a healthy life. Despite further explanations can be offered, it is well known that resources (fossil fuels, crops, animals…) are being overexploited in a way that may be harmful for every life form on Earth. Thus, a change has to be done. In the next section, the researchers offer a possible solution for the private sector. This must not be interpreted as a complete problem-solving idea. The main goal followed by the authors is to offer some suggestions to be discussed among researchers to converge in actions that enhance changes to achieve sustainable development, so following proposals must be interpreted as a possible starting point to finally reach sustainability.

MOVING FROM PROFIT MAXIMIZATION TO LONGEVITY

Maximization, in a mathematical sense, refers to reaching the highest value in a function. Applying this to economics, when profit maximization is exposed, it means obtaining the highest output possible in relation to each unit of resources used. To allow comparison among companies, both inputs and outputs are expressed in monetary terms and related to each other, so profit can be conceptually defined as follows:

$$Profit = \frac{Monetary\ units\ recovered}{Monetary\ units\ invested}$$

As can be seen, the whole activity of firms is concentrated in one single variable. This kind of proxies allows all stakeholders assessing performance of companies in an easy manner. However, reality is way more complex, so summarizing it all in one indicator may distort day to day action within organizations. It is obvious that companies use more indicators (and not all of them are financial) but, at the end of the day, companies that are considered the best are those that give the greatest profit. The problem of having focused that much on benefits over decades, in part to prove from firms (microeconomics) to markets (macroeconomics) that they are doing well, is that the concept has been distorted in a way that it no longer makes sense (Drucker, 1958).

The problem of assessments mainly based on profits is that other perspectives are relegated to the background. For example, in public tenders, costs often have a higher weighting than it should, especially in times of crisis. However, if a change from profit maximization to a broader perspective is aimed, new results will emerge for the same problems humanity has been addressing up to date. This change to a whole of new perspectives (in the case of the private sector) can be done under the umbrella of business longevity.

Longevity, in a management sense, can be defined as “the state an organization reaches when it has proven its self-sustainability along time uninterruptedly”. This brief but meaningful definition can be compared to longevity of living beings: given a species, a living being needs both health (inner functions) and embeddedness with the environment (adaptation) to reach a certain age. If this concept is properly applied to companies, sustainability can be reached as both the company itself and its environment (which includes nature, society, economy…) would be considered together in every decision-making activity.

From Concept to Reality

One thing is to present a theoretical idea as a solution, but doing so without providing operative initiatives to make it work would be useless. Some possible actions to address this problem are given in the next section, while here the main issues to be solved in this conversion from concept to reality are pointed out.

The first stone in the path is simplification. Despite distortion, profit maximization gives an easy, comprehensive way to assess business performance. If the view is widened, different approaches must be considered and, the more approaches are embraced, the more difficult it will be to make them all work together. The easier way to explain this problem would be incompatibilities from stakeholders. When deciding business strategies, one of the things that must be carefully analyzed is compatibility of each strategy with the goals every stakeholder that can influence on it has. By doing so, incompatibilities emerge as every stakeholder has its own, individual goals. For example, in a company that faces crisis, divestments may need to be done in order to save the company. This can be approved by investors as they do not want the company to lose all its value, but workers and union representatives may perceive this as a threaten for job conservation.

As goals cannot be changed suddenly, the only way to make stakeholders’ aims similar is through time and effort. Future generations perceive the danger current actions are inflicting, so this is an opportunity to harmonize perspectives from who will be future stakeholders. However, this is not an easy task as it involves several agents that currently do have different aims, so awareness of the forthcoming situation is crucial. Among these agents the following can be highlighted:

- Politicians
- Researchers
- Educators
- Entrepreneurs
- Role models for the young (sportsmen and sportswomen, gamers and streamers…)

Politicians and researchers must share a common vision as the knowledge generated by the last needs to be applied by the first ones. Giving tools for producing scientific knowledge to optimize decision-making is crucial in order to take the right steps from now on. Regarding educators, it is obvious that their imprint in the youth is huge as they present students a world they have never seen before and, thus, it is critical to transmit the right values in this sense. Finally, role models are key on the process as they highly influence through behaviors and opinions shown, even more nowadays considering the impact made through social networking sites. Finally, entrepreneurs need to do some self-criticism regarding the influence they have in the future: on the one hand, the use of resources they do will influence how future generations will be able to live. On the other, they also act in many cases as role models for those who start a career. Consequently, as they are the first example for those that move from the academic system to labor, it is important that they reformulate their values in a way that meets sustainable development.

There are many agents that can influence sustainable development success or failure, but the ones stated above are some of the most influential ones. As their positions are often really far from one another, the only way to reach a common point is through assessing their own actions. If this does not work, then future generations will have to do so, although the later it is done, the more difficult the problem will become. That is why educators' influence is critical: if those in charge cannot handle the issue, next generations must be ready to do so.

Going back to the earlier-mentioned multidisciplinarity, if business assessment is based on diverse perspectives, it cannot be done by simple metrics. Sustainability (what is the aim of longevity) is so complex that human rationality has to take action, what means problems are not just mathematical nor economic. Despite including these perspectives, a prospective analysis will always be needed, and there is where intuition, self-reflection and experience play a main role. Thus, training critical thinking is maybe the most important part of sustainability: without criticism, nothing will be questioned, and no advances will occur.

As can be seen, plenty of work has to be done, and it is not an easy one. Even though this debate transcends the aims of this chapter, some possible actions that may help to deal with the problem are given in the section "solutions and recommendations".

Longevity and Sustainable Development Goals

Sustainable Development Goals (SDGs) were proposed in the 2030 Agenda by the United Nations (2015b) as a way for achieving sustainable development. They consist of 17 goals and 169 targets that give a guideline for actions at different levels (mainly political, private sector and individuals). Despite the proposed concept of longevity would not meet the 2030 deadline, it must be understood that changes should have been made earlier. For example, claims made by scientists about global warming are currently addressing the critical urge for measures to mitigate its effects as a critical point is being reached (Ekwurzel et al., 2021). However, making long-lasting changes is as important as making fast ones. In this sense, mitigation actions should actually be happening while further, deeper and stronger changes (where business longevity can be included) are shaped.

So, despite not reaching the 2030 deadline, longevity can help to reach the SDG goals and targets in the long term. In the following lines, a comparison between profit maximization and longevity in terms of achieving SDGs is developed to justify the need for a change in the business assessment model.

Regarding SDGs 1 (no poverty) and 2 (zero hunger), as business longevity needs an adequate, healthy environment to be successful, it would empower companies to offer better working conditions. If longevity is the way to assess companies, the ones that offer proper wages, stability and security for workers and reject child labor will be considered as more suitable and, thus, should capture larger market shares. In this sense, a committed society is needed. If clients and suppliers reject to deal with companies that do not meet the premise, the last ones will disappear, generating a cleaning effect that would allow the sustainable ones to remain in the market in the long run, it is, reaching longevity while helping in sustainable development. In the case of those companies that pursue profit maximization, actions as outsourcing to low-cost producing countries (as stated above) are too tentative to make a change to adopt sustainability.

SDGs 3 (good health and well-being) and 4 (quality education) go on the same way. In the case of the third goal, offering good conditions (namely wages and occupational safety and health) would contribute to health improvement as workers spend a considerable part of the day at work. With regard to SDG 4, if child labor is rejected by companies, the only choice for children will be schooling. As shown in Figure 2, countries with higher schooling years are also the most developed ones in technology and economy, what would also help directly reaching SDGs 5 (gender equality) and 10 (reduced inequalities), as well as other SDGs related to knowledge development. In the case of companies pursuing profit maximization, the same that is stated in the above paragraph is applicable.

SDGs 6 (clean water and sanitation) and 7 (affordable and clean energy) are one of the most evident goals that companies can help to reach, even with current technologies in the market. In case of business longevity, as one of the main conditions to become a long-lasting company is congruence with the environment, optimizing the use of resources is key. As a consequence, nonrenewable resources as water and those that can be renewable but not unlimitedly available (as energy) will be used in the best way possible to prevent harming firms' breeding ground. As it has already been seen with profit maximization, the search for the best results has sometimes ended up in questionable actions as polluting discharges in water (heavy metals, fertilizers…) that make water unable for human consumption permanently or temporally, also leading to problems as eutrophication.

Decent work and economic growth (SDG8) are more the way to achieve longevity rather than a result. As stated earlier, giving proper tools and conditions to workers will enhance businesses to remain in the market as they will be the ones chosen. However, this needs commitment from stakeholders as those mentioned in the preceding subsection.

SDG9 (industries, innovation and infrastructure) cannot be a result of longevity. Instead, it is one of the conditions needed to reach it. In this sense, last state-of-the-art technologies need to be used worldwide to optimize resource usage. As can be inferred, most developed countries must help those with shortcomings in this sense to finally reach sustainable development. Despite being more a political issue rather than a business one, part of the problem comes from geopolitical competition. Although this has to be solved by the corresponding power, the private sector has to prepare solutions for underdeveloped countries that meet both the current knowledge on technologies and existing conditions in those territories to make sustainability not just a utopia but both pragmatic and reachable.

Reduced inequalities (SDG9) is probably one of the most notorious output business longevity adoption would bring. Given more considerations than it is actually done with profit maximization, more controls in terms of ethic behavior will be applied to firms' operative. Once business longevity becomes broadly accepted worldwide, opportunities for all human beings (as stated above) will emerge and, consequently, gaps between countries will become scarcer.

SDGs 11 (sustainable cities and communities), 12 (responsible consumption and production), 13 (climate action), 14 (life below water) and 15 (life on land) are also approachable by business longevity. As it has already been exposed, business longevity depends on a series of actions addressed to optimizing the use of resources. That means not only avoiding waste, but also using the resources in the best way so the others do not become affected (e.g. using renewable sources of energy instead of fossil fuels that diminish availability of sanitary water or soil for crops due to acid rain). In this sense, and in contrast to profit maximization (as it has been proven by the current situation), longevity would lead to a better use of the resources available and, consequently, contributing to improve the performance in both cities and industries, thus enhancing climate change countermeasures.

Despite being further than the others from the private sector, SDGs 16 (peace, justice and strong institutions) and 17 (partnerships for the goals) are also supported by business longevity. As previously stated, the adoption of business longevity requires all stakeholders to share common mission, vision and values. The present competitiveness among countries is leading to destructive dynamics in the form of commercial wars (and even armed conflicts). By a general adoption of business longevity, the environment remains the key regardless of borders as lack of sustainability is a global issue. Thereby, positioning the variables already shown above profit maximization in the private sector will lead to changes in geopolitical approaches and, as a consequence, strengthening collaboration and fair institutions.

SOLUTIONS AND RECOMMENDATIONS

In the first sections, some of the issues the adoption of business longevity must face have been exposed. Those problems, as it has been clearly warned, are really difficult to overcome. Nonetheless, it is not an excuse to start developing changes in order to solve the worsening situation humanity is suffering.

The first thing that needs to be considered is that initial solutions will not be the final ones. Given the tremendous complexity of the current non-sustainable society, changes will be done as people find out misfunctions. In this sense, three main pillars cannot be ignored:

- Actions will give results in the long term.
- Changes must be done in the operative, not in goals.
- Timing has to be considered unavoidably.

The actual society has a problem regarding to seeking fast results. Complexity and dynamism in the environment make people choose solutions that give acceptable results in the short term with a huge cost in longer periods of time. Global warming, inequalities, resource overexploitation and pollution have been present for decades, even centuries, so their inertia has a considerable magnitude. As a consequence, to change this dynamic, time is required in order to appreciate proper changes. In this sense, new technologies as forecasting models are an allied because, if used correctly, they will give a prospective view to get ahead of events.

Regarding points two and three, a really tentative solution in case of not reaching the milestones agreed is to change or postpone them, or even not establishing deadlines. A positive view is given by the Paris Agreement (United Nations, 2015a) and Glasgow Climate Pact (United Nations, 2021) as the 1.5ºC temperature increase limit established in the first is maintained in the second. However, establishing halfway goals would improve performance as postponement of actions slows down recovery. Summing up, intermediate goals, timing and their non-modification are crucial to work on the problem in a proper way.

Once clarified the problem, it is time to offer solutions to the issues stated previously. The first one is the damage pollution has already inflicted. Big spaces of land, water and air have unhealthy concentrations of toxics that have to be removed. For example, the Spanish Ministry for Ecologic Transition and Demographic Challenge (MITECO) in collaboration with the Spanish Ministry for Agriculture, Fisheries and Food have published in their geoportal a map that shows affected water sources by the presence of nitrates. The situation at May 2022 can be seen in Figure 4 (Ministerio de Agricultura, Pesca y Alimentación & Ministerio para la Transición Ecológica y el Reto Demográfico, 2022):

Figure 4. Water sources affected by the presence of nitrates
Source: Ministerio de Agricultura, Pesca y Alimentación & Ministerio para la Transición Ecológica y el Reto Demográfico, 2022

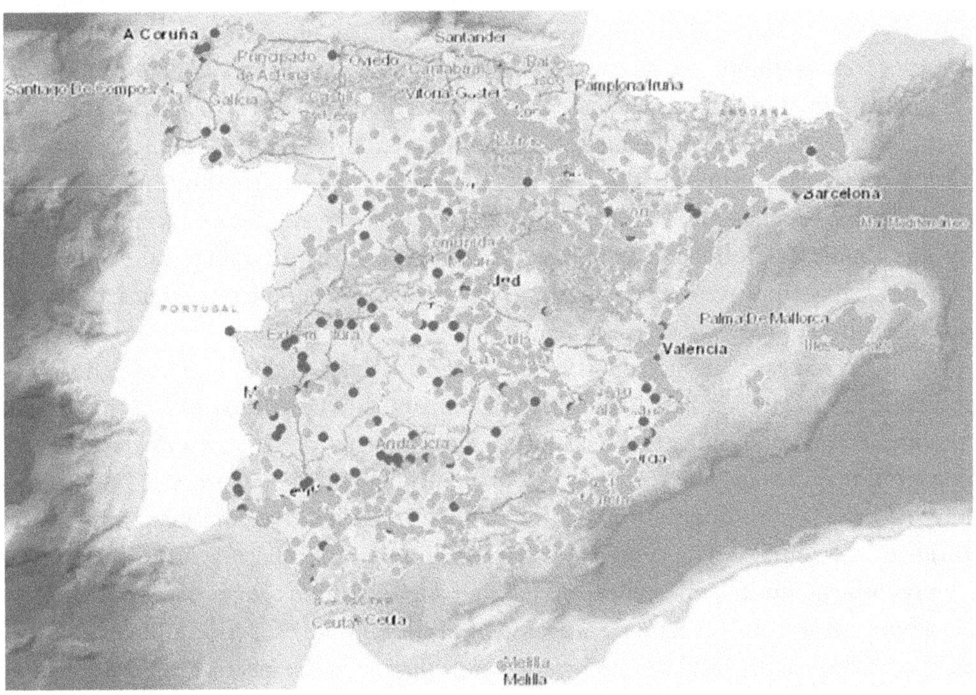

In this case, problems that emerge from this are the aforementioned eutrophication, food poisoning and economic losses, to name a few. However, more situations like the one showed exist. For example, the presence of microplastics and heavy metals in water and its acidification, pesticides in soil and pollutants in air as the already mentioned oxides, PM_{10} and $PM_{2.5}$. The only way to solve this is through removal. However, it is not financially attractive for companies as the costs they would incur to do so in their properties would force them to business exit. As the problem is extended all around the world and has been partially produced by laxity in legislation and controlling, government subsidy programs must be designed to promote decontamination. In this sense, grants should be given to the following activities:

- Research and development in decontamination techniques.
- Creation of businesses that carry out decontamination activities.
- Demand by businesses for decontamination services.

These initiatives need considerable budgets. One way to partially cover funds needed is at the expense of those who keep polluting indiscriminately. It is, the first step would be to tighten controls to trigger changes in businesses and other organizations. Those who do not adapt their processes to current legislation despite moratoriums should face sizable fines as a compensation for getting an unfair advantage at the expense of those who comply with regulations.

Another problem earlier exposed is the impossibility of simplification if business longevity is applied. In fact, as the view is broadened, more incompatibilities emerge. As a consequence, it must be understood that neither single nor compound measurements can be used, so the previously presented human critical thinking is needed. The first step in this sense is to do a self-assessment by part of different stakeholders and recognize the errors that have been done. Once they have been recognized, scientific literature is the basis for new values to transmit to future generations. Valid, contrasted and refutable knowledge has to be a main pillar for sustainable development and societies. One of the keys is refutability: scientific production gives an understanding of existence that changes in the light of new discoveries, allowing both to improvements in actions undertaken and to enhance critical thinking. As science must be the core, it needs reinforcement by part of institutions in terms of funding and accessibility for the best human talent. In this point, education has to play a key role both as earlier formative steps and knowledge quarry. When this part is finally consolidated, the only thing that has to be guaranteed is feedback: producing scientific knowledge that improves decision-making by its transmission from scientists to governors and providing resources in the opposite direction.

Ending the problem-solving proposals, social inequalities are faced. As it has been exposed, lack of decent wages, child labor, gender discriminations, racism and corrupted institutions have become a high barrier that cannot be avoided. In the case of child labor, international sanctions have to be applied. A good example would be the case of North Korea (officially known as Democratic People's Republic of Korea), where infringement of international agreements has carried out sanctions that forbid the selling of certain goods to the country. The same should be applied to child labor, as they are one of the most affected by inequalities, and its persistence ballast their opportunities for prosperity. However, a sanctions regime would bring hostility among developed and underdeveloped countries, so the first ones should do an effort and provide funding, knowledge and support to the last ones so that, in general terms, eradicating child labor seems beneficial for them from the very first moment.

Regarding decent wages and corrupted institutions, markets can play a key role (as well as in the case of child labor). If buyers avoid deals with companies and countries that do not pay enough to their employees or do not give enough guarantees for human rights to have a good living standard in the area they are based, actions would converge to remediating the situation.

The problems of gender discrimination and racism need different solutions than the ones presented for the other issues. As they are rooted in social and even cultural thoughts and beliefs, the only way to make a change is through education. To do so, strengthening the educational system and persecuting fake news and opportunistic behaviors in this sense (while spreading the consequences this kind of actions have) should help to improve the situation. The share for common values pointed out earlier can build a bridge for mutual understanding among cultures. However, it is obvious that these measures are necessary but not sufficient, and deeper debate on the topic has to be done.

FUTURE RESEARCH DIRECTIONS

As it has been exposed, sustainability consists of several dimensions and is influenced by many others. Thus, research in all those areas are necessary. In this sense, some of the directions that may be taken by researchers from different disciplines can be highlighted.

In the case of law research and ethics, the main path to follow is analyzing the current state of the rules, detecting incompatibilities, unethical precepts, gaps and legal loopholes that impede the implementation of sustainable development. With a deep understanding of the legal framework in different scopes (international, national and regional) changes can be done both in rules and activities to make plans for reaching sustainability fit as much as possible.

Other disciplines with big potential are formal (mathematics, statistics, logic…) and natural sciences (biology, physics, chemistry…). These areas establish the basic knowledge from where to start in both incremental and disruptive changes, mainly in technology. In this sense, if undertaking a deep transformation of the current behavior as a society is wanted, new technological discoveries are needed if a quality leap regarding human actions is desired. Thus, trying to discover new materials, processes and methodologies to assess and simulate certain scenarios will fiercely enhance evolution as a society to a new level.

The next step after formal and natural sciences comes by the hand of engineering. Using the knowledge generated by the prior and collaborating with those disciplines will bring brand new solutions that will allow to face challenges in an easier, faster way. For example, additive manufacturing (3D printing) has supposed a huge development in a matter of years. Compared to machining, it leads to a better use of materials as less waste is produced (at the expense of longer production times). However, it has made possible to create certain high-complexity parts in a much cheaper way than other techniques (that were the only choice not long ago) do, even at home as prices for personal 3D printers are relatively low. Therefore, investment in engineering (both private and public) will help reaching a more sustainable development and enhance business survival as producing costs and waste will both decrease.

Obviously, a shift towards sustainability cannot be accomplished without the intervention of social sciences such as economics, sociology, communication and many others. As change has to be made by humans, employing sciences that generate knowledge about them seems a must. In this sense, further understanding of economics (to know causes and predict consequences for the changes that have to be proposed in terms of production, potential offer, demand coverage and evaluation in economic terms) and human behavior (to know the reaction of population to the changes that are proposed and the most efficient ways to communicate carry out them) is necessary, so support from all stakeholders is needed again if the best technical solutions are wanted to fit within the acceptance of citizens.

CONCLUSION

Actual situation regarding development needs deep changes. Resources available, whether natural or human, are being used in a way that will compromise the ability for future generations to satisfy their own needs. As it has been exposed, pollution, inequalities and overexploitation of limited resources are driving the world to a critical point that, if exceeded, will bring consequences of immeasurable size that will endure over a large period of time. The problem is not just its importance but also the urge to solve it. The aforementioned critical point is already being reached, and the line between avoiding the problem and having to face it directly has become blurrier than anyone would desire. Consequently, deep, firm changes must be done in order to keep the situation under a reasonable control.

As pointed out earlier, collaboration among different agents is key in a change to a sustainable development model. In the case of private sector, the model of business longevity is proposed. Although deadlines cannot be accomplished for 2030 as the United Nations established, SDGs may be reached if longevity becomes the priority in all economic sectors and territories. The fact of understanding a needing for good conditions in both companies and their environment should lead to a collaborating behavior from both parts, building a feedback relationship that strengthens all of them, although some conditions must be fulfilled.

The first one is the already mentioned collaboration among different agents. Only a common vision will bring enough commitment to implement the actions that give the best solutions, even if they are detrimental in the short term. Humanity has been working on fast results too much time and it has been proven that is not the way to be taken. Self-assessment and real commitment to take necessary action cannot be ignored.

Another thing to highlight is the fact that trying to make the problem easier will indeed make it harder. Simplifying reality has already been tried, but reality is too complex to be expressed in a few terms or perspectives. Awareness that new ways for approaching problems are needed is a must, even more given the actual VUCA environment (volatile, uncertain, complex and ambiguous). This justifies participation by all stakeholders.

As changes have to be deep and consistent but also interdisciplinary, knowledge is one of the most essential bases for any project taken to reach sustainable development, and business longevity perspective is not an exception. Thus, linking different research and knowledge areas seems the most appropriate way to do so. However, science cannot stand on its own as funds are required: if the best outcomes are wanted, the best people, the best equipment and the best conditions are needed.

Finally, a deep reflection on SDGs and business longevity has to be done. SDGs mostly show the final result that should be achieved, and give possible indicators through targets that can be used to assess outcomes. However, they do not provide specific actions to do so. In fact, actions are the most difficult to undertake. Despite so, SDGs are absolutely necessary as a starting point. As SDGs give the finish line, it is time for experts, policymakers, entrepreneurs and individuals to agree a common path to follow. In this sense, business longevity can help assessing the principles SDGs share regarding the private sector. Firms can only be understood by their embeddedness in the environment. If the later is harmed, firms will so. Consequently, establishing a model that considers both the environment and companies (not as individuals but as a group) at the same level avoids tensions and facilitates mutual feedback and collaboration, what should bring better results than the ones reached up to date. However, it is important to bear in mind that business longevity is just part of the solution. There are many aspects (as the abovementioned legislation) that have to be ready prior to a change of paradigm. Facets of society that need to be deeply checked, reframed and modified are cultural mantras, stigmas and axioms that have been ballasting human progress.

As a conclusion, it can be affirmed that a change from profit maximization to a business longevity assessment model would help in achieving sustainable development and, more concretely, basic SDG precepts, but it will not be enough without strong reflection, coordination, action and considering the views from different perspectives, disciplines and two essential elements: resources and time. Solutions must be global, unbiased and seeking for outcomes in the long run. Development has been made in a way that is harmful for everyone involved on it as society has suffered from short-sightedness. Changes needed to do are huge in number, complexity and diversity plus incompatible in the current situation. Nevertheless, there is no plan B: years of bad practices have led to a situation where drastic decisions are the only change to revert it. In case of avoiding or postponing these decisions, despite the hardness that they bring, consequences may raise the problem exponentially as time and complexity will increase.

"Our task must be to free ourselves by widening our circle of compassion to embrace all living creatures and the whole of nature and its beauty."

Albert Einstein

REFERENCES

Bilan, Y., Nitsenko, V., Ushkarenko, I., Chmut, A., & Sharapa, O. (2017). Outsourcing in international economic relations. *Montenegrin Journal of Economics*, *13*(3), 175–185. doi:10.14254/1800-5845/2017.13-3.14

Drucker, P. F. (1958). Business objectives and survival needs: Notes on a discipline of business-enterprise. *The Journal of Business*, *31*(2), 81–90. doi:10.1086/294178

Edmonds, E. V. (2008). Child Labor. Handbook of Development Economics, 4(9), 3607-3709. doi:10.1016/S1573-4471(07)04057-0

Edmonds, J., Nichols, C., Adamantiades, M., Bistline, J., Huster, J., Iyer, G., Johnson, N., Patel, P., Showalter, S., Victor, N., Waldhoff, S., Wise, M., & Wood, F. (2020). Could congressionally mandated incentives lead to deployment of large-scale CO2 capture, facilities for enhanced oil recovery CO2 markets and geologic CO2 storage? *Energy Policy*, *146*, 111775. doi:10.1016/j.enpol.2020.111775 PMID:35444362

Ekwurzel, B., Mann, M. E., Clement, J., Santer, B. D., Edwards, L., Zelikova, T. J., Frumhoff, P., Kapuscinski, A. R., Ehrlich, P. R., Kailath, T., Michaels, D. H., Lubensky, T., Dumas, M., Grey, D., Jacobs, N., Rector, T., Warwick, A., Crider, D. G., Kennedy, T., . . . Reardon, D. (2021). *Letter from Union of Concerned Scientists to Joseph R. Biden Jr.* https://ucsusa.org/sites/default/files/2021-04/scientist-biden-letter.pdf

European Commission. (n.d.). *International carbon market.* https://ec.europa.eu/clima/eu-action/eu-emissions-trading-system-eu-ets/international-carbon-market_en

Marco-Lajara, B., Zaragoza-Saez, P., Falcó, J. M., & Millan-Tudela, L. A. (2022). Analysing the Relationship Between Green Intellectual Capital and the Achievement of the Sustainable Development Goals. In Handbook of Research on Building Inclusive Global Knowledge Societies for Sustainable Development (pp. 111-129). IGI Global.

Ministerio de Agricultura Pesca y Alimentación & Ministerio para la Transición Ecológica y el Reto Demográfico. (2022). *GeoPortal.* https://sig.mapama.gob.es/geoportal/

National Ocean Service. (n.d.). *A brief history of pollution.* https://oceanservice.noaa.gov/education/tutorial_pollution/02history.html#:~:text=Pollution%20is%20not%20a%20new,broke%20out%20all%20across%20Europe

Nishi, D., Ishikawa, H., & Kawakami, N. (2019). Prevalence of mental disorders and mental health service use in Japan. *Psychiatry and Clinical Neurosciences*, *73*(8), 458–465. doi:10.1111/pcn.12894 PMID:31141260

United Nations. (1987). *Report of the World Commission on Environment and Development: Our common future.* http://www.un-documents.net/our-common-future.pdf

United Nations. (1990). *Human Development Report 1990.* https://hdr.undp.org/sites/default/files/reports/219/hdr_1990_en_complete_nostats.pdf

United Nations. (2015a). *Paris agreement.* https://unfccc.int/sites/default/files/english_paris_agreement.pdf

United Nations. (2015b). *Transforming our world: The 2030 Agenda for Sustainable Development.* https://sdgs.un.org/2030agenda

United Nations. (2020). *The next frontier. Human development and the Anthropocene.* https://hdr.undp.org/sites/default/files/hdr2020.pdf

United Nations. (2021). *Glasgow Climate Pact.* https://unfccc.int/sites/default/files/resource/cop26_auv_2f_cover_decision.pdf

KEY TERMS AND DEFINITIONS

Dimension: Perspective from which understand reality, shaped by professional and personal experiences.

Eutrophication: Inorganic nutrient excess in water sources that produces a proliferation of seaweed in sufficient amount that impedes sunlight to go through it, affecting life underwater.

Human Development Index: Quantitative measure developed by the United Nations in 1990 to assess living standards in different countries.

Longevity: Feature that is linked to a company that has proven self-sustainability uninterruptedly over a considerable period of time.

Profit Maximization: Action consisting of prioritizing economic and financial results over any other consideration, completely or partly.

Survival: Condition met by any organization that has neither used legal instruments for its dissolution nor suffered a process of merger/acquisition.

VUCA Environment: Situation that happens when external elements are characterized by the confluence of changes that are fast, unpredictable and complex at the same time.

Chapter 6
Immigration and Unemployment Nexus:
A Micro-Level Investigation of Ugandan Youth

Esra Karapınar Kocağ
https://orcid.org/0000-0002-2239-0519
Gümüşhane University, Turkey

ABSTRACT

Youth unemployment is a rising concern for many countries across the world. The gap between youth and adult is even wider in Sub-Saharan Africa than the world average. There might be several reasons to explain, yet this chapter focuses on one controversial potential reason: immigration. This continent has experienced considerable migration flows and one could expect that immigration worsens labour market conditions for native youth. Uganda as one of the Sub-Saharan countries is investigated to see if immigrants have a significant impact on unemployment probability of young Ugandans using cross-sectional census data for the years of 1991, 2002, and 2014. Data set was drawn from IPUMS-International. Findings indicate that regional share of immigrants does not have a significant large effect on unemployment probability of youth in Uganda. A further investigation showed that higher share of immigrants in a given region lowers the probability of being not in the labour force across specifications. This means immigrants do not push native youth out of the labour force in the Uganda case.

INTRODUCTION

Unemployment in the labour markets is commonly regarded as a serious issue particularly due to efficiency concerns as it is "a potential wastage of resources" (Casson, 1979). According to the International Labour Organization data, unemployment rate has persistently exceeded the world average in Sub-Saharan African countries, with the exception of the year of the global economic crisis in 2009. Considering the fact that the highest annual population growth rate has been observed in this region,

DOI: 10.4018/978-1-6684-6750-3.ch006

it seems unemployment or job creation will remain as a severe issue at least in the near future. Annual population growth was 2.66 per cent in Sub-Saharan Africa, while the world average was 1.07 per cent. This very high population growth in the region creates pressure on the labour market to provide job opportunities for new entrants.

Apart from own population growth, African continent experience a considerable intraregional migration flows. That is to say, 79 per cent of international immigrants in Africa in 2019 were born in Africa (IOM & AU, 2020). This considerable flow of people in Africa is likely to influence labour market outcomes in receiving countries. Although it has widely been examined in developed country cases, a few attempts (see for example, Biavaschi et al., 2018; Del Carpio et al., 2015; Gindling, 2009; Karapınar Kocağ & Kambhampati, 2020) exist to empirically investigate how a particular developing country was affected by such an inflow.

Labour markets consist of a variety of groups of individuals. Among those who are not employed, youth is one of the most vulnerable groups. Disadvantages such as lack of labour market experience and educational attainment, as well as market structure make this group of people more vulnerable than adults. This situation is reflected by an important gap between adult and youth unemployment rate which is generally two to three times higher for youth (International Labour Organization, 2017). Additional labour supply through immigration is another factor to influence labour market opportunities for young people. However, it is hard to say that empirical evidence in the relevant literature supports a clear relationship between these two variables.

In the case of Africa, Donkor (2021) argues that even if international organisations declare a low rate of unemployment amongst young population in comparison with developed countries, common informal works, underemployment, and poverty via low wages and lack of social safety need to be considered in such comparisons. He also criticises that attitudes towards some fields like art, music, fashion, and drama are not that positive as these fields are considered as hobbies for many African families. If not sorted out, this may not be a national concern but rather a global concern through looting, insurgencies, and terrorism as a result of increased poverty and inequality. Therefore, the author highlights job creation process in all professional fields to be supported by government and private sector cooperation to prevent difficulties on the entering labour market. Limited number of studies in the field and its vast array of effects make the subject more crucial to be investigated. This chapter aims to shed some light on youth unemployment and immigration nexus.

This chapter focuses particularly on the case of Uganda as one of the least developed Sub-Saharan African countries according to UNDESA (2020) classification. The objective of this study is therefore to investigate the impact of immigration on the labour market outcomes of youth in a developing country. To be precise, this chapter estimates the impact of the share of immigrants in the region on the probability of being unemployed for Ugandan youth.

The plan of this chapter is as follows. Section 2 presents the background and the relevant literature on the youth unemployment and immigration nexus. In Section 3 provides the empirical strategy that covers data and methodology along with the empirical findings. Section 4 presents future research directions. Finally, Section 5 concludes the chapter.

BACKGROUND

Concerns and discussions about youth unemployment are not a recent issue for countries all over the world because of the gap between youth and adult unemployment. According to the ILO Statistics (2020), unemployment rate for people over 15 years old was 4 per cent of the total labour force, while it was 13.5 per cent for people in the age group of 15-24 in 2019.

Starting from early studies (e.g. Casson, 1979; Folk, 1968; Matthews, 1937; Miller, 1941), the problem of youth unemployment has been addressed particularly in the case of English and American youth. Folk (1968) in his study highlighted that the reason behind the high rate of unemployment among young population, especially after 1962, is related with the number of youths entered into the labour force, and seasonal surplus of young labour that exceeds the number of available jobs. Study also suggested that individual characteristics such as race and gender are important to explain youth unemployment.

Individual characteristics were widely recognised in the literature. Gender difference is one of the important factors that influence labour market outcome of young individuals. Girls, in this respect are more likely to experience unemployment (Hammarström, 1994; O'Higgins, 2001). Usual activity out of labour force is education for boys and housework for girls that lowers job market opportunities for girls (O'Higgins, 2001). Beside the unemployment experience, gender difference also appears to be in the re-entrance into the labour force. Clark & Summers (1982) suggest that young women are more likely to withdraw from the labour force when they leave unemployment.

Unemployment experience faced by young people of society may also differ in terms of where they locate and what racial background they come from. Clark and Summers (1982) found that the probability of quitting a job is higher for non-white young men in comparison with young white men. Moreover, O'Regan (1993) investigated how minority concentration influence minority youth. Her findings suggested that population size significantly affect unemployment outcome for Black youth, although it is not statistically significant for Hispanic minority youth. This finding was suggested due to more efficient use of network to get employment in Hispanic society than Black ones.

Education level is one of the most important factor to achieve success in the labour market. Biavaschi et al. (2013) highlight that low qualification is often accompanied by lack of access to employment, along with high risk of exclusion for young people. Unemployment level is generally higher for those who have less qualification (Bell et al., 2010) and school-to-work transition badly influence young individuals (Dietrich, 2012). Although educational enrolment increases among young people (ILO, 2019), it may not always translate into higher success in the labour market because of quality of education and the link between education system and the labour market (Biavaschi et al., 2013).

Along with education level, labour market experience of an individual is another input into the production of human capital (Green & Riddell, 2001) that affect labour market outcome. The risk exposed by young people increases as they have relatively lower level human capital such as labour market experience or education (Mortimer, 2006). Therefore, lack of years of work experience place youth in a disadvantaged situation in obtaining employment.

Apart from individual characteristics, additional labour supply through immigration may also influence labour market opportunities of young people. The effect of immigration on the labour market outcome of natives is a controversial issue in the field. Although considerable number of studies investigated how wage level and/or employment opportunities are influenced by the inflow of immigrants (e.g., Biavaschi et al., 2018; Card, 1990, 2001; Del Carpio & Wagner, 2015; Dustmann & Preston, 2013; Facchini et al., 2013; Karapınar Kocağ & Kambhampati, 2020; Pischke & Velling, 1997), it is hard to conclude a significant positive or negative effect on the natives' outcome. Within these natives, youth as a special group of them has not been deeply analysed in the literature.

A limited number of studies have investigated how young natives are affected by immigration in the labour market. De Göer (2018) examined if density of immigrants in a county gives rise to a higher probability of unemployment among youth in French labour market. Findings showed that higher share of immigrants decreases the probability of youth unemployment for low skilled ones. On the contrary, Zulfiqar & Akhtar (2016) in their study, which investigates long run relationship between net immigration and youth unemployment, found that an increase in immigration caused an increase in youth unemployment in Ontario/Canada case. In another study, Winegarden & Khor (1991) analysed the relationship between undocumented alien population and youth in the US case. Findings did not show a large impact between these variables, which means US youth were not severely suffered in the labour market due to non-natives. As seen, empirical findings in the literature widely diverges from each other.

The gap between unemployed youth and adult is even wider in Sub-Saharan Africa than the world average. Unemployment rate for adult was 3.7 in 2019. However, unemployment for young people with age from 15 to 24 was 23.8 per cent. The gap between them was twice higher than the world average. This huge gap attracts attention to investigate the determinants and implications of youth unemployment in the region. Youth unemployment in Uganda case has been addressed by limited number of studies in the literature. Lakuma et al. (2016) adopted the Kaplan-Meier estimator using Uganda National Household Survey 2005/06 and Uganda National Panel Survey 2009/10, 2010/11, 2011/12 data to analyse unemployment duration of youth in Uganda. Their findings showed that over a year Eastern and Northern residents experience longer duration of unemployment, although there is no long run regional difference. To the best of my knowledge, this study is the first attempt to econometrically analyse the relationship between the share of immigrants in a given region and youth unemployment in the Uganda case using census-based data.

Youth unemployment is not only an economic inefficiency problem, but it is also likely to cause some non-economic situations such as political radicalisation (Bay & Blekesaune, 2002) and health consequences (Hammarström, 1994). In the case of Africa, Donkor (2021) argues that even if international organisations declare a low rate of unemployment amongst young population in comparison with developed countries, common informal works, underemployment, and poverty via low wages and lack of social safety need to be considered in such comparisons. He also criticises that attitudes towards some fields like art, music, fashion, and drama are not that positive as these fields are considered as hobbies for many African families. If not sorted out, this may not be a national concern but rather a global concern through looting, insurgencies, and terrorism as a result of increased poverty and inequality. Therefore, the author highlights job creation process in all professional fields to be supported by government and private sector cooperation to prevent difficulties on entering labour market.

Limited number of studies in the field and its vast array of effects make the subject more crucial to be investigated. This study aims to shed some light on youth unemployment and immigration nexus in almost an untouched case country, Uganda.

AN EMPIRICAL INVESTIGATION OF YOUTH UNEMPLOYMENT

In this section of the chapter, author offers an empirical investigation of the relationship between the share of immigrants in a given region and the probability of youth unemployment. For this purpose, first, the data set that were utilised for empirical test was introduced. The data set was obtained from the Minnesota Population Center: Integrated Public Use Microdata Series (IPUMS)-International and it covers considerable numbers of observation.

Along with the introduction of the data set, this section also provides information on the methodological preference and reasoning on choosing this particular methodology. Besides, descriptive statistics and intuitive figures were also presented to give a better idea on the selected topic.

This section ends with the findings of the empirical investigation. Because of the nature of the probit model that was utilised in this investigation, coefficients are not directly interpretable. Therefore, the marginal effects were calculated and presented to make the interpretation more meaningful.

Data and Methodology

In order to estimate the relationship between the share of immigrants in a given region and the probability of youth unemployment, the author uses Ugandan data for the years of 1991, 2002, and 2014 which were drawn from Minnesota Population Center: Integrated Public Use Microdata Series (IPUMS)-International that was originally produced by Bureau of Statistics in Uganda.

Age range for young people is defined in a few ways. First, as commonly used by organisations such as UN and ILO, youth is defined as individuals aged from 15 to 24 years inclusive. Although this definition of youth is common in the official statistics, it may depend on country characteristics as well. Cultural, political and institutional factors (O'Higgins, 1997) in each country may influence this definition. Statutory minimum school-leaving age in industrial countries corresponds to the lower age limit (O'Higgins, 1997). Therefore, considering the national structure of Uganda as highlighted by Ahaibwe et al. (2013), second definition of age cohort covers individuals whose age is between 18 and 30 years inclusive. Finally, taking international lower limit and national upper limit, the third definition of youth covers individuals in age group between 15 and 30 years inclusive. This differentiation in age grouping is expected to show whether definition of youth affect the outcome in the Ugandan labour market. Age group intervals of natives and immigrants were given in Figure 1, Figure 2, and Figure 3 below.

Figure 1. Distribution of natives and immigrants across age groups in 1991, percentage
Source: *Author's calculation based on IPUMS-International data.*

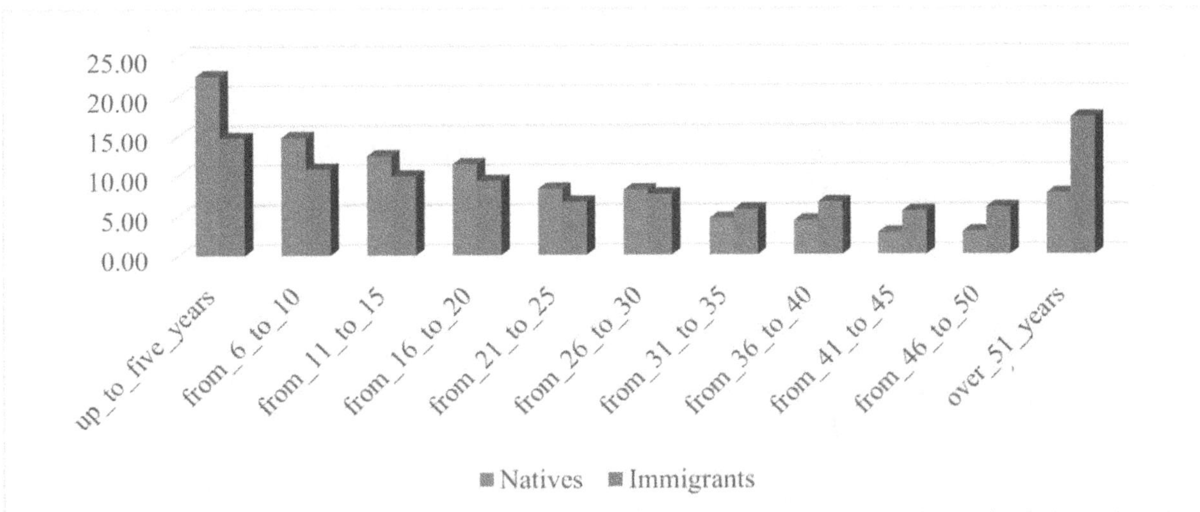

According to the distribution in Figure 1, almost half of the native population was under 16 years old, while it was only 35.5 per cent for immigrant population in 1991. In terms of the percentage of individuals in age cohorts of 16-20, 21-25, and 26-30, native population was higher than immigrants. However, following these cohorts, the difference between natives and immigrants increased and it turned against immigrants. More clearly, the percentage of immigrants in the older age groups was higher than natives. Overall, Figure 1 shows that immigrants were older than natives in 1991.

Figure 2. Distribution of natives and immigrants across age groups in 2002, percentage
Source: *Author's calculation based on IPUMS-International data.*

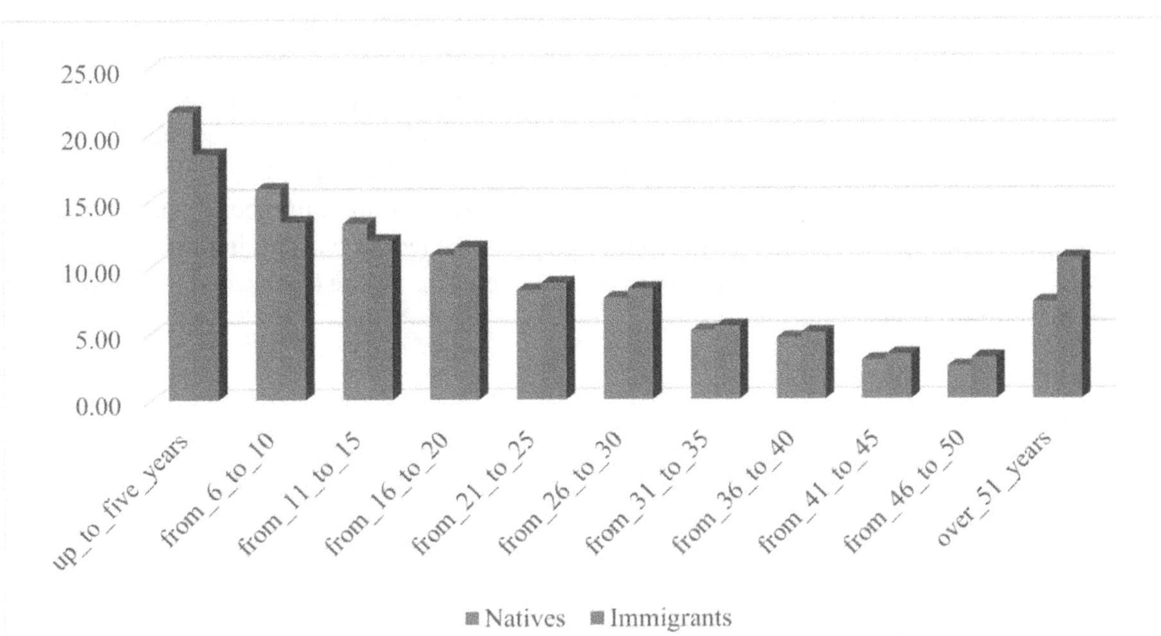

The share of native people who are younger than 16 years old slightly increased in the next census year, 2002 as shown in Figure 2. Yet, the percentage of young immigrants increased remarkably from 35 per cent in 1991 to nearly 44 per cent in 2002. Although immigrant population still represents the older group, the gap between these groups was reduced in this census year.

Figure 3. Distribution of natives and immigrants across age groups in 2014, percentage
Source: *Author's calculation based on IPUMS-International data.*

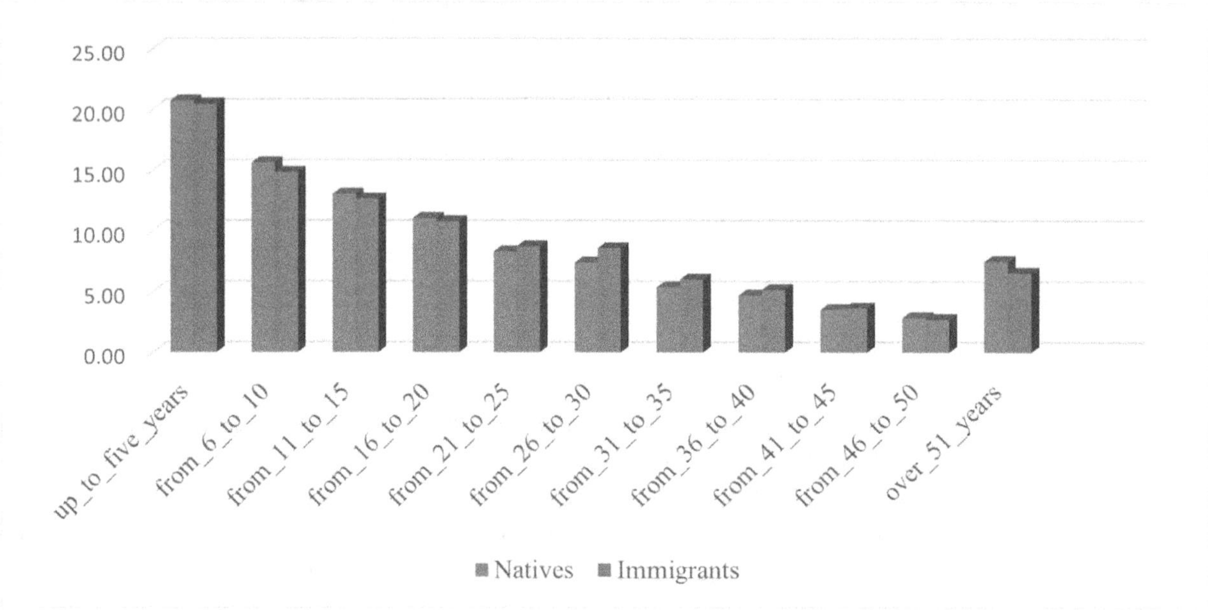

While there was considerable difference in terms of the share of young population between immigrant and native groups in the first two waves of censuses, that difference subsequently disappeared in the final census year, 2014. Figure 3 shows very similar distribution of individuals in both groups.

In this study, being immigrant is defined based on citizenship. If a person is not a Uganda citizen, he or she was considered as an immigrant. The independent variable of interest is the regional share of immigrant in the empirical part of this study. There are four regions of Uganda, i.e., central, western, eastern, and northern. In the calculation of the share of immigrants, total number of immigrants in a given region is divided by total number of population (so, natives and immigrant) in that region. Finally, it is multiplied by 100 to express this variable in percentage term. Figure 4 presents the share of non-Ugandans over census years.

Figure 4. Regional immigrant share, percentage
Source: *Author's calculation based on IPUMS-International data*

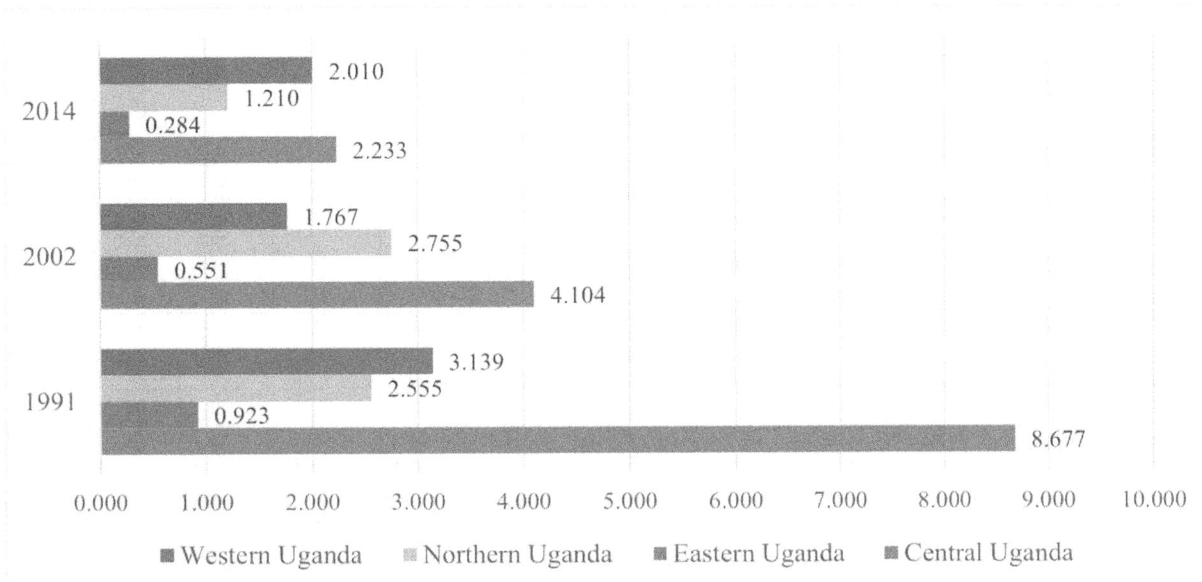

Non-Ugandan population was mostly clustered in Central Uganda over years. The percentage share of immigrants over total population was 8.7 per cent in 1991. However, this share decreased over years to 4.1 per cent in 2002 and 2.2 percent in 2014. Second largest immigrant hosting region was Western part of the country with 3.1 per cent in 1991, then Northern and Eastern region hosted 2.5 and 0.9 per cent of the share of immigrant, respectively. That distribution slightly changed in 2002. The second largest percentage was observed in the Northern region, not in Western region as in 1991. Yet, it reversed again in the final census year, 2014. In all over the census years, Eastern part of the country had the least percentage which was less than 1 per cent.

IPUM-international data set provides information on the employment status of individuals that allows us to identify who is unemployed. Based on that information, a dependent dichotomous youth unemployment variable was generated to use in the analysis. In order to predict this dichotomous dependent variable, probit regression technique was used. So, this approach consists of computing the probit estimates of Equation 1 below:

$$P(U_{ir,y}=1)=\beta_0+\beta_1 IM_{r,y}+\beta_2 X_{ir,y}+\mu_{ir,y} \quad (1)$$

where $U_{ir,y}$ is a dummy dependent variable that stands for unemployment status of young Ugandan i in region r in year y. The independent variable of interest $IM_{r,y}$ is the share of non-Ugandan population in region r in year y. $X_{ir,y}$ presents individual characteristics that are likely to influence labour market outcome of young Ugandan i in region r in year y. Finally, $\varepsilon_{ir,y}$ is error term which is normally distributed with mean zero.

The summary statistics of dependent and independent variables used in empirical estimation in this chapter is presented in Table 1 below. Apart from the independent variable of interest, regional immigrant share, some other variables that are likely to influence young individuals' situations in the labour market, such as marital status, family size, and number of own children in the household were also included in the empirical specification.

Table 1. Summary statistics of the variables of interest

Variable	Label	Obs	Mean	SD	Min	Max
U_int	Youth unemployment: international classification	2149730	.02	.141	0	1
U_nat	Youth unemployment: national classification	2149730	.022	.147	0	1
U_mix	Youth unemployment: mixed classification	2149730	.027	.164	0	1
Imm_s	Regional immigrant share (%)	2149730	2.217	1.737	.281	7.946
Sex	**Sex**					
	Male	2149730	.474	.499	0	1
	Female	2149730	.526	.499	0	1
Yrschool	Years of schooling	2149730	6.17	3.894	0	18
Famsize	Family size	2149730	5.798	3.456	1	46
N_child	Number of own children in household	2149730	.902	1.46	0	9
Age	Age	2149730	21.823	4.675	15	30
Marst	**Marital Status**					
	Single/never married	2149730	.481	.5	0	1
	Married/in union	2149730	.478	.5	0	1
	Separated/divorced/spouse absent	2149730	.035	.183	0	1
	Widowed	2149730	.007	.083	0	1
Religion	**Religion**					
	No religion	2149730	.003	.057	0	1
	Buddhist	2149730	0	.006	0	1
	Hindu	2149730	0	.01	0	1
	Jewish	2149730	0	.01	0	1
	Muslim	2149730	.127	.333	0	1
	Christian	2149730	.854	.353	0	1
	Other	2149730	.016	.125	0	1
Mortmot	**Mortality status of mother**					
	Alive	2149730	.854	.353	0	1
	Dead	2149730	.146	.353	0	1
	Does not know	2149730	0	.009	0	1
Year	**Year**					
	1991	2149730	.205	.404	0	1
	2002	2149730	.33	.47	0	1
	2014	2149730	.464	.499	0	1
Regnug	**Region**					
	Central	2149730	.288	.453	0	1
	Eastern	2149730	.238	.426	0	1
	Northern	2149730	.209	.406	0	1
	Western	2149730	.265	.441	0	1

Source: Author's calculation based on IPUMS-International data.

Moreover, the correlation matrices of three dependent variables that are based on different definitions of youth and independent variables are provided in Table 2. Accordingly, based on the matrix, the low correlations of the variables suggest that multi-collinearity is not a potential problem in the estimation here. As seen from table, correlation coefficients are not very high that would sign a multi-collinearity problem. This finding suggests that the estimation of this model is not likely to suffer multi-collinearity problem.

Table 2. Pairwise correlations

Variables	U_int	U_nat	U_mix	Imm_s	Sex	Yrschool	Famsize	N_child	Age	Marst	Religion	Mortmot	Year	Regnug
U_int	1.000													
U_nat	0.699*	1.000												
U_mix	0.859*	0.892*	1.000											
Imm_s	0.008*	0.013*	0.012*	1.000										
Sex	-0.011*	-0.015*	-0.016*	-0.005*	1.000									
Yrschool	0.048*	0.077*	0.064*	-0.011*	-0.110*	1.000								
Famsize	0.008*	-0.008*	0.001	-0.086*	0.038*	-0.010*	1.000							
N_child	-0.066*	-0.038*	-0.054*	-0.038*	0.240*	-0.176*	0.060*	1.000						
Age	-0.071*	0.033*	-0.012*	0.022*	0.007*	0.005*	-0.185*	0.532*	1.000					
Marst	-0.070*	-0.029*	-0.052*	-0.005*	0.236*	-0.171*	-0.203*	0.483*	0.521*	1.000				
Religion	-0.018*	-0.019*	-0.020*	0.002**	0.004*	-0.032*	-0.022*	-0.011*	-0.005*	-0.012*	1.000			
Mortmot	-0.007*	0.005*	0.001	0.038*	0.011*	-0.057*	-0.093*	0.095*	0.137*	0.104*	-0.002**	1.000		
Year	0.051*	0.041*	0.050*	-0.475*	-0.001*	0.269*	-0.008*	-0.019*	-0.016*	-0.044*	-0.044*	-0.014*	1.000	
Regnug	-0.063*	-0.070*	-0.074*	-0.284*	-0.002**	-0.214*	0.055*	0.023*	-0.020*	0.015*	0.138*	-0.032*	-0.048*	1.000

** $p<0.01$, ** $p<0.05$*

Findings

To estimate the dichotomous variable of youth unemployment, probit model was used. This type of analysis requires to calculate marginal effects for variables to interpret the results. Marginal effects of three models were given in Table 3 below. First model in which international definition of youth (i.e., ages between 15 to 24, inclusive) was considered to construct the dependent variable. The second column presents findings of the model where dependent variable was generated by using national definition of youths who were aged from 18 to 30, inclusive. Finally, the last column presents the marginal effects of the third model which covers national and international age categories in the construction of the last dependent variable.

Table 3. Marginal effects, dependent variable is being unemployed

Variables	U_int	U_nat	U_mix
Imm_s	0.000*	-0.001***	-0.000**
	(0.000)	(0.000)	(0.000)
Yrschool	0.000***	0.001***	0.001***
	(0.000)	(0.000)	(0.000)
N_child	-0.004***	-0.004***	-0.005***
	(0.000)	(0.000)	(0.000)
Famsize	-0.000	0.000***	0.000***
	(0.000)	(0.000)	(0.000)
Age	-0.001***	0.002***	0.001***
	(0.000)	(0.000)	(0.000)
Sex: Female	0.000***	0.001***	0.000
	(0.000)	(0.000)	(0.000)
Marital status: Married/in union	-0.006***	-0.009***	-0.012***
	(0.000)	(0.000)	(0.000)
Separated/divorced/spouse absent	-0.003***	-0.005***	-0.007***
	(0.000)	(0.000)	(0.001)
Widowed	-0.004***	-0.007***	-0.008***
	(0.001)	(0.001)	(0.001)
Religion: Buddhist	0.025	0.019	0.023
	(0.020)	(0.021)	(0.023)
Hindu	-0.005	-0.014**	-0.015*
	(0.007)	(0.007)	(0.009)
Jewish	-0.011**	-0.009	-0.016**
	(0.005)	(0.008)	(0.008)
Muslim	-0.005***	-0.010***	-0.010***
	(0.002)	(0.002)	(0.002)
Christian	-0.009***	-0.014***	-0.015***
	(0.002)	(0.002)	(0.002)
Other	0.001	-0.003	-0.001
	(0.002)	(0.002)	(0.002)
Disable	-0.002***	-0.003***	-0.004***
	(0.000)	(0.000)	(0.000)
Observations	2,149,730	2,149,730	2,149,730
Pseudo R2	0.0886	0.0801	0.0669
Robust standard errors in parentheses			
*** p<0.01, ** p<0.05, * p<0.1			

Negative sign of a variable means there is an adverse relationship between that variable and youth unemployment. The main independent variable of this chapter is the regional share of immigrants, and it is statistically significant over three models. The sign of the coefficient is positive in the first specification, while it is negative in the second and third specifications. However, the impact of regional share of immigrants is very small. That means existence of immigrants in a given region in Uganda does not harm young Ugandans' employment opportunities considerably.

Most of the variables has negative and statistically significant impact on the probability of being unemployed. Nevertheless, coefficients of years of schooling, being female, family size in the second and third model, and age in the second and third model are positive. More clearly, an extra year of schooling increases the probability of youth unemployment; being female increases the probability of being unemployed; an additional member in the family increases the probability of being unemployed, additional year of age increases the probability of being unemployed.

Negative sign of the coefficient of the independent variable of interest might be due to the fact that young natives might be pushed out of the labour force. If they are not actively looking for a job, they will be classified as not in the labour force which would lower youth unemployment. To test this possibility, the same model as above was utilised, but the dependent variable is dichotomous "being not in labour force" this time.

Table 4. Marginal effects, dependent variable is being not in labour force

	U_int		U_nat		U_mix	
Variables	**being unemployed**	**being not in labour force**	**being unemployed**	**being not in labour force**	**being unemployed**	**being not in labour force**
Imm_s	0.000*	-0.006***	-0.001***	-0.002***	-0.000**	-0.006***
	(0.000)	(0.000)	(0.000)	(0.000)	(0.000)	(0.000)
Yrschool	Yes	Yes	Yes	Yes	Yes	Yes
N_child	Yes	Yes	Yes	Yes	Yes	Yes
Famsize	Yes	Yes	Yes	Yes	Yes	Yes
Age	Yes	Yes	Yes	Yes	Yes	Yes
Sex	Yes	Yes	Yes	Yes	Yes	Yes
Marital status	Yes	Yes	Yes	Yes	Yes	Yes
Religion	Yes	Yes	Yes	Yes	Yes	Yes
Disable	Yes	Yes	Yes	Yes	Yes	Yes
Obs.	2,149,730	2,149,730	2,149,730	2,149,730	2,149,730	2,149,730
Pseudo R2	0.0886	0.310	0.0801	0.0735	0.0669	0.160
Robust standard errors in parentheses						
*** p<0.01, ** p<0.05, * p<0.1						

Table 4 presents marginal effects of the model in which the dependent variable is binary and equal to 1 if a young individual is not in labour force. The coefficients of the variable of interest, regional share of immigrants, are negative and statistically significant across specifications. Results indicate that the higher share of immigrants in a given region, the lower probability of being not in the labour force. This means immigrants do not cause young Ugandans to be pushed out of labour force.

FUTURE RESEARCH DIRECTIONS

Youth are an interesting group of population. Welfare of this group has been dealt with by several countries across the world. Protecting and improving welfare of these people find place on the political agendas of the governments. It should be accepted that it has multifaceted dimensions with macro and micro level factors.

In this chapter, the author investigated how existence of immigrants influence employment opportunities of young population at individual level. This constitutes a small piece of a huge range of factors. In this respect, having more indicators on different aspects of youth employment would be useful to get a clearer picture. Additionally, as factors affecting unemployment status may differ based on development level of countries, a comparison findings from developed, developing, and least developed countries would help to understand the difference in terms of development level which could help to offer more specific policy recommendations to implement on the particular countries.

Furthermore, enlarging and more up to date data set would be more desirable in the empirical investigation. Also, further examination on complementarities between young Ugandan and non-Ugandan population in the country would be useful to shed light on labour market opportunities of youth.

CONCLUSION

This chapter overviews determinants of youth unemployment particularly focusing on the effect of immigration. Concerned with relatively higher growth of young population in Sub-Saharan Africa, youth unemployment is one of the biggest struggles for governments and public. Finding effective policies to reduce youth unemployment requires a great deal of effort to understand the roots of the problem. Among several potential reasons, immigration flows might seem an important mechanism to change labour market opportunities of youth. Therefore, in this study, the author estimates the determinants of youth unemployment in Uganda as one of top displaced immigrant hosting countries in the region.

The findings of the chapter suggest that definition of youth matters in terms of the size of the impact on unemployment. The share of non-Ugandan population in a given region does not have a considerable negative effect on youth unemployment. This finding of negligible effect is consistent with studies in the literature that looks at labour market impacts of immigrants on working age natives (e.g., Card, 1990).

Based on this finding, one might relate this negligible effect to another labour market effect of non-natives. That is to say, if they push young Ugandans out of labour force, this will result a small effect on the youth unemployment. Therefore, the author also tested this possibility and found that higher existence of non-Ugandans does not increase the probability of being not in labour force of Ugandan youth. In other words, non-Ugandans do not push native young people out of labour force.

From a policy point of view, even if existence of immigrants in the region do not worsen employment opportunities of young Ugandans, still there is need for improvement of youth unemployment prospect. Schooling seem to be an important factor to tackle with this problem. Therefore, early school leaving should be prevented which would help decreasing entries of insufficient skills into labour market. Besides, local programmes to help needy young people might be applied. This can reduce early entries into labour market as well. Furthermore, government and private sector cooperation to support for job creation process in all professional fields seem necessary interventions as suggested by Donkor (2021).

REFERENCES

Ahaibwe, G., Mbowa, S., & Lwanga, M. M. (2013). Youth Engagement in Agriculture in Uganda : Challenges and Prospects. *Research Series*, *7*(106), 4–20.

Bay, A.-H., & Blekesaune, M. (2002). Youth, unemployment and political marginalisation. *International Journal of Social Welfare*, *11*(2), 132–139. doi:10.1111/1468-2397.00207

Bell, D. N. F., Blanchflower, D. G., Bell, D. N. F., & Blanchflower, D. G. (2010). *Youth Unemployment : Déjà Vu ?* Academic Press.

Biavaschi, C., Eichhorst, W., Giulietti, C., Kendzia, M. J., Muravyev, A., Pieters, J., Schmidl, R., & Zimmermann, K. F. (2013). *World Development Report on Youth Unemployment and Vocational Training*. Academic Press.

Biavaschi, C., Facchini, G., Mayda, A. M., & Mendola, M. (2018). South-South migration and the labor market: Evidence from South Africa. *Journal of Economic Geography*, *18*(4), 823–853. doi:10.1093/jeg/lby010

Card, D. (1990). The Impact of the Mariel Boatlift on the Miami Labor Market. *Industrial & Labor Relations Review*, *43*(2), 245–257. doi:10.1177/001979399004300205

Card, D. (2001). Immigrant Inflows, Native Outflows, and the Local Labor Market Impacts of Higher Immigration. *Journal of Labor Economics*, *19*(1), 22–64. doi:10.1086/209979

Casson, M. (1979). *Youth Unemployment*. The Macmillan Press Ltd. doi:10.1007/978-1-349-16120-1

Clark, K., & Summers, L. (1982). The Dynamics of Youth Unemployment. In *The Youth Labour Market Problem* (Vol. I). Its Nature, Causes and Consequences., doi:10.3386/w0274

De Göer, E. F. (2018). *Are immigrants responsible for France ' s low-skilled youth unemployment*. The Public Sphere.

Del Carpio, X., Özden, Ç., Testaverde, M., & Wagner, M. (2015). Local labor supply responses to immigration. *The Scandinavian Journal of Economics*, *117*(2), 493–521. doi:10.1111joe.12099

Del Carpio, X. V., & Wagner, M. (2015). *The Impact of Syrian Refugees on the Turkish Labor Market*. Policy Research Working Paper 7402.

Dietrich, H. (2012). Youth Unemployment in Europe: Theorical Considerations and Empirical Findings. *Friederich Ebert Stiftung*, 42. http://library.fes.de/pdf-files/id/ipa/09227.pdf

Donkor, A. (2021). *Africa's Youth Unemployment Crisis Is a Global Problem. Foreign Policy*. https://foreignpolicy.com/2021/10/19/africa-youth-unemployment-crisis-global-problem/

Dustmann, C., & Preston, I. A. N. P. (2013). The Effect of Immigration along the Distribution of Wages. *The Review of Economic Studies*, *80*(1), 145–173. doi:10.1093/restud/rds019

Facchini, G., Mendola, M., Facchini, G., & Mayda, A. M. (2013). *South-South Migration and the Labor Market : Evidence from South Africa.* IZA Discussion Paper Series No:7362.

Folk, H. (1968). *The Problem of Youth Unemployment*. Institute of Labor and Industrial Relations, University of Illinois. https://files.eric.ed.gov/fulltext/ED022048.pdf

Gindling, T. H. (2009). South-South Migration: The Impact of Nicaraguan Immigrants on Earnings, Inequality and Poverty in Costa Rica. *World Development*, *37*(1), 116–126. doi:10.1016/j.worlddev.2008.01.013

Green, D. A., & Riddell, W. C. (2001). *Literacy, numeracy and labour market outcomes in Canada.* http://en.copian.ca/library/research/nls/ials/numeracy/english/numeracy.pdf

Hammarström, A. (1994). Health consequences of youth unemployment-review from a gender perspective. *Social Science & Medicine*, *38*(5), 699–709. doi:10.1016/0277-9536(94)90460-X PMID:8171348

ILO. (2019). *World Employment Outlook Social Trends 2019.* ILO. https://www.ilo.org/wcmsp5/groups/public/---dgreports/---dcomm/---publ/documents/publication/wcms_670542.pdf

International Labour Organization. (2017). *Profiling youth labour market disadvantage: A review of approaches in Europe.* https://www.ilo.org/wcmsp5/groups/public/---ed_emp/documents/publication/wcms_613361.pdf

IOM & AU. (2020). *Africa Migration Report 2020.* https://reliefweb.int/sites/reliefweb.int/files/resources/africa-migration-report.pdf

Karapınar Kocağ, E., & Kambhampati, U. (2020). Impact of Immigration on Employment: The Case of Turkey. *Empirical Economics Review*, *10*(4), 291–312.

Lakuma, C. P., Marty, R., & Kuteesa, A. (2016). Survival Analysis of Regional Unemployment in Uganda: Evidence from the Uganda National Panel Survey (UNPS). *African Development Review*, *28*(1), 140–154. doi:10.1111/1467-8268.12173

Matthews, E. N. (1937). Unemployed Youth of New York City. *Monthly Labor Review*, *44*(2), 267–284. https://www.jstor.org/stable/41815043

Miller, D. C. (1941). Youth and National Morale. *Journal of Educational Sociology*, *15*(1), 17–28. doi:10.2307/2262093

Mortimer, J. T. (2006). *Youth Unemployment and Society* (A. C. Petersen & J. T. Mortimer, Eds.). Cambridge University Press. https://books.google.com.tr/books?id=_UwF3QsAuG4C&dq=youth+unemployment&lr=&source=gbs_navlinks_s

O'higgins, N. (1997). The challenge of youth unemployment. *International Social Security Review*, *50*(4), 63–93. doi:10.1111/j.1468-246X.1997.tb01084.x

O'Higgins, N. (2001). *Youth unemployment and employment policy.* Academic Press.

O'Regan, K. M. (1993). The effect of social networks and concentrated poverty on black and hispanic youth unemployment. *The Annals of Regional Science*, *27*(4), 327–342. doi:10.1007/BF01583572

Pischke, J.-S., & Velling, J. (1997). Employment effects of immigration to Germany. *The Review of Economics and Statistics*, *79*(4), 594–604. doi:10.1162/003465397557178

UNDESA. (2020). Inequality in a Rapidly Changing World. In *World Social Report 2020*. https://www.un.org/development/desa/dspd/wp-content/uploads/sites/22/2020/02/World-Social-Report2020-FullReport.pdf

Winegarden, C. R., & Khor, L. B. (1991). Undocumented Immigration and Unemployment of U.S. Youth and Minority Workers: Econometric Evidence. *The Review of Economics and Statistics*, *73*(1), 105–112. doi:10.2307/2109692

Zulfiqar, K., & Akhtar, S. (2016). *Youth Unemployment and Immigration : A Case Study of Ontario, Canada*. doi:10.3968/8413

ADDITIONAL READING

Ahaibwe, G., Mbowa, S., & Lwanga, M. M. (2013). Youth Engagement in Agriculture in Uganda : Challenges and Prospects. *Research Series*, *7*(106), 4–20.

Baah-Boateng, W. (2016). The youth unemployment challenge in Africa: What are the drivers? *Economic and Labour Relations Review*, *27*(4), 413–431. doi:10.1177/1035304616645030

Boutin, D. (2018). The role of internal migration in accessing a first job: A case study of Uganda. *International Labour Review*, *157*(4), 631–650. doi:10.1111/ilr.12123

Broussar, N. H., & Tekleselassie, T. G. (2012). Youth Unemployment, Ethiopia Country Study. *International Growth Centre (IGC) Working Paper*, 1–39. https://www.theigc.org/wp-content/uploads/2014/09/Broussar-Tekleselassie-2012-Working-Paper.pdf

Cartmel, F., & Furlong, A. (2000). *Youth Unemployment in Rural Areas. Work and Opportunity Series.* https://search.proquest.com/docview/62249330?accountid=14511%0Ahttps://ucl-new-primo.hosted.exlibrisgroup.com/openurl/UCL/UCL_VU2?url_ver=Z39.88-2004&rft_val_fmt=info:ofi/fmt:kev:mtx:book&genre=report&sid=ProQ:ProQ%3Aeric&atitle=&title=Youth+Unemployment+

Eichhorst, W., Hinte, H., & Rinne, U. (2013). *Youth Unemployment in Europe: What to Do about It? - pp65.pdf*. http://ftp.iza.org/pp65.pdf

Frenz, M. (2013). Migration, Identity and Post-Colonial Change in Uganda: A Goan Perspective. *Immigrants & Minorities*, *31*(1), 48–73. doi:10.1080/02619288.2012.746864

Lam, D., Leibbrandt, M., & Mlatsheni, C. (2009). Education and youth unemployment in South Africa. In Labor Markets and Economic Development (Issue 22). doi:10.4324/9780203881699

Magelah, P., & Ntambirweki-Karugonjo, B. (2014). *Youth unemployment and job creation in Uganda*. https://www.fao.org/fsnforum/sites/default/files/discussions/contributions/infosheet_26.pdf

O'higgins, N. (1997). The challenge of youth unemployment. *International Social Security Review*, *50*(4), 63–93. doi:10.1111/j.1468-246X.1997.tb01084.x

O'Higgins, N. (2016). *Youth unemployment* (2nd ed.). Routledge Handbook of Youth and Young Adulthood., doi:10.4324/9781315753058

Otaki, O. A. (2003). Youth Unemployment in Nigeria: Some Implications for The Third Millennium. *Global Journal of Social Sciences*, *2*(1), 21–26.

World youth report 2013. (2013). In *World youth report 2013*. doi:10.18356/613c6857-en

KEY TERMS AND DEFINITIONS

Probit Model: This is regression model in which the dependent variable is binary. This means dependent variable takes only two values such as "1" for unemployed, and "0" for employed.

Youth Unemployment: Youth unemployment is the case of young people, whose age is between 15–24 years as defined by international organisations such as the United Nations, are searching for a job, but cannot find a job.

Chapter 7
The Pandemic:
Learning the Way of Continuous Communication With Customers

Nilsah Cavdar Aksoy
Galatasaray University, Turkey

Alev Kocak Alan
Albeka Consulting, Turkey

ABSTRACT

Using primary and secondary data, this case study analyzes the issue KORFEZ must face during the COVID-19 pandemic and demonstrates how KORFEZ may deal with its lack of digital marketing-related initiatives and digital communication weaknesses throughout the pandemic. It highlights the need of making judgments while considering all promotional instruments in marketing, including digital ones, and provides a real-world example that can be addressed from both an academic and a practical standpoint. The teaching case's subject field is marketing, specifically marketing communication. The teaching case may be utilized at the undergraduate and MBA levels. Successful students will be able to improve their theoretical knowledge of strengths and weaknesses analysis, critique elements of the promotional mix in integrated marketing communication, critique a digital marketing strategy, and learn how to lead unusual situations such as a pandemic in terms of marketing-related issues after completing this case study.

INTRODUCTION

KORFEZ is a B2B firm that was founded in Turkey in 1988 and has since provided business solutions for the cement and mining industries. KORFEZ's major business is alloyed steel castings, with an emphasis on heat resistance, wear resistance, and impact resistance. The items are manufactured and supplied according to client designs and specifications, with extra processes including machining, surface treatment, and assembly. Figure 1 illustrates the KORFEZ milestones.

DOI: 10.4018/978-1-6684-6750-3.ch007

Figure 1. History of KORFEZ
Source: Case authors

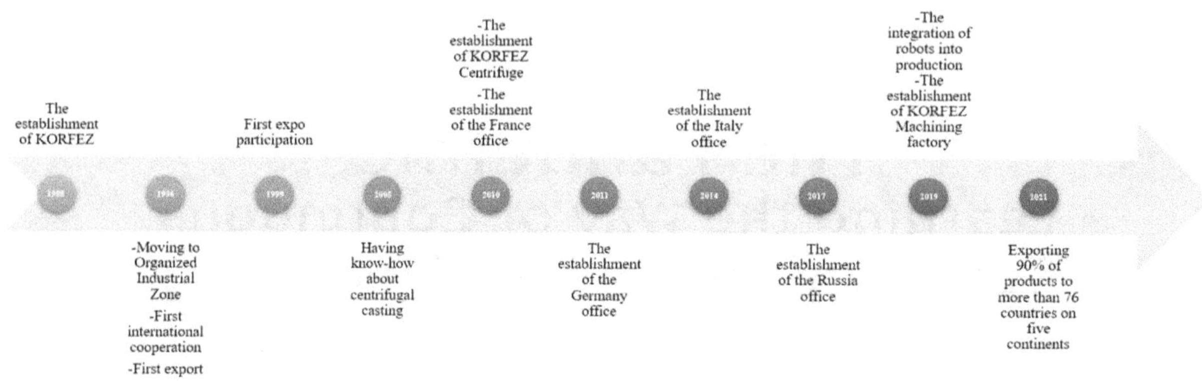

KORFEZ relocated to the Organized Industrial Zone in 1996. The first shipment to Belgium was produced the same year that the first international strategic collaboration was created. In 1999, KORFEZ took part in its first trade show. KORFEZ has centrifugal casting management expertise in 2005. In 2010, as part of its worldwide strategy, KORFEZ created a France office and a sibling business, KORFEZ Centrifuge, to increase its footprint in Turkey. In 2011, the engineering office in Germany was formed, followed by the sales office in Italy in 2014, and the sales office in Russia in 2017. In 2019, robots were introduced into manufacturing, and the KORFEZ Machining plant was founded at the same time. KORFEZ is now operating in the Dilovasi facility, which has a total area of 40.000m^2 and is covered by a 20.000m^2 roof. They now export 95% of their goods to over 78 countries across five continents, and their archive has over 40.000 designs. They can create items with unit weights ranging from 0.5 to 8,000 kgs and have a monthly capacity of 800 tons. According to KORFEZ's General Manager, the company's competitive edge is having the best quality manufacturing owing to its know-how and innovative technology, as well as giving rapid and effective solutions to its clients via its extensive sales network.

The aim of this study is to emphasize the importance and necessity of digital marketing by highlighting a fundamental flaw in the marketing approach in the pandemic, which is an unusual occurrence for a company that has won awards for its local and global production and service understanding and can be described as successful in this regard. This firm is said to have overlooked the need of digital marketing owing to the nature of the industry in which it works, but when the pandemic struck, it had considerable difficulty interacting with customers. Secondary data regarding the firm was included in the research, as well as in-depth interviews performed inside the company. Cagdas Alan, the company's general manager, was interviewed twice in detail at separate periods. First and foremost, an interview was made with Mr. Alan. The goal was to learn about the company's characteristics and marketing strategşes. After the archive was studied, the second step was to conduct an interview in which each of materials used until the pandemic was appraised. The outcomes of the research indicate how strict adherence to established procedures might actually push events to occur at inopportune times. Despite the fact that numerous activities were carried out using the traditional techniques, *digital* was mostly disregarded, and the constant communication provided by digital could not be profited in this way. However, the pandemic has shown that maintaining engagement with the target audience is one of the most important aspects for a company.

BACKGROUND

The Foundry Industry in Turkey

Casting is one of the oldest and most well-established industries of Turkish industry, as well as the whole globe, and is regarded as a necessary component of the country's economy (TUDOKSAD, 2020). In terms of casting production, Turkey has a growing potential. Since 2008, Turkey's casting sector has exported more than 60 percent of its output. Since then, the rate has been steadily growing, and it is projected to continue. When looking at global casting production, Turkey has consistently ranked in the top 10 for many years. Turkey ranks tenth in the world and second in Europe in casting production, according to statistics from 2021 (TUDOKSAD, 2020). In this regard, it can be seen that KORFEZ, on the one hand, continues to operate in a market where local rivalry is fierce, and on the other hand, it has a geographical advantage in terms of maintaining its global presence.

COVID-19 in Turkey

On March 11, 2020, COVID-19 was first seen in Turkey. Turkey has been in the top 10 nations with the most COVID-19 instances since then. The pandemic has had a significant impact on Turkey's business sector, as it has on the rest of the globe, and the way they conduct business has altered dramatically. To adapt to the pandemic, new plans were devised, and several steps were adopted. Quarantine techniques, factory shutdowns, and tighter border restrictions when items are trafficked are some of the activities used within the pandemic scope. Exports in Turkey declined by 17.81 percent compared to the same month the previous year, totaling 13 billion 426 million dollars, according to statistics obtained on the subject. Imports, on the other hand, grew by 3.13 percent over the previous year, totaling 18 billion 821 million dollars. As a consequence, international trade volume declined by 6.76 percent in 2020, reaching 32 billion 247 million dollars, with a 71.3 percent export-to-import ratio. The effects of the pandemic in Turkey are assumed to be the primary cause of these alterations (KMPG, 2020a). According to a study conducted to assess the effects of COVID-19 from the perspective of the business world, a large percentage of respondents (88%) believe that COVID-19 has had a significant impact on the Turkish economy, more than 80% of these company representatives predict a contraction of more than 3%, and 50% of them claim that COVID-19 has had a significant impact on the sector in which they operate. According to a comprehensive examination of the sectors, the COVID-19 situation in Turkey mostly impacts micro and small-scale businesses, with 64 percent of businesses deferring new investment and expansion plans (Business for Goals Platform, 2020). When looking at the direct impacts of COVID-19 on the foundry industry, order cancellation/postponement in domestic buyer sectors was 75%, while order cancellation/postponement in foreign buyer sectors was 74% (TUDOKSAD, 2020). The pandemic, on the other hand, has resulted in a 48 percent order loss rate. Furthermore, 39% of foundries have ceased operations. However, industry leaders stress that there are still many unknowns, and that challenges will persist during the epidemic since casting procedures cannot be done online.

When KORFEZ Faced the Pandemic

Present your perspective on the issues, controversies, problems, etc., as they relate to theme and arguments supporting your position. Compare and contrast with what has been, or is currently being done as it relates to the chapter's specific topic and the main theme of the book.

"And now, COVID-19 has started to be seen in our country as well." said Cagdas Alan, General Manager of KORFEZ, at the meeting on March 11, 2020. On the one hand, they had to redesign the operation of the factory during the pandemic process. At the production facility, serious measures had to be taken to prevent this virus among workers. On the other hand, new decisions had to be made on what strategy to follow to communicate with customers. KORFEZ was a successful company in its field, but it had deficiencies in terms of marketing activities. They planned to invest in marketing activities in that year. However, it did not seem possible to establish continuous communication with the customers based on the existing marketing strategies. When the pandemic conditions came together with the company's lack of a central strategy for alternative applications in terms of marketing, it could be seen that a challenging process started for KORFEZ. "Well, where should we start? We need to design the process down to the last in detail and put it into practice as soon as possible." said Mr. Alan.

"And now, COVID-19 is also being witnessed in our nation," remarked Cagdas Alan, KORFEZ's General Manager, during a meeting on March 11, 2020. On the one hand, they had to rethink the factory's functioning during the epidemic. Serious steps had to be made at the industrial site to prevent the virus from spreading among the personnel. New choices on how to interact with customers, on the other hand, needed to be made. KORFEZ was a successful corporation in its industry, but its digital marketing initiatives were lacking. On that year, they intended to spend in marketing initiatives. However, present marketing tactics did not seem to make it practicable to maintain constant connection with clients. When the pandemic circumstances were combined with the company's absence of a central digital marketing plan for alternate uses, it was clear that KORFEZ was in for a difficult task. "So, where should we begin?" Mr. Alan said, "We need to develop the procedure down to the last detail and put it into effect as quickly as feasible."

KORFEZ's Marketing Communication Strategy Before the Pandemic

KORFEZ Foundry, KORFEZ Centrifuge, and KORFEZ Engineering are three sub-brands under the KORFEZ umbrella brand. To take advantage of umbrella branding, KORFEZ continues to brand all of its initiatives with the same leading brand name (Wernerfelt, 1988; Montgomery and Wernerfelt, 1992). They claim to be able to generate over 40,000 goods, and they are constantly improving their facilities in order to execute this flexible manufacturing strategy. KORFEZ uses a lean manufacturing approach, which entails the systematic removal of waste by all members of the organization in all activities that contribute to the transformation of a product from raw material to finished product, such as design, order taking, and physical production (Worley and Doolen, 2006), as well as an agile manufacturing system, which entails the ability to survive and prosper in a competitive environment by taking quick and effective actions based on a customer-oriented approach. Their most crucial competitive edge is the modern technology they use. They highlight the need of investing in technology, people, and information on a regular basis. Customers in the cement, mining, and energy industries are KORFEZ's target market. With its high-quality product and extensive representative network placement, KORFEZ continues to succeed at an ever-increasing level on its journey to become a global brand.

KORFEZ is the top supplier of big OEM (Original Equipment Manufacturer) firms and certain multinational corporations because of its quality-production timeliness. Most OEM businesses consider KORFEZ to be a gold supplier. Cagdas Alan highlighted in our interviews that they believe that being a reliable supplier to the world's leading OEM firms and global cement companies boosts the value of WOM (word of mouth). As a result, they seek for their consumers to act as brand ambassadors. As a result, the system they built, which was based mostly on direct marketing, could continue to function in the event of a pandemic.

KORFEZ's Marketing Communication Activities Before the Pandemic

Present your perspective on the issues, controversies, problems, etc., as they relate to theme and arguments supporting your position. Compare and contrast with what has been, or is currently being done as it relates to the chapter's specific topic and the main theme of the book.

Before the pandemic, KORFEZ is highly committed to traditional methods in marketing communication. Based on in-depth interviews performed by researchers at KORFEZ, we now give a detailed evaluation of how each marketing communication element was employed prior to the pandemic. Figure 2 depicts the review framework in this regard.

Figure 2. Integrated marketing communication tools
Source: Kotler and Armstrong, 2020

Advertising

Printed media, a prominent advertising tool (Kotler and Armstrong, 2020), was one of KORFEZ's most often utilized advertising tactics prior to the pandemic. Cagdas Alan describes the value placed on printed media as follows: "Being included in sectoral journals is critical for our exposure in the industry. We are aware that these periodicals are read by firms in our sector. As a result, we make it a point to be present in these locations."

Advertisements in numerous national and international periodicals were routinely put in this context before to the pandemic. Figure 3 presents print media examples retrieved from the KORFEZ collection and shot by the researchers.

Figure 3. Some magazines in which KORFEZ has been appeared

Magazine: sektör, DÜNYA

Magazine: CEMENT INTERNATIONAL

Magazine: cemenTürk

Personal Selling

The fundamental promotion method of KORFEZ was personal selling, one of the oldest professions known (Kotler and Armstrong, 2020). They used this tool indefinitely until the pandemic occurs, utilizing a variety of approaches. For instance, the major emphasis of KORFEZ's marketing communication strategy was sales offices. Figure 4 depicts the Germany office. Through these offices, KORFEZ adopted a personal selling technique, emphasizing the need of maintaining close, face-to-face client relationships. Customers' requirements were addressed both personally and via the appropriate institution in this way.

Cagdas Alan summarizes the contribution of using sales offices to them as follows:

"KORFEZ could easily contact clients because to its broad worldwide offices until the pandemic. We were able to supply services such as engineering assistance without interruption. For instance, the technical team in Germany held technical seminars for the businesses. It was feasible for KORFEZ to retain its presence overseas without losing intimate ties."

Figure 4. Germany office of KORFEZ

Below are the images of such technical training that the researchers obtained from the KORFEZ offices:

Figure 5. Technical seminars of KORFEZ

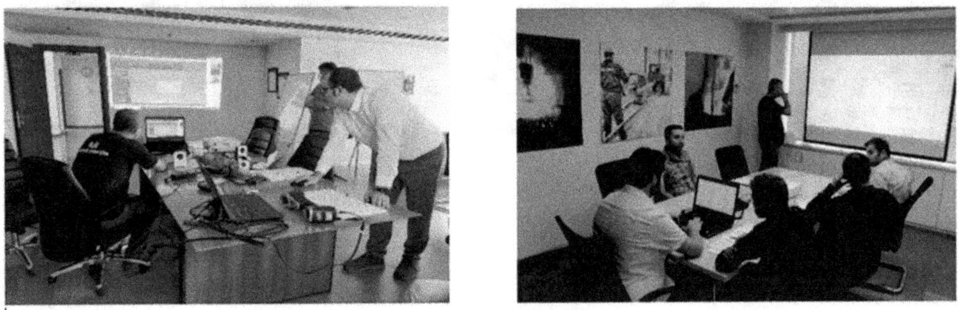

Figure 6. Sales representatives of KORFEZ

KORFEZ also has worldwide sales representatives on staff. This was a team with a strong understanding of technical challenges, familiarity with KORFEZ's goods and services, and strong problem-solving abilities. Those salespeople give on-site help to customers. In this approach, KORFEZ's goods with many technological characteristics could be detailed introduced, and KORFEZ services could be supplied at the appropriate customer's location at the same time. Figure 6 may be considered as an excellent example.

Expos were another avenue for KORFEZ to build strong and deep relationships with customers before to the epidemic. They visited the most well-attended expos in their field and kept up with local and international expos on a regular basis (please see Figure 7). At these expos, they arranged parts and offered training. The major activity they engage in to promote new items to current clients, maintain contact, and obtain new consumers is attending expos. Various actions are done out to actively market their goods and services at the expos, ranging from proper booth preparations to helpful training for participants.

Figure 7. Expos that KORFEZ attended

Public Relations

KORFEZ employed public relations as a major mass-publicity tool (Kotler and Armstrong, 2020). KORFEZ is regularly mentioned in the press, according to the interviews we conducted.

This is how Cagdas explains that approach: "The impact of a firm on society is significant. As much as we value the quality in manufacturing, we also want to ensure that our firm has a positive brand image and a good corporate reputation. One method to do this is explaining KORFEZ by senior management and our expert personnel. Therefore, you'll often find our interviews in trade journals and newspapers."

Here, as another action, we can examine the company magazine published by KORFEZ periodically. KORFEZ shares the developments within the company with its employees through these magazines. The journal cover was photographed by the researchers (Please see Figure 8).

They are very socially sensitive, according to Cagdas Alan. They take care to engage in humanitarian initiatives and are concerned about the environment and nature, he claims. In this respect, Cagdas Alan underlines KORFEZ's attitude as follows:

"The more we place a premium on our company's development and globalization, the more we place a premium on social responsibility. As a result, the KORFEZ brand is always participating in social responsibility initiatives."

Figure 9 is a certificate from a tree-planting campaign campaign example in which KORFEZ took part.

Figure 8. KORFEZ journal

Figure 9. A tree-planting campaign

Sales Promotion

KORFEZ was also using sales promotion. There were two methods they used here. One is to organize events, although not often, and the other is to use various customer promotions. Figure 10 shows the USBs produced for KORFEZ's customers and agents, and an event organized by KORFEZ that brought together actors from the business world.

Figure 10. Sales promotion efforts of KORFEZ

Direct And Digital Marketing

Catalog marketing was the sole instrument they employed for direct marketing. They utilize it to promote their products and services. The feature images of all items and services, as well as short descriptions of each, were presented in these catalogs. They gave these catalogs to their clients in face-to-face meetings or sent it to customer or potential customers. Figure 11 is an example catalog taken from the KORFEZ archive.

Figure 11. KORFEZ's print catalog

When it comes to direct marketing activities by using digital tools, Cagdas Alan claimed that they did not use any method in this regard until the pandemic. The only tool they created was their website but through this channel they did not sell their products. KORFEZ had a website with basic features. For example, although the firm exports to many countries, its website was only bilingual (Turkish and English). This site was not mobile compatible and informative enough. As for social media, the company had an inactive Facebook account. They ignored most digital channels, tools, methods since they believed that digital world does not provide an efficient way of communication with their customers, they should communicate with their current customers face-to-face better and explain their products, services, and technologies in traditional ways more effectively, as Cagdas Alan said. This understanding lasted from the establishment of the company until before the pandemic. In this respect, it is possible to summarize KORFEZ's 'until the pandemic' communication strategy as the close customer contact based on traditional methods far from the digital world.

DISCUSSION

As schematized in Figure 12, although there are many direct and digital marketing opportunities, the main challenge faced by KORFEZ at the beginning of the pandemic was the absence of any digital marketing initiatives.

Figure 12. The option for digital marketing as a promotion tool
Source: Chaffey and Ellis-Chadwick, 2019; Kotler and Armstrong, 2020

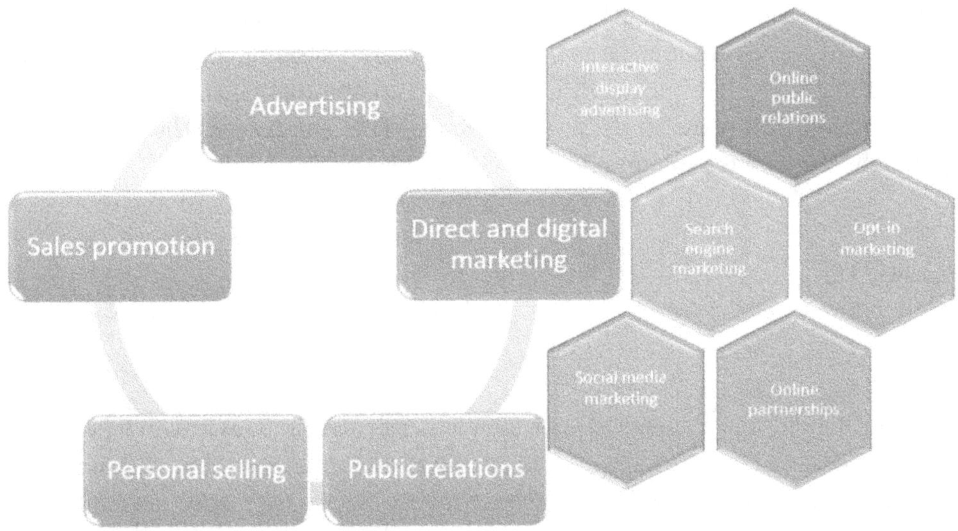

Digital marketing is marketing approach that allows companies to interact with their current and future clients over the internet (Chaffey and Ellis-Chadwick, 2019). The importance of two-way communication in this regard cannot be overstated. In other words, digital marketing has spawned a marketing strategy in which the target audience has a voice and interacts with the business. Customers are not just loyal towards the company but also engaged in digital marketing. In other words, consumers may become marketing message creators, volunteer to assist the firm, provide feedback, and promote the brand to other customers.

Chaffey and Ellis-Chadwick (2019) provide various digital media to implement digital marketing strategies, such as interactive display advertising, online public relations, search engine marketing, opt-in marketing, social media marketing, and online collaborations. Each digital media has some key characteristics, such as providing personalized and customer-engaging ads in interactive display advertising, carrying out various interactive promotional activities in online public relations, enabling individuals to access and interact with the relevant brand in search engine marketing, ensuring customer consent and then reaching them through interactive methods in opt-in marketing, transmitting messages and presenting personalized content to interact with customers in social media marketing, and transmitting content to interact with wider audiences through collaborations in online collaborations. There are several contributions made by each approach that are not confined to these aspects. The most important thing here is to establish an approach for engagement, to make an attempt to contact customers with personalization, and to generate engaged people. Isn't it true that not using these media would put us in a lot of trouble in this age? An unusual event like COVID-19 pandemic would flip everything upside down, even if not immediately.

CONCLUSION

Through the marketing strategy of KORFEZ, a B2B company, this case demonstrates the importance of each aspect in marketing communication, while also demonstrating that we should never neglect the necessities of the age we live in. KORFEZ struggled to communicate with its clients throughout the pandemic and was unable to reach its target audience. This emphasizes the significance of a more integrated approach to marketing communication going ahead.

TEACHING NOTE

Synopsis

In the year 2020, KORFEZ was confronted with the pandemic. Businesses are now facing a new danger as a result of the pandemic. Businesses would be unable to continue operating without being disrupted. Direct sales, for example, would not be employed indefinitely in terms of marketing communication since it requires being face-to-face and developing direct contact. KORFEZ was a brand that relied heavily on conventional means and had no need for a digital presence. Cagdas Alan, KORFEZ's General Manager, was well aware that the company had to cope with pandemic-related warnings as well as digitization, particularly in marketing, at the same time. This case study examines KORFEZ's challenging condition during the pandemic. The case study examines a B2B brand's digitization journey in terms of marketing, specifically how it had to fix its flaws during the pandemic time, how the issue could not be identified until then, and how and where to begin.

Teaching Objectives

Using primary and secondary data, this case study analyzes the issue KORFEZ must face during the pandemic and demonstrates how KORFEZ may deal with its lack of digital marketing-related initiatives and digital communication weaknesses throughout the epidemic. Although digitization is changing the way work is done (i.e., production) in certain areas, it is not reflected in the way work is done (i.e., customer service), which causes significant challenges. Although these negative aspects are not always obvious in the near term, they might develop over time or become considerably more visible in extreme conditions like as a pandemic. This case study highlights the importance of making marketing choices while taking into account all promotional activities.

Furthermore, in terms of dealing with a real-time unusual experimental environment shown by the pandemic, this case study provides a real-world example that may be addressed in tandem with academic and practice-based approaches (Cohen, 2020).

Students who successfully complete this case study will be able to:

- Improve their theoretical understanding of strengths and weaknesses analysis
- Evaluate aspects of the promotional mix in integrated marketing communication
- Evaluate the necessity of a digital marketing plan
- Learn how to manage uncommon events, such as a pandemic, in terms of marketing difficulties

Target Audience

This case study may be utilized in marketing management, integrated marketing communication, digital marketing, and B2B marketing courses at the undergraduate and MBA levels. The case study provides students with a realistic decision-making scenario in which they must build marketing communication strategies based on the company's existing status in an atypical context.

Teaching Plan

Table 1. Teaching plan for the case

Activity	Time (Minutes)
Opening	10
Assignment Question 1	20
Assignment Question 2	25
Assignment Question 3	25
Conclusion	10

Assignment Questions

Q1 What were the strengths and weaknesses of KORFEZ's marketing strategy before to the pandemic? During the pandemic, which of these has grown more critical/less important?

To respond to this question, you may create a conversation environment. Individual responses may be obtained, and students can debate them with one another.

KORFEZ's customer service, capacity to help its customers via training, ability to incorporate artificial intelligence technologies into its production processes, and realization of digitalization in production as a pioneer in its field are some of the company's strengths. The weaknesses of KORFEZ are that it cannot effectively communicate its unique aspects, including all of these strengths, to its target audience on digital channels, they view marketing as a sales-oriented field, and as a result, the KORFEZ team focused primarily on current customers, ignoring digital-related issues such as the need to revisit value definition/propositions and positioning in the digital age. Although KORFEZ is adept at anticipating digital trends in order to digitalize manufacturing, it has yet to accomplish digitalization in marketing. KORFEZ may discover and build brand positioning and values (Keller, 2013) based on digital marketing needs and digital trends in integrated marketing communication as a first step.

"Are there adequate resources available to express the position effectively?" is one of the concerns to be addressed while defining the positioning strategy and making the positioning choice stage. Although KORFEZ's resources are adequate, a fundamental flaw is the company's lack of attention on digital marketing strategy creation, digital marketing-related expenditures, and the long-term communication that digital technologies primarily assure. Offering high-quality goods and the finest custom-based solutions with technical skills based on many years of experience, as well as assisting clients whenever they need it via both conventional and digital channels, may be KORFEZ's value proposition. KOFEZ should have a competitive analysis and a list of points-of-parity and points-of-difference, including comparisons based on digital channels, tools, and methods, and had been able to position itself appropriately by not ignoring the power of digital marketing.

Q2 What method would you use if you were Cagdas Alan to keep in contact with your target audience throughout the pandemic? What would you do first, and how would you go about it?

Based on KORFEZ's pre-pandemic strategy, students may evaluate each aspect in integrated marketing communication components and debate which should be used in the pandemic. Group discussion is suggested here.

Advertising, personal selling, sales promotion, public relations, and direct and digital marketing are all parts of the promotional mix that may assist a firm in developing a marketing communication plan (Belch and Belch, 2005). The brand should first determine its communication goals and then map out a strategy to achieve them. In the pandemic, it is possible to inform the target audience about products/services and pandemic-related actions, persuade the target audience to work based on the needs that the pandemic brings into the business world, and present advertisements that remind the target audience about the unique aspects of products/services, KORFEZ's value propositions, and positioning.

Using methods like personal selling, event marketing, or any other technique that requires face-to-face engagement will be very difficult during the epidemic. Due to the nature of KORFEZ's operational area, sales promotion also does not seem to be particularly readily applied in the pandemic.

In an unusual event such as the COVID-19 pandemic, reaching out to clients and target customers through digital media may be one approach to engage with them swiftly and efficiently.

Q3 What made the pandemic particularly difficult for KORFEZ in terms of marketing? How can you use digital marketing strategies to address KORFEZ's principal deficiency?

Based on KORFEZ's pre-pandemic strategy and the pandemic-related circumstances, students may examine each aspect in direct and digital marketing as an integrated marketing communication element. You can group students into two big groups and they can discuss the topic as a group member.

Direct and digital marketing operations are carried out via interactive display advertising, online public relations, search engine marketing, opt-in marketing, social media marketing, and online collaborations (Chaffey and Ellis-Chadwick, 2019). Of course, although each one has its own set of advantages for businesses (Clow and Baack, 2018), it may not be practical to apply all of them in a pandemic situation. On the other hand, integrating all of them into a business's procedures will be challenging for a company that has never utilized any of them.

When the pandemic was started, the key problem that caused the halt of KORFEZ's ongoing communication was its concentration on face-to-face methods. KORFEZ entirely disregarded internet channels until the pandemic. However, so many digital tools are very essentials for companies from several different industries. Corporate web sites, on the other hand, are an important part of digitally communicating the brand identity and image. KORFEZ did not have a webpage that made all of these details obvious. The initial stage in this process should be to assess the website, create interactive material for social media, and engage in interactive marketing activities that direct people to the website.

Blogs and newsletters are another way that KORFEZ may deliver value through information. An excellent technique will be to publish blogs, bulletins, commercial and technical catalogues online and to send e-mails including all these materials by showing them in a precise design framework and time schedule. It will be the most effective approach to contact and engage with the target audience by describing product/service solutions, identifying trends, and emphasizing features that are appropriate for these trends, guaranteeing that they are followed and shared online.

In a nutshell, consumers and prospective customers of KORFEZ may be contacted by creating informative, persuasive, and reminder materials. The business website, social media platforms, and other digital industry forums may all be useful tools for disseminating KORFEZ-related information. As a consequence, precise information about the brand may be given, increasing brand awareness, improving search results, and increasing social interaction.

What Happened?

When KORFEZ discovered marketing flaws during the pandemic, it opted to start by creating marketing goals that included digital marketing technologies. Mr. Alan opted to outsource marketing tasks and have them completed outside of the firm, and he invested more in digital marketing than he had in the pre-pandemic period. While the required marketing choices were taken and implemented, the focus was to establish a digital identity, and the assessment of the website and social media channels served as the beginning point. The website was updated, a corporate video was filmed, a LinkedIn profile was created, and marketing activities were carried out through the website, LinkedIn, and online sectoral publications. For example, they have made the website available in all of the target audience's languages. They shuffled the things about products and services. The website was created that directs visitors to the sales staff. They employed opt-in marketing to establish an email list at the same time. They also digitized practically all of their marketing materials and shared them with consumers via relevant channels (e.g., online events, LinkedIn page, online supervising, online trainings). Furthermore, they did claim that they had begun to work on SEO marketing.

REFERENCES

Belch, G. E., & Belch, M. A. (2021). *Advertising and Promotion: An Integrated Marketing Communications Perspective* (12th ed.). McGraw-Hill.

Business for Goals Platform. (2020). https://www.business4goals.org/en/the-survey-results-on-the-impacts-of-the-covid-19-crisis-on-enterprises-are-published/

Chaffey, D., & Ellis-Chadwick, F. (2019). *Digital Marketing* (7th ed.). Pearson Education.

Clow, K. E., & Baack, D. (2018). *Integrated Advertising, Promotion and Marketing Communications* (8th ed.). Pearson Education.

Cohen, M. J. (2020). Does the COVID-19 outbreak mark the onset of a sustainable consumption transition? *Sustainability: Science. Practice and Policy, 16*(1), 1–3.

Gunasekaran, A. (1999). Agile manufacturing: A framework for research and development. *International Journal of Production Economics*, *62*(1-2), 87–105. doi:10.1016/S0925-5273(98)00222-9

Keller, K. L., Parameswaran, M. G., & Jacob, I. (2020). *Strategic Brand Management: Building, Measuring, and Managing Brand Equity* (5th ed.). Pearson Education.

Kotler, P., & Armstrong, G. (2020). *Principles of Marketing* (18th ed.). Pearson Education.

Montgomery, C. A., & Wernerfelt, B. (1992). Risk reduction and umbrella branding. *The Journal of Business*, *65*(1), 31–50. doi:10.1086/296556

TUDOKSAD. (2020). *Türkiye Döküm Sektörü* [Foundry Sector in Turkey]. https://tudoksad.org.tr/turkiye-dokum-sektoru

TUDOKSAD. (2020). *Türkiye Dünya Döküm Üretiminde 9. Avrupa'da İse 2. Sıraya Çıktı* [Turkey Ranks 9th in Casting Production in the World and 2nd in Europe]. https://tudoksad.org.tr/turkiye-dunya-dokum-uretiminde-9-avrupa-da-ise-2-siraya-cikti

TUDOKSAD. (2020). *Covid - 19 Pandemisinin Türk Döküm Sektöründe Çalışma Hayatına Etkileri* [Effects of the Covid - 19 Pandemic on Working Life in Turkish Foundry Industry]. https://tudoksad.org.tr/upload/files/T%C3%BCrkd%C3%B6k%C3%BCm_56-s%C4%B1k%C4%B1%C5%9Ft%C4%B1r%C4%B1ld%C4%B1%20%281%29.pdf

Wernerfelt, B. (1988). Umbrella branding as a signal of new product quality: An example of signalling by posting a bond. *The RAND Journal of Economics*, *19*(3), 458–466. doi:10.2307/2555667

Worley, J. M., & Doolen, T. L. (2006). The role of communication and management support in a lean manufacturing implementation. *Management Decision*, *44*(2), 228–245. doi:10.1108/00251740610650210

ADDITIONAL READING

Arslan, A., Golgeci, I., Khan, Z., Ahokangas, P., & Haapanen, L. (2021). COVID-19 driven challenges in international B2B customer relationship management: Empirical insights from Finnish high-tech industrial microenterprises. *The International Journal of Organizational Analysis*, *30*(7), 49–66. doi:10.1108/IJOA-04-2021-2719

Bond, E. U. III, de Jong, A., Eggert, A., Houston, M. B., Kleinaltenkamp, M., Kohli, A. K., Ritter, T., & Ulaga, W. (2020). The future of B2B customer solutions in a post-COVID-19 economy: Managerial issues and an agenda for academic inquiry. *Journal of Service Research*, *23*(4), 401–408. doi:10.1177/1094670520960230

Corsaro, D., & D'Amico, V. (2022). How the digital transformation from COVID-19 affected the relational approaches in B2B. *Journal of Business and Industrial Marketing*. Advance online publication. doi:10.1108/JBIM-05-2021-0266

Fready, S., Vel, P., & Nyadzayo, M. W. (2022). Business customer virtual interaction: Enhancing value creation in B2B markets in the post-COVID-19 era–an SME perspective. *Journal of Business and Industrial Marketing*. Advance online publication. doi:10.1108/JBIM-01-2021-0074

Hansen, J. M., Hansen, J. W., & Madsen, S. R. (2022). Improving how we lead and manage in business marketing during and after a market crisis: The importance of perceived status, certainty, autonomy, relatedness and fairness. *Journal of Business and Industrial Marketing*. Advance online publication. doi:10.1108/JBIM-01-2021-0073

Hartmann, N. N., & Lussier, B. (2020). Managing the sales force through the unexpected exogenous COVID-19 crisis. *Industrial Marketing Management*, *88*, 101–111. doi:10.1016/j.indmarman.2020.05.005

Obal, M., & Gao, T. T. (2020). Managing business relationships during a pandemic: Conducting a relationship audit and developing a path forward. *Industrial Marketing Management*, *88*, 247–254. doi:10.1016/j.indmarman.2020.05.025

Oehmen, J., Locatelli, G., Wied, M., & Willumsen, P. (2020). Risk, uncertainty, ignorance and myopia: Their managerial implications for B2B firms. *Industrial Marketing Management*, *88*, 330–338. doi:10.1016/j.indmarman.2020.05.018

Rangarajan, D., Sharma, A., Lyngdoh, T., & Paesbrugghe, B. (2021). Business-to-business selling in the post-COVID-19 era: Developing an adaptive sales force. *Business Horizons*, *64*(5), 647–658. doi:10.1016/j.bushor.2021.02.030

Yaghtin, S., Safarzadeh, H., & Zand, M. K. (2021). B2B digital content marketing in uncertain situations: A systematic review. *Journal of Business and Industrial Marketing*. Advance online publication. doi:10.1108/JBIM-03-2021-0174

KEY TERMS AND DEFINITIONS

Advertising: Bringing a product or service to the attention of a large number of people using a variety of different forms of media in order to advertise, remind, sell that product/service or provide information about it.

B2B Firm: A firm that targets other companies rather than individual customers when it engages in marketing or sales operations.

Digital Marketing: The sort of marketing in which a company connects with its consumers and maintains engagement via the use of digital methods and techniques in order to provide its goods and services to the market, communicate with said customers, and so on.

Direct Marketing: A kind of marketing in which the company does not go through any third parties in order to present the product or service that is being provided on the market, instead, the company engages in direct interaction with the customer.

Marketing Communication: The combined efforts of businesses to connect with members of their target customers via various forms of marketing tools and approaches.

Personal Selling: Sales activities are carried out by making direct contact with the intended customers via face-to-face interaction.

Public Relations: The coordinated series of activities that are carried out by the company in order to win the support of the public.

Sales Promotion: Incentives used in the near term to capture the attention of the consumer in the hopes of persuading her to buy a product or service and, as a result, complete the transaction.

Strategy: All of the strategies and procedures that companies put into play in order to accomplish the goals they have established for themselves.

Synopsis: A text that outlines the fundamental concepts that will be discussed in the case study as well as the primary focus of the investigation.

Chapter 8
Current High-Powered Challenges and High-Reaching Reforms:
Moving to a New Economic Model Based on Green Energy, Digitalization, and Shock Resistance

Cristina Raluca Gh. Popescu
https://orcid.org/0000-0002-5876-0550
University of Bucharest, Romania & The Bucharest University of Economic Studies, Romania

Arturo Luque González
Universidad Técnica de Manabí, Ecuador & Observatorio Euromediterráneo de Espacio Público y Democracia URJC, Ecuador

ABSTRACT

Knowledge has the miraculous power to advance the United Nations Sustainable Development Goals (SDGs) at an international level, with the notable help provided by courageous reforms due to promoting a new economic model based on quality, green energy, digitalization, and shock resistance. Environmental sustainability relies on collaboration in achieving the SDGs and on communication in making the SDGs a way of living. The unforgettable challenges brought in today's society by the COVID-19 pandemic and the COVID-19 crisis posed even a greater pressure than before to achieve a better and more sustainable future for all, thus placing on pivotal positions the answers for the following questions: "What steps are due to be taken for ensuring affordable and clean energy?" "What role do sustainable cities and communities play in people's lives?" "What does climate action involve in terms of the partnerships for the global goals?" and "What does digitalization implicates in terms of supporting long term positive economic, social, and environmental links in the post-COVID-19 era?"

DOI: 10.4018/978-1-6684-6750-3.ch008

INTRODUCTION

According to the United Nations (UN) Sustainable Development Goals (SDGs) Report published for the year 2021 it has been mentioned that "since the start of the COVID-19 pandemic, policymakers and business leaders have routinely had to make time-sensitive decisions, many of which have life-or-death consequences", especially in the context in which the pandemic has severely and irreversibly accentuated the inequalities between individuals in terms of "health, the society and the economy" (United Nations (UN), 2021, p.1). What is more, the stage where currently the society finds itself is a critical one, which has been acknowledged by specialists as follows: "As the pandemic continues to unfold, and the world moves further off track in meeting the 2030 SDG deadline, timely and high-quality data are more essential than ever" (United Nations (UN), 2021, p.1). Furthermore, based on the Eurostat document on "Sustainable development in the European Union Monitoring report on progress towards the SDGs in an EU context" which was released in May 2022, Paolo Gentiloni – Commissioner, European Commission Responsible for Economy and for Eurostat, emphasizes the importance of the Sustainable Development Goals (SDGs) and stresses the following decisive aspects: "Despite the challenges brought about by the COVID-19 pandemic and more recently Russia's invasion of Ukraine, the European Commission has been focusing on concrete actions to bring tangible progress in the areas of the Sustainable Development Goals (SDGs). Several deeply transformative initiatives have been launched since the beginning of this mandate, such as the European Green Deal, the Climate Law and the European Pillar of Social Rights Action Plan" (Eurostat, 2022, p.4).

Based on the ideas mentioned in the lines above, the authors of this book chapter believe that it is high time for individuals to move to a New Economic Model based on green energy, digitalization, and shock resistance, in the context in which the society in which people live in has become more and more affected by social and economic shocks which generated an increased level of diseases, disasters, inequality, poverty, hunger, and wars at a global level. Also, the authors of this current book chapter display a great concern towards the current high-powered challenges with which humankind confronts itself with and show a tremendous worry towards the process of implementing new and high-reaching reforms due to support the transition to a New Economic Model, knowing the manner in which human nature works and the fact that individuals are more likely to ignore change and to continue the activities without taking any concrete actions in order to change, to improve, and to progress.

In the same line with the elements aforementioned, Mariana Kotzeva – Director-General, Eurostat, stresses in the Eurostat document on "Sustainable development in the European Union Monitoring report on progress towards the SDGs in an EU context" the fact that the most recent figures published by Eurostat in May 2022 will have a major impact on both individuals and entities all around the Globe and "will inspire European citizens, policy-makers, researchers and businesses to undertake sound sustainable development actions, particularly as part of the recovery from the COVID-19 crisis, so that European societies can become more resilient to future challenges" (Eurostat, 2022, p.5).

These days, specialists worldwide have come to the worth mentioning idea that knowledge has the miraculous power to advance the United Nations (UN) Sustainable Development Goals (SDGs) at an international level, with the notable help provided by courageous reforms due to promote a New Economic Model based on quality, green energy, digitalization, and shock resistance. These are times in which Environmental Sustainability relies on the collaboration in achieving the Sustainable Development Goals (SDGs) and on the communication in making the Sustainable Development Goals (SDGs) a way of living. Besides all these aspects aforementioned, the authors feel the necessity to bring to light the unforgettable and the unprecedented challenges brought in today's society by the COVID-19 pandemic and the COVID-19 crisis which posed even a greater pressure than before to achieve a better and more sustainable future for all, thus placing on pivotal positions the answers for the following questions: (1) "What steps are due to be taken for ensuring Affordable and Clean Energy?"; (2) "What role do Sustainable Cities and Communities play in people's lives?"; (3) "What does Climate Action involve in terms of the partnerships for the Global Goals?"; and (4) "What does digitalization implicates in terms of supporting long term positive economic, social and environmental links in the Post-COVID-19 Era?"

Also, the authors take this opportunity to draw the attention on specific keywords that profoundly and irreversibility resonates with today's context represented by the current high-powered challenges that humanity faces and the high-reaching reforms targeted, while looking for solutions to move to a New Economic Model based on green energy, digitalization, and shock resistance, among which can be mentioned: business, knowledge, human resources, innovation, intangible assets, intellectual capital (IC), Sustainable Development Goals (SDGs), digitalization, global economic environment, restart the economy, and the COVID-19.

The authors believe that their work is extremely bold and might be regarded as groundbreaking in the context in which a book chapter on "Current high-powered challenges and high-reaching reforms: Moving to a New Economic Model based on green energy, digitalization, and shock resistance" is due to shed a new light on the manner in which individuals and organizations should focus their efforts in terms of creating a better world for all and of offering constant supports towards supporting the 2030 Agenda for Sustainable Development and its 17 Sustainable Development Goals (SDGs), adopted by the United Nations (UN) in September 2015. Thus, there are several steps taken into consideration in this regard by the authors, as follows:

Step 1: The book chapter centers on finding an answer to the key question (research question RQ1): "What steps are due to be taken for ensuring Affordable and Clean Energy?"

Step 2: The book chapter focuses on better understanding (research question RQ2: "What roles do Sustainable Cities and Communities play in people's lives?"

Step 3: The book chapter concentrates on presenting and describing the implications of the following pivotal question, as follows (research question RQ3): "What does Climate Action involve in terms of the partnerships for the Global Goals?"

Step 4: The book chapter has as area of interest to offer answers to the following vital question, as follows (research question RQ4): "What does digitalization implicates in terms of supporting long term positive economic, social and environmental links in the Post-COVID-19 Era?"

The authors of this current book chapter on "Current high-powered challenges and high-reaching reforms: Moving to a New Economic Model based on green energy, digitalization, and shock resistance" believe that knowledge seems to be the catalysts of the 17 United Nations Sustainable Development Goals (SDGs), since it represents, on the one hand, a source of motivation to all individuals in order to act together for the fulfillment of these noble and important targets, and it provides, on the other hand, a powerful impulse to help people to better understand the meaning and the implications of ending poverty, protecting the planet, and ensuring that by the year 2030 all people will be able to "enjoy peace and prosperity" (United Nations (UN), 2022d). In addition, knowledge, creativity, and innovation are regarded as determining sources of inspiration for the achievement of the 17 United Nations Sustainable Development Goals (SDGs), which can be successfully displayed and promoted at different major international scientific events (Luque, 2021). An international event of utmost importance both for human life preservation and for the maintenance of the ecosystems of our Planet will soon take place at Altice

Arena, in Lisbon, Portugal, between the 27th of June 2022 and the 1st of July 2022, namely the "United Nations (UN) Ocean Conference". This global event which is an integrating part of the series of activities on the subject "UN Takes Ocean Action" – expected to seek solutions capable to "conserve and sustainably use the oceans, seas and marine resources for sustainable development" – will be centered on theme "Save our Ocean, Protect our Future", being "co-hosted by the Governments of Kenya and Portugal", and is believed to take place "at a critical time as the world is seeking to address many of the deep-rooted problems of our societies laid bare by the COVID-19 pandemic and which will require major structural transformations and common shared solutions that are anchored in the SDGs", and "will seek to propel much needed science-based innovative solutions aimed at starting a new chapter of global ocean action." (United Nations (UN), 2022d).

This book chapter on "Current high-powered challenges and high-reaching reforms: Moving to a New Economic Model based on green energy, digitalization, and shock resistance" starts with an introduction in which the authors have successfully managed to present the vision of specialists regarding the importance of the United Nations (UN) Sustainable Development Goals (SDGs), drawing attention to the most recent analysis and the most recent data published by the United Nations (UN) and by Eurostat. Also, the introduction has the power to accentuate the vision of several important figures at an international level, among which could be mentioned Paolo Gentiloni (Commissioner, European Commission Responsible for Economy and for Eurostat) and Mariana Kotzeva (Director-General, Eurostat). In this matter, the introduction presents the importance of the subject chosen for analysis and emphasizes the four research question (RQ) selected by the authors for this book chapter. In continuation, the following sections of this book chapter are represented by: the background – which presents the most representative literature review on the topic chosen for analysis; the main focus of the chapter – which highlights the content of this book chapter, bringing numerous arguments towards the creation of a New Economic Model based on green energy, digitalization, and shock resistance; the discussion and synthesis of results – which intends to reiterate the importance of the subject chosen for analysis and to prompt the most relevant aspects due to be considered by specialists in order to ensure Affordable and Clean Energy, support Sustainable Cities and Communities, take Climate Action in the Post-COVID-19 Era; the solutions and recommendations – which come to call for immediate action and display a variety of opportunities due to be considered by leaders and by specialists on the road to ensure better and more secure lives for all individuals; the future research directions – which have the scope of presenting in what manner this current research can be continued and enlarged in order to offer new dimensions of future analysis and debate; the conclusion – which supports the benefits of the 17 Sustainable Development Goals (SDGs) for our Planet and the ecosystems; the acknowledgment, the references, and the key terms and definitions – which come to complete this scientific work and bring new arguments for its originality and novelty.

BACKGROUND

The background section of this book chapter focuses on drawing the attention on the current high-powered challenges that our society is striving with in the unfortunate economic, social, and political context generated by the COVID-19 pandemic and the COVID-19 crisis, while seeking the creation of high-reaching reforms capable to move the society in which human beings live in to a New Economic Model based on green energy, digitalization, and shock resistance. There are certain keywords that require immediate analysis and among which the authors have extracted the following ones, namely: business, knowledge, human resources, innovation, intangible assets, intellectual capital, Sustainable Development Goals (SDGs), digitalization, global economic environment, restart the economy, and the COVID-19.

The Eurostat document on "Sustainable development in the European Union Monitoring report on progress towards the SDGs in an EU context" highlights the importance of two key concepts, namely sustainability and Sustainable Development (SD), stressing the fact that: "Sustainable development has long been a core principle for the European Union, enshrined in its Treaties since 1997, and a priority objective for the EU's internal and external policies" (Eurostat, 2022, p.22).

Also, the Eurostat document on "Sustainable development in the European Union Monitoring report on progress towards the SDGs in an EU context" addresses the following pivotal question for the social and economic context these days, as follows: "How has the EU progressed towards the SDGs?", while answer offered is meant to display "a statistical overview of progress towards the SDGs in the EU" (Eurostat, 2022, p.9). In this matter, the most recent data available have shown the following key aspects:

Step 1: As presented in the past years, "the EU continued to make the strongest progress towards fostering peace and personal security within its territory and improving access to justice and trust in institutions (SDG 16)", which has brought unequivocal opportunities for individuals and businesses to progress and to further develop (Eurostat, 2022, p.9).

Step 2: Also, it has been noted that "significant progress was also visible for the goals on reducing poverty and social exclusion (SDG 1), on the economy and the labor market (SDG 8), on clean and affordable energy (SDG 7) and on innovation and infrastructure (SDG 9)", which brought tremendous hope in terms of become closer to ensuring individuals better lives and higher levels of satisfaction when it comes to fostering health, social inclusion, equality, and decent lives for all (Eurostat, 2022, p.11).

Step 3: In continuation, "the EU has also achieved good progress towards the goals on health and well-being (SDG 3), life below water (SDG 14) and gender equality (SDG 5)", which has shown the importance of health and the desire to increase the standards of living for all (Eurostat, 2022, p.11).

It is the authors' strong opinion that a New Economic Model represents the key for a better future for all individuals at a global scale. In this matter, the highly-praised solution of creating a New Economic Model calling into question today's practices and coming to support life, well-being, heath, happiness, and synergies amongst the Sustainable Development Goals (SDGs) represents the key looked-for by specialists and leaders worldwide, especially as a result of the COVID-19 pandemic and the COVID-19 crisis. Also, it ought to be pointed out that there is the need of creating this New Economic Model which mainly has its roots in the sustainability barriers that were identified by specialists and by practitioners over the last years, thus offering individuals the possibility to focus, in the Post-COVID-19 Era, much more on the most urgent or on the fundamental needs of the Planet and of the communities they are part of.

Figure 1. Creating and implementing a new economic model seeking to help the achievement of the United Nations' (UN) Sustainable Development Goals (SDGs)
Source: The Authors based on the references mentioned in the book chapter

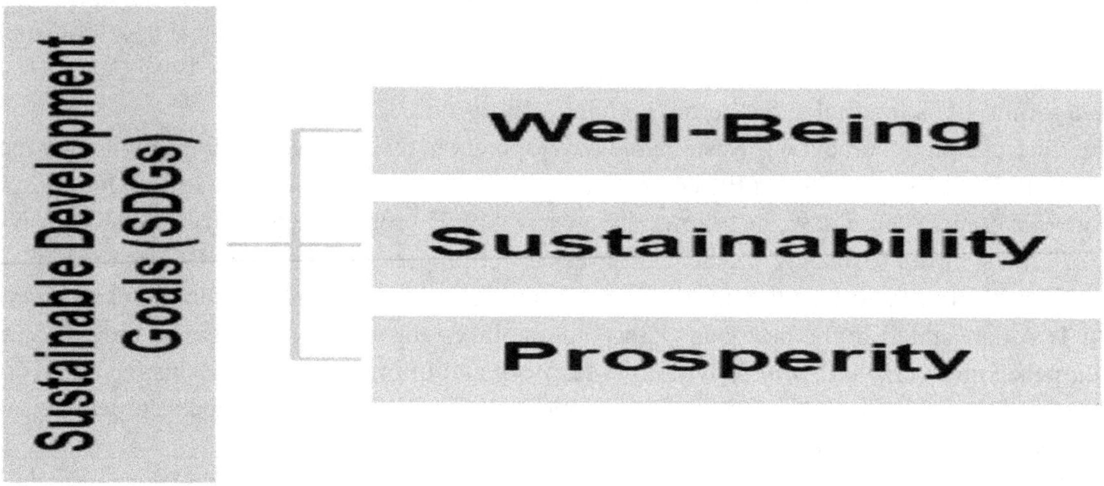

In the same line with the idea of creating and implementing a New Economic Model, the authors have noticed the high-powered challenges that have come to life in the process to create a New Economic Model (see, in this matter, Figure 1: Creating and Implementing a New Economic Model seeking to help the achievement of the United Nations' (UN) Sustainable Development Goals (SDGs)). In this matter, on the one hand, these days, the COVID-19 pandemic and the COVID-19 crisis represent overpowering threats for the society and for the economy, especially when seeking to achieve the United Nations' (UN) Sustainable Development Goals (SDGs) which represent, through their indented outcomes, putting an end to poverty, finding the necessary solutions capable to protect the Planet, and striving to ensure that by the year 2030 all people will get the opportunity to enjoy the well-deserved peace and the well-praised prosperity (United Nations Development Program (UNDP), 2022). Also, on the other hand, in the Post-COVID-19 Era the solution for a bright future is seen in the context in which a New Economic Model is being foreseen and created, with a particular emphasis on "affordable and clean energy" expected to encourage growth and Sustainable Development (SD) for all, "sustainable cities and communities" envisioned to support green energy, green public spaces, digitalization, inclusion, and shock resistance in all senses, and "climate action" counted on fostering the partnerships for reaching the Global Goals in a world that seems more and more inclined to alter the meaning of life, to lack global participation in helping the human rights, and to become more subjective in terms of banning harmful practices for ecosystems and humanity (United Nations Development Program (UNDP), 2022).

In support of the aforementioned ideas, the authors believe that the society in which we live in should rely on the high-reaching reforms to create a New Economic Model. In this situation, the success of the United Nations' (UN) Sustainable Development Goals (SDGs) as well as the achievement of the partnerships capable to support the United Nations' (UN) Sustainable Development Goals (SDGs) in present days and in the future relies on creating strong reforms in all domains. Moreover, in this matter, these reforms should address a wide range of objectives due to be based on all the 17 Sustainable

Development Goals (SDGs), in the attempt to find solutions to support all the implications and all the benefits that these 17 Sustainable Development Goals (SDGs) will come to represent for the economic, the socio-political, and the environmental dimensions, Furthermore, in like manner, creating these reforms should target accomplishing progress in terms of supporting research at all levels, namely: interdisciplinary, multidisciplinary, and trans-disciplinary research for the economic, the socio-political, and the environmental dimensions.

It is the authors' strong belief that digitalization represents a must when referring to reaching the Sustainable Development Goals (SDGs), since digitalization is expected to be part of the present as well as part of the future. Hence, digitalization supporting the 17 Sustainable Development Goals (SDGs) brings to the attention of the individuals and the entities the possibility to make use of the digital technologies in order to change certain business models, while seeking, on one hand, an increase in the businesses' profitability, revenue, global visibility, international recognition, and while striving, on the other hand, to accomplish unprecedented opportunities in terms of giving new meaning to the values of the businesses. In continuation, this is a process which has the power to bring information and knowledge closer to both individuals and organizations, while fostering the benefits of 17 Sustainable Development Goals (SDGs), in a world that has come to rely more and more on the benefits of this phenomenon, namely: unlimited and unrestricted access to information, accessibility, automation, data quality, preservation, integration, interaction, interconnection, searching ability, and income generation.

Green Energy represents a top priority on the United Nations' (UN) Sustainable Development Goals (SDGs) Agenda, and is believed to be one of targets embedded in the United Nations' (UN) Sustainable Development Goals (SDGs) and is known as the energy obtained through the use of natural resources, renewable energy sources, such as sunlight, wind or water. Thus, the goal of this form of energy is to place life and the environment on the highest positions, since this specific form of energy is not harmful for the environment, as the release of the greenhouse gases into the atmosphere would represent in today's context.

The COVID-19 pandemic and the COVID-19 crisis have represented tremendous challenges for today's society and for today's economy. Shock resistance represents the desiderate for the future in the context designed to accomplish and to support the United Nations' (UN) Sustainable Development Goals (SDGs), in a world dominated by the effects generated by the COVID-19 pandemic and the COVID-19 crisis. In addition, it has been remarked the danger represented, in this context, by the systemic resistance to change, to novelty, and to progress (known as "business-as-usual") which should be fully avoided in the Post-COVID-19 Era, since it would only promote chaos, insecurity, and uncertainty, while generating a severe decline in the individuals' standards of living and businesses profitability and success. Nevertheless, a shock resistant society and a shock resistant economy are robust and inclusive systems capable to increase the utilization of information, value the benefits of knowledge, support the Sustainable Development Goals (SDGs) frameworks that "leave now one behind" and that fight for the "general good" of all individuals in the present days and in the future.

Furthermore, the synergies amongst the Sustainable Development Goals (SDGs) are extremely powerful. Hence, the world people live in these days seeks new meanings for committeemen, development, environment, equality, life, love, health, sustainability, sustainable development (SD), power, preservation, progress, profit, and well-being, which are due to be formed and to be promoted only in the context in which everyone has the opportunity to participate and to have the voice heard during the process. Also, according to the United Nations' (UN) the Synergies amongst the Sustainable Development Goals (SDGs) are due to be encountered in a cross-impact matrix that is born from the interaction of all the objectives considered to be accomplished (United Nations Development Program (UNDP), 2022). However, this cross-impact matrix represents an essential tool that facilitates the process of better understanding the manner in which the individuals and the entities can help in order to give life to the targets proposed, in the context in which sustainability requires committed actions from all involved parties in a society.

According to the Organization for Economic Co-operation and Development (OECD) reputed specialists, "the Sustainable Development Goals (SDGs) are broad and ambitious, calling on all countries – be they upper, middle or low income – to make tangible improvements to the lives of their citizens", since these particular "goals social, environmental and economic aspects", while the importance of these targets resides in all the nations capacity to value, at all times and in all given circumstances, their "existing knowledge" and their "unique tools and experience" in order to ensure the great success of the 2030 Agenda for Sustainable Development (SD) (Organization for Economic Co-operation and Development (OECD), 2022a).

MAIN FOCUS OF THE CHAPTER

This current section that constitutes, in essence, the main focus of the current book chapter presents the main part of the scientific work entitled the "Current high-powered challenges and high-reaching reforms: moving to a New Economic Model based on green energy, digitalization, and shock resistance", has the following aspects to be presented: (a) has the purpose of centering on the SDG 7 "Affordable and clean energy" – which is believed to be "is strongly influenced by the measures taken in response to the COVID-19 pandemic and the related restrictions on public life and lower economic activity" (Eurostat, 2022, p.12); (b) has the objective of addressing the SDG 11 "Sustainable cities and communities" – which is believed to "show largely favorable developments concerning the quality of life in cities and communities, whereas the picture is more mixed for sustainable mobility and environmental impacts" (Eurostat, 2022, p.13), while seeking green energy, digitalization (smart cities), inclusive ways of living, and shock resistance; (c) has the target of analyzing the SDG 13 "Climate action" – which is believed to "moderately positive, even though the trends in the monitored areas – climate mitigation, adaptation and finance – show a somewhat mixed picture" (Eurostat, 2022, p.14); and (d) has the scope of finding solutions for the SDG 17 "Partnerships for the goals" (Eurostat, 2022, p.15).

Figure 2. Current high-powered challenges in creating and implementing a new economic model seeking to help the achievement of the United Nations' (UN) Sustainable Development Goals (SDGs)
Source: The Authors based on the references mentioned in the book chapter

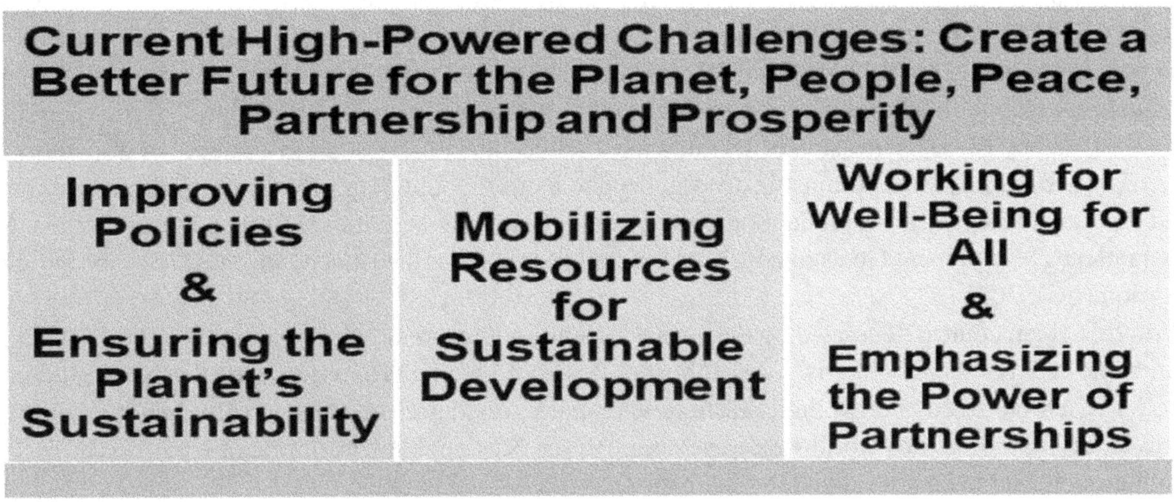

Hence, knowledge and innovation are regarded as crucial when it comes to help today's communities prosper and aid the creation of partnerships capable to bring together the valuable results and the inestimable work of specialists from the business sectors and the education sectors (research centers, research institutes, and universities) (European Union (EU) & European Institute for Innovation and Technology (EIT), 2022) (see, in this matter, Figure 2: Current High-Powered Challenges in Creating and Implementing a New Economic Model seeking to help the achievement of the United Nations' (UN) Sustainable Development Goals (SDGs)). In this matter, there are several questions that ought to be addressed in order to foster stronger communities based on knowledge and innovation, as follows: (a) In what way the creation of innovative products and novel services can bring change in the Post-COVID-19 Era and can facilitate the creation of bold reforms capable to support life, health, well-being, and sustainability, in a world that suffers from accentuated disequilibrium in terms of climate change?; (b) In what manner is entrepreneurship expected to facilitate the creation of new businesses in the context in which a new generation of entrepreneurs are expected to be trained in the spirit of Active Reforms, Healthy Living, and Sustainable Development (SD)?; and (c) How can cooperation and partnerships between businesses, research centers, research institutes and organizations, and universities is expected to give birth to the largest innovation network ever encountered, in order to make the Sustainable Development Goals (SDGs) reality and act in the benefit of us all? (European Union (EU) & European Institute for Innovation and Technology (EIT), 2022).

The document entitled "Halfway to 2030: UNECE report shows we must accelerate progress to achieve SDGs in the region" published on the 25th of March 2022 by the United Nations Economic Commission for Europe (UNECE) presents "the halfway mark between the adoption and finish line of the 2030 Agenda for Sustainable Development" and showed the fact that both the Covid-19 pandemic and "the war in Ukraine still to be assessed" have sadly slowed down the rhythm required in order to obtain the United Nations' (UN) Sustainable Development Goals (SDGs) (United Nations Economic Commission for Europe (UNECE), 2022).

It ought to be mentioned that on the 23rd of May 2022, in Brussels, the European Commission (EC) (Eurostat) published the 2022 report on the Sustainable Development Goals (SDGs) in the European Union (EU), which represented the moment in which Paolo Gentiloni (Commissioner, European Commission Responsible for Economy and for Eurostat) mentioned the following crucial aspects: "Europe is facing its second 'black swan' event in three years. But while managing the impact of the economic shock caused by Russia's invasion of Ukraine must not lead us to lose sight of our goal of transforming the EU's economic model. It must instead galvanize us to redouble our efforts to boost our resilience and the sustainability of our production processes and everyday activities. In this collective effort, the Sustainable Development Goals remain both our compass and our measure of success" (European Commission (EC), 2022a).

In this given context generated by the global instability which has mainly its roots in the COVID-19 pandemic and the COVID-19 crisis, the authors of this book chapter propose moving to a New Economic Model based on green energy, digitalization, and shock resistance, in order to offer better chances to individuals and to entities worldwide to accomplish the Sustainable Development Goals (SDGs). The main aspects due to be considered in this matter are the following ones:

Step 1: The first step is finding an answer to the following key question, namely: "What are the steps needed in order to support Affordable and Clean Energy for all individuals, in all areas?" It is the authors' opinion that this objective is very bold, especially due to the existing discrepancies' between the way in which individuals perceive life priorities as well as the way in which people regard the idea of having access to affordable, reliable, sustainable and modern energy for all, all around the Globe. The inequalities between individuals have generated serious differences in terms of prioritizing the daily problems with which individuals have come to confront themselves. As it can be seen from the most recent statistics, some people are having absolutely no access to electricity due to the life conditions that they have and, also, due to the economic and the social environment they are forced to live in. Nevertheless, it ought to be mentioned that there is a growing demand for cheap energy, especially in the context in which there are numerous groups of individuals worldwide who cannot afford minimum life conditions and a decent way of living and of supporting themselves (Luque & Jiménez, 2019). Also, as the global population continues to rise, the climate system will become more at risk mainly because of the harm caused to human lives and to the environment as a whole by the "fossil fuels and the increase of greenhouse gas emissions" (United Nations (UN), 2022a). The authors envision a world focused on ensuring climate balance and stability, governed by a great concern towards the health of the environment and the well-being of individuals, in an era which encourages alternative energy sources based on renewable energy, starting from the assumption that there is still the need for "a substantial increase in the production of renewable energy across the world" in order to be able to achieve the Sustainable Development Goals (SDGs) (United Nations (UN), 2022a).

Step 2: The second step is finding an answer to the following key question, namely: "What roles do Sustainable Cities and Communities play in people's lives and how can Sustainable Cities and Communities be created in the Post-COVID-19 Era?" The authors promote their vision about creating a New Economic Model based on green energy, digitalization, and shock resistance, in the context of building and supporting Sustainable Cities and Communities, which are expected to make the human settlements safe places for living, in a world governed by reforms capable to foster an inclusive, safe, resilient and sustainable way of living for all. The most recent statistics on building and supporting Sustainable Cities and Communities in the Post-COVID-19 Era have managed to display the necessity to create modern, smart, and sustainable cities as a result of the constant increase in the world's population (United Nations (UN), 2022a). These are times in which the authors show a great worry in terms of building and supporting Sustainable Cities and Communities since the current living conditions are not always the best alternative for life for all individuals in order to be able to survive and to prosper. The New Economic Model envisioned by the authors is in accordance with the Sustainable Development Goals (SDGs) and puts an emphasis on creating novel, modern, intelligent planning, in the context in which this accent should be placed on healthier ways of living governed by green living conditions which place the environment on the top positions.

Step 3: The third step is finding an answer to the following key question, namely: "What does Climate Action involve in terms of the partnerships for the Global Goals?" The Climate Action is in a strong connection with the first two steps mentioned in the lines above, since according to the authors offering Affordable and Clean Energy to all individuals worldwide and creating and supporting Sustainable Cities and Communities are part of the process that ensures taking coherent Climate Action in the Post-COVID-19 Era (United Nations (UN), 2022a). The authors of this book chapter would like to draw the attention to the United Nations (UN) Secretary-General António Manuel de Oliveira Guterres video message on the launch of the third Intergovernmental Panel on Climate Change (IPCC) report, in New York which took place on the 4th of April 2022, which states the following aspects: "This report of the Intergovernmental Panel on Climate Change is a litany of broken climate promises. It is a file of shame, cataloguing the empty pledges that put us firmly on track towards an unlivable world" (United Nations (UN), 2022b). Of great concern are, also, the following remarks, namely: "We are on a fast track to climate disaster. Major cities under water. Unprecedented heat waves. Terrifying storms. Widespread water shortages. The extinction of a million species of plants and animals. This is not fiction or exaggeration. It is what science tells us will result from our current energy policies. We are on a pathway to global warming of more than double the 1.5°C limit agreed in Paris. Some Government and business leaders are saying one thing, but doing another. Simply put, they are lying. And the results will be catastrophic. This is a climate emergency" (United Nations (UN), 2022b).

Step 4: The fourth step is finding an answer to the following key question, namely: "What does digitalization implicates in terms of supporting long term positive economic, social and environmental links in the Post-COVID-19 Era?" The authors of this book chapter believe that the success of accomplishing the Sustainable Development Goals (SDGs) is to be found in creating and supporting long term partnerships for sustainability and for sustainable development. In this matter, the United Nations (UN) Secretary-General António Manuel de Oliveira Guterres shows the importance of addressing the Sustainable Development Goals (SDGs) with a unitary vision, as follows: The "IPCC report is an atlas of human suffering and a damning indictment of failed climate leadership. With fact upon fact, this report reveals how people and the planet are getting clobbered by climate change. Nearly half of humanity is living in the danger zone – now. Many ecosystems are at the point of no return – now. Unchecked carbon pollution is forcing the world's most vulnerable on a frog march to destruction – now. The facts are undeniable. This abdication of leadership is criminal. The world's biggest polluters are guilty of arson of our only home. It is essential to meet the goal of limiting global temperature rise to 1.5 degrees. Science tells us that will require the world to cut emissions by 45 percent by 2030 and achieve net zero emissions by 2050. But according to current commitments, global emissions are set to increase almost 14 per cent over the current decade. That spells catastrophe. It will destroy any chance of keeping 1.5 alive. Today's report underscores two core truths. First, coal and other fossil fuels are choking humanity.

(…)The second core finding from this report is slightly better news: investments in adaptation work. Adaptation saves lives. As climate impacts worsen – and they will – scaling up investments will be essential for survival" (United Nations (UN), 2022c).

The authors acknowledge in this section the importance of the four steps presented and analyzed in the lines above and exhibit a genuine concern for promoting the drivers of climate action and "climate innovation in Europe and beyond", in the attempt to put on view the benefits and the opportunities that "a strong, digital Europe" might have to offer to both the present and the future generations (European Union (EU) & European Institute for Innovation and Technology (EIT), 2022). Also, in the spirit of the aspects laid out in the lines above, the authors appreciate and recognize the implications of "joint research initiatives and EU action to promote" research and innovation especially when building a New Economic Model based on green energy, digitalization, and shock resistance (European Commission (EC), 2022b). In this context, the European Commission (EC) published in the year 2014 the "Commission Regulation (EU) No 316/2014 of 21 March 2014 on the application of Article 101(3) of the Treaty on the Functioning of the European Union to categories of technology transfer agreements Text with EEA relevance" which mentions the following elements: "Technology transfer agreements concern the licensing of technology rights. Such agreements will usually improve economic efficiency and be pro-competitive as they can reduce duplication of research and development, strengthen the incentive for the initial research and development, spur incremental innovation, facilitate diffusion and generate product market competition" (European Commission (EC), 2014, p.17). Hence, competitiveness resides in the individuals and the entities capacity to foster research and innovation – due to be advanced by the international "innovation-friendly legislation", in a world that relies on healthy development and that depends on the success of the Sustainable Development Goals (SDGs) (European Commission (EC), 2022b). Nevertheless, while referring to the case of the support due to be received at the European level in terms of development, innovation and research, the European University Association (EUA) is renowned for its programs that are meant to invest "in a sustainable and inclusive future", on the road "to foster resilience, accelerate the green and digital transitions" at a local and at a global level (European University Association (EUA), 2022).

All in all, Paolo Gentiloni (Commissioner, European Commission Responsible for Economy and for Eurostat) delivered a speech on the 16th of June 2022, in Brussels, at the Eurogroup press conference, in which the following vital points were highlighted, as follows: humanity is "navigating troubled waters" these days "because of the Russian invasion of Ukraine"; "and this is casting a shadow over our economy – at the global level, and in Europe, in particular", which is testing "the resilience of our economy"; moreover, the society in which we live in has "to use the lessons learned – thanks to our strong policy response and unity showed during the COVID-19 crisis"; furthermore, "the latest figures from Eurostat point to a stronger-than-expected growth in the first quarter, at 0.6% in the euro area, 0.7% in the Union as a whole" (European Commission (EC), 2022c).

The Organization for Economic Co-operation and Development (OECD) document on "The Sustainable Development Goals: An overview of relevant OECD analysis, tools and approaches" brings to light the need to focus on the targets due to be accomplished while having "a holistic plan for action on all fronts – social, economic and environmental" and "emphasizes" the importance of centering all the actions due to be taken on the necessity of reaching "well-being and sustainability in all countries", based on "the universal nature of the Sustainable Development Goals (SDGs)" (Organization for Economic Co-operation and Development (OECD), 2022b, p.3; Popescu, 2021, 2022a,b,c).

In this matter, it ought to be pointed out the Organization for Economic Co-operation and Development (OECD) visionary specialists believe that the success of the 2030 Agenda for Sustainable Development (SD) can be accomplished by following closely and with profound dedication two sets of actions, namely: (a) first of all, "a strong track record in policy work with developed and developing countries", and (b) second of all, "measures and systems for monitoring performance" (Organization for Economic Co-operation and Development (OECD), 2022a). What is more, the authors have noticed that there is a great opportunity that might be found in the individuals and in the entities desire to accomplish the objectives which are part of the 2030 Agenda for Sustainable Development (SD) and this magnificent opportunity is represented by the organizations ability in creating different types of partnerships, as mentioned in the lines below: the "OECD partnerships are creating synergies among private and public, domestic and international, and donor and developing country resources to provide countries with a strong support mechanism on which to build towards a better future" (Organization for Economic Co-operation and Development (OECD), 2022a). Furthermore, the Organization for Economic Co-operation and Development (OECD) Council highlighted on 13th December 2016, in the document on "Better Policies for 2030. An OECD Action Plan on the Sustainable Development Goals" – which was built on an earlier draft presented at the Organization for Economic Co-operation and Development (OECD) Ministerial Council Meeting (that took place between the 1st and the 2nd of June 2016) – the fact that there is a tremendous pressure in "identifying the OECD's strengths and assets in relation to the 2030 Agenda", which includes the following main aspects: (a) "Assessing economic, social and environmental progress through measures going beyond GDP (e.g. multidimensional well-being)"; (b) "Generating solid evidence and recommendations on global public goods and "bads", and relevant national efforts, with a focus on OECD countries and Key Partners"; (c) "Measuring and improving development finance by helping governments mobilize the broad suite of financial resources (taxes, foreign and domestic investments, remittances, aid and philanthropy) that will be necessary to achieve the SDGs in many countries"; (d) "Enhancing policy and institutional coherence by identifying policy interactions, trade-offs and synergies across economic, social and environmental areas; and considering trans-boundary and intergenerational effects"; (e) "Dismantling intellectual and policy silos to undertake integrated diagnostics and provide policy advice to both Member and partner countries"; (f) "Facilitating the exchange of knowledge and data across countries through global fora, expert groups, peer review mechanisms, inclusive partnerships, and open data platforms."; and (g) "Supporting sector-specific initiatives and partnerships, some of which are being tailored to support a broader range of countries in the achievement of specific Goals, and are helping to strengthen capacity in countries" (Organization for Economic Co-operation and Development (OECD), 2016, pp.3-4). All the aspects mentioned in the lines above have the purpose of demonstrating that being able to create a better future for all is to be found in all individuals as well as in all entities at a wide level, and the actions that are due to be taken need to rely solely on good intentions, on the relentless desire to be of help and to participate in the process of creating a better world for the present and for the future generations. Besides all these, the connections between the current high-powered challenges generated by the most recent economic and social shocks, and the need for the creation of high-reaching reforms capable to move our society to the next level and to a new dimension – namely the one represented by a New Economic Model based on green energy, digitalization, and shock resistance, are extremely clear in today's general context and have come to support the following three questions addressed by the Organization for Economic Co-operation and Development (OECD) at the Meeting of the Members of the Council on the 2030 Agenda for Sustainable Development that took place on the 1st of March 2021: (a) "What can countries do to leverage finance to address the public health dimension of the 2030 Agenda amidst the COVID-19 crisis, and ensure human security for all, including the most vulnerable?"; (b) "How can countries collectively address the "scissor-effect" of SDG financing, which has been further magnified by the COVID-19 crisis? What can the OECD do to support such efforts?"; and (c) "How can countries better mobilize and align public and private resources with the 2030 Agenda as a framework for long-term sustainable and inclusive recovery? Along the investment chain, how can countries ensure policy coherence across domestic and international financing strategies?" (Organization for Economic Co-operation and Development (OECD), 2021, p.2).

DISCUSSION AND SYNTHESIS OF RESULTS

The discussion and synthesis of results section of this book chapter presents the most important outcomes regarding the theme chosen for examination.

According to the great philosopher Aristotle happiness should be placed at the core of individuals and the Planet's existence, as follows: "Happiness is the meaning and the purpose of life, the whole aim and end of human existence." (Royal Government of Bhutan, 2012, p.8). In the same line with these ideas, Alicia Bárcena – Executive Secretary, Economic Commission for Latin America and the Caribbean (ECLAC), points out in the "Foreword" section of the document on "The 2030 Agenda for Sustainable Development in the New Global and Regional Context: Scenarios and Projections in the Current Crisis", presented in Santiago, that: "In this framework, the 2030 Agenda for Sustainable Development and the 17 Sustainable Development Goals (SDGs) are more important and relevant than ever, because they form the foundation established by the international community in 2015 for advancing towards a new development model capable of eradicating extreme poverty, generating quality employment, ensuring healthy lives and promoting well-being for all at all ages, and tackling the climate crisis leaving no one behind" (Economic Commission for Latin America and the Caribbean (ECLAC), 2020, p.9).

First of all, the New Economic Model due to be created and implemented in the Post-COVID-19 Era is centered on frameworks capable to offer long term benefits to individuals and to the Planet, since it focuses on the new Sustainable Development Goals (SDGs). The idea of a New Economic Model that comes to ensure life and to foster health and well-being for all, has been promoted by the authors of this book chapter in accordance to other renown scientific works due to be encountered at an international level, among which should be mentioned the ones belonging to World Economic Forum (WEF), as part of the Sustainable Development Impact Summit (World Economic Forum (WEF), 2019). Hence, sustainability both for the individuals and for markets can be found in the progress that the human indicators are registering from one time period to another, and the COVID-19 pandemic and the COVID-19 crisis have both represented consistent arguments to find new solutions to the rapid environmental degradation that has been noted in the last decades (Luque, 2022). This New Economic Model relies on finding massive sources of financing the Sustainable Development (SD), which should be integrated with the sustainability Global Goals and with the benefits of individuals and corporations responsibility towards achieving a better life for us all.

Second of all, the New Economic Model due to be created and implemented in the Post-COVID-19 Era is based on governmental decisions that have to support programs capable to offer clean and green energy for all, digitalization, and shock resistance solutions in terms of creating new markets and novel technologies. In this matter, the actions that must be taken in order to be able to cope with the current "changes" which "affected the economic, social and environmental dynamics" require preserving "the comprehensive spirit of the 2030 Agenda" and stresses that: "Only by mobilizing resources to finance the achievement of the SDGs, enhancing implementation at the national and local levels, institution-building, problem-solving via international cooperation and the uptake of science, innovation and technology can we concentrate on the poorest and most vulnerable to leave no one behind" (Economic Commission for Latin America and the Caribbean (ECLAC), 2020, pp.9-10).

SOLUTIONS AND RECOMMENDATIONS

The solutions and recommendations section of this book chapter take into consideration the implications of the COVID-19 pandemic and the COVID-19 crisis for our economy and for our society, and are intended to promote the process of building a New Economic Model capable to offer better chances for the achievement of the Sustainable Development Goals (SDGs).

The importance of the Sustainable Development Goals (SDGs) has been regarded by the World Business Council for Sustainable Development as reasoning for making important investments, based on the idea that by achieving the proposed aims that are part of Sustainable Development Goals (SDGs) there is the possibility to "unlock trillions in new market value" (World Business Council for Sustainable Development, 2022). In addition, the Organization for Economic Co-operation and Development (OECD) highlighted in the Report of the Secretary General's Advisory Group on a New Growth Narrative published in the year 2019 and entitled "Beyond Growth: Towards A New Economic Approach", the following pivotal aspects which shed a new light on the necessity to "create a 'new economic narrative'" which "consists of three elements", namely: (a) "A new conception of economic progress – a deeper understanding of the relationship between growth, human wellbeing, a reduction in inequalities and environmental sustainability, which can inform economic policymaking and politics"; (b) "New frameworks of economic theory and analysis – a richer basis of understanding and evidence on how economies work, and new tools and techniques to help policymakers devise policy"; and (c) "New approaches to economic policy – a wider set of policy and institutional reforms, based on the new frameworks and analysis, to achieve the new social and economic goals" (Organization for Economic Co-operation and Development (OECD), 2019, p.5).

In terms of solutions and recommendations, the aspects aforementioned represent the arguments capable to support change at a global level, and to these aspects, there are several other issues that ought to be pointed out, as follows:

First of all, in the Post-COVID-19 the Sustainable Development Goals (SDGs) achievement has the power to attract investments in education, research, and innovation, which may foster cooperation and valuable partnerships in all domains and at all levels. It is generally known and accepted that education is one of the most important sources of well-being in a society, since it empowers individuals to look for themselves and for the good of their families, based on the opportunities that education and life-long learning programs and training session have to offer. Hence, it is the authors' strong belief that investments in education, research, and innovation help making consistent improvements in addressing health issues and promoting well-being.

Second of all, in the Post-COVID-19 the Sustainable Development Goals (SDGs) achievement has the power to attract a more responsible behavior for both individuals and entities, in the context in which the standards of living at a global level have been severely affected by the current demographic, economic, financial, political, and social situation in addition to the prevailing lack of ethics (Luque & Herrero-

García, 2019). The achievement of the Sustainable Development Goals (SDGs) is threatened on a daily basis by the economic and the social insecurity, while the inequalities in our society are becoming more and more accentuated by the political actions that seem to have unleashed a wave of instability, inequalities, and migration. In this matter, for instance, the section dedicated to the case of the "Economic and social progress and the goals of economic policy" mentions the following threats for human life and for the environment: "(…) GDP growth is no longer correlated with improvements in wellbeing. The study of wellbeing has advanced greatly in recent decades. Income is important, particularly for those whose incomes are low. But we now understand that people' sense of a fulfilled and flourishing life comes also from a wide variety of other factors: from the security and satisfaction they experience in work; their physical and mental health, social networks and personal and family relationships; and from social goods such as the levels of crime and trust in society, and the quality of public services such as health and education. None of these are automatically improved simply by higher GDP, and can often be harmed by the ways it is generated – particularly for those on lower incomes and in more precarious work, and where private consumption is prioritized over public goods. For most people today, rising GDP is no longer a sufficient measure either of their own wellbeing or their sense of society's economic progress" (Organization for Economic Co-operation and Development (OECD), 2019, p.6).

FUTURE RESEARCH DIRECTIONS

In this case, the future research directions are numerous and may start from the desire to monitor the progress of the implementation of the Sustainable Development Goals (SDGs), or from the need to present the benefits and the opportunities of a New Economic Model mainly based on green energy, digitalization, and shock resistance.

The authors' intention in the near future is to continue their scientific work on the benefits of the Sustainable Development Goals (SDGs) for our society and for our economy, by offering more examples of good practices and successful implementation of the objectives represented by these Global Goals for certain communities and for specific organizations.

Also, the authors' desire is to expend the construction of a New Economic Model by taking into account all the components of the Sustainable Development Goals (SDGs), not solely the ones that refer to green energy, digitalization, and shock resistance.

Nevertheless, a bright future for all has the power of offering people and entities worldwide the chance to reflect to those decisions that were wrongfully taken, while seeking the opportunities of changing the past and making better assumptions and wiser choices that are due to be in line with the necessities of the present and the future generations. In this matter, the authors' future research directions should embrace the most recent trends in terms of fostering education, knowledge, innovation, and research, in the context in which education has the unique attribute of keeping us in line with everything that is novel and positive in life and in the society.

CONCLUSION

In conclusion, the society in which people live in these days has become subject to the current high-powered challenges and has become dependent on the high-reaching reforms due to be expected in order to facilitate the process of successfully and securely moving to a New Economic Model mainly based on green energy, digitalization, and shock resistance. Thus, development, information, innovation, knowledge, and research are considered the miraculous power capable to advance the United Nations Sustainable Development Goals (SDGs) at an international level, with the notable help provided by courageous reforms due to promote a New Economic Model based on quality, green energy, digitalization, and shock resistance.

Besides all these, the authors believe that Environmental Sustainability relies on the individuals and on the entities collaboration in achieving the Sustainable Development Goals (SDGs) and on communication in making the Sustainable Development Goals (SDGs) a way of living. These are decisive times in which the unforgettable challenges brought in today's society by the COVID-19 pandemic and the COVID-19 crisis posed even a greater pressure than before to achieve a better and more sustainable future for all.

Thus, the authors of this book chapter on "Current high-powered challenges and high-reaching reforms: Moving to a New Economic Model based on green energy, digitalization, and shock resistance" have placed on pivotal positions the answers for the following questions that were asked in this scientific work and which have represented the research objectives for this study, namely: "What steps are due to be taken for ensuring Affordable and Clean Energy?"; "What role do Sustainable Cities and Communities play in people's lives?"; "What does Climate Action involve in terms of the partnerships for the Global Goals?"; and "What does digitalization implicates in terms of supporting long term positive economic, social and environmental links in the Post-COVID-19 Era?"

Hence, a New Economic Model is seen as the highly-praised solution of creating a New Economic Model calling into question today's practices and coming to support life, well-being, heath, happiness, and synergies amongst the Sustainable Development Goals (SDGs) represents the key looked-for by specialists and leaders worldwide, especially as a result of the COVID-19 pandemic and the COVID-19 crisis. Also, on top of that, there is an overgrowing desire and an overwhelming need of creating a New Economic Model that has its roots in the sustainability barriers that were identified by specialists and by practitioners over the last years, thus offering individuals the possibility to focus, in the Post-COVID-19 Era, much more on the most urgent or on the fundamental needs of the Planet and of the communities they are part of.

ACKNOWLEDGMENT

This research received no specific grant from any funding agency in the public, commercial, or not-for-profit sectors.

REFERENCES

Economic Commission for Latin America and the Caribbean (ECLAC). (2020). *The 2030 Agenda for Sustainable Development in the New Global and Regional Context: Scenarios and Projections in the Current Crisis (LC/PUB.2020/5).* https://repositorio.cepal.org/bitstream/handle/11362/45338/4/S2000207_en.pdf

European Commission (EC). (2014). *Commission Regulation (EU) No 316/2014 of 21 March 2014 on the application of Article 101(3) of the Treaty on the Functioning of the European Union to categories of technology transfer agreements Text with EEA relevance.* https://ec.europa.eu/competition/antitrust/legislation/transfer.html

European Commission (EC). (2022a). *Commission (Eurostat) publishes 2022 report on Sustainable Development Goals in the European Union. Press release.* https://ec.europa.eu/commission/presscorner/detail/en/IP_22_3212

European Commission (EC). (2022b). *Research and Innovation.* https://ec.europa.eu/info/research-and-innovation_en

European Commission (EC). (2022c). *Remarks by Commissioner Gentiloni. Remarks by Commissioner Gentiloni at the Eurogroup press conference.* Speech. https://ec.europa.eu/commission/presscorner/detail/en/SPEECH_22_3804

European Union (EU) & European Institute for Innovation and Technology (EIT). (2022). *Knowledge and Innovation Communities.* https://eit.europa.eu/our-communities/eit-innovation-communities

European University Association (EUA). (2022). *EU Research & Innovation Programmes.* https://eua.eu/issues/16:eu-research-innovation-programmes.html

Eurostat. (2022). *Sustainable development in the European Union Monitoring report on progress towards the SDGs in an EU context 2022 edition* (6th ed.). https://ec.europa.eu/eurostat/web/products-statistical-books/-/KS-09-22-019 doi:10.2785/313289

Luque, A. (2021). Implications and Asymmetries of the Knowledge Society: An Analysis of 82 Constructs. In C. Popescu (Ed.), *COVID-19 Pandemic Impact on New Economy Development and Societal Change* (pp. 154–176). IGI Global. doi:10.4018/978-1-6684-3374-4.ch008

Luque, A. (2022). Analysis of the concept of informal economy through 102 definitions: Legality or necessity. *Open Research Europe*, *2022*(1), 134. doi:10.12688/openreseurope.13990.2

Luque, A., & Herrero-García, N. (2019). How corporate social (ir)responsibility in the textile sector is defined, and its impact on ethical sustainability: An analysis of 133 concepts. *Corporate Social Responsibility and Environmental Management*, *26*(6), 1–22. doi:10.1002/csr.1747

Luque, A., & Jiménez, A. (2019). Procesos de sostenibilidad textil: éxito, o nueva forma de contaminar bajo un paradigma amable. *Revista Inclusiones, 6*, 259-288.

Organization for Economic Co-operation and Development (OECD). (2016). *Better Policies for 2030. An OECD Action Plan on the Sustainable Development Goals.* https://www.oecd.org/dac/sustainable-development-goals.htm

Organization for Economic Co-operation and Development (OECD). (2019). *Beyond Growth: Towards A New Economic Approach.* Report of the Secretary General's Advisory Group on a New Growth Narrative. OECD Conference Centre. SG/NAEC(2019)3. https://www.oecd.org/naec/averting-systemic-collapse/SG-NAEC(2019)3_Beyond%20Growth.pdf

Organization for Economic Co-operation and Development (OECD). (2021). *Meeting of the Members of the Council on the 2030 Agenda for Sustainable Development 1 March 2021*. Draft Agenda. https://www.oecd.org/sdgs/

Organization for Economic Co-operation and Development (OECD). (2022a). *OECD and the Sustainable Development Goals: Delivering on Universal Goals and Targets*. https://www.oecd.org/dac/sustainable-development-goals.htm

Organization for Economic Co-operation and Development (OECD). (2022b). *The Sustainable Development Goals: An overview of relevant OECD analysis, tools and approaches*. https://www.oecd.org/dac/sustainable-development-goals.htm. https://www.oecd.org/dac/The%20Sustainable%20Development%20Goals%20An%20overview%20of%20relevant%20OECD%20analysis.pdf

Popescu, C. R. G. (2021). Sustainable and Responsible Entrepreneurship for Value-Based Cultures, Economies, and Societies: Increasing Performance Through Intellectual Capital in Challenging Times. In C. Popescu & R. Verma (Eds.), *Sustainable and Responsible Entrepreneurship and Key Drivers of Performance* (pp. 33–58). IGI Global. doi:10.4018/978-1-7998-7951-0.ch002

Popescu, C. R. G. (2022a). Mindfulness at Work, a Sound Business Investment: Focusing on the Employee Well-Being While Increasing Creativity and Innovation. In C. Popescu (Ed.), *Handbook of Research on Changing Dynamics in Responsible and Sustainable Business in the Post-COVID-19 Era* (pp. 1–34). IGI Global. doi:10.4018/978-1-6684-2523-7.ch001

Popescu, C. R. G. (2022b). Mindfulness Business Principles: Producing Outstanding Value and Encouraging Community Connections. In C. Popescu (Ed.), *COVID-19 Pandemic Impact on New Economy Development and Societal Change* (pp. 196–228). IGI Global. doi:10.4018/978-1-6684-3374-4.ch010

Popescu, C. R. G. (2022c). Impressive, Inspiring, and Profound Mindfulness Movement in Organizations: Boosting Productivity, Cultivating Joy, and Sharping Awareness. In C. Popescu (Ed.), *Handbook of Research on Building Inclusive Global Knowledge Societies for Sustainable Development* (pp. 60–96). IGI Global. doi:10.4018/978-1-6684-5109-0.ch003

Royal Government of Bhutan. (2012). *The Report of the High-Level Meeting on Wellbeing and Happiness: Defining a New Economic Paradigm*. New York: The Permanent Mission of the Kingdom of Bhutan to the United Nations. https://sustainabledevelopment.un.org/content/documents/617BhutanReport_WEB_F.pdf

United Nations Development Program (UNDP). (2022). *Sustainable Development Goals (SDGs). The SDGs in action. What are the Sustainable Development Goals?* https://www.undp.org/sustainable-development-goals

United Nations Economic Commission for Europe (UNECE). (2022). *Halfway to 2030: UNECE report shows we must accelerate progress to achieve SDGs in the region*. https://unece.org/media/press/366086

United Nations (UN). (2021). *The Sustainable Development Goals Report 2021*. https://unstats.un.org/sdgs/report/2021/The-Sustainable-Development-Goals-Report-2021.pdf

United Nations (UN). (2022a). *Goal 7: Affordable and Clean Energy*. https://www.jointsdgfund.org/sustainable-development-goals/goal-7-affordable-and-clean-energy

United Nations (UN). (2022b). *Meetings Coverage and Press Releases. Secretary-General Warns of Climate Emergency, Calling Intergovernmental Panel's Report 'a File of Shame', While Saying Leaders 'Are Lying', Fuelling Flames. The 4th of April 2022.* Author.

United Nations (UN). (2022c). *Secretary-General. Secretary-General's video message to the Press Conference Launch of IPCC Report.* https://www.un.org/sg/en/content/sg/statement/2022-02-28/secretary-generals-video-message-the-press-conference-launch-of-ipcc-report-scroll-down-for-languages

United Nations (UN). (2022d). *Department of Economic and Social Affairs. Sustainable Development (SD). Make The SDGs A Reality.* https://sdgs.un.org/

World Business Council for Sustainable Development. (2022). *Achieving the Sustainable Development Goals can unlock trillions in new market value.* https://www.wbcsd.org/Overview/News-Insights/General/News/Achieving-the-Sustainable-Development-Goals-can-unlock-trillions-in-new-market-value

World Economic Forum (WEF). (2019). *Sustainable Development Impact Summit. Article on Sustainable Development entitled "We need an economic model that works for people and the planet".* https://www.weforum.org/agenda/2019/09/how-to-make-markets-more-sustainable/

KEY TERMS AND DEFINITIONS

Digitalization Supporting the 17 Sustainable Development Goals (SDGs): Brings to the attention of the individuals and the entities the possibility to make use of the digital technologies in order to change certain business models, while seeking, on one hand, an increase in the businesses' profitability, revenue, global visibility, international recognition, and while striving, on the other hand, to accomplish unprecedented opportunities in terms of giving new meaning to the values of the businesses; in continuation, this is a process which has the power to bring information and knowledge closer to both individuals and organizations, while fostering the benefits of 17 Sustainable Development Goals (SDGs), in a world that has come to rely more and more on the benefits of this phenomenon, namely: unlimited and unrestricted access to information, accessibility, automation, data quality, preservation, integration, interaction, interconnection, searching ability, and income generation.

Economic Globalization: This is a phenomenon in expansion that causes profound changes on the world stage. It revolves around trade, the flow of investment, financial capital, division of labor and specialization. The concept is not limited only to economic variables since its effects extend to individuals, society to the state. Developing countries are experiencing stagnation in the face of their inability to cope with globalization, which is compounded by poor management of their financial markets, leading to an increase in the income inequality gap. Economic globalization brings with it the mobilization of goods and capital, reduces distance between borders and energizes international trade with some alterations to sovereignty.

Green Energy: Represents one of targets embedded in the United Nations' (UN) Sustainable Development Goals (SDGs) and is known as the energy obtained through the use of natural resources, renewable energy sources, such as sunlight, wind or water; the goal of this form of energy is to place life and the environment on the highest positions, since this specific form of energy is not harmful for the environment, as the release of the greenhouse gases into the atmosphere would represent in today's context.

High-Powered Challenges to Create a New Economic Model: on the one hand, these days, the COVID-19 pandemic and the COVID-19 crisis represent overpowering threats for the society and for the economy, especially when seeking to achieve the United Nations' (UN) Sustainable Development Goals (SDGs) which represent, through their indented outcomes, putting an end to poverty, finding the necessary solutions capable to protect the Planet, and striving to ensure that by the year 2030 all people will get the opportunity to enjoy the well-deserved peace and the well-praised prosperity (United Nations Development Program (UNDP), 2022); on the other hand, in the Post-COVID-19 Era the solution for a bright future is seen in the context in which a New Economic Model is being foreseen and created, with a particular emphasis on "affordable and clean energy" expected to encourage growth and Sustainable Development (SD) for all, "sustainable cities and communities" envisioned to support green energy, green public spaces, digitalization, inclusion, and shock resistance in all senses, and "climate action" counted on fostering the partnerships for reaching the Global Goals in a world that seems more and more inclined to alter the meaning of life, to lack global participation in helping the human rights, and to become more subjective in terms of banning harmful practices for ecosystems and humanity (United Nations Development Program (UNDP), 2022).

High-Reaching Reforms to Create a New Economic Model: The success of the United Nations' (UN) Sustainable Development Goals (SDGs) as well as the achievement of the partnerships capable to support the United Nations' (UN) Sustainable Development Goals (SDGs) in present days and in the future relies on creating strong reforms in all domains; in this matter, these reforms should address a wide range of objectives due to be based on all the 17 Sustainable Development Goals (SDGs), in the attempt to find solutions to support all the implications and all the benefits that these 17 Sustainable Development Goals (SDGs) will come to represent for the economic, the socio-political, and the environmental dimensions; in like manner, creating these reforms should target accomplishing progress in terms of supporting research at all levels, namely: interdisciplinary, multidisciplinary, and trans-disciplinary research for the economic, the socio-political, and the environmental dimensions.

New Economic Model: The highly-praised solution of creating a New Economic Model calling into question today's practices and coming to support life, well-being, heath, happiness, and synergies amongst the Sustainable Development Goals (SDGs) represents the key looked-for by specialists and leaders worldwide, especially as a result of the COVID-19 pandemic and the COVID-19 crisis; the need of creating this New Economic Model has its roots in the sustainability barriers that were identified by specialists and by practitioners over the last years, thus offering individuals the possibility to focus, in the Post-COVID-19 Era, much more on the most urgent or on the fundamental needs of the Planet and of the communities they are part of.

Resilience: Transformations within a complex system related to the capacity for self-organization while maintaining internal structure, together with the ability to create adaptive responses, generate knowledge, experience, and learning. Resilience and sustainability are directly related to changes within societies, economies, and the human system as a whole. The transformation of systems is inevitable since it allows systems to strengthen.

Shock Resistance: Represents the desiderate for the future in the context designed to accomplish and to support the United Nations' (UN) Sustainable Development Goals (SDGs), in a world dominated by the effects generated by the COVID-19 pandemic and the COVID-19 crisis; it has been remarked the danger represented, in this context, by the systemic resistance to change, to novelty, and to progress (known as "business-as-usual") which should be fully avoided in the Post-COVID-19 Era, since it would only promote chaos, insecurity, and uncertainty, while generating a severe decline in the individuals standards of living and businesses profitability and success; in addition, a shock resistant society and a shock resistant economy are robust and inclusive systems capable to increase the utilization of information, value the benefits of knowledge, support the Sustainable Development Goals (SDGs) frameworks that "leave now one behind" and that fight for the "general good" of all individuals in the present days and in the future.

Social Economy: Encompasses a variety of businesses, organizations, and different legal entities. They share the objective of systematically putting people first, producing a positive impact on local communities and pursuing a social cause.

Synergies Amongst the Sustainable Development Goals (SDGs): The world people live in these days seeks new meanings for committeemen, development, environment, equality, life, love, health, sustainability, sustainable development (SD), power, preservation, progress, profit, and well-being, which are due to be formed and to be promoted only in the context in which everyone has the opportunity to participate and to have the voice heard during the process; according to the United Nations' (UN) the Synergies amongst the Sustainable Development Goals (SDGs) are due to be encountered in a cross-impact matrix that is born from the interaction of all the objectives considered to be accomplished (United Nations Development Program (UNDP), 2022); this cross-impact matrix represents an essential tool that facilitates the process of better understanding the manner in which the individuals and the entities can help in order to give life to the targets proposed, in the context in which sustainability requires committed actions from all involved parties in a society.

Chapter 9
Application of Sustainable Projects in the Paper Industry in Rio de Janeiro

Wenderson dos Santos Alvarenga
Universidade Federal Fluminense, Brazil

Sergio Luiz Braga França
Universidade Federal Fluminense, Brazil

Luis Perez Zotes
Universidade Federal Fluminense, Brazil

ABSTRACT

This chapter analyzes the environmental, social, and governance (ESG) risk management practices currently used in sustainable projects in the paper industry in the state of Rio de Janeiro. This is exploratory research in which a case study was carried out supported by structured interviews with 17 specialists who work in the main paper industries in Rio de Janeiro. The results indicate that the approaches of preliminary risk analysis, failure mode analysis, and WHAT–IF (WI) are the main practices used by the consulted managers. These practices are incomplete, in the search for convergence of objectives and expansion of the life cycle of products and processes, as they comprise industrial processes in a fragmented way, without systematically covering the entire life cycle of products or the socio-environmental interests of the community. Critical points for sustainable industrial projects were also pointed out as the possibility of a power outage in the global economy and society's lack of adaptability to the ongoing structural changes.

DOI: 10.4018/978-1-6684-6750-3.ch009

1. INTRODUCTION

1.1 Research Contextualization

Mastering the principles of environmental, social, and governance (ESG) risk analysis is one of the key factors when considering the professional performance of engineers in their relationship with the industry (Rampasso et al., 2020). Currently, sustainability assessments are required from the first stages of any project, since they impact the life cycles and resilience of projects, consolidating themselves as strategic aspects both for investment decision-making and risk assessments in industrial activities (NBR ISO 31000: Risk Management - Guidelines, 2018).

Considerations about sustainable development have been debated for more than four decades (Ipiranga et al., 2011). In this trajectory, the assessment of factors associated with sustainability has become relevant for organizational objectives, given the growing search for harmonizing social, financial, and environmental results.

Sustainability indicators are publicly evaluated through corporate governance indices and similar, which have been widely used for decision-making, producing impacts from the initial financing of projects to the termination of strategic activities, such as the closing of coal plants in Australia, or the shutdown of fossil fuel vehicle production in the European Union, for example (Carey & Steitz, 2021; Roden, 2021).

Such changes have implications for the development of new research on risk analysis processes focused on sustainability.

Roden (2021) shows that communities are divided on the social impacts of sustainability-related changes, although there is a perception among the actors consulted that the transition to the green economy generates development opportunities for society as a whole. Only 12% of the interviewees reported perceiving positive impacts on their health, as a result of the closing of fossil fuel power plants, for the author, there is a tendency toward the extinction of the culture of ignorance about the social and environmental aspects of products and services. To this end, investment in education and training is necessary to adapt to the new reality, so that communities perceive the added value of producing clean energy and implementing sustainable projects.

From this perspective, many of the technological solutions being applied in the industry carry emerging environmental and social risk factors, which lack updated objective assessments, demanding the readjustment of risk analysis methodologies to the post-pandemic reality and the transition to a green economy. In this environment of rapid changes and constant tests of organizations' resilience, research on the analysis of risks associated with ESG is imposed, presenting itself as a determining factor for strategic decision-making in the industry.

This research shows a case study related to the paper industry in Rio de Janeiro, which presents a similar reality to the aforementioned aspects, being of significant relevance due to the environmental, social, and governance (ESG) impact on the production chain of the sector.

1.2 Formulation of the Problem Situation

Given the context, the following research problem arises: how can risk management and analysis contribute to the implementation of sustainability principles focused on environmental, social, and governance (ESG) management in industrial projects?

1.3 Research Objectives

As a general objective of this study, the research question suggests analyzing environmental, social, and governance (ESG) risk management practices in risk analysis for the management of sustainable industrial projects. The researcher's scope of interest delimits the object of study to the context of the paper industry in the state of Rio de Janeiro.

To make the general objective viable and answer the research problem, the literature review on risk analysis approaches in the industry and the consultation of specialists working in Rio de Janeiro was appropriated as specific objectives. Furthermore, the research also aims to identify the critical factors for the implementation of sustainable projects.

1.4 Aspects of Interdisciplinarity

Regarding interdisciplinarity, the aim is to disseminate, mainly, the following impacts: critical factors for the success of risk analysis technologies used by industry managers in the region, as well as fostering debate on improving the industry's ESG risk management strategies.

The disclosure of the critical factors for the success of the risk analysis used by managers of the paper industry in the region can be framed as a technological impact of the research, since it contributes to disseminating the best management practices, preventing systemic risks and favoring the development of new technologies, with the potential to disseminate techniques and knowledge, including social technologies, to all sectors of society (CAPES, 2022, p. 9). This impact is justified by the potential for mitigating and preventing risks associated with ESG in the local industry.

In addition, the debate on the need to improve risk management systems for the social and environmental governance of organizations can be considered a positive social impact of this research, since it meets the requirement of contributing either to the improvement of public and social management or to the improvement of the population's living conditions and the resolution of today's most important social problems (CAPES, 2020, p. 9).

The research also has a positive environmental impact, since the improvement in ESG risk levels directly implies improving the balance and sustainability of socio-environmental aspects, valuing the maintenance of biodiversity, nature, and traditional peoples and communities, which are directly influenced by the socio-environmental performance of the paper industry in Rio de Janeiro (CAPES, 2020, p. 10). From this perspective, the assessment of ESG risk analysis practices has the interdisciplinary potential to produce positive technological, social, and environmental impacts.

1.5 Relationship between ESG and Sustainable Development Goals (SDGs)

At the United Nations (Rio + 20), replacing the Millennium Goals SDGs, replacing the Millennium Goals SDGs. They were guided by the protection of the Earth's life support system and the reduction of poverty. This is necessary because human influences have no environment an emergence of a new geological epoch, the Antropoc characterized by the non-approximation of limits whose transposition for living beings is because the changes can be abrupt since environmental and irreversible is safe on the planet. Among the environmental conditions and the increase in the production capacity of the environmental conditions and the production capacity of environments, ocean water et al. (Grigg, 2013).

The authors draw attention to the difficulty of harmonizing shared goals and individual interests. However, they consider it possible to do so based on six provisional SDGs, based on consolidated scientific knowledge and the millennium goals. The goals highlighted by Griggs et al. (2013) are: fighting poverty through education and reducing social inequalities; ending hunger and promoting food security; universal access to water and sanitation; universalizing the generation of clean energy; improving the management of ecosystems and environmental services; and transform governance at all levels to include previous objectives in institutional guidelines.

Ten years after the Rio+20 summit, entitled "Green Economy in the context of sustainable development and eradication of poverty", the SDGs are multiplied and divided into targets by the dozen, producing indicators by the hundreds in October 2014, when the 68th session of the United Nations General Assembly ratified the report of the Open Working Group established in 2012 to define the goals and indicators for the SDGs (Hák et al., 2016).

This exponential nature of social, environmental, and governance indices and targets makes them less and less realistic and makes it clear that the SDGs, as the millennium goals, were nothing more than protocols of unbelievable intentions. However, three aspects of this protocol stand out in terms of the possibility of being converted into management technologies, namely: environmental management, social responsibility, and corporate governance, which are currently grouped under the acronym ESG. This administrative approach makes it possible to associate social responsibility with objectives related to the fight against poverty and hunger, in addition to providing clear goals for environmental management, which could focus on water resources, the energy matrix, and environmental services. All these goals can be organized from the strengthening of governance, understood as respect for laws and the interests of the parties involved in management systems at all levels of society.

1.6 Relevance of ESG Initiatives for the Circulation of Wealth

Corporate governance strategies, that is, those that aim to obey the law and seek to meet the interests of the parties involved in each organizational activity in the context of the private sector, have historically privileged profit over the law and the law over the environment. Ethical management, in turn, that is, management focused on social responsibility, has traditionally been ignored by financial institutions, since in many cases there are no commercial arguments to act morally (Richardson & Cragg, 2010). This fact highlights a conflict between the public interests of governance, that is, respect for the law, and the private intentions of investors, profit. In this context, the main motivator of investment is the relationship between risk and reward, since in the absence of punishment, whether due to lack of supervision or lack of negative advertising, the basic organizational objective of maximizing results must prevail in the investors' decision.

Richardson and Cragg (2010) propose that investors should pay attention to the social risks of their financial decisions, which implies the internalization of public and environmental costs in private organizations, with reduced gains. This is a contradiction in terms since the fundamental objective of any private investment is to maximize profits. Such a contradiction, when applied to corporate governance, fosters a set of articulations about business risks, which are subject to punishment for breaking the law, as well as the vulnerability of the brand to negative advertising that, currently, can arise both from social irresponsibility by the lack of empathy with the suffering of the community, as well as through the community perception of the externalization of environmental costs.

Based on these considerations, ESG strategies can be approached as ways of harmonizing the internalization of socio-environmental costs with the maximization of profits. In the current environment, where negative propaganda and public oversight are progressively more articulated with the media, evaluating and controlling ESG risks becomes necessary for organizations to demonstrate to investors their commitment to the best economic, environmental and social interests. This makes it possible to raise funds from investors who are more aware of the SDGs, as well as taking part in funds, socio-environmental indices and public resources aimed at reducing environmental impact (Owen, 2021).

According to Owen (2021), even small and medium-sized companies have a significant potential to take part in the transition to the green economy, being able to contribute in a disruptive way in a wide variety of productive sectors, especially with regard to innovation, research and development.

Notably, the contradiction between profit and socio-environmental investment limits the ability of large corporations to assume preponderance in the pursuit of the SDGs, so that it is mainly up to governments to finance new technologies at an accelerated pace, which climate change demands. A rational way of doing this is through venture capital, allocating it in a dispersed way to a greater number of small and medium-sized companies, which allows the public sphere to follow the governance standard established by the SDGs by reducing costs. social gaps, as well as orienting technological innovations towards cleaner production.

2. SYSTEMATIC REVIEW OF THE LITERATURE

2.1 PICO Method (Population, Intervention, Comparison, and Outcome)

For a better understanding of the main concepts involved in ESG risk analysis, focused on sustainable industrial projects, a systematic literature review was carried out between January and March 2022, using the Web of Science (WoS) and EBSCOhost databases, accessed from the Portal of Periodicals of the Coordination for the Improvement of Higher Education Personnel (CAPES, 2022).

In the systematic review of the literature, the query method guided by population, intervention, comparison, and outcome (PICO) was used, presented in the Cochrane protocol, widely used in the health sciences as an evidence-based research practice (Kolahi et al., 2020; Santos et al., 2007; Shaffer et al., 2019). In this step of the review, the following keywords were defined by criteria of relevance:

- Population: <RISK ANALYSIS>.
- Intervention: <INDUSTRIAL PROJECTS>.
- Comparison: <GOVERNANCE> and <SOCIAL or ENVIRONMENTAL>
- Outcome: <SUSTAINABILITY> or <ESG>.

The ordering of keywords generated the following search key:
<risk analysis> AND <industrial project> AND
<governance AND social OR environmental> AND
<sustainability OR ESG>

The query, carried out in February 2022, on the EBSCOhost database, in full-text peer-reviewed, showed 65,766 results. When refining the search by subject, in the <Title> field, the EBSCOhost engine highlighted 73 results, among which 13 searches were selected by criteria of relevance, which is considered suitable for peer-reviewed articles, dedicated to related areas of interest with industrial management of sustainable projects, risk analysis, and ESG practices. The selected articles are referenced in Table 1.

The search key was also applied to the Web of Science database, in the same period, and presented 13 results when selected <all fields>, confirming the high rate of innovation in this research topic. The studies identified in this collection were classified by criteria of relevance, and one article was excluded for dealing with a topic outside the field of interest. Table 2 shows the results selected in the WoS database.

Table 1. Articles reviewed from the EBSCOhost database

Author (data)	Title	Method	Contributions
(Lee, 2017)	A Bridge Back to the Future: Public Health Ethics, Bioethics, and Environmental Ethics.	Analytical	History of environmental ethics.
(Fantke et al., 2018)	Advances in Life Cycle Human Exposure and Toxicity Characterization	Case study	Assessment of human exposure and toxicity impacts. Life cycle analysis.
(Malloy et al., 2017)	Advancing Alternative Analysis: Integration of Decision Science.	Case study	Decision analysis and analysis of alternatives.
(Bauer et al., 2020)	Associations of a Metal Mixture Measured in Multiple Biomarkers with IQ: Evidence from Italian Adolescents Living near Ferroalloy Industry	Case study (cross-sectional)	Higher levels of Mn, Pb, and Cr in adolescents were associated with lower IQ scores.
(Laskaris et al., 2019)	Derivation of Time-Activity Data Using Wearable Cameras and Measures of Personal Inhalation Exposure among Workers at an informal Electronic-Waste Recovery Site in Ghana.	Case study	Exposure to particles in informal e-waste recovery is higher than recommended by the World Health Organization (WHO).
(Covert et al., 2020)	Environmental Health Risk Relationships, Responsibility, and Sources of Information among Vietnamese Americans in coastal Mississippi	Case study (focus groups)	Impact of environmental disasters on community resilience. Environmental health. A relational theory of risk.
(Roden, 2021)	Exploring the Perceived Health, Community, and Employment Impacts of an Announced Closure of a Coal-Fired Power Station in Upper Hunter Valley, Australia	Case study (focus groups)	Impacts of closing coal-fired power plants.
(Uccelli et al., 2016)	Female Lung Cancer Mortality and Long-Term Exposure to Particulate Matter in Italy	Case study	Impact of inhaled particulate matter on human health.
(Shaffer et al., 2019)	Improving and Expanding Estimates of the Global Burden of Disease due to Environmental Health Risk Factors	Analytical	Classification of evidence for environmental health risk assessment and global risk analysis.
(Portelinha et al., 2021)	Links between Health and Environmental Sustainability.	Integrative review	Importance of leveraging resources for ESG.
(Ablah et al., 2018)	Need for Transparency and Ongoing Communication After Residents with Contaminated Water Wells are Connected to City Water.	Case study (focus groups)	Effects of water contamination by tetrachlorethylene: the need for transparency in communication.
(Stumpf et al., 2020)	Noise Exposure of Sugar Cane Mill Workers in Guatemala	Case study	Findings of hazardous exposure to noise in the industry.
(Yang et al., 2018)	The Productivity Dynamics of China's Environmentally Friendly Production Technologies in terms of Wastewater Treatment Techniques	Case study (Productivity Index)	Technological progress contributes to improving sustainability indices.

Source: Own elaboration, 2022

Table 2. Articles reviewed from the Web of Science database

Author (date)	Title	Method	Contributions
(FRASER, 2021)	Mining Companies and Communities: Collaborative Approaches to Reduce Social Risk and Advance Sustainable Development	Comparative analysis	The common interest in water creates opportunities for the industry to contribute to sustainable development. There is financial value to a good reputation.
(TETTEH et al., 2021)	Key drivers for Implementing International Construction Joint Ventures (ICJVs): Global Insights for Sustainable Growth	Case study	Example of application of the methodology. Sample definition.
(MARCOULAKI et al., 2021)	Project for a Self-Sustaining European Center for Service Delivery in Safe and Sustainable Innovation for Nanotechnology	Multiple case study	Proposal for a governance scheme for self-sustaining projects.
(GUMIRAN; DAAG, 2021)	Negotiated Participatory Action Research for Multi-Stakeholder Implementation of Early Warning Systems for Landslides	Participatory action research	The inclusion of the community in the development process can improve the credibility and relevance of the developed system. Risk reduction is a common interest and can unite diverse actors with conflicting expectations.
(TARIQ; WANGCHUK; MUTTIL, 2021)	A Critical Review of Water Resources and Their Management in Bhutan	Critical review	It systematically exposes the main issues related to the management of water resources.
(SUN et al., 2020)	Comprehensive Partitions and Different Strategies Based on Ecological Security and Economic Development in Guizhou Province, China	Ecological quantification	Offers a quantitative approach in order to calculate environmental impacts.
(DING et al., 2020)	Land Degradation Sensitivity Assessment and Convergence Analysis in Korla of Xinjiang, China	Convergence analysis	Describes the main threats to soil integrity.
(BĂRBUȚĂ-MIȘU; MADALENO; ILIE, 2019)	Analysis of Risk Factors Affecting Firms' Financial Performance - Support for Managerial Decision-Making	Integrative factor analysis	Financial analysis of the impact of critical factors in times of crisis as a means of promoting the assessment of socio-environmental risks.
(CREED et al., 2019)	Managing Risks to Canada's Boreal Zone: Transdisciplinary Thinking in Pursuit of Sustainability	Bibliographic review with scenario analysis	It identifies the main risk factors for the sustainability of the boreal zone, including atmospheric changes, demand for ecosystem services, demographic and social values, industrial, infrastructure, and governance innovation.
(ZHANG; WANG, 2019)	How Does Paired Assistance to Disaster-Affected Areas (PADAA) Contribute to Economic Sustainability? A Qualitative Analysis of Wenchuan County	Case study	It addresses the relationship between social assistance and financial sustainability in post-crisis times.
(SUGIYAMA et al., 2017)	Transdisciplinary Co-Design of Scientific Research Agendas: 40 Research Questions for Socially Relevant Climate Engineering Research	Convergence analysis	Examples of relevant questions for research on social and environmental governance.
(TAYLOR; HARMAN, 2016)	Governing Urban Development for Climate Risk: What Role for Public-Private Partnerships?	Case study	It addresses the relationship between the State and the private sector in the context of environmental sustainability.

Source: Own elaboration, 2022

The systematic review was complemented by automated semantic analysis of abstracts and titles, using the VOSviewer software, provided by the University of Leiden (Kolahi et al., 2020; University of Leiden, 2022).

The objective of this research phase was to generate an ontology, highlighting the most relevant concepts and categories in the group of articles analyzed. The software was parameterized to highlight the 11 most significant terms, among the words with more than four occurrences in the abstracts and titles of the 25 articles reviewed, excluding the terms <paper>, <china>, and <study>, by pertinence criterion. The automated semantic analysis generated the ontology shown in Figures 1 and 2.

Figure 1. Selection of search categories in order of relevance
Source: Own elaboration, 2022

Create Map

Verify selected terms

Selected	Term	Occurrences	Relevance
☑	stakeholder	5	1.74
☑	community	8	1.40
☐	paper	7	1.35
☐	china	4	1.29
☑	climate change	4	0.93
☑	management	4	0.80
☑	sustainability	11	0.79
☑	development	10	0.76
☐	study	7	0.66
☑	risk	10	0.66
☑	analysis	12	0.62

Figure 2. Mind map representing the ontology of the systematic literature review prepared by the author using the VOSviewer program
Source: Own elaboration, 2022

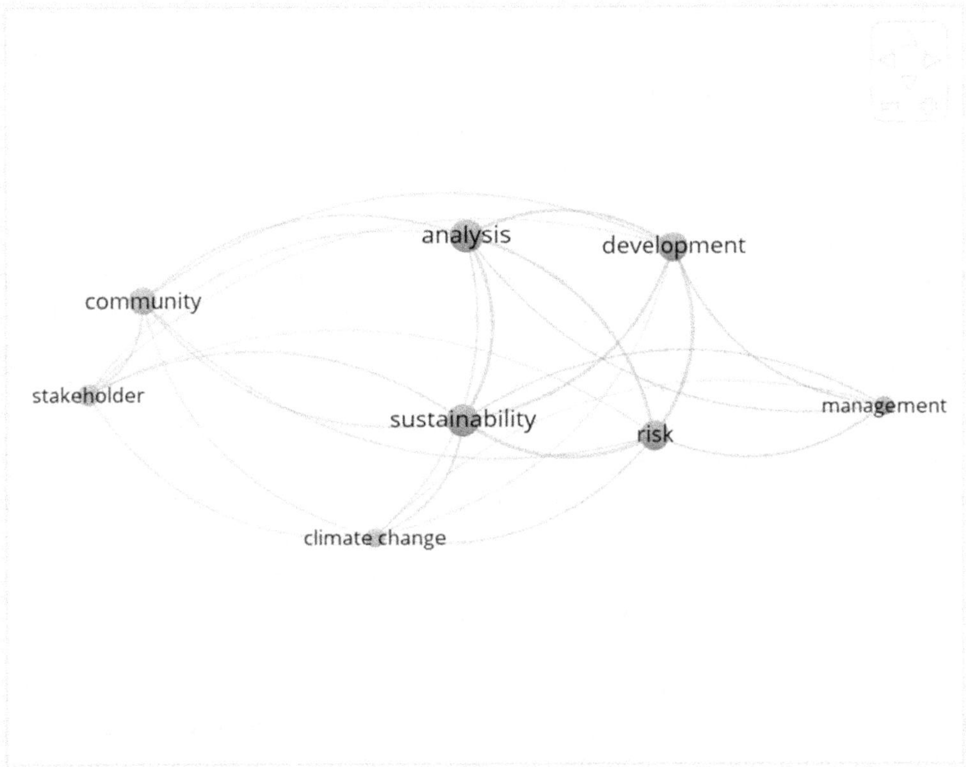

The terms highlighted by semantic analysis can be grouped as follows:
Group 1: <stakeholder> (stakeholder); <community> and <climate change>.
Group 2: <management>; <sustainability>; <development> and <risk analysis>.

The main objective of this type of semantic analysis is to represent a complex set of data from simple components, which are evidenced and grouped from standardized statistical calculations forming an ontology, that is, a group of keywords that represent a phenomenon. (Andrade, 2013; Kolahi et al., 2020). The highlighted categories are used as a guide for the next topics in the review.

2.2 Relationship between Community and Stakeholders

According to Lee (2017), environmental ethics was developed by Leopold and Potter, back in the 1940s and 1970s, respectively. Such paradigms tend towards the perception of a connected biosphere, in which different agents are mutually impacted by their activities.

From this perspective, there is an evolution of the debate from individual autonomy to solidarity, about community and environmental health. Although such areas of knowledge are based on bioethics, which considers the interaction between human values and biological facts necessary, there is an evolution in the multifactorial complexity of emerging problems, related to human health and the environment, so risks at both individual, collective and environmental levels must be mitigated. In this view, risk management is a way of fostering the connection between the health of the individual and that of the planet. With this in mind, Lee (2017) considers the concern with solidarity, justice, health protection, and social engagement fundamental.

Regarding these risk prevention factors, few sectors have established themselves in such conflicting relationships, in terms of social and environmental governance, as in the case of mining. For this reason, there is a growing demand for a reduction in the many negative impacts of extractivism, especially after the serious accidents in the cities of Mariana and Brumadinho, which exposed the presence of unacceptable risks to local communities, as well as interference, subsidized by analysis of fragile, biased and ineffective risks (Di Noi & Ciroth, 2018; Oliveira et al., 2019).

In those cases, the lack of assertiveness in risk management brought incalculable losses to all interested parties in the extraction of iron ore from Minas Gerais and the region, in addition to favoring the achievement of the biggest environmental disaster that had occurred in Brazil until then. The emergence of this new reality has brought to the mining industry the need to develop and apply new collaborative approaches, aiming at reducing and addressing socio-environmental risks (Fraser, 2021).

In the case of the paper industry in Rio de Janeiro, a relevant aspect is recycling, characterized in Brazil by the precariousness of work and informality in the collection phase, which exposes workers to various risks, such as supporting higher levels of inhalable particles, as indicated by the World Health Organization (WHO), similar to the recovery of e-waste in Ghana, as observed by Laskaris et al. (2019). A study carried out in Italy found that the inhalation of particulate matter above the recommended has a potential annual impact of 300 deaths from lung cancer, for an analyzed population of 8,146,520 women (Uccelli et al., 2016).

Another consequence of the socio-environmental risks assumed by many organizations was highlighted by Bauer et al. (2020) in the vicinity of an Italian ferroalloy industry. In that case, an association was found between low intelligence quotients (IQ) and high levels of manganese (Mn), lead (Pb), and chromium (Cr) in the body of adolescents between 10 and 14 years old.

Among the many socio-environmental problems produced by industrial activity, the management of water resources stands out, which can put the industry and the local community in direct competition for scarce and indispensable factors for the sustainability of their activities. Groundwater contamination by tetrachlorethylene, derived from dry cleaning, is reported by Ablah et al. (2018), who consider transparency an essential tool to deal with the negative environmental impacts of activities associated with the use of water resources.

Although on a smaller scale, variants of the same problems can be identified in the pulp and paper industry, parts of the socio-environmental governance solutions available for mining may be appropriate for the paper industry in Rio de Janeiro, given that in that activity the debate on ESG is more mature.

2.3 Relationship between Risk Management, Development, and Analysis

Of the tools currently available to measure the effect of industrial activities on human life and the environment, life cycle analysis stands out, considered an effective way to compare the cumulative burden of diseases arising from industrial activities, as well as the potential negative impacts to the community (Fantke et al., 2018). Portelinha et al. (2021) highlight the importance of reusing materials to amplify the positive social impacts of human activities. This is due to the potential to increase the life cycle of products, reducing thus the demand for natural resources.

In addition to environmental risks, work in the industry involves severe risks to human health, among which those derived from noise pollution can be highlighted. According to Stumpf et al. (2020), who analyzed working conditions in the Guatemalan sugar industry, the majority of workers surveyed were subjected to hazardous occupational noise, which exceeded the recommended annual exposure limit in Guatemala and in the USA (a time-weighted average of 85 dBA).

The complexity of environmental, social, and governance (ESG) risks present in the contemporary industry requires approaches aimed at risk analysis that are capable of integrating decision and alternative analysis, as discussed by Malloy et al. (2017). These and other observations, found in the literature review, were selected to enable the construction of a preliminary questionnaire, presented to specialists in order to elaborate the field research data.

3. RESEARCH METHODOLOGY

This is an exploratory study, based on a systematic review of the bibliography and a case study, supported by consultations with experts from the paper industry in Rio de Janeiro.

To prepare the collection instruments used in these consultations, a preliminary questionnaire was created (Table 3) to assess the perception of research subjects on the analysis of environmental, social, and governance risks in the paper industry in Rio de Janeiro. The criterion for defining the questions was that of relevance to the scope of the research, associated with the presence of problems in the literature consulted. The questions were elaborated from three axes of interest: environment; society and governance.

After the initial proposal (Chart 3), the construct was submitted to four experts and researchers in the area for face validation. Employees sent several suggestions for improvement in the collection instrument, which, after corrections, were sent to respondents through electronic tools such as e-mail, social networks, and electronic forms.

In the literature review, the survey prepared by Magalhães (2021) was found, which points out 59 corrugated cardboard companies in the state of Rio de Janeiro. In addition to these, in field research, the presence of two large paper producers in the region was observed, limiting the universe of interest to 61 companies.

The choice of research subjects was made for convenience, given the low availability of managers and engineers from these companies to participate in the interviews. Of the 61 contacts made with managers from the various paper industries identified, 18 questionnaires were answered, with randomization of the order the questions were presented. In the data processing phase, responses from one of the participants were excluded due to his lack of experience in the paper industry.

The field study had 17 research subjects, who currently perform executive functions (two respondents); eight managers; two engineers; a supervisor; three consultants, and one analyst. The experience of most research subjects in the paper industry (10 of them) is four years or more, as shown in Figure 3:

The training of research subjects is mostly concentrated (relative frequency of 58.8%) at the graduate level, with three participants having master's and four bachelor's degrees.

To measure the nominal qualitative variables, a Likert scale from 0 to 5 points was used, with <0> corresponding to "I don't know", <1> equivalent to "I don't agree", and <5> representing "I fully agree".

Table 3. A questionnaire was used to assess the perception of experts on the analysis of environmental, social, and governance risks

Research problem: how can risk management and analysis contribute to the implementation of sustainability principles aimed at the analysis of environmental, social, and governance risks in industrial projects?						
Do you agree with the statement below?		Disagree	Agree Slightly	Partially	Agree	Agree Completely
Environmental						
Q1	Generation of hydroelectric power; irrigation; industry; population increase; changes in lifestyle (urbanization); economic advances and tourism are risks to water availability for sustainable projects (TARIQ; WANGCHUK; MUTTIL, 2021).					
Q2	"Returning agricultural land to forests" reduces soil-associated risks in sustainable industrial projects (DING et al., 2020).					
Q3	Forestry, mining, use of fossil fuels, and increased demand for renewable energy are critical factors for sustainable industrial projects (CREED et al., 2019).					
Q4	Low energy in the global economy and society's lack of adaptability to change are risk factors for sustainable industrial projects (CREED et al., 2019).					
Social						
Q5	The on-demand approach is sufficient for risk analysis in sustainable industrial projects (MARCOULAKI et al., 2021).					
Q6	Collaborative approaches reduce social risk and promote sustainable development (FRASER, 2021).					
Q7	Convergence analyses reduce social risk and promote sustainable development (DING et al., 2020).					
Q8	Risk management oriented towards the involvement of people is capable of empowering those involved and has greater governance potential for sustainability (GUMIRAN; DAAG, 2021).					
Q9	Community commitment is a critical factor for the success of sustainable industrial projects (GUMIRAN; DAAG, 2021).					
Q10	Political support is a critical factor for the success of sustainable industrial projects (GUMIRAN; DAAG, 2021).					
Q11	Increased external dependence can delay the economic development of communities involved in sustainable industrial projects (ZHANG; WANG, 2019).					
Q12	Local economic poverty is a risk factor for sustainable industrial projects (SUN et al., 2020).					
Governmental						
Q13	Planning policies are a critical factor for the success of sustainable industrial projects (GUMIRAN; DAAG, 2021).					
Q14	Scenario analysis is a sufficient technique for risk analysis in sustainable industrial projects (CREED et al., 2019).					
Q15	NBR ISO 31000 contains sufficient guidelines for risk analysis in sustainable industrial projects (ABNT, 2018; CREED et al., 2019).					
Q16	The convergence of objectives makes it possible to reduce conflicts of interest and advance toward sustainable development objectives (FRASER, 2021).					

Continued on following page

Table 3. Continued

Research problem: how can risk management and analysis contribute to the implementation of sustainability principles aimed at the analysis of environmental, social, and governance risks in industrial projects?						
	Do you agree with the statement below?	**Disagree**	**Agree Slightly**	**Partially**	**Agree**	**Agree Completely**
Q17	The integration between public and private objectives is a success factor for sustainable industrial projects (TAYLOR; HARMAN, 2016).					
Q18	There is a positive correlation between liquidity; leverage; productivity and financial success of sustainable industrial projects (BĂRBUŢĂ-MIŞU; MADALENO; ILIE, 2019).					
Q19	What are the main deficiencies in the governance, social and environmental aspects of your company?					
Q20	What risk management practice(s) do you consider most appropriate for sustainable industrial projects?					
Q21	What are the main risk analysis techniques (Tools) in use in your company?					

Source: Own elaboration, 2022

Figure 3. Research subjects' time of work in the paper industry in Rio de Janeiro
Source: Own elaboration, 2022

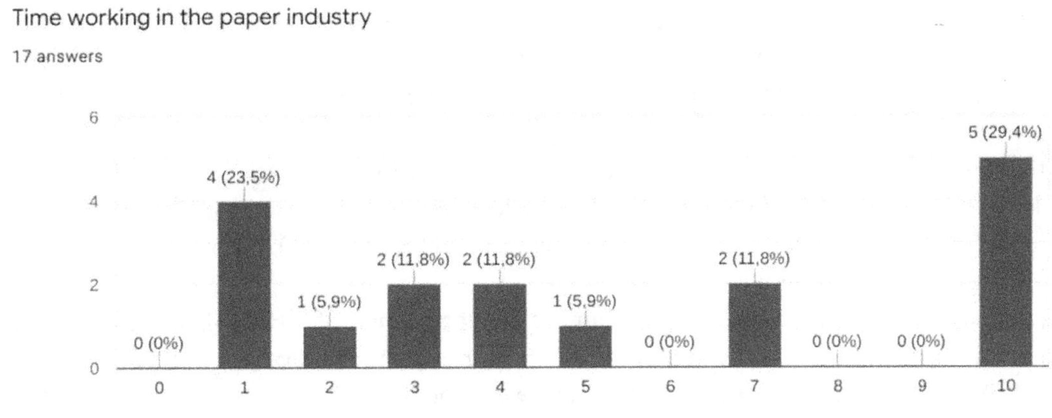

4. ANALYSIS OF RESPONDENTS' PERCEPTION

4.1 Risk Analysis Techniques and Tools

Research subjects were asked about the main techniques or risk analysis tools in use in the paper industry in which they work. They pointed to the preliminary risk analysis (APR) as the main approach used for risk management, with a relative frequency of 58.8% of the observations. In addition to this, the respondents highlighted the failure mode analysis (FMEA) in 29.4% of the questionnaires; the WHAT–IF (WI) analysis tool was mentioned by 23.5% of respondents as one of the risk analysis techniques in use in the company where they work.

The cause tree and the fault tree are evidenced by three and two research subjects, respectively. Other management techniques, listed only once in the consultation, were SWOT analysis; Ishikawa; PDCA; SDCA; Pareto diagram; brainstorming; 5 Whys, and Critical Incident Technique. One of the research subjects reports that "The company has low know-how with risk analysis," while one of the interviewees considers that this type of analysis does not apply to their activity.

When asked about the most appropriate risk management practice for application in sustainable industrial projects, 76.5% of managers highlighted the preliminary risk analysis (APR). In addition to this, failure modes analysis (FMEA) was highlighted by 52.9% of the research subjects, and the WHAT–IF (WI) technique by 41.2% of the participants.

4.2 Governance Concerns

The research subjects were also asked about the main deficiencies in the social and environmental governance of the company they work for. The most frequently mentioned factors were: clarity in the alignment of objectives between the State, communities, and the private sector (relative frequency = 58.8%); list of governance problems (52.9%); monitoring and eliminating the causes of risks (47.1%); measuring the socio-environmental impacts of the activity (41.2%); development of planning policies (35.3%), and society's involvement (29.4%).

Regarding approaches in risk management and governance for sustainability, the absolute majority of respondents (70.5%) agree with the statement that collaborative approaches reduce social risk and promote sustainable development (Fraser, 2021). In addition, 67.7% of respondents corroborate the thesis pointed out by Ding et al. (2020), that convergence analyses reduce social risk and promote sustainable development.

Among the administrative factors with the greatest potential to positively influence the success of sustainable industrial projects, the following stand out, according to the research subjects: influence of top management (relative frequency of 76.5%); sustainable advantage (70.6%); innovation (64.7%); legal factors (58.8%); and identification with the brand (52.9%).

The data collected did not prove to be significant on the application of NBR ISO 31000, since most respondents claim to be unaware of the standard (29.4%), or to be undecided about its impact on risk management (29.4%). Also, no significant differences were found in the responses on the analysis of scenarios, the on-demand approach, and the return of agricultural land to the forest as a reduction of soil risks in sustainable industrial projects.

4.3 Social Factors

Regarding the risk factors for sustainable industrial projects, most respondents (nine subjects) said they agree or completely agree with the statement that the drop in energy in the global economy and society's lack of adaptability to socio-environmental changes are risk factors for sustainable industrial projects (Creed et al., 2019), while six of them were undecided on the subject and one of them disagreed with the proposition.

The results also point to a strong agreement with the statement that risk management oriented towards the involvement of people is capable of empowering those involved and has a greater governance potential for sustainability (Gumiran & Daag, 2021), given that 14 respondents said they agree, or completely agree with it, while three of the research subjects were undecided and none disagreed.

Although a significant part of the respondents (35.3%) is undecided about the statement that community commitment is a critical factor for the success of sustainable industrial projects (Gumiran & Daag, 2021), most of them (52.9%) agrees, or completely agrees with the proposition, while two subjects indicated partial disagreement. Another assertion corroborated by most respondents (64.7%) is that political support is a critical factor in the success of sustainable industrial projects (Gumiran & Daag, 2021).

Most of the managers consulted (70.6%) agreed with the statement that the integration between public and private objectives is a success factor for sustainable industrial projects (Taylor & Harman, 2016). Similarly, 76.5% of respondents agreed that the benefit/cost ratio is favorable in sustainable industrial projects (Sugiyama et al., 2017).

No significant differences were found in the answers about the relationship between economic poverty, or the assistance dependence of communities and sustainable industrial projects.

4.4 Environmental Factors

The research subjects were also asked to identify critical factors for sustainable industrial projects in the paper industry in Rio de Janeiro, based on a list of factors found in a literature review and corroborated in consultation with experts in this research area. Among the main critical factors pointed out by the interviewees, the following stand out: development of planning policies (relative frequency of 64.7%); energy availability (58.8%); increased demand for renewable energy (52.9%); society involvement (47.1%); and clarity in the alignment of objectives between the State, communities and the private sector (41.2%).

5. ANALYSIS OF RISK ANALYSIS TECHNIQUES AND TOOLS

5.1 Preliminary Risk Analysis (APR), Failure Mode Analysis (FMEA), and What–If (WI).

Field data reveals a greater appreciation of managers for preliminary risk analysis (APR), failure mode analysis (FMEA) and WHAT-IF (WI) approaches. The APR-type approach has been used at least since 1977 in the area of nuclear science (Fullwood et al., 1977). It represents just one of the stages of risk analysis, which unfolds in risk estimation. The objectives of the first phase are to produce a clear statement about the problem under consideration, identify the various groups involved in resolving the issue as well as their responsibilities, and identify potential stakeholders. This is a feature provided for in consolidated standards such as ISO-14121 and ISO-17776, according to Komljenovic et al. (2008, p. 796).

Failure mode analysis is a technique developed by the automotive industry and defined in manuals such as QS9000. It is a corrective approach, based on an in-line process-oriented value stream. The objective of the technique is to identify how and when a process may fail to produce the desired value by the system (potential failure mode). In addition, the potential effects, severity, and causes of failures are analyzed. Records and controls of occurrences are also prepared, as well as the processes involved, and the ways of detecting and recovering failures. FMEA also provides for the definition of priorities and risk levels, records of responsibility, recommended actions, remedies, and treatment outcomes (Rotondaro, 2002).

The third risk analysis approach in use in the paper industry in Rio de Janeiro, according to the respondents, was identified as WHAT-IF (WI), a qualitative model of unique and oversimplified analysis that uses brainstorming, that is, the meeting of stakeholders to answer the question: What would happen if ... (there was a structural integrity failure). In this way, it is sought to predict, based on speculation, the ability to maintain and deliver the structural integrity (well integrity - WI) of the values, assets, or processes analyzed (Dethlefs & Chastain, 2012).

The discussion of the main risk analysis approaches used by the paper industry in Rio de Janeiro shows an incompleteness regarding the global view of the impact industrial activities have on society and the environment. In the preliminary risk analysis, the approach most used by the managers consulted, there is a limitation of the procedures to the identification of immediate problems and the interested parties, in search of accountability, without a clear concern with the global governance of organizations, expansion of the life cycle, or stakeholder engagement.

The second most used approach, the FMEA, although it is much more systematized and rigorous than the others, is structured based on orientation by online industrial processes, which can easily be decontextualized and converted into bureaucracy, making ESG solutions difficult, as well as the convergence of interests and community engagement, when considered in a global context of prevention. The third format, WHAT–IF (WI), although showing itself to be quite flexible and with the potential to involve the community, suffers from superficiality.

5.2 Deficiencies and Solutions in Social and Environmental Governance

The consultation with the managers of paper industries in RJ made it possible to identify the main social and environmental governance difficulties faced by the sector today. The lack of alignment between the objectives of the main stakeholders involved in the industrial ecosystem of the region was highlighted, namely: the State, communities, and private sector organizations.

In addition, the research subjects show difficulties in identifying and listing governance problems, as well as in eliminating the causes of social and environmental risks inherent to their activities.

Difficulties in measuring socio-environmental impacts were also reported, as well as the precariousness of the companies' planning policies and the lack of involvement of society in the search for social and environmental governance solutions.

The approaches to risk management identified as most relevant to solving such difficulties are collaborative and convergence analysis, highlighting the importance of community involvement for the development of better levels of social and environmental governance. Unfortunately, this type of approach is not favored by the risk management methods most used today in the RJ paper industry. When this occurs, it is through superficial wealth management techniques, such as brainstorming, WHAT –IF (WI), fault trees, etc., or in society, to value high levels of governance for organizations and community engagement, with a view to the convergence of interests.

5.3 Critical Factors for the Governance of Sustainable Industrial Projects

Respondents identified the main administrative factors associated with the success of sustainable projects in the paper industry in Rio de Janeiro, the influence of top management, which needs to be engaged in promoting sustainability as a necessary principle to make such initiatives viable. In addition, taking advantage of sustainable advantages, such as the availability of renewable resources, or the possibility of expanding the life cycle of products and processes, stands out as an important differential for the success of initiatives aimed at improving social and environmental governance.

The innovation capacity of the industries, associated with the corroboration of legal factors and the identification of the community with the organization's brand is evidenced by the research subjects as relevant opportunities to enhance the development and achieve success in sustainable industrial projects in the paper industry of Rio de Janeiro.

The main critical factor, pointed out by managers as impediments to such achievements, is the possibility of a drop in energy in the global economy, which would reduce demand and make it difficult for organizations in the sector to generate value, in addition to society's lack of adaptability to the ongoing structural changes, about the transition to a green economy and the need to adopt new consumption practices, relationship with the environment and respect for social norms, these factors are essential for the ascension to new levels of social governance and ESG in contemporary industry.

6. CONCLUSION

This research identified the methodologies used in risk management for ESG in sustainable industrial projects in the state of Rio de Janeiro. Research subjects identified the approaches of preliminary risk analysis, failure mode analysis, and WHAT–IF (WI) as the main practices in use in organizations in the region. These practices are incomplete in terms of the search for convergence of objectives, community engagement, and expansion of the life cycle of products and processes.

To achieve our objective, a case study was carried out, in consultation with experts and managers, based on a systematic review of the literature on risk analysis approaches in use in contemporary industry. The review and consultation pointed to collaborative perspectives and convergence analysis as structuring to enable stakeholder engagement in sustainable industrial projects in the paper industry in Rio de Janeiro.

Another specific objective of the research was to identify the critical factors for the implementation of sustainable projects in the analyzed case, among which the managers consulted highlighted the possibility of a drop in energy in the global economy and the lack of society's adaptability to the structural changes in course. Such critical factors have the potential to harm organizations in their search for better levels of social and environmental governance (ESG) in contemporary industry.

It must be considered that these results are limited by the small size of the paper industry in Rio de Janeiro and by the selection of a convenience sample, lacking further details to corroborate or refute the hypotheses raised herein.

REFERENCES

Oliveira, W.K. de, Rohlfs, D.B., & Garcia, L.P. (2019). The Brumadinho disaster and the role of Health Surveillance. *Epidemiology and Health Services, 28*(1). https://doi.org/10.5123/S1679-49742019000100025

Ablah, E., Oslon, C., Brown, J., Merriman, V., & Lee, C., Konda, Bronleewe, T., & Buzard, A. (2018). Need for Transparency and Ongoing Communication After Residents With Contaminated Water Wells Are Connected to City Water. *Journal of Environmental Health, 81*(3), 26–31.

Andrade, P. (2013). Sociological ontology of the Digital Public Sphere: The case of the Web 2.0/3.0. *Communicatio Socialis*, *23*, 186–201.

Bărbuță-Mișu, N., Madaleno, M., & Ilie, V. (2019). Analysis of Risk Factors Affecting Firms' Financial Performance—Support for Managerial Decision-Making. *Sustainability*, *11*(18), 4838. https://doi.org/10.3390/su11184838

Bauer, J. A., Devick, K. L., Bobb, J. F., Coull, B. A., Bellinger, D., Benedetti, C., Cagna, G., Fedrighi, C., Guazzetti, S., Oppini, M., Placidi, D., Webster, T. F., White, R. F., Yang, Q., Zoni, S., Wright, R. O., Smith, D. R., Lucchini, R. G., & Claus Henn, B. (2020). Associations of a Metal Mixture Measured in Multiple Biomarkers with IQ: Evidence from Italian Adolescents Living near Ferroalloy Industry. *Environmental Health Perspectives*, *128*(9), 097002. https://doi.org/10.1289/EHP6803

Capes, C. de A. de P. de N. S. (2022, January 11). *Portal. periodicals.* CAPES - *Who we are*. https://www-periodicos-capes-gov-br.ezl.periodicos.capes.gov.br/index.php/sobre/quem-somos.html]

Carey, N., & Steitz. (2021, July 14). *UE proposes a ban on sales of combustion cars from 2035*. Agência Brazil. https://agenciabrasil.ebc.com.br/internacional/noticia/2021-07/ue-propoe-proibicao-de-vendas-de-carros-combustao-partir-de-2035]

Covert, H. H., Sherman, M., Le, D., & Lichtveld, M. Y. (2020). Environmental health risk relationships, responsibility, and sources of information among Vietnamese Americans in coastal Mississippi. *Health Risk & Society*, *22*(5–6), 362–376. https://doi.org/10.1080/13698575.2020.1840528

Creed, I. F., Duinker, P. N., Serran, J. N., & Steenberg, J. W. N. (2019). Managing risks to Canada's boreal zone: Transdisciplinary thinking in pursuit of sustainability [1]. *Environmental Reviews*, *27*(3), 407–418. https://doi.org/10.1139/er-2018-0070

de Magalhães, S. (2021). *Our Everyday Role: Recycle, Reuse and Learn—A Pedagogical and Environmental Proposal in a Carioca Public Extension School* [Dissertation]. West Zone State University Center Foundation – UEZO, Sectorial Center for Computing and Applied Mathematics.

Dethlefs, J. C., & Chastain, B. (2012). Assessing Well-Integrity Risk: A Qualitative Model. *SPE Drill & Compl, 27*(2), 294–302. doi:10.2118/142854-PA

Di Noi, C., & Ciroth, A. (2018). Environmental and Social Pressures in Mining. Results from a Sustainability Hotspots Screening. *Resources*, *7*(4), 80. https://doi.org/10.3390/resources7040080

Ding, J., Chen, Y., Wang, X., & Cao, M. (2020). Land degradation sensitivity assessment and convergence analysis in Korla of Xinjiang, China. *Journal of Arid Land*, *12*(4), 594–608. https://doi.org/10.1007/s40333-020-0057-y

Fantke, P., Aylward, L., Bare, J., Chiu, W. A., Dodson, R., Dwyer, R., Ernstoff, A., Howard, B., Jantunen, M., Jolliet, O., Judson, R., Kirchhübel, N., Li, D., Miller, A., Paoli, G., Price, P., Rhomberg, L., Shen, B., Shin, H.-M., … McKone, T. E. (2018). Advancements in Life Cycle Human Exposure and Toxicity Characterization. *Environmental Health Perspectives, 126*(12), 125001. doi:10.1289/EHP3871

Fraser, J. (2021). Mining companies and communities: Collaborative approaches to reduce social risk and advance sustainable development. *Resources Policy, 74*, 101144. https://doi.org/10.1016/j.resourpol.2018.02.003

Fullwood, R., Straker, E., & Aron, W. (1977). Preliminary risk analysis of transportation of nuclear waste. *Transactions of the American Nuclear Society, 26*, 271–272.

Gumiran, B. A., & Daag, A. (2021). Negotiated participatory action research for multi-stakeholder implementation of early warning systems for landslides. *International Journal of Disaster Risk Reduction, 58*, 102184. https://doi.org/10.1016/j.ijdrr.2021.102184

Ipiranga, A. S. R., Godoy, A. S., & Brunstein, J. (2011). Introdução. *RAM. Revista de Administração Mackenzie, 12*(3), 13–20. https://doi.org/10.1590/S1678-69712011000300002

Kolahi, J., Khazaei, S., Bidram, E., Kelishadi, R., Iranmanesh, P., Nekoofar, M. H., & Dummer, P. M. (2020). Science Map of Cochrane Systematic Reviews Receiving the Most Altmetric Attention Score: A Network Analysis. *Journal of Scientometric Research, 9*(3), 293–299. https://doi.org/10.5530/jscires.9.3.36

Komljenovic, D., Groves, W. A., & Kecojevic, V. J. (2008). Injuries in U.S. mining operations – A preliminary risk analysis. *Safety Science, 46*(5), 792–801. https://doi.org/10.1016/j.ssci.2007.01.012

Laskaris, Z., Milando, C., Batterman, S., Mukherjee, B., Basu, N., O'neill, M. S., Robins, T. G., & Fobil, J. N. (2019). Derivation of Time-Activity Data Using Wearable Cameras and Measures of Personal Inhalation Exposure among Workers at an Informal Electronic-Waste Recovery Site in Ghana. *Annals of Work Exposures and Health, 63*(8), 829–841. https://doi.org/10.1093/annweh/wxz056

Lee, L. M. (2017). A Bridge Back to the Future: Public Health Ethics, Bioethics, and Environmental Ethics. *The American Journal of Bioethics, 17*(9), 5–12. https://doi.org/10.1080/15265161.2017.1353164

Malloy, T. F., Zaunbrecher, V. M., Batteate, C. M., Blake, A., Carroll, W. F., Corbett, C. J., Hansen, S. F., Lempert, R. J., Linkov, I., McFadden, R., Moran, K. D., Olivetti, E., Ostrom, N. K., Romero, M., Schoenung, J. M., Seager, T. P., Sinsheimer, P., & Thayer, K. A. (2017). Advancing Alternative Analysis: Integration of Decision Science. *Environmental Health Perspectives, 125*(6), 066001. https://doi.org/10.1289/EHP483

Marcoulaki, E., López de Ipiña, J. M., Vercauteren, S., Bouillard, J., Himly, M., Lynch, I., Witters, H., Shandilya, N., van Duuren-Stuurman, B., Kunz, V., Unger, W. E. S., Hodoroaba, V.-D., Bard, D., Evans, G., Jensen, K. A., Pilou, M., Viitanen, A.-K., Bochon, A., Duschl, A., … Dulio, V. (2021). Blueprint for a self-sustained European Centre for service provision in safe and sustainable innovation for nanotechnology. *NanoImpact, 23*, 100337. doi:10.1016/j.impact.2021.100337

NBR ISO 31000: Risk Management—Guidelines, no. NBR ISO 31000 Second Edition. (2018).

Portelinha, M. K., Almeida, C., Vargas, N. R. C., & Lopes, C. V. (2021). Interlaces among health, sustainability and environment: An integrative review. *Research Journal Care is Fundamental Online, 13*, 1001–1006. doi:10.9789/2175-5361.rpcfo.v13.9767

Rampasso, I. S., Quelhas, O. L. G., Anholon, R., Pereira, M. B., Miranda, J. D. A., & Alvarenga, W. S. (2020). Engineering Education for Sustainable Development: Evaluation Criteria for Brazilian Context. *Sustainability*, *12*(10), 3947. https://doi.org/10.3390/su12103947

Roden, J. (2021). Exploring the Perceived Health, Community, and Employment Impacts of an Announced Closure of a Coal-Fired Power Station in Upper Hunter Valley, Australia. *Journal of Environmental Health*, *83*(7), 26–35.

Rotondaro, R. G. (2002). SFMEA: Analysis of the effect and mode of failure in services – applying prevention techniques to improve services. *Production*, *12*(2), 54–62. https://doi.org/10.1590/S0103-65132002000200006

Santos, C. M. da C., Pimenta, C. A. de M., & Nobre, M. R. C. (2007). The PICO strategy for the research question construction and evidence search. *Revista Latino-Americana de Enfermagem*, *15*(3), 508–511. https://doi.org/10.1590/S0104-11692007000300023

Shaffer, R. M., Sellers, S. P., Baker, M. G., de Buen Kalman, R., Frostad, J., Suter, M. K., Anenberg, S. C., Balbus, J., Basu, N., Bellinger, D. C., Birnbaum, L., Brauer, M., Cohen, A., Ebi, K. L., Fuller, R., Grandjean, P., Hess, J. J., Kogevinas, M., Kumar, P., … Hu, H. (2019). Improving and Expanding Estimates of the Global Burden of Disease Due to Environmental Health Risk Factors. *Environmental Health Perspectives, 127*(10), 105001. doi:10.1289/EHP5496

Stumpf, A. M., Erlandson, G., Ruths, J., Meinke, D. K., Newman, L. S., Krisher, L., Pilloni, D., Cruz, A., & Asensio, C. (2020). Noise exposures of sugar cane mill workers in Guatemala. *International Journal of Audiology*, *59*(Suplemento), S48–S53.

Sugiyama, M., Asayama, S., Kosugi, T., Ishii, A., Emori, S., Adachi, J., Akimoto, K., Fujiwara, M., Hasegawa, T., Hibi, Y., Hirata, K., Ishii, T., Kaburagi, T., Kita, Y., Kobayashi, S., Kurosawa, A., Kuwata, M., Masuda, K., Mitsui, M., … Yoshizawa, G. (2017). Transdisciplinary co-design of scientific research agendas: 40 research questions for socially relevant climate engineering research. *Sustainability Science, 12*(1), 31–44. doi:10.1007/s11625-016-0376-2

Sun, M., Li, X., Yang, R., Zhang, Y., Zhang, L., Song, Z., Liu, Q., & Zhao, D. (2020). Comprehensive partitions and different strategies based on ecological security and economic development in Guizhou Province, China. *Journal of Cleaner Production*, *274*, 122794. https://doi.org/10.1016/j.jclepro.2020.122794

Tariq, M. A. U. R., Wangchuk, K., & Muttil, N. (2021). A Critical Review of Water Resources and Their Management in Bhutan. *Hydrology*, *8*(1), 31. https://doi.org/10.3390/hydrology8010031

Taylor, B. M., & Harman, B. P. (2016). Governing urban development for climate risk: What role for public-private partnerships? *Environment and Planning. C, Government & Policy*, *34*(5), 927–944. https://doi.org/10.1177/0263774X15614692

Tetteh, M. O., Chan, A. P. C., Darko, A., Yevu, S. K., Boateng, E. B., & Nwaogu, J. M. (2021). Key drivers for implementing international construction joint ventures (ICJVs): Global insights for sustainable growth. *Engineering, Construction and Architectural Management*. doi:10.1108/ECAM-07-2020-0512

Uccelli, R., Mastrantonio, M., Altavista, P., Caiaffa, E., Cattani, G., Belli, S., & Comba, P. (2016). Female lung cancer mortality and long-term exposure to particulate matter in Italy. *The European Journal of Public Health*. doi:10.1093/eurpub/ckw203

Universidade de Leiden. (2022). *VOSviewer—Visualizing scientific landscapes* (1.6.15) [Computer software]. https://www.vosviewer.com/

Yang, F., Yang, M., & Xu, J. (2018). The Productivity Dynamics of China's Environmentally Friendly Production Technologies in terms of Wastewater Treatment Techniques. *BioMed Research International*, *2018*, 1–10. https://doi.org/10.1155/2018/6878741

Zhang, X., & Wang, Z. (2019). How Does Paired Assistance to Disaster-Affected Areas (PADAA) Contribute to Economic Sustainability? A Qualitative Analysis of Wenchuan County. *Sustainability*, *11*(14), 3915. https://doi.org/10.3390/su11114391

Chapter 10
Waste Management Analysis for Energy Generation: An Interdisciplinary Study

Marcio Batista Pereira
https://orcid.org/0000-0001-6645-7087
Universidade Federal Fluminense, Brazil

Osvaldo Gonçalves Quelhas
https://orcid.org/0000-0001-6816-1677
Universidade Federal Fluminense, Brazil

Julio Vieira Neto
Universidade Federal Fluminense, Brazil

ABSTRACT

Currently, sustainable means of production and consumption are insufficient to meet the Sustainable Development Goals, requiring high awareness from managers of organizations and consumers. The production of urban solid waste, climate change, the emission of greenhouse gases, as well as energy demands are complex problems that require solutions from various branches of knowledge, including in the post-COVID-19 era. Considering the challenges of urban solid waste management and energy recovery technology, it is important to reflect on the level of understanding of municipal managers, in addition to observing the economic, social, and environmental impacts of the pandemic. Through a structured literature review, the study highlights multiple perspectives that can understand and seek alternatives for socio-environmental liabilities.

INTRODUCTION

Due to global changes, knowledge has become fundamental for participation in the development of society and insertion in professional sectors. The question that arises is to know the level of understanding of

DOI: 10.4018/978-1-6684-6750-3.ch010

municipal managers about the energy recovery of solid waste, as well as whether the pandemic affected the zero waste goal, implicit in the Sustainable Development Goals - SDGs 11 and 12, the survey intends to answer in five topics.

The first topic lists the theoretical foundations of interdisciplinarity, waste and energy, the sustainability of the SDGs and the Convid-19 Pandemic, all duly referenced. It is concluded that the current sustainable means of production and consumption are insufficient, requiring high awareness from managers of organizations and consumers. It is not by chance that the high production of solid waste and the emission of greenhouse gases are complex problems that require several branches of knowledge. It can be seen that the long-term success of businesses and their respective economic, social and environmental impacts depend on sustainability. From then on, the hypothesis of transforming urban waste into energy appears as an alternative to the dilemma of managing urban solid waste in municipalities, undoubtedly one of the main obstacles to making cities sustainable, in addition to consumption and production responsible.

Following, the study addresses how the pandemic demonstrated poverty, extreme inequality, both pre-existing, but now revealing total contempt for human life across the planet. Therefore, the large-scale availability of cheap energy, accessible to the population, prevails. The main impacts of scientific research are reported in the second topic, as a way of enabling solutions, recovering the stagnation and barriers imposed by the Coronavirus-19 and in the application of the SDGs.

In the third topic, the method of structured literature review was presented, which served as the basis for the critical analysis and with an interdisciplinary approach to the study. In addition, the fourth topic portrays the descriptive analysis, followed by the results and discussions specified in the fifth topic.

Finally, in the sixth topic, the conclusion of multiple perspectives with interdisciplinary adherence, capable of understanding, studying and seeking theoretical support from the various urban and socio-environmental sciences in practice, structuring the SDGs, such as the generation of energy from urban solid waste, mitigating disasters like the Coronavirus.

1. THEORETICAL BACKGROUND

1.1. Interdisciplinarity

The transformative scientific developments of the 20th century can be explored as alternatives to solve emerging problems, such as climate change. These are complex issues, whose amplitude and integration demand a holistic, joint vision for a proper (necessary or true) understanding of presente day phenomena (events).

Increasingly, the integration of different experts in diverse field of knowledge is becoming necessary to understand and critically analyze complex problems that require an integrated and interdisciplinary approach (Di Giulio, et al., 2017).

The joint work of different areas, when properly executed, provides achieving more effective and innovative results, transposing the knowledge reached in individual research (Ambrizzi, et al., 2017). The ability of transformative approaches to face complex problems and their polycentric nature has increased their value and prominence in recent years (Nhamo et al. 2020).

The interdisciplinarity applicable in urban dynamics and environmental changes emerges as a stable proposal to put people back in control of knowledge (Waldman, et al., 2017). All this, consolidates new ways of thinking in relation to science and technology in modern society in an interdisciplinary framework.

1.2. Waste and Energy

Due to evolution, in recent decades, households have increased their absolute level of energy consumption, as they have also equipped themselves with more efficient machines and appliances. As happens in highly complex systems, tensions always manifest between efficiency and resilience, the ability to anticipate, absorb, recover, and adapt to unexpected disruptions (Hynes et al., 2020; Pnum and ILRI, 2020).

Driven by state efforts around the world, the "green industrial revolution" should be seen as an attempt to transform existing infrastructure into energy infrastructure (Mazuccato, 2016). The effects of the socio-environmental crisis arising from the mismanagement of solid waste show that the economic potential to be extracted with the reutilization or reuse, proves to be lower than expected, making it difficult to adopt the perspective of a sustainable management with social inclusion (Selau, 2018)

Not coincidentally, the choice for one of the thermal processes for pre- or post-recycling waste treatment should be guided by technical, social, economic, and political issues, in line with strategies pertinent to integrated waste management that prioritize energy generation from waste (Themelis et al., 2016).

It is urgent to clarify that developed countries in relation to waste generated tend towards the "upstream avoidance" type of solutions, while less developed countries use "downstream remediation" solutions (Chalhoub, 2018). Understanding trends and changes in energy demand, implies analyzing the dynamics of social practices.

Therefore, issues related to energy and sanitation with an interdisciplinary spectrum have the potential to generate applicable knowledge in economic and political decisions, especially regarding the internal and external discrepancies of developed and developing countries (Batista, et al., 2021).

1.3. Sustainability

Countries of continental dimensions such as Brazil present deep infrastructure challenges, where the provision of public energy services needs to be accompanied by affordable and uniform prices (Bercovici, et al., 2021).

Most likely as a result of the low insertion of research and also the reduced appropriation of knowledge generated in Academia by the industrial sector, the generation of innovation is very restricted in developing countries, where government and business need to act in harmony and in an integrated manner to generate technologies and innovations for economic growth and development (Dall'Agnol, et al. 2017).

Therefore, sustainability is critical to the long-term success of business and progressively requires correlating the non-financial, economic and administrative, but also environmental and social impacts of all the organization's activities (Zhang, et al., 2021).

In this way, the search for sustainable results does not reside solely in the company's finances, but depends on the results in the social and environmental spheres. (Barszcz, 2007)

The interconnectedness of challenges currently by humanity has reignited the discussion on the importance of transformative approaches to achieve sustainability in world surrounded by a host of problems (Burch et al., 2019).

It is noted that sustainable development can improve production processes, reducing environmental impacts, as well as responding to society's demands on environmental issues.

1.4. Sustainable Development Goal

The integrative aspect of this research occurs when it addresses the hypothesis of transforming urban waste into energy, emphasizing an environmental problem of great relevance. Then, production processes can be improved by reducing environmental impacts based on sustainable development.

Hence, the interconnection of the current challenges imposed on humanity, which reignite the discussion about the importance of transformative approaches to achieve sustainability in a world surrounded by a host of problems (Burch et al., 2019).

Challenge targets set in the ODS encounter barriers to practical implementation, far from responding to society's key demands. The pandemic and social isolation have affected the consolidation of the goals contained in the ODS, as well as caused the economic slowdown, affecting families, businesses, financial sectors, etc.

The main challenges are to recover the implementation of the Sustainable Development Goals lost in the pandemic, as well as to enable future progress in this direction.

1.5. Pandemic Covid-19

The coronavirus merely exposed the pre-existing pandemic of poverty. Covid-19 has arrived in a world in which poverty, extreme inequality, and contempt for human life are spreading, not least because economic policies and legal structures are designed to generate and sustain wealth for the most powerful, not to eradicate poverty (Philip Alston, 2020).

Health, social inequality, and other sustainable development goals must be addressed together based on multiple environmental processes that integrate simultaneously (Sunyer et al., 2021). On the other hand, many scholars have found that the closure of industrial activities during the Pandemic caused economic losses (Bashir et al. 2020; Goolsbee and Syverson, 2021, Versschuur et al., 2021).

The pandemic has impacted companies, families, corporations, the financial sector, and the rules set forth in the ODS Accessible and affordable energy must be used on a large scale for the population.

2. IMPACTS ON SCIENTIFIC RESEARCH

Along the lines of enabling solutions to recover from the stagnation and barriers imposed on ODS by Coranavirus-19, the major impacts of this scientific research can be reported. Many scholars have found that the closure of industrial activities during the pandemic caused economic losses (Bashir et al., 2020, Goolsbe and Syverson, 2021, Versschuur, 20121), in addition to other social, legal, professional, health, technological, and other impacts.

The social impact is present when the research values public policy actions in municipalities, through sustainable energy management from the reuse of urban waste. The economic impact is verified when the study envisions the commercialization of energy recovered from solid waste, which provides revenue for the players involved in the urban cleaning segment.

There is also a legal impact when the theme requires further study with the regulation of Energy Recovery Plants, Basic Sanitation, Players in the Electricity Sector, among others. The professional impact of research resides in projects focused on GRSU that use waste as a source of innovative solutions for infrastructure, basic services, consulting, and qualification, both in the academic and corporate spheres.

Sanitary and technological impacts can be observed in this study, as it signals an effective alternative related to energy, climate, and health, as well as the aspects of integrated and technological management with theoretical and practical application.

Finally, other impacts can be explored by employing the technology of reusing energy from RSU. This is an alternative with the potential to stimulate strategic solutions in energy and environmental liabilities, in the medium and long term.

3. METHODOLOGY

In this paper, a structured literature review was conducted in order to enable a critical analysis about solid waste management for energy generation and with an interdisciplinary focus, without prejudice to technical measures and validation and reliability techniques (Massaro et al., 2016).

The literature survey comprised combinations of the following key words: (i) economic model and social inequality; (ii) environmental liabilities and urban solid waste; (iii) sustainable development and post covid 19, and (iv) interdisciplinarity and energy demand.

Then, the keywords were combined with the Booleans "AND" and "OR", precisely between January and February, 2022, in the Scopus database, having as references the year of publication, the countries, and the areas of knowledge.

It should be noted that Scopus is considered by the academic community as the largest interdisciplinary database and, according to (Azevedo, Scavarda and Caiado, 2019). The reason why the mentioned database referenced this research was not otherwise, given that it is the largest data collection of citations and abstracts of peer-reviewed literature, in addition to providing instruments for tracking, analyzing, and visualizing research (Elsevier, 2019).

Subsequently, interviews with Brazilian municipal managers were conducted so as to verify their familiarity with the subject matter of **SUW** energy recovery so as to establish an understanding of the questions and replies of interviewees that operate in the management of solid waste in Brazilian cities.

Chart 1 illustrates Boolean combinations with keywords, raw and net results, after considering priority criteria adherent to the theme.

Table 1. Search results with Boolean combinations with key words

Search	Base	Boolean combinations with key words	Raw result	Net result
1. economic model and social inequality	Scopus	"econ AND model AND social AND inequality"	31	10
2. Environmental Passive and Urban Solid Waste	Scopus	"ambient AND liabilities AND solid AND waste"	5	2
3. Sustainable Development and Post Covid 19	Scopus	"Sustainable Development" and "Post Covid 19"	414	10
4. Interdisciplinarity and Energy Demand	Scopus	"Interdisciplinary" and "Energy Demand"	528	10
		Total Scopus	978	32

Source - The author himself

The screening process for the selection of articles included the reading of titles and abstracts, evaluation of the texts, as well as their adherence and alignment with the theme under discussion, totaling a quantity of 32 (thirty-two) searches.

4. DESCRIPTIVE ANALYSIS OF THE RESULTS

This topic highlights the descriptive results of the bibliographical survey adhering to the thematic axis, year of publication, countries and areas of knowledge.

4.1. Economic Model and Social Inequality

Regarding the sources related to the Economic Model and Social Inequality in the period between 2017 and 2020, there is no information.

Figure 1. Economic model and social inequality by year
Source Scopus

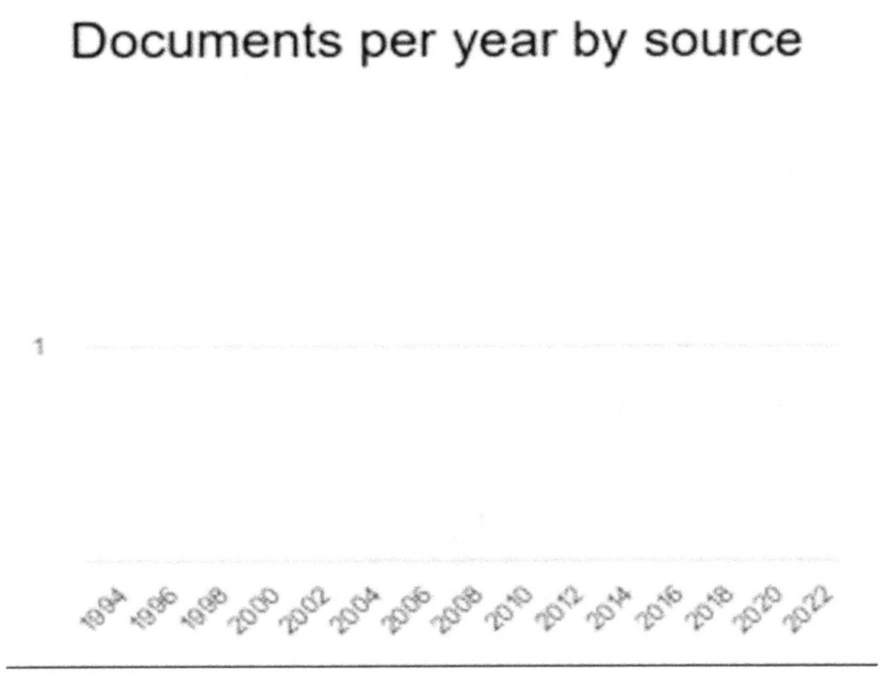

In turn, the data segregated by the top five countries, Italy, Germany, England, the United States, and Ireland.

Figure 2. Economic model and social inequality by country
Source Scopus

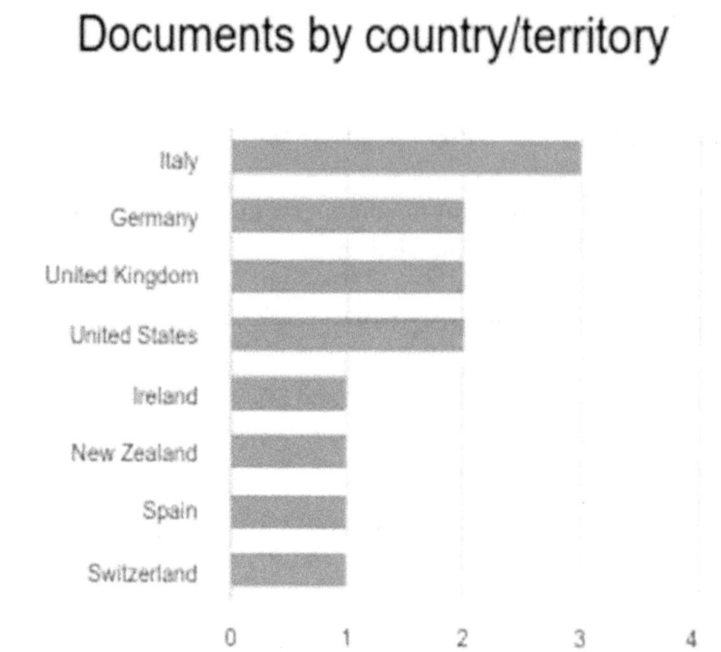

As for the section referenced by the five areas of knowledge, they follow the following order: Economics, Social Sciences, Psychology, Human Sciences, Computer Sciences.

Figure 3. Economic model and social inequality by knowledge area
Source Scopus

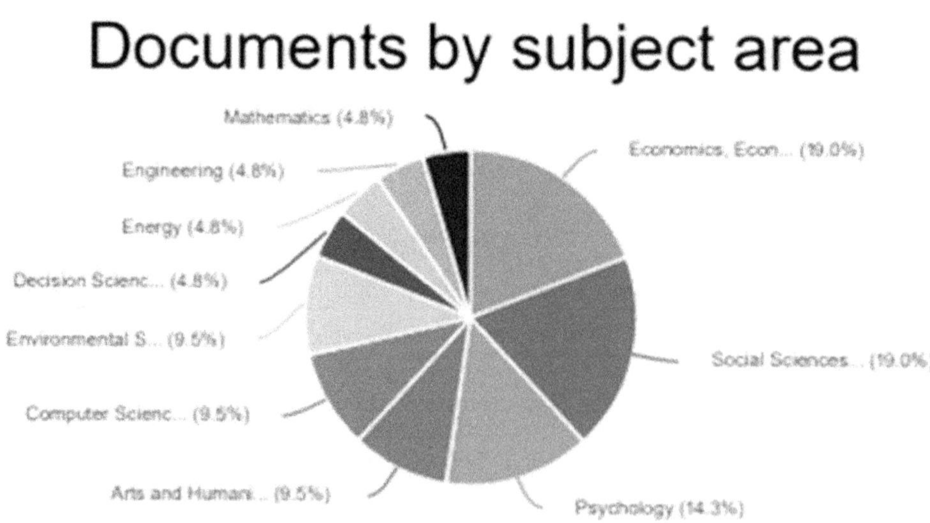

4.2. Environmental Passive and Urban Solid Waste

Regarding the Environmental Passive and Urban Solid Waste axis, the absence of information concerning the year is repeated.

Figure 4. Environmental passive and urban solid waste by year
Source: Scopus

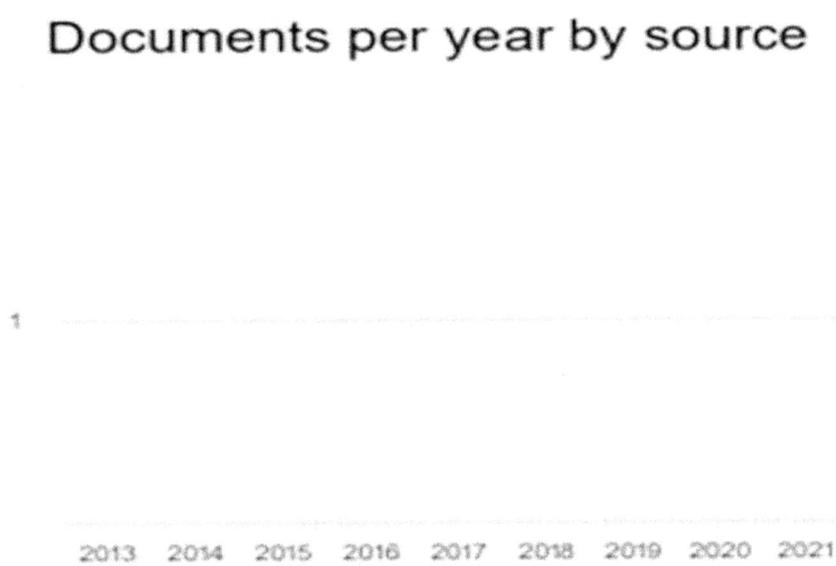

In the sequence, the description by country is observed, with Canada and India, among others, standing out.

Figure 5. Environmental passive and municipal solid waste by country
Source Scopus

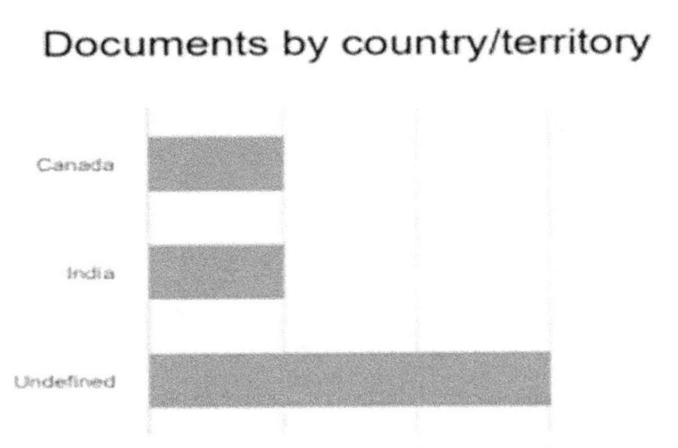

In conclusion, the specifications by knowledge area ordered by Environmental Sciences, Energy, Social Sciences, Business Management, and Engineering.

Figure 6. Environmental passive and urban solid waste by knowledge area
Source: Scopus

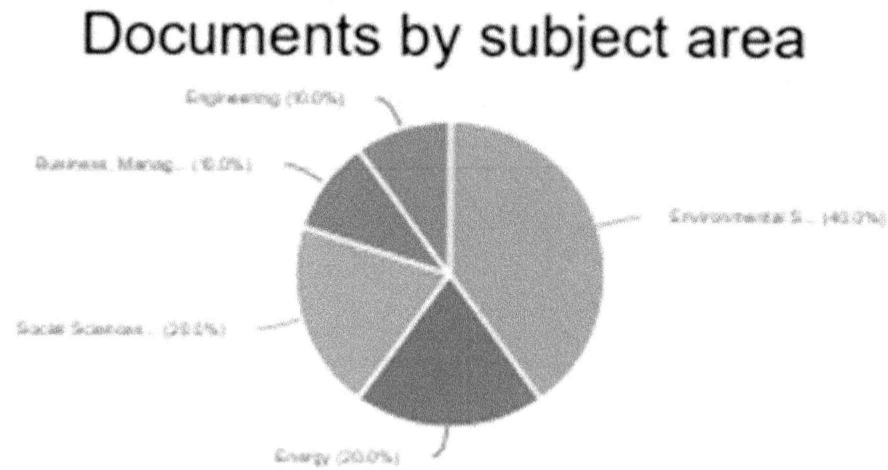

4.3. Sustainable Development and Post Covid 19

The following is descriptive about the Sustainable Development and Post Covid 19 axis, where a peak of documents in the year 2021, the peak of the pandemic, emerges.

Figure 7. Sustainable development and post Covid 19 by year
Source: Scopus

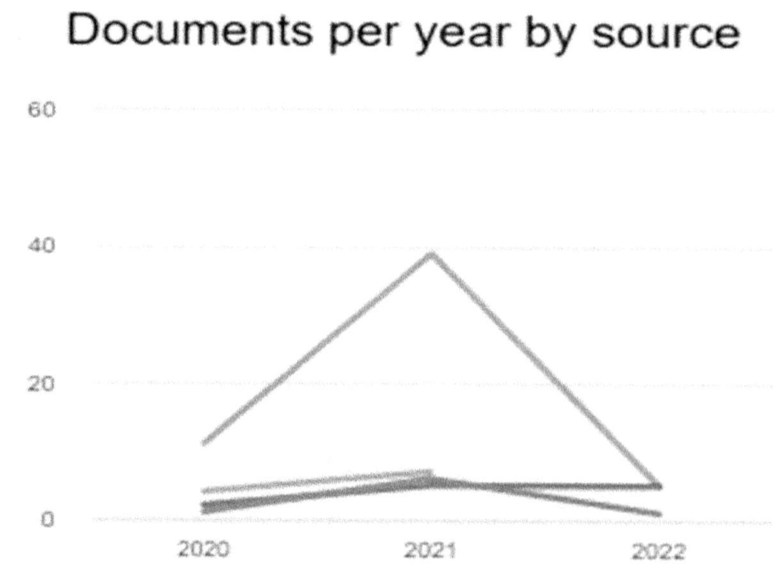

The list of the top five countries points to the United States, China, Spain, England, India.

Figure 8. Sustainable development and post Covid 19 by country
Source: Scopus

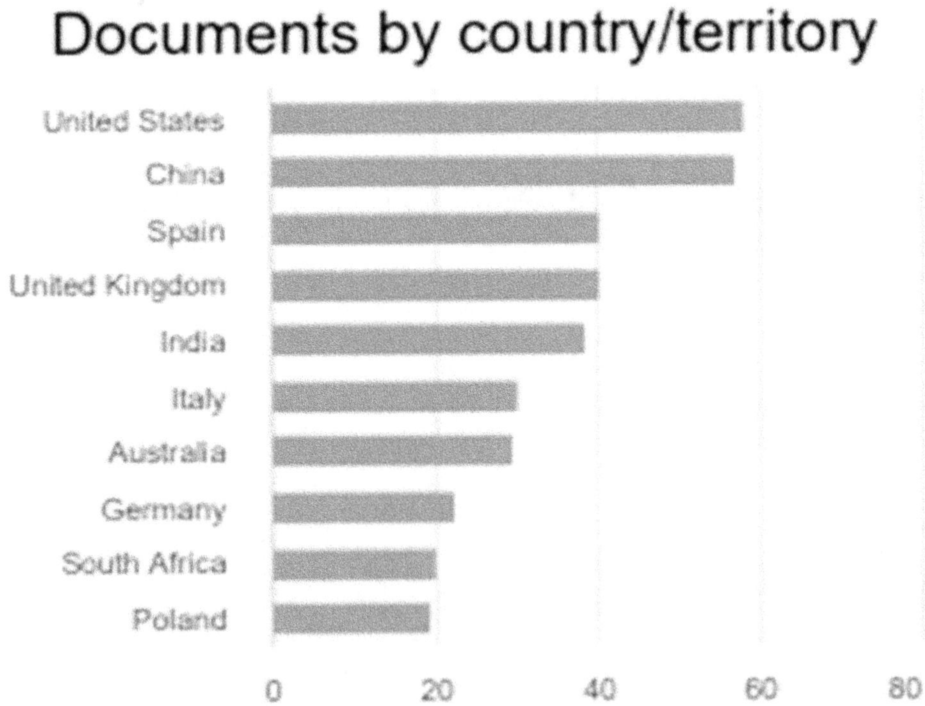

Going forward, the five major areas are ordered as follows: Social Sciences, Environmental Sciences, Energy, Business Management, Engineering.

Figure 9. Sustainable development and post Covid by knowledge area
Source Scopus

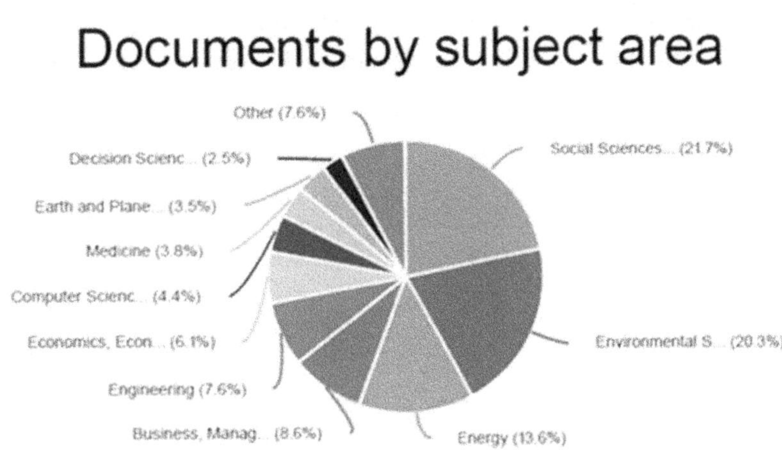

4.4. Interdisciplinarity and Energy Demand

There is a significant rise between the years 2019 to 2021 focused on the themes of interdisciplinarity and energy demand.

Figure 10. Interdisciplinarity and energy demand by year
Source Scopus

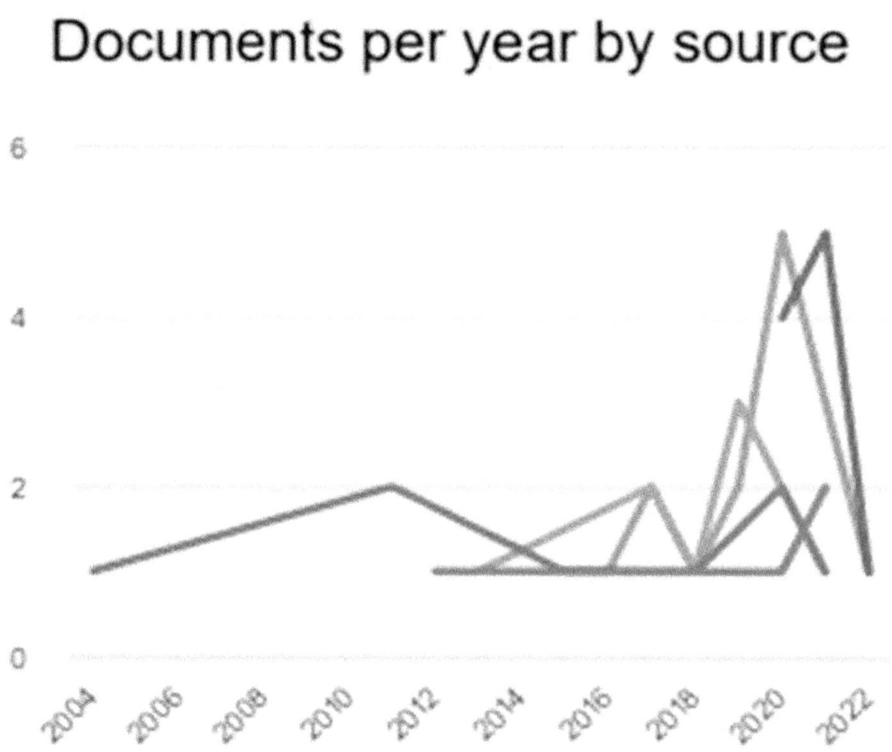

Otherwise, the top five countries are: United States, Germany, England, China and Italy.

Finally, the five areas, namely: Engineering, Environmental Science, Energy, Social Sciences, and Computer Science.

Figure 11. Interdisciplinarity and energy demand by country
Source Scopus

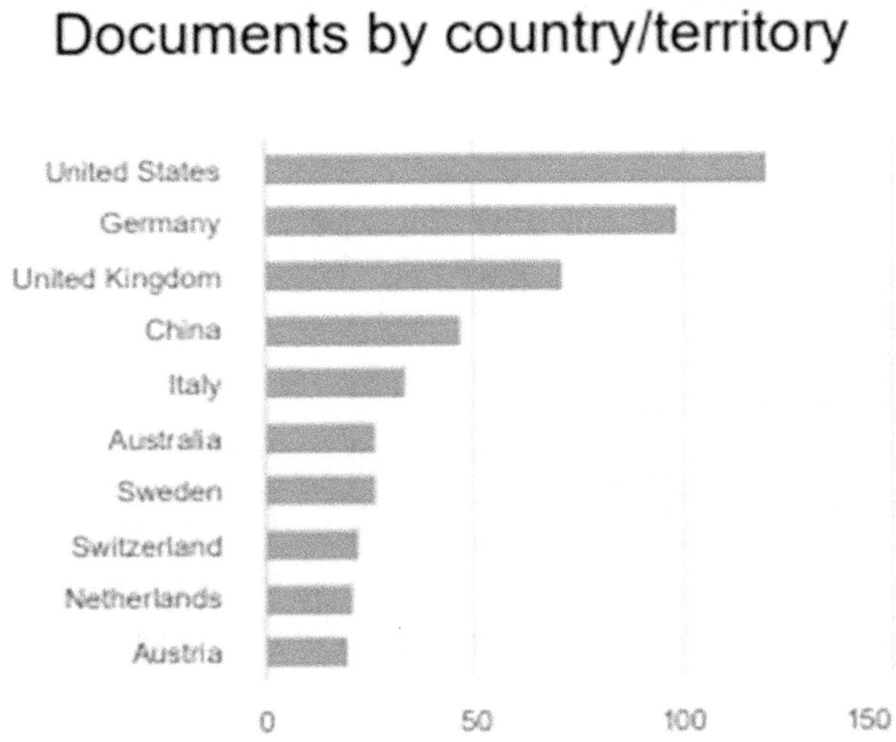

Figure 12. Interdisciplinarity and energy demand by area of knowledge
Source Scopus

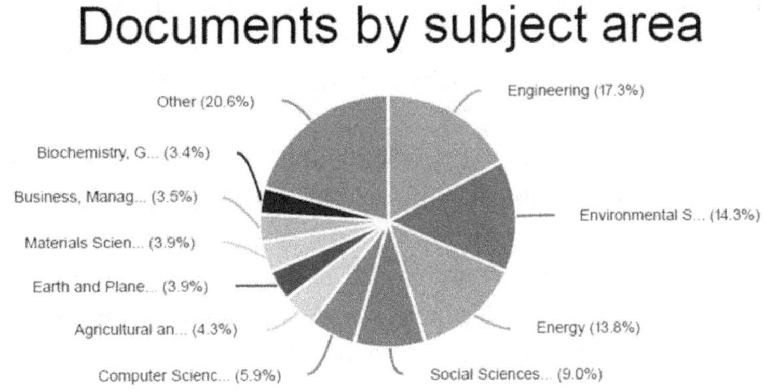

4.5 Knowledge Level of the Managers

It is found that the professional respondents have low or very low knowledge on the subject of energy recovery from urban waste (Pereira, 2022).

Figure 13. Level of knowledge of the managers on energy recovery
Source prepared by the author

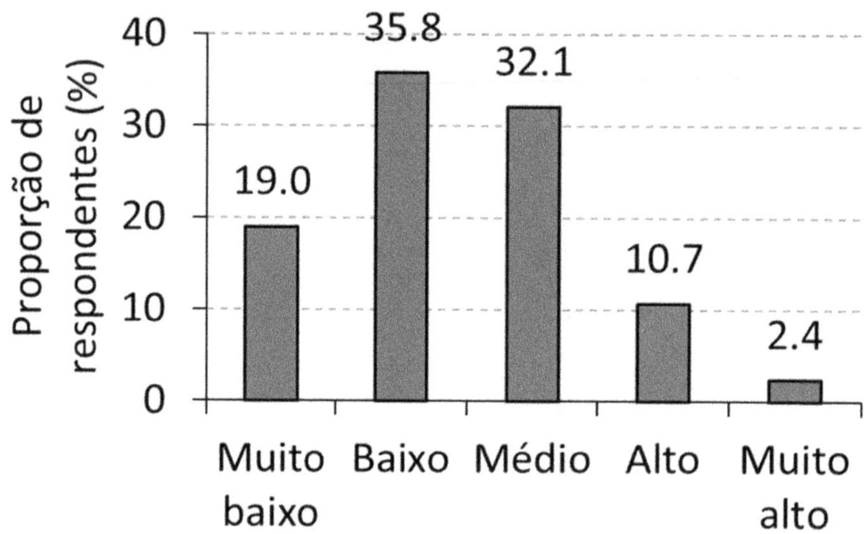

5. RESULTS AND DISCUSSIONS

As for the Economic Model and Social Inequality, there are no relevant movements in the last five years. Only developed countries present highlights concerning the theme. The knowledge areas presented are Economics, Social Sciences, Psychology and Computer Sciences. Therefore, the trend is to maintain the concentration of income and social inequality in developed countries, with no relevance for Energy and Environmental Sciences.

For the combination of movements on Environmental Passive and Urban Solid Waste, the non-existence observed in the previous combination from 2018 to 2022 is repeated. One developed country (Canada) and one developing country (India) showed movements related to the topic in the last five years. Therefore, Environmental Sciences, Energy and Social Sciences make up the relevant knowledge areas.

Concerning the topic Sustainable Development and Post Civid-19, a peak of movements are visualized in 2021, the year of the lethal effects of the pandemic. Once the pandemic effects are under control in 2022, the movements have equalized. Developed countries ranked between first and fourth, with the exception of India (a developing country) which ranked fifth. Interestingly, the knowledge areas of Environmental Sciences, Energy, and Social Sciences were also relevant.

Regarding Interdisciplinarity and Energy Demand, in the same way it was verified a significant increase in movements during the pandemic period (2020 and 2021), returning to normality after the control of Covid-19. In this topic no developing countries were found with related movements, with Environmental Sciences, Energy, and Social Sciences remaining the relevant fields of knowledge. The professional respondents had low or very low knowledge about energy recovery from waste.

6. CONCLUSION

It is concluded that the level of understanding of municipal managers about energy recovery from waste is below what is required and that the pandemic has sensitively affected the goals of zero waste and eradication of open dumps and landfills present in the items of the Sustainable Development Goals. There is also the predominance of Environmental, Energy, and Social Sciences as areas of knowledge.

It is necessary to understand the actions and procedures, especially regarding the management of solid waste in cities, which are far from establishing methods that meet society's expectations. On the other hand, once the concentration of income and inequality in developed countries is maintained, reversing this accentuated context in developing countries, characterized by the lack of resources and basic infrastructure, reveals a dilemma of complex solution.

The shortage of energy and the urban solid waste disposed of to the contrary of environmental rules are interdisciplinary issues of complex solution. As it is known, promoting mechanisms that recover and transform solid waste into energy, is a key element for everyday environmental management systems, especially to help operational activities to work efficiently and correctly. The contribution of this work is to propose a holistic, interdisciplinary approach in order to hypothesize affordable, reliable, and modern energy from the reuse of municipal solid waste, aligned with sustainable consumption and production.

Finally, the study aims to facilitate the approximation of managers from different fields or branches of knowledge, whether from the engineering, legal, financial or administrative areas, without prejudice to other forms of managed experiments with mutual enrichment that may result in new ideas and strategic solutions.

REFERENCES

AMBRIZZI. (2017). *Tercio Ambrizzi, Cintia Barcellos Lacerda e Lívia Márcia Mosso Dutra. Construção de núcleo de pesquisa interdisciplinar em mudanças climáticas: o caso INCLINE da USP. Ensino e Pesquisa da Inovação Desenvolvendo a Interdisciplinaridade*. Manole.

Batista, M., Caiado, R. G. G., Yparraguirre, I. T. R., Filho, W. L., Lima, G. B. A., & Quelhas, O. L. G. (2021). A framework for sustainable and integrated municipal solid waste management: Barriers and critical factors to developing countries. *Journal of Cleaner Production*, *312*, 127516. Advance online publication. doi:10.1016/j.jclepro.2021.127516

Bercovici, Costa. (2021). Nacionalização: Necessidade e Possibilidade. Academic Press.

Burrch, S. (2019). New directions in earth system governance research. *Earth Syst. Govern.*, *1*, 100006. Advance online publication. doi:10.1016/j.esg.2019.100006

Chalhoub, M. S. (2018). Public policy and technology choices for municipal solid waste management a recent case in Lebanon. *Cogent Environmental Science*, *4*(1), 1–18. doi:10.1080/23311843.2018.1529853

DALL'AGNOL. (2017). *Roberto, José Oswaldo Siqueira, Maria Cristina Maneschy, Pedro Walfir Martins e Souza Filho e Everaldo Barreiros de Souza. Interdisciplinaridade em instituto vinculado a empresa: experiências, desafios e perspectivas do Instituto Tecnológico Vale Desenvolvimento Sustentável. Ensino e Pesquisa da Inovação Desenvolvendo a Interdisciplinaridade*. Manole.

Di Giulio, Vasconcellos, & Ribeiro. (2017). Megacidades e mudanças climáticas: compreendendo problemas e desafios do município de São Paulo sob enfoque interdisciplinar. In *Ensino e Pesquisa da Inovação Desenvolvendo a Interdisciplinaridade*. Elsevier. https://hdl.handle.net/1884/66700

Goolsbee, A., & Syverson, C. (2021). Fear, lockdown, and diversion: Comparing drivers of pandemic economic decline 2020. *Journal of Public Economics, 193*(C). doi:10.1016/j.jpubeco.2020.104311

Govindarajan, V. (2016). A Estratégia das 3 Caixas. Academic Press.

Massaro, M., Dumay, J., & Guthrie, J. (2016). On the shoulders of giants: Undertaking a structured literature review in accounting. *Accounting, Auditing & Accountability Journal*, *29*(5), 767–801. doi:10.1108/AAAJ-01-2015-1939

Mazzucato, M. (2016). *O Estado Empreendedor: desmascarando o mito do setor público vs. setor privado*. Portfolio-Penguin.

Nhamo, L., Ndlela, B., Mpandeli, S., & Mabhaudhi, T. (2020a). The water-energy-food nexus as an adaptation strategy for achieving sustainable livelihoods at a local level. *Sustainability (Switzerland), 12*(20), 1–16. doi:10.3390u12208582

Pereira. (2021). *Marcio Batista. Análise de modelos e práticas de gestão de resíduos sólidos: o caso do aproveitamento energético do lixo urbano no Brasil. Pag. 69*. Editora Dialética.

Philippi, Fernandes, Pacheco, & Roberto. (2017). *Ensino, pesquisa e inovação: Desenvolvendo a interdisciplinaridade*. Editora Manole.

PNUMA/ILRI. (2020). *Preventing the Next Pandemic: Zoonotic Diseases and How to Break the Chain of Transmission*. Author.

Selau, C. C. (2018). Gestão E Gerenciamento De Resíduos Sólidos No Município de Criciúma/Sc [Solid Waste Management in the Municipality of Criciúma/Sc. Academic Press.

Sunyer & Dadvand. (2021). Environment and the COVID-19 pandemic. *Environmental Research, 195*(1). doi:10.1016/j.envres.2021.110819

Themelis, N. J., Barriga, M. E. D., Estevez, P., & Valesco, M. G. (2016). *Guia Para Recuperar Energia E Materiais (Rem) de Resíduos Sólidos* [Guide to Recovering Energy and Materials (Rem) from Solid Waste]. Vitória: Wtert-brasil. Available in: http://www.wtert.com.br

Waldamn & Dalpia. (2017). *A Universidade e a construção da interdisciplinaridade. Ensino, pesquisa e inovação: Desenvolvendo a interdisciplinaridade*. Editora Manole.

Xue, B., Zhang, Z., & Li, P. (2020). Desempenho ambiental corporativo, gestão ambiental e risco firme. Estratégia Empresarial e Meio Ambiente, 29(3), 1074-1096. doi:10.1002/bse.2418

Zhang, T., Wu, Q., & Zhang, Z. (2020). Probable Pangolin Origin of SARS-CoV-2 Associated with the COVID-19 Outbreak. *Current Biology*, *30*(7), 1346–1351. doi:10.1016/j.cub.2020.03.022 PMID:32197085

Chapter 11
Are There Sustainable Development Trends in Chinese Ecotourism Policies?

Poshan Yu
https://orcid.org/0000-0003-1069-3675
Soochow University, China & Australian Studies Centre, Shanghai University, China

Keyi He
Independent Researcher, China

Emanuela Hanes
Independent Researcher, Austria

ABSTRACT

Defined as a type of tourism uniting conservation, communities, and sustainable travel, ecotourism is becoming increasingly important. For governments, developing guidance for the industry which helps address the potential conflicts between ecological conservation and economic development is of utmost importance. Thus, the changes of government policies in tourism have significantly driven the ecotourism development in China. However, most current research findings on ecotourism paid insufficient attention on the significance of the interlinked relationships among policies and research studies and the trends inside them. Implementing research methods including literature analysis and institutional analysis, this chapter aims to examine these dynamic relationships from the regulators' perspectives. This chapter contributes to the field by demonstrating a sustainable development trend of Chinese ecotourism driven by the unique institutional settings with Chinese characteristics and analyzing the potential implications for various stakeholders due to the rising standards of ecotourism.

DOI: 10.4018/978-1-6684-6750-3.ch011

INTRODUCTION

Defined as a type of tourism uniting conservation, communities and sustainable travel, ecotourism is becoming increasingly important. For governments, developing guidance for the industry which helps address the potential conflicts between ecological conservation and economic development is of utmost importance. Thus, the changes of government policies in tourism have significantly driven the ecotourism development in China. However, most of current research findings on ecotourism paid insufficient attention on the significance of the interlinked relationships among policies & research studies and the trends inside them. Implementing research methods including literature analysis and institutional analysis, this paper aims to examine these dynamic relationships from the regulators' perspective. This chapter contributes to the field by 1) demonstrating a sustainable development trend of Chinese ecotourism driven by the unique institutional settings with Chinese characteristics and 2) analyzing the potential implications for various stakeholders due to the rising standards of ecotourism. The findings have indicated that the Chinese government has imposed the ideology of the ecotourism development for promoting the concept of ecological conservation while harmonizing the conflicting interests of various stakeholders.

LITERATURE REVIEW

Although there are numerous studies about Chinese ecotourism, most of them concentrate on ecotourism content or influence. Ren et al. (2021) in their study examine residents' behaviors under different types of ecotourism participation and how these behaviors impact the surrounding ecosystem. By using quantitative analysis, Zhou et al. (2013) evaluate the impact of ecotourism on mammals in a protected area. A number of studies also explore the relationship between ecotourism and local communities (Ma et al., 2019; Qiu & Tang, 2020) and ecotourism management (Li, 2004; Xu et al., 2017). However, only few studies have investigated Chinese ecotourism-related policies. Amongst these, the work of Liu and Cai (2009) discusses the need of public participation in ecotourism policies' formulation. A seminal study in this area is the work of Xiao & Zhong (2017), in which they used cluster analysis to describe policy evolution in China synthetically and trace the change of objectives, contents and patterns in Chinese ecotourism policies. Specific terms such as scenic spots and forest parks are introduced in their data collection, which in turn help advance the comprehensiveness of collected data. However, their study neglected the significance of ecotourism and failed to distinguish the difference between simple natural tourism and sustainable ecotourism. Moreover, policies that show only weak association included in their study led to deviations during the conduct of the study.

Based upon previous studies, it can be stated that misinterpretations or malpractices of ecotourism are particularly serious in China. The work of Li et al. (2019) indicated that there may be misunderstanding or misuse of ecotourism in China by analyzing the distribution of Chinese ecotourism sites and found no correlation between the provincial distribution pattern of Chinese ecotourism sites and natural factors such as the number of protected areas or forest coverages. Liu et al. (2009) indicated institutionalizing and formalizing the whole process of public participation is an important prerequisite to achieving effective participation in formulating Chinese eco-tourism policies. Driven by economic interests, some ecotourism operators may selectively ignore the environmentally friendly requirements of "ecotourism" and use the term "ecotourism" just for attracting tourists (Qin et al., 2006; Chen, 2013). Meanwhile, in some ecotourism sites, the excessive number of tourists and the over-development of tourist facilities construction generate negative impacts, such as, environment pollution to the community (Wang et al., 2014; Zhao & Jiao, 2019).

According to The International Ecotourism Society (TIES) (n.d.), ecotourism is described as "responsible travel to natural areas that conserves the environment, sustains the well-being of the local people, and involves interpretation and education". The World Tourism Organization defines sustainable ecotourism as "tourism that takes full account of its current and future economic, social and environmental impacts, addressing the needs of visitors, the industry, the environment and host communities", while The Global Sustainable Tourism Council Criteria (n.d.) defines "sustainable tourism in an actionable, measurable and credible way". These definitions offer much room for various interpretations and implementation, particularly in the Chinese tourism sector. Due to the confusion about the definition of ecotourism, the study as to whether and how the Chinese regulators lead the entire tourism sector to achieve its sustainable tourism goals is of utmost importance.

METHODOLOGY

Since the complexity of interpreting the meanings of ecotourism in practice, this paper attempts to sort out the interlinked relationships between literature and government policies regarding Chinese ecotourism development from Chinese and English literature sources. To investigate Chinese ecotourism policies' changes, we divided the study into two parts. Firstly, CiteSpace, which is a Java application for text mining and visualization in scientific literature, will be used as analysis tool. By applying co-occurrence analysis, Cluster analysis and the Strongest Citation Bursts analysis to different factors, such as keywords and references, CiteSpace can help researchers trace literature hotspots and trends quickly and comprehensively (Chen, 2006 & 2017). Many researchers have utilized CiteSpace to measure academic publications' hotspots and development trends (Fang et al., 2018; Xiao et al., 2017; Shi & Liu, 2019). Since keywords are usually considered as the summary of article subject, here we use CiteSpace to build up keyword co-occurrence network models for literature hotspots assessment on Chinese ecotourism. The analysis result will be treated as the focus of sustainable ecotourism development and Chinese academic circles' concerns about sustainable ecotourism. We will then examine Chinese ecotourism policies' development trends and verify whether the trend is consistent with literature analysis results or sustainable development philosophy. A hypothesis test is also made between the results of two parts.

To better understand the dynamic relationships among policies & research studies and the trends inside them, this study adopting from the regulators' perspective tries to answer the three questions below.

1. When and what policy changes occurred?
2. Is there a certain trend in policy changes? Does this trend conform to the direction of sustainable development?
3. What are the driving factors for this kind of change?

Data Collection

In order to improve the accuracy of data collection in this study, the names of China's "national parks" and "natural reserves" were used as proxies for the search terms of the literature. National parks and nature reserves are currently the first two protected areas with the most stringent protection requirements in China (General Office of the Central Committee of the Communist Party of China & General Office of the State Council, 2019). At the same time, due to the rich and diverse natural landscape resources, China's national parks and nature reserves are also major or potential destinations for sustainable ecotourism. (Zhang et al., 2016; Li, 2021). Since Chinese national parks were newly established after 2015 during the so-called Chinese protected area reform, the term "national park" itself reflects future development trends of Chinese ecotourism development. We separately analyze the literature on China's national parks and nature reserves to obtain more information on policy changes.

To ensure our literature analysis results meet the requirements of sustainable ecotourism, this paper captures the analysis time interval from 2015 to 2020 matching with the respective policies introduced by the Chinese authorizes. In April 2015, The Central Committee of the CPC and The State Council issued the "Opinions on Accelerating the Construction of Ecological Civilization", which is the first comprehensively special deployment document released by Chinese government for ecological civilization construction (Xinhua News Agency, 2015). Soon after, Chinese 13th Five-Year Plan released in September 2015 clearly stated that innovation, coordination, greenness, openness, and sharing would be the key development philosophy during the 13th five-year plan period (The National People's Congress of the People's Republic of China, 2016). The reform of the Chinese protected area system has been also carried out since 2015 (Huang et al., 2018). Overall, the Chinese government has given unprecedented emphasis on ecological civilization[1] since 2015.

We used the data collection platforms Web of Science Core Collection (English literature source) and China National Knowledge Infrastructure (CNKI) as Chinese literature source. For data sufficiency, this paper merged two search terms together.

For Chinese literature of national parks (NP), the search criteria can be expressed as follows: "subject = ("national park" or title = "national park") AND main subject = ("national park" or "national park system" or "national park (in English)"), document types = (academic journal)". For Chinese literature of natural reserves (NR), the search criteria can be expressed as follows: "subject = ("natural reserve" or title = "natural reserve") AND main subject = ("natural reserve" or "national natural reserve"), document types = (academic journal)".

For English literature (EL), the search criteria can be expressed as follows: "tittle = ("Chin* national park " or "Chin* natur* reserve"), language = (English) and document types = (article)". In order to make the document data more reliable, only the cited documents are used. Finally, after excluding articles unrelated to foreign national parks / natural reserves or other types of protected areas, articles 445 (NP), 971 (NR) and 267 (EL) were selected respectively.

Results

Literature Results in Chinese

In order to ensure the validity of the analysis, some irrelevant words were excluded (in the analysis of national parks: "China", "national park"; in the analysis of nature reserves: "China", "natural reserve", "National Nature Reserve"). For the same reason, keywords with close meanings are combined in each analysis, such as "protected area" and "protected area system", "ecological protection" and "natural protection". Finally, 229 and 256 different keywords were found for national park and natural reserve respectively. Figures 1 & 2 show the networks of keyword co-occurrence of the selected literature. In both Figures 1 and 2, we represent the frequency of the mentions with the circle or font size of a Chinese character. Tables 1 & 2 list top 15 keywords with highest appearance frequency.

Figure 1. Top 15 counts—keyword co-occurrence network of Chinese literatures on Chinese sustainable ecotourism ("national park" as search term)
Source: China National Knowledge Infrastructure

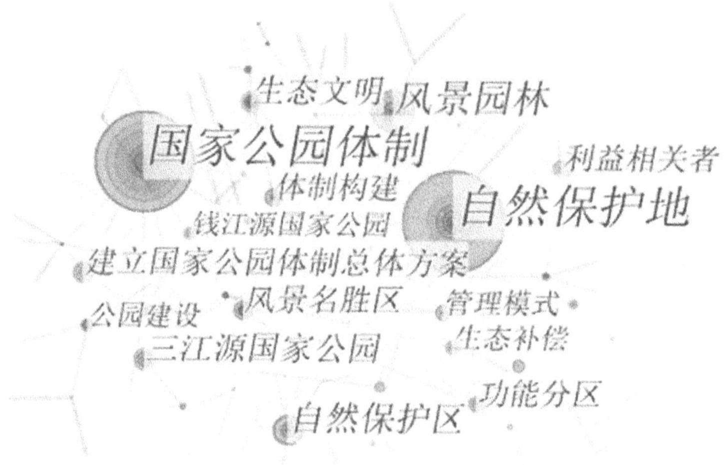

Table 1. Top 15 counts keywords in keyword co-occurrence analysis of Chinese literatures on Chinese sustainable ecotourism ("national park" as search term)

Ranking	Count	Centrality	Year	Keywords
1	66	0.37	2015	自然保护地 (protected area)
2	65	0.22	2015	国家公园体制 (national park system)
3	29	0.18	2015	风景园林 (landscape architecture)
4	20	0.23	2015	自然保护区 (natural reserve)
5	17	0.09	2015	三江源国家公园 (Three-river source national park)
6	16	0.08	2015	生态文明 (Ecological civilization)
7	15	0.06	2017	建立国家公园体制总体方案 (The overall plan for establishing the national park system)
8	14	0.18	2015	风景名胜区 (Scenic spot)
9	13	0.11	2015	体制构建 (System construction)
10	13	0.09	2017	利益相关者 (Stakeholder)
11	13	0.02	2016	功能分区 (Functional zoning)
12	11	0.06	2017	生态补偿 (Ecological compensation)
13	11	0.12	2016	管理模式 (management pattern)
14	10	0.08	2015	公园建设 (Park construction)
15	10	0.03	2017	钱江源国家公园 (Qianjiangyuan national park)

Source: China National Knowledge Infrastructure

Figure 2. Top 15 counts—keyword co-occurrence network of Chinese literatures on Chinese sustainable ecotourism ("natural reserve" as search term)
Source: China National Knowledge Infrastructure

Table 2. Top 15 counts keywords in keyword co-occurrence analysis of Chinese literatures on Chinese sustainable ecotourism ("natural reserve" as search term)

Ranking	Count	Centrality	Year	Keywords
1	69	0.27	2015	生物多样性 (Biodiversity)
2	69	0.19	2015	生态旅游 (Ecotourism)
3	51	0.05	2015	管理 (Management)
4	49	0.16	2015	生态保护 (ecological protection)
5	37	0.07	2015	可持续发展 (Sustainable development)
6	36	0.08	2015	¥ (Countermeasure)
7	26	0.14	2015	湿地 (Wetland)
8	26	0.21	2015	评价 (Evaluate)
9	22	0.14	2015	野生动物 (Wildlife)
10	21	0.09	2015	多样性 (diversity)
11	21	0.05	2016	林业资源 (forest resource)
12	18	0.11	2016	保护对策 (Protection countermeasures)
13	18	0.04	2015	生态补偿 (Ecological compensation)
14	16	0.11	2015	建设 (construction)
15	14	0.07	2015	区系 (Biota)

Source: China National Knowledge Infrastructure

The keyword co-occurrence analysis results indicated that the results for natural reserve contain much more keywords related to natural or ecological topics, such as biodiversity and wildlife, than the results of national park. Simultaneously, keywords of topics like "system construction" or "other types of protected area" did not appear in the results of natural reserve. For comparison, we calculated the occurrence rate of the top 15 keywords in each analysis. Keywords related to the same topic were added up to roughly show the hotspot level. All findings were rounded to four decimal places. It's worth noting that one keyword may be listed more than once as it may fit in more than one topic.

Table 3. Occurrence rate of different topics in the Chinese literature analysis on Chinese sustainable ecotourism ("national park" as search term)

Chinese literature analysis of Chinese sustainable ecotourism ("natural reserve" as search term)					
Topic	**Environment & Nature &Ecology**	**Management**	**Changes**	**Social-related**	**Ecotourism**
Keywords	Biodiversity; Ecological protection; Sustainable development; Wetland; Wildlife ; diversity; Forest resource; Protection Countermeasures; Biota	Management; Countermeasure; Protection Countermeasure; construction	Evaluate	Ecological compensation	ecotourism
Rate	0.2340	0.1022	0.0177	0.0152	0.0583

Source: China National Knowledge Infrastructure

Table 4. Occurrence rate of different topics in the Chinese literature analysis on Chinese sustainable ecotourism ("natural reserve" as search term)

Chinese literature analysis of Chinese sustainable ecotourism ("national park" as search term)						
Topic	**Environment & Nature &Ecology**	**Management**	**Social-related**	**Other types of protected area**	**System**	**Pilot national park**
Keywords	Ecological civilization	Functional zoning; management pattern; park construction; landscape architecture	Stakeholder; Ecological compensation	protected area; natural reserve; Scenic spot	national park system; The overall plan for establishing the national park system; System construction	Three-river source national park; Qianjiangyuan national park
Rate	0.0222	0.0875	0.0333	0.1389	0.1292	0.0375

Source: China National Knowledge Infrastructure

The occurrence rates in tables 3 & 4 demonstrate that the majority of Chinese literature on sustainable ecotourism focuses on three topics, "environment & nature & ecology", "management", "social-related". The distinction lies on the presence of other three themes, including "other types of protected area", "system" and "pilot national park", that only occurs in the analysis result using national park as search terms. Topics like "other types of protected area" and "system" performed highest occurrence rates in the table 3. The reasoning behind this may be related to the following issues: China's protected area system has long been criticized for issues such as unclear definitions of power and responsibilities and conflicts between governance and commercial interests (Ma et al., 2019; Xia et al. 2016). In the past few years, the Chinese government has continuously attempted to resolve these issues by unifying responsible administrative departments, merging various protected area types and improving ecological compensation system. Our findings tend to support our view that the ideology of promoting a better protected area system in China can effectively regulate the development of ecotourism institutionally and help maintain a balance between environmental protection and stakeholders.

Turning now to table 4, its topic frame appears more consistent with sustainable ecotourism definition than that of table 3. Topics of "environment & nature & ecology", "management" account for the highest occurrence rate. Occurrence rate for keywords about "environment & nature & ecology" is 0.2340 that is significantly higher than other topics' rates.

Literature Results in English

We followed the same approach like above: After excluding insignificant keywords, including "China", "national park" and "nature reserve", 234 different keywords were found. As four keywords are tied for 15th simultaneously, totally 18 keywords are showed in figure 3 and table 5. The calculation method of the theme incidence is the same as in the previous section. The results also showed a structure similar to the previous analysis results ("Nature Reserve" as the search term), with the most concerned topic being "Environment and Nature and Ecology".

Figure 3. Top 15 counts—keyword co-occurrence network of English literatures on Chinese sustainable ecotourism ("national park" and "natural reserve" as search term)
Source: Web of Science

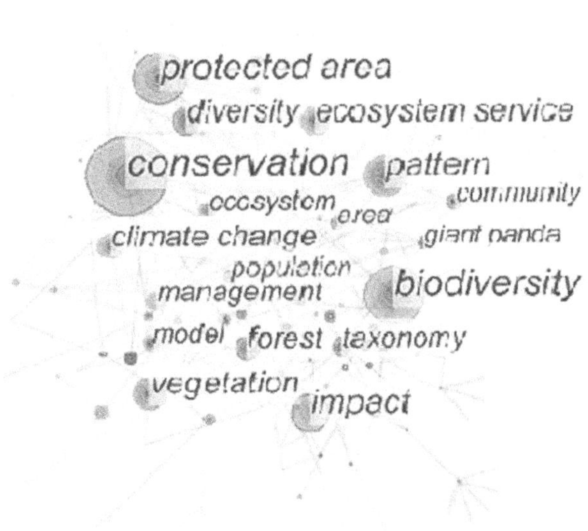

Table 5. Top 15 counts keywords in keyword co-occurrence analysis of English literatures on Chinese sustainable ecotourism ("national park" and "natural reserve" as search term)

Rank	Count	Centrality	Year	Keywords
1	49	0.23	2015	conservation
2	33	0.13	2015	protected area
3	33	0.11	2015	biodiversity
4	27	0.11	2015	pattern
5	24	0.28	2015	impact
6	22	0.07	2015	vegetation
7	20	0.04	2015	ecosystem service
8	18	0.1	2015	diversity
9	18	0.06	2015	climate change
10	16	0.25	2015	forest
11	13	0.06	2016	management
12	13	0.23	2015	taxonomy
13	12	0.08	2015	model
14	12	0.14	2015	ecosystem
15	11	0.11	2015	community
16	11	0.16	2015	giant panda
17	11	0.21	2015	area
18	11	0.11	2017	population

Source: Web of Science

Table 6. Occurrence rate of different topics in the English literature analysis on Chinese sustainable ecotourism ("national park" and "natural reserve" as search term)

English literature analysis of Chinese sustainable ecotourism					
Topic	**Environment & Nature &Ecology**	**Management**	**Social-related**	**Changes**	**Others**
Keyword	Conservation; Biodiversity; vegetation; Ecosystem service; Diversity; Climate change; Forest; Ecosystem; Giant panda; Taxonomy	Pattern; Management	Community; Population	Impact	Protected area; Model; Area
Rate	0.2317	0.0437	0.0240	0.02623	0.0612

Source: Web of Science

Hypothesis Development about Hotspot-Based Analysis

After summarizing three analysis results, we draw a more comprehensive research hotspot table.

Table 7. Summary of counts

	Total Counts of all keywords	Total Counts of top 15 keywords	Total occurrence rate of top 15 keywords
English literature analysis of Chinese sustainable ecotourism	915	354	0.386885246
Chinese literature analysis of Chinese sustainable ecotourism ("national park" as search term)	720	323	0.448611111
Chinese literature analysis of Chinese sustainable ecotourism ("natural reserve" as search term)	1184	493	0.416385135

Source: China National Knowledge Infrastructure, Web of Science

Table 8. Summary of occurrence rates

	Environment & Nature & Ecology	Management	Social-related	Changes	Other types of protected area	System	Pilot	Others
English literature analysis of Chinese sustainable ecotourism	0.2317	0.0437	0.024	0.0262				0.0612
Chinese literature analysis of Chinese sustainable ecotourism ("national park" as search term)	0.0222	0.0875	0.0333		0.1389	0.1292	0.0375	
Chinese literature analysis of Chinese sustainable ecotourism ("natural reserve" as search term)	0.234	0.1022	0.0177	0.0152				0.0583

Source: China National Knowledge Infrastructure, Web of Science

Tables 7 & 8 demonstrate that in the literature analysis results on Chinese sustainable ecotourism using data from the specified three sources, the three hot topics, "Environment & Nature & Ecology", "Management" and "Social-related", are overlapping. Keywords about subjects "change & trend" also appear in two analyses. It can be inferred that "change & trend" is also one of the most important study hotspots within studies of Chinese sustainable ecotourism but not as significant as the previous three topics. The keywords in topics of "other types of protected area", "system" and "pilot" can be understood as the increasing efforts the Chinese government made to balance issues between ecology and development. Besides, keywords in "others" column, such as "model" and "area", are negligible in our hypothesis test.

Figure 4. Model of the improving process of sustainable ecotourism development
Source: Authors

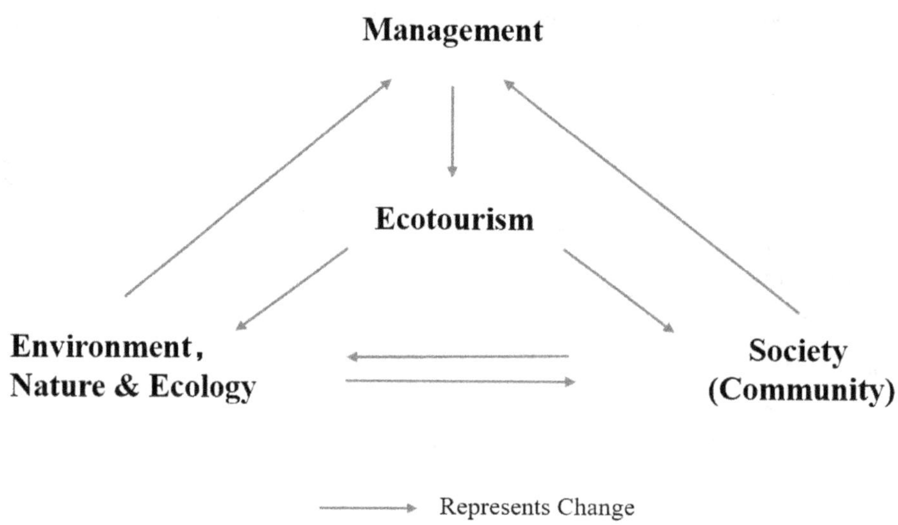

Using the topics found above, we can then build a hotspot-based model which explains the improving process of sustainable ecotourism development.

In general, the research hotspots and hotspots-based models based on the results of our literature analysis show a high degree of consistency with TIES's core definition of ecotourism (namely environmental conservation, local community development and interpretative experience to visitors).

Consequently, we have reached two conclusions

1. After 2015, the research topic of sustainable ecotourism in China's academic community basically coincides with the internationally recognized definition of ecotourism.
2. The themes of "environment and natural ecology", "management", "change" and "related to society" are the core of China's sustainable ecotourism development.

Based on the above discussion, the following hypotheses are proposed:

H: The change of Chinese policies related to ecotourism follows the sustainable development trend, while most of Chinese ecotourism policies are associated with topics of "environment & nature & ecology", "management", "social related" and "changes".

INSTITUTIONAL CHANGE ANALYSIS

In this section, we will analyze Chinese ecotourism policies' change based on institutional change theory and the research results from the previous discussion.

North (1990) defines institutions as "humanly devised constraints that structure political, economic and social interactions". Institutional changes are the ways in which institutions are created, changed, and broken over time. It is institutional changes that constitute a source of long-term economic growth.

Usually, Institutional changes are gradual, and are connected to institutional characteristics, institutional costs, and change mechanisms. The institution itself is predictable or path dependent (Wang & Wang, 2007). Lin (1989) in his study divided the institutional change into two types: induced and imposed change. Institutional change refers to the process of institutional substitution, conversion and transaction, i.e. the process of replacing a less effective institution with another institution with higher effectiveness and benefit. Induced institutional changes indicate the spontaneous changes made by individual(s) in response to profit opportunities caused by institutional imbalances. On the other hand, imposed institutional changes suggest changes due to government decrees. Institutional changes will be conducted as long as government expects the revenue to exceed cost (Shi & Shen, 2002). Since most of institutional changes in China were propelled by the Chinese government, our study focuses on imposed institutional changes of Chinese ecotourism, which represented by policies changes.

Soon after Ceballos-Lascurain (1987) first proposed the concept of ecotourism formally, the Chinese government introduced it into China and popularized it as one of key industries to develop a sustainable economy. In a regional planning outline released by Chinese national planning Commission in 1993 (1993), ecotourism that was then described as "return to nature" was promoted to accelerate regional economic development. Noteworthily, in contrast to the misuse in practice, ecotourism definition in Chinese policies from its beginnings has been the same as the internationally recognized sustainable ecotourism. However, similar definition does not mean that it has been implemented in the institutional establishment and changes. Our study is aiming to fill this gap and investigate whether the change of related Chinese ecotourism institution and policies follows the sustainable trend, and if so, what are the influence factors of these changes.

In the previous section, we have demonstrated Chinese sustainable ecotourism academic hotspots through literature analysis. In order to analyze the institutional changes, we will select key policies that can represent the dynamics of China's eco-tourism, and try to analyze the trends from them. Since Chinese government has been emphasizing sustainable notion in relevant ecotourism documents, we used "ecotourism" as search term in data collection of this part (The State Environmental Protection Administration, 2002). The Peking University laws and regulations database was used as data collection platform. Search criteria can be expressed as follows: "title or full text = ("ecotourism"); policy type = ("administrative regulations" or "departmental regulations"); release department = ("Chinese the National People's Congress " or "Chinese National People's Congress Standing Committee" or " Chinese State Council departments") ". Altogether 497 policies were found. And the first policy contains the word "ecotourism" was promulgated in 1993. Therefore, 1993 was regarded as the beginning of the time interval. Only policies illustrated essential ecotourism-related institutional changes were selected. In order to maintain accuracy, we deleted the policy of repeated expressions and retained the original policy and selected 18 relevant policy documents.

We will discuss in detail the changes in China's eco-tourism policy according to different periods, and examine whether the focus of other policies is related to the literature concerns found in the previous paragraph. If any major policy mentions the content of the first four topics, it is recorded as a concern for sustainable ecotourism development. In the most ideal case, all key Chinese eco-tourism policies that reflect institutional changes will focus on the above four themes at the same time. Therefore, the upper limit of the number of followers is 72 (that is, 18 policies x 4 topics). However, considering that our research goal is whether the changes in China's ecotourism policy are in line with sustainable development trends, and most policies are not only issued for ecotourism development, the 50% coverage rate will be used as the threshold for hypothesis testing. In other words, if the total exceeds 36, the hypothesis will be accepted.

During the 8th and 9th Five-Year Plan Period (1990-2000)

In this period, "ecotourism" was just introduced into China. As a whole, the Chinese ecotourism industry in this period stayed in introduction phase. Only few policies mentioned ecotourism. In parallel, this period is also one of the most important economic reform periods in Chinese history. Following the deepening of reform and opening-up, China's primary goal in this period was to promote economic development and transform economic system from a planned economic system to a new socialist market economic system (Shi, 2006). As an emerging concept, ecotourism is simply used as one of the economic stimulation tools at this period.

Table 9. Summary of Chinese ecotourism related policies during the 8th and 9th five-year plan period

Policy title\ Serving president\ Five-year plan	Issue department	Released data\ Tenure of office\ Five-year plan period	Ecotourism related highlight\ President's key governing philosophy\ Key development concepts or goals of Five-year plan	Domestic visitors number (million people)	Gross national income (trillion yuans)	Mentioned topics
President Jiang Zemin served in office		1989 - 2002	The Three Represents: Put forward in 2000, The Three Represents defines the role of the CCP, and stresses that the Party must always represent the requirements for developing China's advanced productive forces, the orientation of China's advanced culture and the fundamental interests of the overwhelming majority of the Chinese people.			
The 8th Five-year plan period		1990 - 1995	Promote reform and opening-up, advance economic system reform, and gradually establish a socialist market economic system			
Notice of the National Planning Commission on the outline of regional planning of some provinces and regions in Southwest and South China	National Planning Commission (reorganized)	1993.06.29	Make full use of the unique advantages of regionally ecological environment, and develop ecotourism that returns to nature as regional advantage project	Null	3559.92	"environment & nature & ecology", "social-related"
The 9th Five-year plan period		1996 - 2000	The key goal is to promote two fundamental transformations with overall significance. The first is to transform the economic system from a traditional planned economic system to a socialist market economic system. The second is to transform the economic growth mode from extensive to intensive, which promotes sustained and healthy development of the national economy and comprehensive social progress.			

Source: The Peking University laws and regulations database, Official website of the state council of China (2022)

During the 10th Five-Year Plan Period (2001 - 2005)

During Chinese 10th five-year plan period, more policies have mentioned the concept of ecotourism. Compared with the previous period, Chinese ecotourism policies in this period pay much more attention on ecotourism's environmental conservation function. Ecotourism regulation approaches such as proper supervision, environmental protection assessment and formulation of rule & standards were emphasized too. In the policy issued in 2005, Chinese government clearly stated for the first time that ecotourism should be developed on the basis of ecological protection. However, from another perspective, most of the measures presented in this period were aimed at promoting ecological tourism while ensuring ecological protection. Chinese government was not aware of the importance of other ecotourism-related factors. Hence, we summarized this period as the initial stage of Chinese ecotourism industry.

Ecotourism-related policies during this period, as shown in Table 10, may also be affected by the goals of five-year plan and leaders' serving ideas. After entering the new millennium, China initially established a socialist market economy system. The government plan during this period led and promoted development. Moreover, after joining the WTO, Chinese economy entered a high-speed economic growth era. The number of tourists and the gross national income grew rapidly. Due to development and market demand, during this period, the development of China's eco-tourism has naturally received more attention and support from the government. The scientific development concept put forward by President Hu Jintao after he took office in 2003 highlights the concept of promoting comprehensive, coordinated and sustainable economic development. This may be one of the reasons why ecotourism and its environmental protection function were "discovered" during this period.

During the 11th Five-Year Plan Period (2006 - 2010)

Entering the time of the 11th Five-Year Plan, ecotourism policy changes during this period have distinctive features. We can perceive a high number of institutional changes related to the local communities or local residents in ecotourism sites, including promoting the establishment of an ecological compensation system, conducting ecological immigration mechanisms, and encouraging the promotion of the development of rural areas through ecotourism. Part of the causes for policy changes was China facing serious problems of relatively backward economic development in rural areas and the growing gap between urban and rural area, which still needs to be resolved urgently (Cao et al., 2010; Wang & Ouyang, 2007). The 11th Five-Year Plan emphasized the basic strategy of persistent overall planning of urban and rural areas' economic and social development, and proposing the establishment of the model of the new socialist countryside[2] for the first time. This was due to the fact that most of the Chinese protected areas greatly overlap with rural and poor areas (Xu et al., 2016; Liu et al., 2020). Developing ecotourism and encouraging rural residents to participate in sustainable ecotourism-related operations can effectively promote local economic development and increase the income of local residents while meeting ecological protection needs. On the other hand, as important ecotourism sites Chinese protected areas were also facing social problems. There was large conflict between protected areas' ecological protection requirements and local residents' needs for development and natural resource utilization. Many residents have low satisfaction with protected areas' management and construction (Song et al., 2018). As an important sustainable industry that balances ecological protection and local development, eco-tourism can and in future should effectively help solve this problem.

Table 10. Summary of Chinese ecotourism related policies during the 10th five-year plan period

Policy title\ Serving president\ Five-year plan	Issue department	Released data\Tenure of office\ Five-year plan period	Ecotourism related highlight\ President's key governing philosophy\ Key development concepts or goals of Five-year plan	Domestic visitors number (million people)	Gross national income (trillion yuans)	Mentioned topics
The 10th Five-year plan period		2001-2005	Taking development as the theme, structural adjustment as the main line, and reform & opening-up, scientific & technological progress as the driving force of the 10th Five-Year Plan			
Notice of the State Council on Further Accelerating the Development of Tourism Industry	The State Council	2001.04.11	Accelerate the development of special tourism products, vigorously develop ecotourism, urban tourism, etc., and plan to build a number of national ecotourism demonstration zones.	784	10927.62	"management"
Notice of the State Environmental Protection Administration on Printing and Distributing the "Tenth Five-Year Plan for National Ecological Environment Protection"	The State Environmental Protection Administration (withdrawn)	2002.03.28	1, Strengthen ecological and environmental protection in the development of tourism resources. Carry out quantitative assessment of environmental protection in tourist attractions. 2, Carry out ecotourism sites demonstration. Guided by the harmony between human and nature, focus on the rational development of tourism resources. Pay attention to tourism environmental protection and improve tourism management and protection capabilities. 3, Improve laws and regulations, reasonably control the scale of tourism, and strictly enforce environmental management of tourism facilities construction projects. 4, Unremittingly carry out ecological protection publicity, and further enhance the ecological protection awareness of the whole people.	878	12048,04	"environment & nature & ecology", "management", "change"
President Hu Jintao served in office		2003 - 2013	Put forward "Adhering to people-oriented" and establish a comprehensive, coordinated and sustainable Scientific outlook on development			
Notice of the Ministry of Education on Issuing the "Guidelines for the Implementation of Environmental Education in Primary and Secondary Schools (Trial)"	The Ministry of Education	2003.10.08	Encourage students to investigate the development of tourism in local region, discuss the potential impact of tourism on the environment and the possibility of developing ecotourism in local region.	870	13657.63	Null
Opinions of the State Forestry Administration on Strengthening the Construction and Management of Nature Reserves	The State Forestry Administration (withdrawn)	2005.04.14	All of business activities in the nature reserve must accept the unified management and supervision of the nature reserve management agency. carrying out business activities such as ecotourism shall not change the affiliation relationship and management system of nature reserves	1212	18599.89	"environment & nature & ecology", "management"
Notice of the National Tourism Administration and the State Environmental Protection Administration on Further Strengthening the Work of Tourism Eco-environmental Protection	The National Tourism Administration (withdrawn), The State Environmental Protection Administration (withdrawn)	2005.06.16	1, Effectively strengthen the environmental supervision of various tourist areas, tourism projects and tourism activities under its jurisdiction, urge tourism operators to strictly implement relevant national laws, regulations, standards and norms, and establish and improve corresponding rules and regulations and assessment methods to effectively prevent tourism environmental pollution and ecological damage in its development and operation. 2, Further speed up the formulation of standards and norms related to tourism environmental protection and ecotourism 3, Actively develop ecotourism on the basis of effectively protecting the ecological environment. 4, Strengthen the application of science and technology in tourism ecological environment protection	1212	18599.89	"environment & nature & ecology", "management", "changes"

Source: The Peking University laws and regulations database, Official website of the state council of China (2022)

During the 12th Five-Year Plan Period (2011 - 2015)

There are three main characteristics within ecotourism-related policies changes during the period of 12th Five-Year Plan. Firstly, the Chinese government began to encourage private capital and enterprises to invest in the ecotourism industry or carry out government & social capital co-operation (namely public-private partnership) projects with government. In this respect, the Chinese government's attitude differs from that in the earlier ecotourism development stage. In the policy issued in 2005, Chinese government highlighted that all operation activities in nature reserves shall be run under the management of the nature reserves management agencies. Since this period, social capitals were welcome to participate in ecotourism sites' management. Secondly, contents and features from tech industries such as smart technology started to appear in ecotourism-related policies, indicating changes for improving Chinese ecotourism industry's overall efficiency and service quality through technology. Thirdly, the Chinese government has also promulgated three ecotourism-related standards and regulations to promote the standardization of China's ecotourism industry. Besides, in this period, the word "ecotourism" appeared in the outline of a five-year plan firstly, which further underlines its significance.

Table 11. Summary of Chinese ecotourism related policies during the 11th five-year plan period

Policy title\ Serving president\ Five-year plan	Issue department	Released data\ Tenure of office\ Five-year plan period	Ecotourism related highlight\ President's key governing philosophy\ Key development concepts or goals of Five-year plan	Domestic visitors number (million people)	Gross national income (trillion yuans)	Mentioned topics
The 11th Five-year plan period		2006-2010	Persisting in taking economic construction as the center, and using development and reform to solve the problems in the process of progress. Development must be scientific. We must adhere to people-oriented philosophy. Change development concepts, innovate development models and improve development quality. implement the "five overall plans". And effectively turn economic and social development onto the track of comprehensive, coordinated and sustainable development.			
Opinions of the State Forestry Administration on the implementation of the "Several Opinions of the Central Committee of the Communist Party of China and the State Council on Promoting the Construction of a New Socialist Countryside"	The State Forestry Administration (withdrawn)	2006.03.29	1, Vigorously develop emerging forestry industries such as ecotourism, and energy forests, and promote rural areas' economic structure adjustment 2, Vigorously develop ecotourism, spur surrounding farmers to develop forest tourism services such as "agritourism" and "forest sightseeing" that expand rural population employment, and increase farmers' income.	1394	21902.85	"Society-related", "management"

Continued on following page

Table 11. Continued

Policy title\ Serving president\ Five-year plan	Issue department	Released data\ Tenure of office\ Five-year plan period	Ecotourism related highlight\ President's key governing philosophy\ Key development concepts or goals of Five-year plan	Domestic visitors number (million people)	Gross national income (trillion yuans)	Mentioned topics
Notice of the State Environmental Protection Administration on Issuing the "Eleventh Five-Year Plan for National Ecological Protection"	The State Environmental Protection Administration (Revoked)	2006.10.13	1, Establish and improve relevant laws, regulations, and standards. Strengthen legislative work and bring ecological and environmental protection into the track of legalization. Formulate as soon as possible the "Nature Reserve Law", "Soil Pollution Prevention Law", "GMO Safety Law", "Ecological Protection Law" and other laws to speed up the establishment of an ecological protection standard system including ecotourism Standards. 2, Strengthen the ecological environment protection of tourism development activities, increase the inspection of environmental pollution and ecological damage in tourist areas.	1394	21902.85	"environment & nature & ecology", "management", "change"
Guiding Opinions of the State Environmental Protection Administration on the Pilot Program of Ecological Compensation	The State Environmental Protection Administration (withdrawn)	2007.08.24	**Explore the establishment of ecological compensation mechanisms in key areas** Attract and help residents in nature reserves to carry out ecological migration by providing funds, material compensation, employment opportunities or preferential policies. Guide residents in natural reserve and surrounding communities to change their production way and lifestyles and develop organic food, ecotourism and other characteristic industries in accordance with local conditions. Increasing employment opportunities and reducing the pressure of surrounding communities on the nature reserves.	1610	27070.4	"environment & nature & ecology", "management", "Society-related"
Notice of the National Tourism Administration on Determining the 2009 as the "China Ecotourism Year"	the National Tourism (withdrawn)	2008.11.07	Chinese government decided to designate the 2009 National Theme Tourism Year as the "China Ecotourism Year" with the theme slogan "Go into Green Tourism and Feel Ecological Civilization"	1712	32122.95	"environment & nature & ecology", "management"

Source: The Peking University laws and regulations database, Official website of the state council of China (2022)

Table 12. Summary of Chinese ecotourism related policies during the 12th five-year plan period

Policy title\ Serving president\ Five-year plan	Issue department	Released data\ Tenure of office\ Five-year plan period	Ecotourism related highlight\ President's key governing philosophy\ Key development concepts or goals of Five-year plan	Domestic visitors number (million people)	Gross national income (trillion yuans)	Mentioned topics
The 12th Five-year plan period		2010 - 2015	To achieve economic and social development goals, we must focus on promoting scientific development, accelerating the transformation of economic development methods. Making overall plans, promoting reforms and innovations, and focusing on solving the problems of imbalance, uncoordinated, and unsustainable in economic and social development.			
Implementation Opinions of the National Tourism Administration on Encouraging and Guiding Private Capital to Invest in Tourism	The National Tourism Administration (withdrawn)	2012.06.05	Encourage private capital to develop various tourism products. Encourage private capital to use its own advantages and develop eco-tourism in accordance with local conditions and resource.	2957	53732.9	"management", "Social-related"
1, State Forestry Administration Announcement No. 5 of 2012-"National Forest City Evaluation Index" and other 103 industry standards catalog 2, Notice of the National Tourism Administration and the Ministry of Environmental Protection on the issuance of the "National Ecotourism Demonstration Zone Management Regulations" and the "National Ecotourism Demonstration Zone Construction and Operation Regulations (GB/T26362-2010) Rating Implementation Rules"	The State Forestry Administration (withdrawn), The National Tourism Administration (withdrawn); The Ministry of Environmental Protection (withdrawn)	2012.02.23\ 2012.09.29	1, Releasing the "General Rules for the Construction of Ecotourism Facilities in Nature Reserves" 2, Releasing the "National Ecotourism Demonstration Zone Management Regulations" and the "National Ecotourism Demonstration Zone Construction and Operation Regulations (GB/T26362-2010) Rating Implementation Rules"	2957	53732.9	"environment & nature & ecology", "management", "Social-related"
President Xi Jinping served in office		2013 -	Since the 18th National Congress of the Communist Party of China, the Party Central Committee with Comrade Xi Jinping at its core has incorporated the construction of ecological civilization into the overall layout of the cause of socialism with Chinese characteristics, and has planned and carried out a series of fundamental, pioneering, and long-term work to promote the historic occurrence of ecological and environmental protection.			
Notice of the State Forestry Administration on Issuing the "Guiding Opinions on the Development of Smart Forestry in China"	The State Forestry Administration (withdrawn)	2013.08.21	Deepen the application of information technology in public service fields such as ecotourism. Vigorously develop ecotourism, and promote the construction of smart ecotourism. Build a smart ecotourism public service platform to provide consumers and forestry producers with convenient, intelligent, and optimized services. Establish an excellent ecotourism brand, and comprehensively enhance the industry image and overall benefits of ecotourism	3262	58814.12	"management"
Several Opinions of the State Council on Promoting the Reform and Development of the Tourism Industry	The State Council	2014.08.09	Formulate the national ecotourism development plan, strengthen the guidance to the national key tourist areas, do a good job in the overall development of tourism resources in concentrated contiguous areas with special difficulties, and guide the healthy development of ecotourism.	3611	64438.02	"management", "Social-related"

Continued on following page

Table 12. Continued

Policy title\ Serving president\ Five-year plan	Issue department	Released data\ Tenure of office\ Five-year plan period	Ecotourism related highlight\ President's key governing philosophy\ Key development concepts or goals of Five-year plan	Domestic visitors number (million people)	Gross national income (trillion yuans)	Mentioned topics
Several Opinions of the General Office of the State Council on Further Promoting Tourism Investment and Consumption	The General Office of the State Council	2015.08.04	1, Support enterprises to invest, construct and operate tourism projects through the government and social capital cooperation (PPP) model. 2, Governments at all levels should increase support for tourism infrastructure and public service facilities such as key national tourist attractions, ecological tourism development in concentrated contiguous areas of poverty, and rural tourism poverty alleviation villages. Let colorful tourism enrich people's lives and help economic development.	3990	68625.57	"management", "Social-related"

Source: The Peking University laws and regulations database, Official website of the state council of China (2022)

During the 13th Five-Year Plan Period (2016 - 2020)

As mentioned above, after 2015, under the advocacy of its national leaders, China's emphasis on the concept of constructing an "ecological civilization" has reached unprecedented heights. Correspondingly, the Chinese government also paid greater attention to ecotourism development during this period. In 2016, the Chinese government issued a detailed plan for ecotourism development from 2016 to 2020, in which it details Chinese ecotourism development goals and strategies. China also vigorously promoted a protected area system reform during this period. A wide range of different types of protected areas were merged under the management of a unified department to build a more reasonable and strict protected area system (Huang et al., 2018). This drastic reform has institutionally regulated ecotourism sites' management and laid a good institutional foundation for long-term sustainable ecotourism construction. Meanwhile, policies in this period also encourage the integration and development of ecotourism industry and other industries. Diversification may become one of the key points of future Chinese ecotourism development.

HYPOTHESIS TEST UNDER THE INSTITUTIONAL CHANGE ANALYSIS

Table 9-13 demonstrates whether the relevant eco-tourism policies are related to the four topics we discussed earlier. We show that most of them have at least a focus on one of the four topics. Finally, the total counts of mentioned topics are 41 > 36. The hypothesis test is accepted, which means the change of Chinese policies related to ecotourism follows a sustainable development trend. Although there were or are many imperfections in the process of Chinese ecotourism development, Chinese ecotourism-related institutional changes have kept aiming at sustainable development since 1993.

Table 13. Summary of Chinese ecotourism related policies during the 13th five-year plan period

Policy title\ Serving president\ Five-year plan	Issue department	Released data\ Tenure of office\ Five-year plan period	Ecotourism related highlight\ President's key governing philosophy\ Key development concepts or goals of Five-year plan	Domestic visitors number (million people)	Gross national income (trillion yuans)	Mentioned topics
The 13th Five-year plan period			The "13th Five-Year Plan" period is the decisive stage for building a moderately prosperous society in all respects. We must actively understand and adapt to the new normal for China's economic development. Comprehensively promote innovative development, coordinated development, green development, open development, and shared development to ensure that a moderately prosperous society is built in an all-round way.			
Notice of the National Development and Reform Commission and the National Tourism Administration on Issuing the National Ecotourism Development Plan (2016-2025)	National Development and Reform Commission (including the former National Development Planning Commission and the former National Planning Commission); National Tourism Administration (withdrawn)	2016.08.22	By 2025, the overall layout of eco-tourism cooperation areas, destinations, routes and scenic roads will be basically established. Regional cooperation mechanisms will be more complete, cooperation models will become increasingly mature, ecotourism resource protection, product development, public services, environmental education, community participation, marketing promotion, and technological innovation is gradually improved. Ecotourism has played a full role in promoting the construction of ecological civilization, and its international competitiveness has been significantly improved, making China a strong country in ecotourism internationally.	4435	74340.83	"environment & nature & ecology", "management", "social related" and "changes".
Notice of the National Development and Reform Commission, the State Forestry Administration, and the Ministry of Finance on the issuance of the "Ecological Poverty Alleviation Work Plan"	National Development and Reform Commission (including the former National Development Planning Commission and the former National Planning Commission); State Forestry Administration (withdrawn); Ministry of Finance	2018.01.18	1, Improve the linkage mechanism between ecotourism development and ecological resource protection, and increase guidance and support for ecotourism poverty alleviation, 2, Actively create diversified eco-tourism products, and promote the deep integration of ecology and tourism, education, culture, health and other industries.	5539	91432.71	"environment & nature & ecology", "management", "social related"
The General Office of the Central Committee of the Communist Party of China and the General Office of the State Council issued the "Guiding Opinions on Establishing a Natural Reserve System with National Parks as the Main Body"	General Office of the Central Committee of the Communist Party of China; General Office of the State Council	2019.06.26	Explore the sharing mechanism for the whole people. Under the premise of protection, delimit appropriate areas within the control area of the nature reserve to carry out activities such as ecological education, nature experience, and eco-tourism to build a high-quality and diversified ecological product system	6006	98417.9	"environment & nature & ecology", "management", "social related"

Source: The Peking University laws and regulations database, Official website of the State council of China (2022)

DISCUSSION

Considering ecotourism is one of the key links in the construction of the Chinese ecological civilization, here we will discuss the development of the construction of the Chinese ecological civilization and the role ecotourism play in this process.

After the reform and opening-up, China has been looking for a suitable sustainable development path. The Chinese government has been trying to avoid the "pollution first, cure later" development approach adopted by most Western countries in the past. However, later practice proved that China did not completely break out of this vicious circle. Driven by development needs and economic benefits, many stakeholders have actively or passively ignored ecological interests and focused on economic benefit (Pang et al., 2021). The negligence of local governments, enterprises and individuals severely damaged

Chinese ecological environment and caused serious problems such as water pollution and air pollution (Wang et al., 2021; Hao et al., 2021).

Nonetheless, the advantage of Chinese institutions lies in their powerful error correction ability. Driven by strong government power, China has a more efficient error correction processes than Western countries. In the 18th National Congress of CPC, China incorporated ecological civilization into the five-in-one overall layout (Huang, 2014). The 19th National Congress of CPC further listed the battle against pollution as one of the three crucial fights to comprehensively build a well-off society (Xi, 2017). After 2015, the Chinese government continued promoting sustainable development by establishing unique institutional settings with Chinese characteristics through the model of constructing the "ecological civilization". There are four major characteristics for the Chinese ecological civilization construction process. Firstly, providing top-to-down institutional power and development foundation for the ecological civilization construction by improving top-level institutional designs. The 13th National People's Congress passed the State Council's institutional reform plan, established the Ministry of Ecology & Environment and Natural Resources to distinguish responsibility for natural resources management and ecological environment monitoring & law enforcement. (Xinhua News Agency, 2018). The management and supervision functions for ecological environment were separated to improve ecological governance capabilities. Government also conducted a lifetime accountability institution to ensure policies can be implemented (China Daily, 2018). Management departments of various protected areas were also unified to avoid policy conflicts and waste of administrative resources. Secondly, ensure the efficiency of policy implementation by conducting unique local accountability institutions. Through policies like the "ecological civilization assessment target system", China incorporated ecological governance and protection effects into the government's official assessment system (China Development and Reform Commission, 2016). For water resource protection, China built a river management system and lake management system. Managers will be held accountable if environmental damage occurs in the water bodies they oversee (Hou, 2018). Thirdly, the trial-and-error system combining demonstration zones and pilot projects provide necessary experience for the construction of the Chinese ecological civilization. "The overall plan for establishing a national park system" was released after a two-year pilot process (Huang, 2018). Fourthly, implementing specified policies to coordinate and balance the interests of stakeholders and ensure the smooth development of ecological civilization construction, such as ecological protection compensation mechanism, tax incentives policy for green industries and marketization of the Mechanism for Environmental Pollution Control (Xinhua News Agency, 2015).

Ecotourism is one of the key industries to coordinate the interests of stakeholders. When advancing protection requirements of the ecological civilization construction and ecotourism development, it is inevitable to harm stakeholders' interests. High-polluting companies were required to withdraw from ecotourism sites or meet local protection standards, both of which may harm companies' interest. In some of ecotourism sites like natural reserves, local residents' demand for farming and natural resources using were greatly limited, resulting to income decline (Song et al, 2018). However, driven by reasonable policies, ecotourism can also provide suitable development methods for harmed stakeholders and coordinate their interests. The summary table and figure below show the increased attention the Chinese government paid to ecotourism development since 1993. There is a trend of continuously incorporating experiences in practice and gradually coordinating with various stakeholders in the changes of Chinese ecotourism-related policies. During the first three five-year plans period, very few policies took stakeholders' interest into account. But from the 11th five-year plan period onward, contents about coordinating stakeholders' interests started to appear in ecotourism-related policies. Ecotourism policies issued during the 11th five-year plan emphasized the role ecotourism plays in the development of local communities and rural areas. In traditional development mode, it's hard to avoid large-scale natural resources utilization when developing. As a sustainable industry, ecotourism is used as a substitute for the above industries to promote the sustainable development of rural areas and poor areas (Qiu & Tang, 2020). Local residents are encouraged to take part in ecotourism operations. Similar industries also included ecological agriculture and eco-friendly industries. As for enterprises that were seriously affected by strict environmental protection policies, the Chinese government encourages them to enter sustainable industries such as ecotourism through various preferential policies. Table 14 lists policy changes encouraging social capital to participate in ecotourism industry and supporting integrated development of ecotourism industry and multi-industry during the 12th and 13th five-year plan periods. In the face of rising market demand, the Chinese government also prompts combinations between information technology industry and ecotourism, developing new ecotourism types such as camping and hiking to diversify and develop on a high quality level in order to meet changing market demand.

In general, China is promoting the overall sustainable national development through the construction of a unique institutional setting with Chinese characteristics, called the construction of the "ecological civilization". Ecotourism is a key industry that coordinates stakeholders' interest in ecological civilization construction process. Ecotourism -related policy changes are based on sustainable development and stakeholders' interest coordination.

In the policies released after 2020, we can still find a coherent develop trend. For example, in the "Opinions on encouraging and supporting the participation of social capital in ecological protection and restoration" document, the Chinese government encourages individuals and enterprises take part in the ecological conservation through a range of cooperative investment patterns. By April 2022, over 50 ecology-oriented development pilots have been licensed.

In this process, the academic sphere seems to play a role of bridge. This does not mean that academic research has always been ahead of government cognition or that academic research has led the changes in government policies. The results of our literature analysis above reflects the focus of sustainable ecotourism under various restrictions. But in fact, literature and research focuses also experience changing trends. The academic sphere and government governance may actually shape or affect each other. Boswell, C. & Smith, K. (2017) describe this effect in their study as follows: "research knowledge and governance are co-produced through an ongoing process of mutual constitution". On one hand, academic research may have paid attention to more social changes and needs earlier than government. Then, these needs may be reflected to government though academic studies. Government may propel institutional changes based on research results: "governance is itself constituted by scientific knowledge" (Boswell, C. & Smith, K., 2017). Take the five-year plan as an example. After the start of the reform and opening-up, each five-year plan in China has gone through a formulation process of one to two years during which a large number of academic experts and people from all walks of life participate in offering information or recommendation (Yan et al, 2012).

The Chinese government collects opinions from academia and society through various methods to promote institutional changes. To close the circle, the topics that the government focuses on also influence academia research. The Government's attention on a certain topic is typically soon noticed by scholars and transformed into academic hotspots. An obvious example is research related to the "One Belt, One Road" Initiative.

Table 14. Summary of Chinese ecotourism related policies changes from 1993-2020

Time period	Key development concepts or goals in Five-year plan	Policies keywords	Development stage of Chinese ecotourism	The overall trend of change during this period
The 8th and 9th five-year plan period	Establish socialist market economy system	Develop ecotourism that returns to nature as a regional advantage project	The introduction phase	Use ecotourism as a tool for economic development
The 10th five-year plan period	Taking development as the theme, structural adjustment as the main line, and reform & opening-up, scientific & technological progress as the driving force of the 10th Five-Year Plan	1, Environmental conservation (Environmental assessment and supervision of tourist areas) 2, Unified management	The initial stage	Emphasizing the environmental conservation function of ecotourism
The 11th five-year plan period	Adhere to people-oriented, change the concept of development, innovate the development model, improve the quality of development, implement the "five overall plan", and effectively put economic and social development into a comprehensive and coordinated sustainable development track. Highlight:For the first time, it proposed to establish a new socialist countryside and focused on solving the three rural issues	1, Rural areas or local communities development 2, Related legal construction 3, Ecological compensation mechanism 4, China Ecotourism Year	The further socialization phase	Emphasizing the social function of ecotourism. The development of Chinese ecotourism was given more social-related significance
The12th five-year plan period	Taking scientific development as the theme, accelerating the transformation of economic development mode as the main line. Insisting on reform and innovation and focusing on solving the problems of imbalance, uncoordinated, and unsustainable in economic and social development Highlight: The term "ecotourism" appears in the five-year plan for the first time	1, The application of information technology and smart technology 2, Encourage the participation of private capital and enterprises. 3, Standardization construction	The optimization phase	Advocate the integration with science and technology and improving the industry image and service quality.
The13th five-year plan period	The "13th Five-Year Plan" period is the decisive stage for building a moderately prosperous society in all respects. We must actively understand and adapt to the new normal for China's economic development. Comprehensively promote innovative development, coordinated development, green development, open development, and shared development to ensure that a moderately prosperous society is built in an all-round way.	1, Ecotour tourism development planning (2016-2025) 2, Deep integration of multiple industries 3, Reform of Chinese protected area institution	The holistic development stage	Emphasizing in-depth and comprehensive development.

Source: The Peking University laws and regulations database, Official website of the state council of China (2022)

In a nutshell, the driving factors model for ecotourism-related institutional changes can be roughly expressed as follows:

Figure 5. The count of Chinese policies issued that included the term "ecotourism" in its content during different five-year period
Source: The Peking University laws and regulations database (2022)

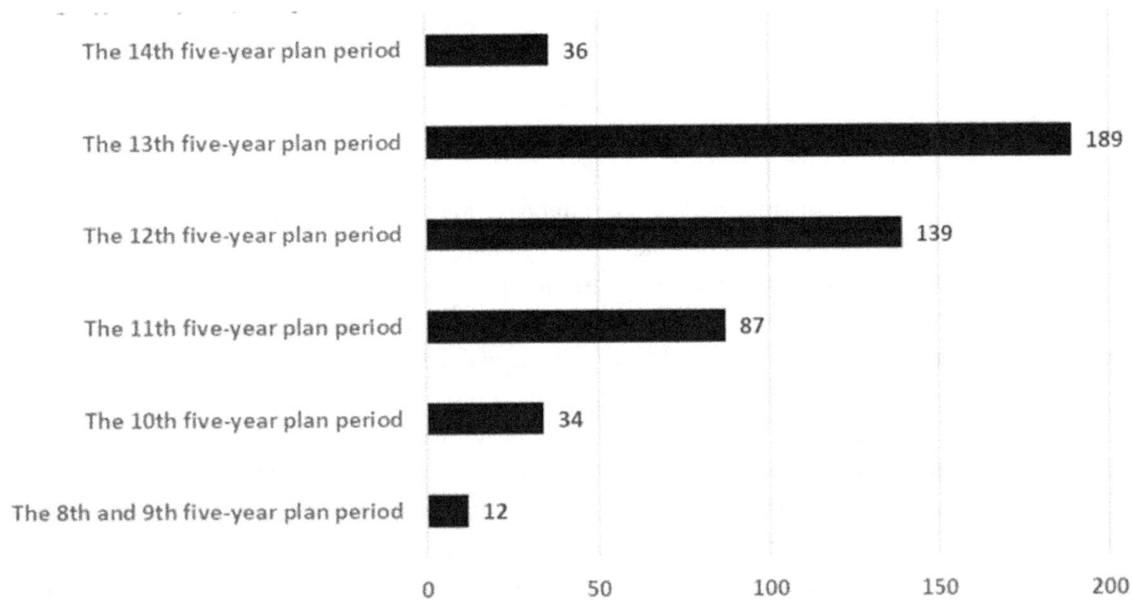

Figure 6. The driving factors model of Chinese ecotourism-related institutional changes
Source: Authors

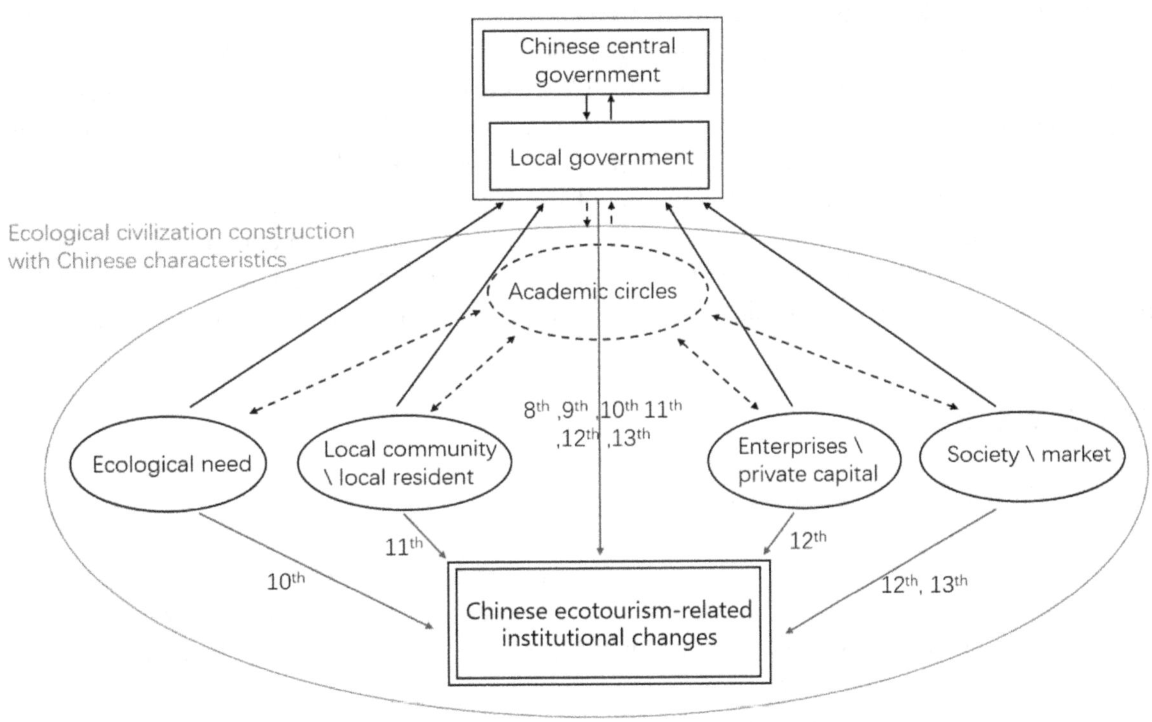

The upper part of the model represents the transmission of information and knowledge between government, academic circles and other parties. The lower part of the model represents the driving factors of ecotourism-related institutional changes. The dashed line indicates non-essential conduction processes. 8th, 9th, 10th, 11th, 12th, 13th represents corresponding five-year plans.

CONCLUSION

Through literature analysis and institutional change analysis, this paper confirms that there is a sustainable development trend in Chinese ecotourism-related policy changes. Analysis of policy changes indicates that since the introduction of the concept of ecotourism, the Chinese government has been continuously promoting the development of sustainable ecotourism though measures like adopting laws and regulations, monitoring and supervision etc. and balancing the needs of environmental protection and economic development. Promoting the sustainable development of ecotourism itself, boosting ecological protection and the Chinese economy similarly the main goals of relevant ecotourism policies. Meanwhile, as an important part of the construction of the Chinese ecological civilization, more and more ecotourism policies are aimed at coordinating the interests of various stakeholders. The interests of stakeholders are also one of the main factors affecting the changes in ecotourism policies.

In the future, Chinese ecotourism related policy development should still focus on achieving two main goals in order to improve sustainability and strengthen the ability to coordinate stakeholders' interests. Firstly, the lack of relevant laws is one of the biggest obstacles for Chinese ecotourism sustainable development. So far, there has been no specified law for protected areas in China. And the legal effect of relevant content in other laws and regulations is relatively too low to regulate complex ecotourism-related behaviors in the market. It is very important to speed up the formulation of relevant laws as much as possible in order to further promote the construction of sustainable ecotourism. Meanwhile, there is an obvious deficiency in the publicity and education of ecotourism. Although the term "ecotourism" has a high popularity, in fact, most people have not clear understanding about the actual sustainable connotation of "ecotourism". On the other hand, to better coordinate stakeholders' interests, the government should continuously pay attention to the demand of stakeholders. Policies measures such as reasonably dividing functional areas to ensure the normal life of residents living in ecotourism sites will not affect ecotourism development and ecological protection, and encouraging companies to participate in ecotourism, eco-agriculture and eco-industry through more preferential policies etc. can be implemented.

ACKNOWLEDGMENT

The authors extend sincere gratitude to:

- Our colleagues from Soochow University, the Australian Studies Centre of Shanghai University and Krirk University as well as the independent research colleagues who provided insight and expertise that greatly assisted the research, although they may not agree with all of the interpretations/conclusions of this chapter.
- Professor Marafa Lawal Mohammed of The Chinese University of Hong Kong for his insightful comments and editorial support in our first draft.

- China Knowledge for supporting our research.
- The Editor and the International Editorial Advisory Board (IEAB) of this book who initially desk reviewed, arranged a rigorous double/triple blind review process and conducted a thorough, minute and critical final review before accepting the chapter for publication.
- All anonymous reviewers who provided very constructive feedbacks for thorough revision, improvement and fine tuning of the chapter.

REFERENCES

Boswell, C., & Smith, K. (2017). Rethinking policy 'impact': Four models of research-policy relations. *Palgrave Communications*, *3*(1), 44. Advance online publication. doi:10.105741599-017-0042-z

Cao, Y., Chen, X., & Ma, Y. (2010). Urbanization, Urban-Rural Income Gap and Economic Growth—An Empirical Research Based on Provincial Panel Data in China. *Statistical Research*, 29–36. doi:10.19343/j.cnki.11-1302/c.2010.03.005

Ceballos-Lascurain, H. (1987). The future of 'ecotourism. *Mexico Journal,* 13-14.

Chen, C. (2006). CiteSpace II: Detecting and visualizing emerging trends and transient patterns in scientific literature. *Journal of the American Society for Information Science and Technology*, *57*(3), 359–377. doi:10.1002/asi.20317

Chen, C. (2017). Science mapping: A systematic review of the literature. *Journal of Data and Information Science*, *2*(2), 1–40. doi:10.1515/jdis-2017-0006

Chen, Q. (2013). Analysis on the Misunderstanding of Ecotourism from the Perspective of China's Practice. *Tourism Overview*, 36–37+40.

China Daily. (2018, March 13). *China plans to establish the Ministry of Natural Resources and the Ministry of Ecology and Environment.* Retrieved from https://baijiahao.baidu.com/s?id=1594805287518566570&wfr=spider&for=pc

Fang, Y., Yin, J., & Wu, B. (2017). Climate change and tourism: A scientometric analysis using CiteSpace. *Journal of Sustainable Tourism*, *26*(1), 108–126. doi:10.1080/09669582.2017.1329310

General Office of the Central Committee of the Communist Party of China & General Office of the State Council, Guiding Opinions on Establishing a Natural Reserve System with National Parks as the Main Body. (2019). The State Council of The people's Republic of China.

Global Sustainable Tourism Council. (n.d.). *GSTC criteria.* Retrieved from https://www.gstcouncil.org/gstc-criteria/

Gössling, S. (1999). Ecotourism: A means to safeguard biodiversity and ecosystem functions? *Ecological Economics*, *29*(2), 303–320. doi:10.1016/S0921-8009(99)00012-9

Hao, Y., Gai, Z., Yan, G., Wu, H., & Irfan, M. (2021). The spatial spillover effect and nonlinear relationship analysis between Environmental Decentralization, government corruption and air pollution: Evidence from China. *The Science of the Total Environment, 763*, 144183. doi:10.1016/j.scitotenv.2020.144183 PMID:33383516

Hou, L. (2018, July 18). *River chiefs keep water bodies clean*. The State Council of The People's Republic of China. Retrieved from http://english.www.gov.cn/state_council/ministries/2018/07/18/content_281476226902566.htm

Huang, B., Ma, Y., Huang, K., Su, L., Zhang, C., Cheng, D., & Wang, Y. (2018). Strategic Approach on Promoting Reform of China's Natural Protected Areas System with National Parks as Backbone. *Bulletin of Chinese Academy of Sciences*, 1342–1351. doi:10.16418/j.issn.1000-3045.2018.12.007

Huang, Q. (2014). *The special function of ecological civilization construction in the "five-in-one" overall layout*. Guangming Daily.

Li, W. (2004). Environmental management indicators for ecotourism in China's nature reserves: A case study in Tianmushan Nature Reserve. *Tourism Management, 25*(5), 559–564. doi:10.1016/j.tourman.2003.06.001

Li, Y., Zhang, L., Gao, Y., Huang, Z., Cui, L., Liu, S., Fang, Y., Ren, G., Fornacca, D., & Xiao, W. (2019). Ecotourism in China, misuse or genuine development? an analysis based on map browser results. *Sustainability, 11*(18), 4997. doi:10.3390u11184997

Li, Z. (2021). Research on Ecotourism Positioning and Effect in Chinese National Park System. *Tourism and Photography*, 82–83.

Lin, J. Y. (1989). An economic theory of institutional change: induced and imposed change. *Cato Journal, 9*(1), 1-33. https://www.cato.org/sites/cato.org/files/serials/fl/1989/5/cj9n1-1.pdf

Liu, T., & Cai, J. (2009). Public participation in Community Tourism Planning. *Tourism Research*, 55–61.

Liu, X., Fu, Z., Wen, R., Jin, C., Wang, X., Wang, C., Xiao, R., & Hou, P. (2020). Characteristics of human activities and the spatio-temporal changes of national nature reserves in China. *Geographical Research*, 2391–2402.

Liu, Y., Shi, D., & Li, X. (2009). A research on phenomena, causes and countermeasures of expansion of eco-tourism in China. *Resources & Industries*, 131–134.

Ma, T., Lü, C., & Lei, G. (2019). The spatial overlapping analysis for China's natural protected area and countermeasures for the optimization and integration of Protected Area System. *Shengwu Duoyangxing, 27*(7), 758–771. doi:10.17520/biods.2019087

Marafa, L. M. (2018). Leisure in nature: The advent of eco-leisure in academic discourse. *World Leisure Journal, 60*(3), 178–180. doi:10.1080/16078055.2018.1496526

National Development and Reform Commission (NDRC), the People´s Republic of China. (2016). *Notice on Issuing the "Green Development Index System" and "Ecological Civilization Construction Assessment Target System"*. Author.

North, D. C. (1990). *Institutions, institutional change, and Economic Performance*. Cambridge University Press. doi:10.1017/CBO9780511808678

Pang, J., Li, N., Mu, H., & Zhang, M. (2021). Empirical analysis of the interplay between shadow economy and pollution: With panel data across the provinces of China. *Journal of Cleaner Production*, *285*, 124864. doi:10.1016/j.jclepro.2020.124864

Peng, S. (2004). Some Environmental Problems and Countermeasures in Developing Ecotourism in China. *Environmental Protection*, 25–30.

Qin, H., Wan, Y., & Xia, Y. (2006). A Study on Over-extending Ecotourism and the Construction of Its Concept Model. *Huanjing Kexue Yu Guanli*, 146–140.

Qiu, S., & Tang, X. (2020). Effect of Ecotourism Development on Precision Poverty Alleviation of Farmers in Ethnic Minority Areas. *Ecological Economy*.

Ren, L., Li, J., Li, C., & Dang, P. (2021). Can ecotourism contribute to ecosystem? Evidence from local residents' ecological behaviors. *The Science of the Total Environment*, *757*, 143814. doi:10.1016/j.scitotenv.2020.143814 PMID:33248787

Shi, J., & Shen, G. (2002). On the classification criteria between institutional change theory and institutional change mode. *Economist*, 41–46.

Shi, K. (2006). *China's ten five-year plans*. Macroeconomic Management. doi:10.19709/j.cnki.11-3199/f.2006.12.023

Shi, Y., & Liu, X. (2019). Research on the literature of Green Building based on The web of science: A scientometric analysis in CITESPACE (2002–2018). *Sustainability*, *11*(13), 3716. doi:10.3390u11133716

Song, W., Li, G., & Yang, Y.-L. (2018). Analysis of residents' willingness to accept compensation of ecological protection and its influencing factors——Based on the research data of 660 households in Shaanxi National Nature Reserve. *Ganhanqu Ziyuan Yu Huanjing*, 63–69. doi:10.13448/j.cnki.jalre.2018.074

The International Ecotourism Society. (n.d.). *What is ecotourism*. Retrieved from https://ecotourism.org/what-is-ecotourism/

The National People's Congress, the People´s Republic of China. (2016). *Outline of the 13th Five-Year Plan for the National Economic and Social Development of the People's Republic of China*. Author.

The State Council. the People's Republic of China. (1993). Circular on the Outline of Regional Planning for Some Provinces and Regions in Southwest and Southern China. Author.

The State Environmental Protection Administration. the People's Republic of China. (2002). Notice on Printing and Distributing the Tenth Five-Year Plan for National Ecological Environmental Protection. Author.

Wang, K.-L., Zhao, B., Ding, L.-L., & Miao, Z. (2021). Government intervention, market development, and pollution emission efficiency: Evidence from China. *The Science of the Total Environment*, *757*, 143738. doi:10.1016/j.scitotenv.2020.143738 PMID:33223188

Wang, L., Zhong, L., Zhang, Y., & Zhou, B. (2014). Ecotourism Environmental Protection measures and their effects on protected areas in China. *Sustainability*, *6*(10), 6781–6798. doi:10.3390u6106781

Wang, S., & Ouyang, Z. (2007). The Rural-urban Income Disparity and Its Effects to Economic Growth in the Case of China. *Economic Research Journal*, 44–55.

Wang, Z., & Wang, L. (2007). North's Theory of Institutional Change and Its Implications for Chinese Reform. *Forward Position,* 45–47.

World Tourism Organization. (n.d.). *Ecotourism and Protected Areas*. Retrieved from https://www.unwto.org/sustainable-development/ecotourism-and-protected-areas

Xi, J. (2017, October 10). *Xi Jinping: Decisive Victory to Build a Well-off Society in an All-round Way and Win the Great Victory of Socialism with Chinese Characteristics in the New Era* [Poster presentation]. The 19th National Congress of the Communist Party of China, Beijing, China.

Xia, X., Wang, Z., Xu, W., Zhang, H., Zhou, D., & Jiang, M. (2016). Problems in Construction of Management System of Nature Reserves in China and Countermeasures. *Journal of Ecology and Rural Environment*, 30–34.

Xiao, F., Li, C., Sun, J., & Zhang, L. (2017). Knowledge domain and emerging trends in Organic Photovoltaic Technology: A Scientometric Review based on CITESPACE analysis. *Frontiers in Chemistry*, *5*, 67. Advance online publication. doi:10.3389/fchem.2017.00067 PMID:28966923

Xiao, L., & Zhong, L. (2017). Quantitative study on the evolution of Ecotourism Policy Development in China. *Journal of Resources and Ecology*, *8*(5), 460–469. doi:10.5814/j.issn.1674-764x.2017.05.003

Xinhua News Agency. (2015). *Opinions of the State Council of the People's Republic of China on Accelerating the Construction of Ecological Civilization*. The State Council. Retrieved from http://www.gov.cn/gongbao/content/2015/content_2864050.htm

Xinhua News Agency. (2018). *The Institutional Reform Program of the State Council*. The State Council of the People's Republic of China. Retrieved from http://www.gov.cn/xinwen/2018-03/17/content_5275116.htm

Xu, S., Mingzhu, L., Bu, N., & Pan, S. (2017). Regulatory frameworks for ecotourism: An application of total relationship flow management theorems. *Tourism Management*, *61*, 321–330. doi:10.1016/j.tourman.2017.02.012

Xu, W., Gao, J., Xia, X., Zhou, D., Li, Z., & Jiang, M. (2016). Distribution of Community Residents in Nature Reserves and Its Impacts on the Reserves in China. *Journal of Ecology and Rural Environment*, 19–23.

Yan, Y., Hu, A., & Wang, S. (2012). The evolution of the Chinese government's decision-making model: taking the five-year plan as an example. *National Report.*

Zhang, H., Qin, W., Zhou, D., Fan, L., Li, Z., & Jiang, M. (2016). Status Quo of Ecological Tourism in Nature Reserves in China. *Journal of Ecology and Rural Environment*, 24–29.

Zhao, Y., & Jiao, L. (2019). Resources development and tourism environmental carrying capacity of ecotourism industry in Pingdingshan City, China. *Ecological Processes*, *8*(1), 7. Advance online publication. doi:10.118613717-019-0161-0

Zhou, Y., Buesching, C. D., Newman, C., Kaneko, Y., Xie, Z., & Macdonald, D. W. (2013). Balancing the benefits of ecotourism and development: The effects of visitor trail-use on mammals in a protected area in rapidly developing China. *Biological Conservation*, *165*, 18–24. doi:10.1016/j.biocon.2013.05.007

ENDNOTES

1 Ecological civilization is a social form with the basic purpose of harmonious coexistence between man and nature, man and man, and man and society, a virtuous circle, all-round development and sustainable prosperity.

2 In the early 1980s, China put forward the concept of "well-off society", in which the construction of a new socialist countryside is one of the important contents of a well-off society. The construction of a "new socialist countryside" proposed at the Fifth Plenary Session of the 16th CPC Central Committee is a new starting point for a comprehensive rural reform under the guidance of new ideas in the new historical background, which will greatly promote the development and construction of rural areas.

Chapter 12
Understanding the Attitude–Behavior Gap in the Context of Green Consumption Behavior

F. Gül Aygen Ispahi
https://orcid.org/0000-0001-6980-7919
Independent Researcher, Turkey

ABSTRACT

The purpose of this chapter is to delineate the attitude-behavior gap phenomenon as it relates to green consumption behavior, an important component of environmental sustainability considerations. After a brief introduction to the topic, a number of possible explanations for the gap are reviewed. Some of the viable steps to overcome the associated problems—in light of various actions that can be taken by governments/public policy makers, environmental non-governmental organizations, the business sector, and individual consumers—are considered in the discussion section. Suggestions for future research and some concluding remarks follow, which, altogether, try to shed some light on the issue and hence encourage consumers be more involved—rather than just concerned—with the environmental betterment of the planet.

INTRODUCTION

Despite the immense amount of technological developments taking place, one of the main problems of our day is environmental deterioration. Global warming from fossil fuels, poor governance, food waste, biodiversity loss, plastic pollution, deforestation, air pollution, melting ice caps and sea level rise, ocean acidification, agricultural issues, food and water insecurity, together with fast fashion and textile waste have been cited by Robinson (2022) as being the twelve biggest environmental problems of 2022.

Due both to biodiversity loss and degradation and also to damages given to the ecosystems, every region in the World is expected to be confronted with huge risks, in the near future: In terrestrial ecosystems, up to 14% of a great variety of species are expected to face a very high risk of extinction at global warming levels of 1.5°C. On the other hand, risk of biodiversity loss ranges between moderate to very

DOI: 10.4018/978-1-6684-6750-3.ch012

high by 1.5°C global warming level, in case of ocean and coastal ecosystems. Likewise, hazards related to water and water availability are also expected to increase in many regions, with risks being more at higher global warming levels. Moreover, change in climate will most likely affect food production and access to food adversely, especially in the rather less-developed regions of the World. What is more, due to global warming, soil health will continuously be weakened which, in turn, will lead to pest and disease increases and a reduction in marine animal biomass, eroding food productivity on land and in the oceans. Leaving aside the economic damages, unfortunately, various diseases (either food, water, or vector-borne), ill health, heat-related mortality, and premature deaths are also expected to increase due mainly to climate change and extreme events related to this change. Besides, further global warming is also expected to affect mental health of different populations and lead to an increase in various psychological problems such as anxiety and stress. Along with many other drastic changes, higher global warming levels are anticipated to lead to extremities in weather and climate, particularly to drought, which might end up in violent intrastate conflicts, as well (IPCC, 2022).

All these problems, together with the issues of overpopulation and depletion of natural resources, make it necessary for different stakeholders to take urgent measures and act more responsibly toward the betterment of the environment.

With respect to these stakeholders, this responsibility belongs not only to governments, non-governmental organizations, or the business sector worldwide, but also to individual consumers. Even if one would be tempted to think that the above mentioned wide-ranging, hard-to-solve problems cannot be dealt with by individual consumer efforts, given that consumer household purchases are responsible for 40% of the environmental damage (Joshi and Rahman, 2015), it is "crucial to acknowledge and accept that individual behavior both significantly contributes to global environmental challenges and that individual behavioral change has the potential to reduce this impact significantly" (Klöckner, 2013, p.1030).

In fact, such a change may be initiated by pro-environmental behaviors and green consumption practices. When talking about pro-environmental behavior, one refers to actions undertaken consciously by an individual so as to bring the negative impact of his/her activities on the environment, to a minimum (Kollmuss and Agyeman, 2002). Examples of pro-environmental behavior include purchasing environmentally friendly products, recycling, using water, electricity and electrical appliances carefully at homes, avoiding to buy products that harm the environment or that cause environmental damage, using public rather than private transportation, and taking part in profit or not-for-profit environmental organizations (Kalamas et al., 2014). Relatedly, green consumption practices refer to consumption behaviors that an individual perceives to have either no impact or a minimum or reduced impact on the environment (Johnstone and Tan, 2015). Likewise, green products are produced so as to minimize natural resource exploitation, toxic material usage, or waste and pollutant emissions (Yan et al., 2021). As such, pro-environmental behaviors and green consumption practices are important topics in environmental sustainability considerations.

Together with this, having lived, at least, some of the adverse effects of environmental deterioration, individuals in most parts of the world have become more concerned about these issues in the recent years and are aware of the fact that there is an immediate need to take action.

The Sustainable Development Goals (SDGs), on the other hand, which have been set forth by the United Nations Member States in 2015 serve as a global roadmap to deal with issues related to poverty and protection of the planet. Likewise, if these goals can be attained, it is hoped that, by 2030, all people will be enjoying peace and prosperity (UNDP, 2022a). There are a total of 17 goals, one of which (the 12th) is on ensuring responsible consumption and production patterns (UNDP, 2022a). As such, it is stated within this goal that if economic growth and sustainable development are to be achieved, there is an urgent need to reduce the ecological footprint humans have on the planet. This, in turn, means changing the way goods and resources are produced and consumed (UNDP, 2022b). The sustainable consumption and production goal (SDG 12) aims at changing both the consumer and producer actions. Yet, although much of the effort on this topic has been put into changing production methods and policies until recent years, it should not be forgotten that altering the behaviors and demands of individual consumers is equally important (UNEP, 2017), as has been mentioned in the above paragraphs, as well.

Based on a number of large-scale attitudinal studies conducted in the diverse regions of the world -inclusive of the European Union, China, and the United States-, Langenbach et al. (2020) indicate that a large number of people not only acknowledge that immediacy but also feel that they have a responsibility to act.

Accomplishing this deed, however, would be less challenging if the below explained phenomenon did not exist!

BACKGROUND

Over the years, numerous environmental research studies have pointed out to an issue called the attitude-behavior gap: Although consumers say that they are 'very concerned' about environmental problems, this concern does not translate into substantive behavior change (Roberts, 1996; Mainieri et al., 1997; Roberts and Bacon, 1997; Kilbourne et al., 2002; Rex and Baumann, 2007; Do Paço and Raposo, 2009; Rettie et al., 2012; Yoon-Na et al., 2013; Kalamas et al., 2014; Nittala, 2014; Rettie et al., 2014; Johnstone and Tan, 2015; Mc Donald et al., 2015; Moser, 2015; Wymer and Polonsky, 2015; Felix and Braunsberger, 2016; Nguyen et al., 2019).

The term 'attitude-behavior gap' is also used interchangeably with the terms 'green attitude-behavior gap', 'green intention-behavior gap', 'motivation-behavior gap' (Wijekoon and Sabri, 2021), and 'green purchasing inconsistency' (Joshi and Rahman, 2015), by different researchers. In their study, ElHaffar et al. (2020) reveal various definitions of the concept that have been made over the past decades and give their own definition as "the inconsistency between what the individual says regarding his/her growing concern about the environmental problems and what he/she does in terms of actions, behaviors, and contributions to lessen the consequences of these problems" (p.4).

In spite of the 'stated' growing rate of concern, the fact that the estimated market share for green products does not exceed 7-8% worldwide (Wijekoon and Sabri, 2021) is an evidence of this gap. Although consumers may have positive attitudes toward green issues, their consumption behaviors are inconsistent and often conflicting (Johnstone and Tan, 2015). According to Shim et al. (2018), this situation indicates that due to different perceived barriers or bottlenecks, people are hampered somehow in their decision-making process.

Within this frame, a number of possible explanations have been made for this gap, by various authors: One of the oldest of these belongs to Kardash (1974) as has been mentioned by Peattie and Charter (2003). Accordingly, Kardash has argued that, for two seemingly identical products, all other things being equal, most consumers would choose the eco-friendly alternative rather than the conventional one. So, if one looks at the 'other things' that are not equal, he/she will have a chance of better understanding green purchase behavior (Peattie and Charter, 2003): In many cases, when one makes a green purchase, he/

she will have to make some compromises such as a higher price, a lower level of technical performance and/or less convenience – fewer distribution outlets – in reaching the item.

The list of such compromises and inhibitors can be extended: Most of the time, an individual will have to make some personal sacrifices if he/she wants to be green and this acts as a barrier to green behavior. There is also a perception that green is just for those people who are ready, implying that it is not for everyone (Johnstone and Tan, 2015). Likewise, some people think of green as something that is "elusive and/or exclusive" (p.317) or that green products are for "weird" people (Rettie et al., 2014, p.10). Moreover, in some cases people will feel a sense of powerlessness where they think that their individual actions will not have any effect on the environment (Johnstone and Tan, 2015). Furthermore, some others have an "all or nothing approach". They think that they can either be a 'totally green' or a 'totally non-green' consumer (p.317). There is also a tendency to be more willing to act if others are seen acting as well. If nobody around is seen as acting, an individual will also be inclined not to act, a notion called "the tragedy of the commons" (WBCSD, 2015, p.18).

According to Johnstone and Tan (2015), "it is too hard to be green" (p.316) – being environmentally friendly has its costs both money-wise, time-wise, and effort-wise –. Besides, in some cases, consumers believe that others (people they live with, marketers, and the government) do not make it easy for them to be green. Moreover, "there is a stigma attached to being green" (p.319), an unfavorable perception associated with being green; hence people prefer not to be green so as to maintain their positive social identity. Furthermore, in some other cases, "being 'green' is not perceived as a pressing matter" (p.320) either because the possible negative consequences of using conventional products cannot be seen, those negative effects have not been directly experienced, or else a significant difference between green and non-green products is not perceived.

Majid and Russell (2015) also point out that the reluctance of consumers to purchase green products stems from at least three factors which they cite as 'perceived inferiority of green products', 'unwillingness to incur greater costs', and 'perceived greenwashing activities of companies'.

As Shim et al. (2018) state, according to Blake who has conducted a study in 1999, there are three factors that hinder consumers from making green purchases and hence that lead to the attitude-behavior gap. These are individual barriers that are present within the person - inclusive of laziness and lack of interest-, responsibility -the feeling that a person will not be able to influence environmental reform-, and practicality – social and institutional constraints preventing pro-environmental behaviors whether or not an individual has the best of intentions or attitudes.

The gap may be a result of certain internal (financial limitations) or external (sociopolitical changes) factors, as well (Leonidou et al., 2010).

In a quite recent study, Riskos et al. (2021) indicate that lack of knowledge, social norms, situational factors, and individual factors such as demographics and lifestyle choices are among the reasons behind the gap.

Various other barriers include immature markets (Lund et al.'s study conducted in 2013 as cited in ElHaffar et al., 2020), missing regulations/standards on the part of governments, and poor marketing messages/practices on the part of businesses. With respect to businesses, even things like confusing package information and bewildering physical surroundings of a store hinder purchase of green products (Johnstone and Tan, 2015; Majid and Russell, 2015; Rettie at al., 2014).

Potential sacrifices in terms of convenience, costs, or performance have also been cited by Moser (2015) as likely inhibitors of green purchase behavior. Moreover, the author points out to prevailing habits and lifestyles as potential barriers to purchase. Force of habit is also mentioned by other authors

(Kollmuss and Agyemann, 2002; Marechal's study conducted in 2010 as cited by ElHaffar et al., 2020; WBCSD, 2015).

Another consideration relates to the rather 'feminine friendly' nature of the green movement which is believed to hold men back from acting environmentally friendly (Bennett and Williams, 2011). As Brough et al. (2016) argue, due to their gender identity ("the extent to which one identifies with being masculine or feminine" (p. 568)), men may be inclined to refrain from or even oppose green behaviors as there is an association between the concepts of 'greenness' and 'femininity' and also "a corresponding stereotype that green consumers are more feminine" (p.567).

The effect of situated cognition has, as well, been studied as a factor leading to the gap. Accordingly, the situation in which an individual is placed influences his/her behavior towards green products and when there is a competition between situational parameters, on the one hand, and moral beliefs, on the other, the resulting heavy cognitive burden may lead a consumer to overlook the issue of green purchase (ElHaffar et al., 2020).

In their study, Langenbach et al. (2020) support the argument that cognitive resources are a relevant variable in explaining the relation between pro-environmental attitudes and behavior and they show that those with low cognitive resources cannot really transform their pro-environmental attitudes into behavior, whereas those with high resources are capable of doing so.

In case of health considerations and also when children are of concern, people tend to perceive that eco-friendly products do not perform as effectively as conventional products. Under such circumstances, the less eco-friendly choice could win out provided that it can "evoke a stronger feeling of security" (Bennett and Williams, 2011, p.49).

Likewise, different types of risks -namely, financial, functional, and temporal risks - perceived in the purchase of green products also lead to the gap between attitudes and behavior (Durif et al., 2012).

Faced with such compromises and hindrances, a consumer needs to have confidence in the environmental benefits involved - inclusive of the extent to which the individual believes that the company offering the product is really environmentally-friendly, that the product addresses a real issue, and that it represents an environmental benefit (Mc Donald and Oates, 2006) -, so as to make the purchase. Hence, when both the compromises involved and the confidence needed are taken into account, it becomes easier to understand why individuals do not take action/purchase green products quite readily (Kardash, 1974).

SOLUTIONS AND RECOMMENDATIONS

As has been revealed in the above section, due to a variety of factors, willingness of consumers often does not translate into sustainable consumer behavior. Given that "sustainable consumption is a systemic challenge" (WBCSD, 2015, p.34), both governments, non-governmental organizations (NGOs), businesses, and consumers, all building blocks of a society, have important roles to play in enhancing more sustainable levels of consumption.

As for governments and policy makers, it should be noted that many pro-environmental behaviors such as recycling and taking public transportation can be performed if the necessary infrastructure is provided. "The poorer such services are, the less likely people are to use them" (Kollmuss and Agyeman, 2002, p.60). Besides, a lack of infrastructure influences the attitude-behavior gap, even when there is a willingness on the part of consumers to adopt sustainable behaviors (Romero et al, 2018). Hence, easy-to-use and readily available (Wijekoon and Sabri, 2021) infrastructure has to be there if one is to expect pro-environmental behaviors to flourish.

Together with infrastructural developments, governments and public policy makers should also pass and/or improve relevant rules, regulations, bans, and industry-wide standards. A related consideration is pointed out by Orquin et al. (2020) who concentrate on the concept of visual ecology and show that those packaging elements which are related to characteristics pertaining to trust (i.e. information regarding sustainability and nutrition) are visually inconspicuous and that consumers tend to ignore sustainability and nutrition information, not because of a lack of motivation but rather due to their visual environment which impedes them from addressing this information. They suggest policy intervention so as to increase the noticeability of sustainability and nutrition information.

In some cases, taxes may be imposed on environmentally harmful activities (Kollmuss and Agyeman, 2002); in some other cases, incentives, particularly non-monetary ones, may be provided (Wijekoon and Sabri, 2021) so as to either punish or reward people on their environment-related behavior, respectively.

Ecological education is of great importance to nurture young generations who are to become adults of the future. Therefore, increasing knowledge on ecological change and the potential threats mankind is confronted with is a vital consideration that should be addressed by public policy makers.

Apart from these, it seems that there is a need for more dialogue between governments and the business world for viable solutions to be developed.

International environmental non-governmental organizations (NGOs) make important contributions to the environment and the society in which they operate. They are mainly responsible for conducting research, building consumer awareness about environmental issues, protecting habitats, reducing human impact on the environment, and lobbying governments so that they enact environmentally friendly legislation. More specifically, some of them give support for environmental protection, some try to provide individuals or groups the capability to develop initiatives, some are dedicated to litigate environmental issues, some work on global warming, ecosystem restoration, oceans, and human health, some are involved in conserving threatened species and ecosystems worldwide, some work to protect ecologically important lands and waters for nature and people, some are dedicated to the conservation and restoration of wetlands (Berkeley Library, 2022).

Among the best known of these international environmental NGOs, one can cite Greenpeace, Earth Institute Center for Environmental Research and Conservation, Earth Island Institute, Earth Justice, Environmental Defense Fund, Fauna and Flora International, Nature Friends International, Global Footprint Network, International Union for Conservation of Nature, Nature Conservancy, Natural Resources Defense Council, Wetlands International, World Agroforestry Centre, and World Wildlife Fund, which all work hard toward advancing sustainable development (Berkeley Library, 2022).

Social norms, a type of social power which are influenced by the values and beliefs of a society, have been shown to affect environmentally friendly product purchase behavior of consumers; the deeds of environmental NGOs such as Friends of the Earth International and the Greenpeace are considered to be one of the driving forces behind these norms (Lin and Niu, 2018).

Social campaigns, which can be developed by the joint efforts of NGOs, environmentalists, companies, and governments, may also be used to increase individual social responsibility toward the environment (Rahimah et al., 2018).

As to the various possible ways to overcome the obstacles mentioned in the above section, one of the main considerations is to understand and assess how and why unfavorable green perceptions are formed: On the part of the business world, companies need to overcome the prevailing negative perceptions of consumers by offering them better quality (so as to deal with the perceived inferiority problem), lower price (both money, time, and effort-wise) green products that can be reached easily (so as to minimize the inconvenience problem). Likewise, there is a need for more honest business practices (so as to deal with the perceived greenwashing issue).

Besides, as poor marketing messages, confusing package information, and even bewildering physical surroundings of a store are all found to be obstacles to green purchase behavior, companies need to find ways to reach their customers through better marketing messages, clearer package information, easily comprehendible labeling, and better-designed stores (Johnstone and Tan, 2015; Majid and Russell, 2015). Furthermore, to deal with the greenwashing issue more effectively, it might be a good idea for companies to increase the transparency of their manufacturing and distribution processes and place the traceability information of their products either on the labels or make them known through some other medium (Calderon-Monge et al., 2020). Another way to improve a company's image in the eyes of potential customers may be through involvement in environmental causes and/or formation of partnerships/ alliances with green distributors or channels (Ghazali et al., 2018).

In their efforts to market green products, companies may make use of product sampling, as well, since both the likelihood of purchase and the willingness to pay higher prices for the green product increase after consumers actually experience it. Besides, the influence of green products on consumer behavior at the consumption stage is also important as using green products improves the associated consumption experiences. Hence, it is recommended that companies should communicate the environmental benefits of their green products effectively (Tezer and Bodur, 2020).

Still, due to health consideration of 'important others' (i.e. babies and children, in particular), some consumers insist on using the 'tried and trusted' conventional products. Hence, well-known, trusted brands in the market may consider to produce greener alternatives so as to deal with these issues of security. This may also lead to new opportunities for these companies in the 'green world'. As such, better and innovative products may be able to penetrate markets, by time (Bennett and Williams, 2011).

Also, companies need to focus on personal benefits of these products and try to convey their messages to customers, accordingly, due to the fact that individuals value their or their families' well-being more than anything else in the world.

Rewarding consumers for their better behaviors or penalizing them for their poor choices may also be considered as a means to increase pro-environmental behaviors or decrease environment-unfriendly deeds. In their review of marketing scholarship on environmental sustainability, Iacobucci et al. (2020) suggest that systems can be designed so as to enable manufacturers or retailers follow consumers via their mobile phones in an effort to reward or charge them, depending on their increased or decreased recycling behaviors, respectively.

As Polonsky (2011) puts, real life-changing solutions may be provided if environmental problems can be made more current and urgent in consumers' minds. Lee et al. (2020) explain the notion of episodic future thinking (EFT) as "projecting the self into the future to pre-experience future events" (p.60) and propose engagement in EFT so as to facilitate the perception of future events as psychologically close and hence increase the risk perceived associated with those events. In their point of view, such a situation, in turn, is expected to lead to pro-environmental behavior. The authors share the view with some other researchers that "increased vividness, availability, and elaboration of environmental imagery may foster pro-environmental behavior" (p.74).

Another perspective relates to the notion of 'death anxiety', proposed by Rahimah et al. (2018), as an effective way to drive green product purchase intention. In their point of view, rather than promoting the positive benefits of green product consumption, "negative consequences of environmental deterioration on individual consumers' and their loved ones' continued existence can be evoked by marketers" (p.486). As such, communicating the likelihood of an individual's death due to environmental worsening can result in anxiety within that individual's mind which may lead the person to take preventive actions, one of which would be the purchase of green products (Rahimah et al, 2018).

On the other hand, there are also researchers who believe that rewards are more motivating than arousal of feelings of fear or punishment and that it is important to encourage good behavior through tangible treats (Bennett and Williams, 2011). As such, Ertz and Sarıgöllü (2019) concentrate on the effect of behavior on attitude and examine the influence of satisfaction on that relationship to suggest that 'satisfaction' is a positive reinforcer of the link between previous pro-environmental behavior and following attitudes related to pro-environmental behavior. Accordingly, they point out that if individuals are satisfied with their past behavior, they will be more inclined to develop positive attitudes toward both the cost and importance of pro-environmental behavior. Likewise, it would be a better idea to support, encourage, and reward consumers to increase the satisfaction they get from their pro-environmental behaviors, rather than penalizing them in some way.

Similarly, there is also a need to reduce barriers to positive behavior and to make it hard for consumers to persist with their old, negative habits, as well (Majid and Russell, 2015).

Furthermore, as Rettie et al. (2014) point out, greener consumer behavior may be encouraged by repositioning such behavior as 'normal' rather than 'green'. This is because behaviors and products that are considered to be 'normal' are more likely to be adopted by consumers and hence, through a process of 'social normalization', even novel activities and products that may be perceived to be different and peculiar, at first, can later be accepted by the society. Again, green marketing efforts may be targeted at mainstream consumers -so as to be positioned as the new normal- instead of only a niche group of green consumers (Rettie et al., 2014). Moreover, it may be possible to redefine unconcerned/uncaring consumption as "abnormal and anti-social" and green behavior as "normal and inclusive" (Bennett and Williams, 2011, p.22).

Together with this, in regard to the 'feminine friendly nature' of the green movement, Borau et al. (2021) studied whether males could benefit from the on-going green-feminine stereotype and concluded that "green consumption (could) act as a signal of altruism and high commitment both as a partner and as a father" (p. 266) and they stated that men could increase their value as long-term mates by engaging in green consumption behavior.

Besides, the issue of consumer perceptions need to be taken into consideration, as well, so as to diminish the gap (ElHaffar et al., 2020). According to Bennett and Williams (2011), it is quite important for marketers to get involved with increasing the perceived value of green products in the eyes of customers through promotional efforts by informing them on the physical and psychological benefits of green products. Moreover, different benefits of a product should be emphasized depending on how it is positioned: If the income level of the target market is rather high, environmental appeals should be conveyed; however, for the low-income consumers who are not able to buy green products frequently, it may be more beneficial to use personal appeals such as health or nutrition claims (Moser, 2015).

As the young generation makes use of social media tools such as Facebook, Twitter, and Instagram, to a great extent, it may make sense to utilize buzz marketing and umbrella branding strategies through digital channels to increase word of mouth and communication among the youth, their families, and friends (Eşsiz and Mandrik, 2022).

In an attempt to discover how individual consumers can be encouraged to behave more sustainably, White et al. (2019) review the literature and introduce the *SHIFT* framework that reflects the importance of considering how *S*ocial influence, *H*abit formation, *I*ndividual self, *F*eelings and cognition, and *T*angibility, five broad psychological routes, can be used in this respect. They conclude that there is no single route that works ‘best’ in changing behavior but rather a combination of strategies can be more fruitful as there often arise more than one barrier to sustainable behavior change, at a time.

Based on the Environmental Impacts of Products (EIPRO) technical report of the European Commission, Tukker and Jansen (2006) argue that housing (mainly building structures, heating, and (electrical) energy-using products), transport (mainly car and air travel), and food (mainly meat and dairy products) are the three main priorities that are responsible for 70% of environmental impacts meaning, we as consumers also have much to do in this respect. As such, Moser (2015) argues that “if individuals are motivated to make a contribution to sustainable development and especially environmental protection, everyday consumption behavior would be an adequate starting point” (p.167). Accordingly, consumers should be informed that their individual consumption behavior can really make a difference and benefits of green products should be conveyed to them as clearly as possible (Moser, 2015).

It is obvious that although green products have a higher price, they can pay for themselves many times over a lifetime of use - such as the case with compact fluorescent light bulbs, low-flow showerheads, hybrid vehicles, and reusable beverage or food containers. Unfortunately, lifetime savings do not say much to consumers who are after instant gratification of needs (Bennett and Williams, 2011). And what is more, consumers care most about things that have a direct impact on their lives. They are not that concerned about issues which are expected to take place in the future and which really do not bother them at present. Besides, they have difficulty in identifying future outcomes and consequences (Johnstone and Tan, 2015). Apart from these, it is important to remember that environmental change takes place at a very slow pace and it is not easy to perceive slow changes. Hence, information pertaining to environmental degradation should be conveyed to consumers in an understandable format, be it in the form of language, pictures, or graphs (Kollmuss and Agyeman, 2002).

In some cases, even if individuals may have high ecological concern, they do not act -as they feel it is the responsibility of the government and/or big corporations to preserve the environment (Laroche et al., 2001; Wymer and Polonsky, 2015). As has been stated above, it is very important to let individual consumers know that although governments and businesses are liable for many deeds, apart from them, consumers themselves have responsibilities to take, as well. “Empowering the consumer-citizen is likely a core element in efforts to bridge the gap between sustainable attitudes and unsustainable behavior” (Prothero et al., 2011, p.33).

FUTURE RESEARCH DIRECTIONS

Besides the ‘attitude-behavior gap’, future research may study actual behavior of consumers as well as their reported behaviors due to the fact that social desirability bias may also influence individuals to a great extent, leading to another gap.

Likewise, more systematic analyses and meta analyses on the topic of green consumer behavior may be recommended since usage of these methods may be helpful in identifying the gaps more thoroughly (Sharma, 2021).

Furthermore, an examination of the reasons behind individuals' "passive state of inconsistent behavior" as well as "the determinants and settings supporting positive eco-friendly compensation behavior, mainly personality traits" may provide valuable insights into the topic (Wijekoon and Sabri, 2021, p.26).

Apart from these, use of neuromarketing research may also be suggested so as to gain insight into consumers' hidden feelings, preferences, and decisions (Sharma, 2021).

It may also be fruitful to conduct multidisciplinary research on the topic, especially integrating aspects of behavioral science and other applied social sciences (UNEP, 2017).

Two of the most recent research areas that deserve attention and that may be fruitful to study are the circular economy paradigm, which defines the 3R's principle of 'reduce', 'reuse', and 'recycle' in producing, transporting, and consuming products (Shao, 2019) - concentrating on take backs, leases, and pay-per-uses – and the sharing economy model -like bike and car sharing initiatives- both of which are aimed at lengthening the life and durability of products (Testa et al., 2021). Like the sharing economy trend, voluntary simplicity "indicate(s) that consumers can fulfill their needs without the possession of tangible products being a focal point" (White et al., 2019, p. 31). Further research on voluntary simplicity would, hence, be worthwhile, as well.

Another topic that might be of interest is whether virtual reality (VR), one of the new realities of our times, can transform consumer experience (Wolhuter, 2021) and be a substitute for, at least, some of the real life experiences. If the answer to the latter is affirmative, then might it be possible somehow to reduce the adverse impact of individual consumers on the environment?

Reasons for the gap may differ depending on countries, as well. In the rather affluent societies, monetary considerations are not expected to play a major role whereas in case of developing nations, economic constraints may hinder purchase behavior even when there is the best of attitudes. Hence, the developed and the developing countries should be analyzed separately so as to create meaningful solutions for each. Besides, more research is surely needed in case of developing nations as relatively much has been conducted in the developed countries.

CONCLUSION

Having reviewed the attitude-behavior gap phenomenon, some of the possible ways to overcome the associated problems, and various actions that can be taken by governments/public policy makers, environmental non-governmental organizations, the business sector, and individual consumers, one can see that even though there is a growing interest in the phenomenon of the green attitude-behavior gap, research on the topic has not come to a stage where solutions can be applied and due, also, to the profound effects of technological innovations, consumers are faced with very frequent changes in their daily lives which lead to a continuous evolution of the gap. Hence, it is not quite likely that the green gap phenomenon will be resolved in the near future and more analyses will surely be needed to further study the subject (ElHaffar et al., 2020).

The world population which was estimated to be around 7.95 billion people in the beginning of 2022 (UNFPA, 2022), is expected to reach 9.7 billion people by 2050 and 11 billion people by the end of the 21st century (UN, 2022). Nevertheless, even today, "humans use as much ecological resources as if (they) lived on 1.7 Earths" (Global Footprint Network, 2022) and nobody knows what the situation will be like by the end of the century! It may be possible to solve most of the prevailing problems associated with environmental deterioration and to have a much healthier planet by that time, due to the immense body of technological developments taking place, almost each passing day. Yet, if huge populations of the world continue to abuse the environment and just wait for the technology to heal it for them, this will most probably lead to a disaster, as Nature is always more powerful than technology.

Hence, taking the SDG12 of 'responsible production and consumption' into consideration once more and looking at the situation from the perspective of consumers again, it will not be wrong to conclude with the following: If individuals can somehow be persuaded to follow the three R's (reduce, reuse, and recycle) in their daily lives, at least to an extent, much will be done in protecting the environment and ecosystems as is indicated in the poem written by Julia A. Carney back in 1845: "Little drops of water, little grains of sand, make the mighty ocean, and the pleasant land…".

REFERENCES

Bennett, G., & Williams, F. (2011). Mainstream green: Moving sustainability from niche to normal. The Red Papers: Issue 4. Ogilvy & Mather.

Berkeley Library, University of California. (2022). *Non-governmental organizations.* Retrieved June 15, 2022, from https://guides.lib.berkeley.edu/c.php?g=496970&p=3427176

Borau, S., Elgaaied-Gambier, L., & Barbarossa, C. (2021). The green mate appeal: Men's pro-environmental consumption is an honest signal of commitment to their partner. *Psychology and Marketing*, *38*(2), 266–285. doi:10.1002/mar.21321

Brough, A. R., Wilkie, J. E. B., Ma, J., Isaac, M. S., & Gal, D. (2016). Is eco-friendly unmanly? The green-feminine stereotype and its effect on sustainable consumption. *The Journal of Consumer Research*, *43*(4), 567–582. doi:10.1093/jcr/ucw044

Calderon-Monge, E., Sanz-Pastor, I., & Garcia, F. J. S. (2020). Analysis of sustainable consumer behavior as a business opportunity. *Journal of Business Research*, *120*, 74–81. doi:10.1016/j.jbusres.2020.07.039

Do Paço, A. M. F., & Raposo, M. L. B. (2009). Green segmentation: An application to the Portuguese consumer market. *Marketing Intelligence & Planning*, *27*(3), 364–379. doi:10.1108/02634500910955245

Durif, F., Roy, J., & Boivin, C. (2012). Could perceived risks explain the 'green gap'in green product consumption? *Electronic Green Journal*, *1*(33). Advance online publication. doi:10.5070/G313310923

ElHaffar, G., Durif, F., & Dube, L. (2020). Towards closing the attitude-intention-behavior gap in green consumption: A narrative review of the literature and an overview of future research directions. *Journal of Cleaner Production*, *275*(122556), 1–20. doi:10.1016/j.jclepro.2020.122556

Ertz, M., & Sarıgöllü, E. (2019). The behavior-attitude relationship and satisfaction in pro-environmental behavior. *Environment and Behavior*, *51*(9-10), 1106–1132. doi:10.1177/0013916518783241

Essiz, O., & Mandrik, C. (2022). Intergenerational influence on sustainable consumer attitudes and behaviors: Roles of family communication and peer influence in environmental consumer socialization. *Psychology and Marketing*, *39*(1), 5–26.

Felix, R., & Braunsberger, K. (2016). I believe therefore I care. The relationship between religiosity, environmental attitudes, and green product purchase in Mexico. *International Marketing Review*, *33*(1), 137–155. doi:10.1108/IMR-07-2014-0216

Ghazali, E. M., Mutum, D. S., & Ariswibowo, N. (2018). Impact of religious values and habit on an extended green purchase behaviour model. *International Journal of Consumer Studies*, *42*(6), 639–654. doi:10.1111/ijcs.12472

Global Footprint Network. (2022). Retrieved February 15, 2022, from https://www.footprintnetwork. org

Iacobucci, D., Gabriel, M. L. D. S., Schneider, M. J., & Hamza, K. M. (2020). Marketing research on environmental sustainability. *Review of Marketing Research*, *17*, 261–292. doi:10.1108/S1548-643520200000017019

IPCC (Intergovernmental Panel on Climate Change). (2022). *Climate change 2022: Impacts, adaptation, and vulnerability*. Retrieved June 15, 2022, from https://www.ipcc.ch/report/ ar6/wg2/downloads/report/IPCC_AR6_WGII_FinalDraft_FullReport.pdf

Johnstone, M.-L., & Tan, L. P. (2015). Exploring the gap between consumers' green rhetoric and purchasing behavior. *Journal of Business Ethics*, *132*(2), 311–328. doi:10.100710551-014-2316-3

Joshi, Y., & Rahman, Z. (2015). Factors affecting green purchase behavior and future research directions. *International Strategic Management Review*, *3*(1-2), 128–143. doi:10.1016/j.ism.2015.04.001

Kalamas, M., Cleveland, M., & Laroche, M. (2014). Pro-environmental behaviors for thee but not for me: Green giants, green Gods, and external environmental locus of control. *Journal of Business Research*, *67*(2), 12–22. doi:10.1016/j.jbusres.2013.03.007

Kardash, W. J. (1974). Corporate responsibility and the quality of life: Developing the ecologically concerned consumer. In Ecological Marketing. AMA.

Kilbourne, W. E., Beckmann, S. C., & Thelen, E. (2002). The role of the dominant social paradigm in environmental attitudes: A multinational examination. *Journal of Business Research*, *55*(3), 193–204. doi:10.1016/S0148-2963(00)00141-7

Klöckner, C. A. (2013). A comprehensive model of the psychology of environmental behaviour – a metaanalysis. *Global Environmental Change*, *23*(5), 1028–1038. doi:10.1016/j.gloenvcha.2013.05.014

Kollmuss, A., & Agyeman, J. (2002). Mind the gap: Why do people act environmentally and what are the barriers to pro-environmental behavior. *Environmental Education Research*, *8*(3), 239–260. doi:10.1080/13504620220145401

Langenbach, B. P., Berger, S., Baumgartner, T., & Knoch, D. (2020). Cognitive resources moderate the relationship between pro-environmental attitudes and green behavior. *Environment and Behavior*, *52*(9), 979–995. doi:10.1177/0013916519843127

Laroche, M., Bergeron, J., & Barbaro-Forleo, G. (2001). Targeting consumers who are willing to pay more for environmentally friendly products. *Journal of Consumer Marketing*, *18*(6), 503–520. doi:10.1108/EUM0000000006155

Lee, P.-S., Sung, Y.-H., Wu, C.-C., Ho, L.-C., & Chiou, W.-B. (2020). Using episodic future thinking to pre-experience climate change increases pro-environmental behavior. *Environment and Behavior*, *52*(1), 60–81. doi:10.1177/0013916518790590

Leonidou, C. N., Leonidou, L. C., & Kvasova, O. (2010). Antecedents and outcomes of consumer environmentally friendly attitudes and behavior. *Journal of Marketing Management*, *26*(13-14), 1319–1344. doi:10.1080/0267257X.2010.523710

Lin, S.-T., & Niu, H.-J. (2018). Green consumption: Environmental knowledge, environmental consciousness, social norms, and purchasing behavior. *Business Strategy and the Environment*, *27*(8), 1679–1688. doi:10.1002/bse.2233

Mainieri, T., Barnett, E. G., Valdero, T. R., Unipan, J. B., & Oskamp, S. (1997). Green buying: The influence of environmental concern on consumer behavior. *The Journal of Social Psychology*, *137*(2), 189–204. doi:10.1080/00224549709595430

Majid, K. A., & Russell, C. A. (2015). Giving green a second thought: Modeling the value retention of green products in the secondary market. *Journal of Business Research*, *68*(5), 994–1002. doi:10.1016/j.jbusres.2014.10.001

Mc Donald, S., & Oates, C. J. (2006). Sustainability: Consumer perceptions and marketing strategies. *Business Strategy and the Environment*, *15*(3), 157–170. doi:10.1002/bse.524

Mc Donald, S., Oates, C. J., Thyne, M., Timmis, A. J., & Carlile, C. (2015). Flying in the face of environmental concern: Why green consumers continue to fly. *Journal of Marketing Management*, *31*(13-14), 1503–1528. doi:10.1080/0267257X.2015.1059352

Moser, A. K. (2015). Thinking green, buying green? Drivers of pro-environmental purchasing behavior. *Journal of Consumer Marketing*, *32*(3), 167–175. doi:10.1108/JCM-10-2014-1179

Nguyen, H. V., Nguyen, C. H., & Hoang, T. T. B. (2019). Green consumption: Closing the intention-behavior gap. *Sustainable Development*, *27*(1), 118–129. doi:10.1002d.1875

Nittala, R. (2014). Green consumer behavior of the educated segment in India. *Journal of International Consumer Marketing*, *26*(2), 138–152. doi:10.1080/08961530.2014.878205

Orquin, J. L., Bagger, M. P., Lahm, E. S., Grunert, K. G., & Scholderer, J. (2020). The visual ecology of product packaging and its effects on consumer attention. *Journal of Business Research*, *111*, 187–195. doi:10.1016/j.jbusres.2019.01.043

Peattie, K., & Charter, M. (2003). Green marketing. In M. J. Baker (Ed.), *The Marketing Book* (5th ed., pp. 726–755). Butterworth Heinemann.

Polonsky, M. J. (2011). Transformative green marketing: Impediments and opportunities. *Journal of Business Research*, *64*(12), 1311–1319. doi:10.1016/j.jbusres.2011.01.016

Prothero, A., Dobscha, S., Freund, J., Kilbourne, W. E., Luchs, M. G., Ozanne, L. K., & Thogersen, J. (2011, Spring). Sustainable consumption: Opportunities for consumer research and public policy. *Journal of Public Policy & Marketing*, *30*(1), 31–38. doi:10.1509/jppm.30.1.31

Rahimah, A., Khalil, S., Ming-Sung, J., Tran, M. D., & Panwar, V. (2018). Understanding green purchase behavior through death anxiety and individual social responsibility: Mastery as a moderator. *Journal of Consumer Behaviour, 17*(5), 477–490. doi:10.1002/cb.1733

Rettie, R., Burchell, K., & Barnham, C. (2014). Social normalisation: Using marketing to make green normal. *Journal of Consumer Behaviour, 13*(1), 9–17. doi:10.1002/cb.1439

Rettie, R., Burchell, K., & Riley, D. (2012). Normalising green behaviours: A new approach to sustainability marketing. *Journal of Marketing Management, 28*(3-4), 420–444. doi:10.1080/0267257X.2012.658840

Rex, E., & Baumann, H. (2007). Beyond ecolabels: What green marketing can learn from conventional marketing. *Journal of Cleaner Production, 15*(6), 567–576. doi:10.1016/j.jclepro.2006.05.013

Riskos, K., Paraskevi, D., Mylonas, N., & Tsourvakas, G. (2021). Ecolabels and the attitude-behavior relationship towards green product purchase: A multiple mediation model. *Sustainability, 13*(12), 6867. doi:10.3390u13126867

Roberts, J. A. (1996). Green consumers in the 1990's: Profile and implications for advertising. *Journal of Business Research, 36*(3), 217–231. doi:10.1016/0148-2963(95)00150-6

Roberts, J. A., & Bacon, D. R. (1997). Exploring the subtle relationships between environmental concern and ecologically conscious consumer behavior. *Journal of Business Research, 40*(1), 79–89. doi:10.1016/S0148-2963(96)00280-9

Robinson, D. (2022). *Twelve biggest environmental problems of 2022*. Retrieved April 27, 2022, from https://earth.org/the-biggest-environmental-problems-of-our-lifetime/

Romero, C. B. A., Golam, M. L., Aurup, M., & Ferraz, S. B. (2018). Ethnicity and acculturation of environmental attitudes and behaviors: A cross-cultural study with Brazilians in Canada. *Journal of Business Research, 82*, 300–309. doi:10.1016/j.jbusres.2017.09.009

Shao, J. (2019). Sustainable consumption in China: New trends and research interests. *Business Strategy and the Environment, 28*(8), 1507–1517. doi:10.1002/bse.2327

Sharma, A. P. (2021). Consumers' purchase behavior and green marketing: A synthesis, review, and agenda. *International Journal of Consumer Studies, 45*(6), 1217–1238. doi:10.1111/ijcs.12722

Shim, D., Shin, J., & Kwak, S.-Y. (2018). Modelling the consumer decision-making process to identify key drivers and bottlenecks in the adoption of environmentally friendly products. *Business Strategy and the Environment, 27*(8), 1409–1421. doi:10.1002/bse.2192

Testa, F., Pretner, G., Iovino, R., Bianchi, G., Tessitore, S., & Iraldo, F. (2021). Drivers to green consumption: A systematic review. *Environment, Development and Sustainability, 23*(4), 4826–4880. doi:10.100710668-020-00844-5

Tezer, A., & Bodur, O. (2020). The green consumption effect: How using green products improves consumption experience. *The Journal of Consumer Research, 47*(1), 25–39. doi:10.1093/jcr/ucz045

Tukker, A., & Jansen, B. (2006). Environmental impacts of products - a detailed review of studies. *Journal of Industrial Ecology, 10*(3), 159–182. doi:10.1162/jiec.2006.10.3.159

UN (United Nations). (2022). *Population*. Retrieved June 15, 2022, from https://www.un.org/en/ global-issues/population

UNDP (United Nations Development Program). (2022a). *Sustainable development goals*. Retrieved May 26, 2022, from https://www.undp.org/sustainable-development-goals

UNDP (United Nations Development Program). (2022b). *Sustainable development goals*. Retrieved May 26, 2022, from https://www.undp.org/sustainable-development-goals#responsible-consumption-and-production

UNEP (United Nations Environment Program). (2017). *Consuming differently, consuming sustainably: Behavioral insights for policymaking*. Retrieved May 26, 2022 from, https://sustainabledevelopment.un.org/content/documents/2404Behavioral%20Insights.pdf

UNFPA (United Nations Population Fund). (2022). *World population*. Retrieved June 15, 2022, from https://www.unfpa.org/ data/world-population-dashboard

WBCSD (World Business Council for Sustainable Development). (2015). *Sustainable consumption facts and trends-from a business perspective*. Retrieved January 5, 2017, from http://www.wbcsd.org/Clusters/Sustainable-Lifestyles/Resources/Sustainable-Consumption-Fact-and-Trends-From-a-Business-Perspective

White, K., Habib, R., & Hardisty, D. J. (2019). How to SHIFT consumer behaviors to be more sustainable: A literature review and guiding framework. *Journal of Marketing*, *83*(3), 22–49. doi:10.1177/0022242919825649

Wijekoon, R., & Sabri, M. F. (2021). Determinants that influence green product purchase intention and behavior: A literature review and guiding framework. *Sustainability*, *13*(11), 6219. doi:10.3390u13116219

Wolhuter, S. (2021). *How VR is transforming customer experience*. Retrieved February 7, 2022, from https://wearebrain.com

Wymer, W., & Polonsky, M. J. (2015). The limitations and potentialities of green marketing. *Journal of Nonprofit & Public Sector Marketing*, *27*(3), 239–262. doi:10.1080/10495142.2015.1053341

Yan, L., Keh, H. T., & Wang, X. (2021). Powering sustainable consumption: The roles of green consumption values and power distance belief. *Journal of Business Ethics*, *169*(3), 499–516. doi:10.100710551-019-04295-5

Yoon-Na, C., Thyroff, A., Rapert, M. I., Park, S.-Y., & Lee, H. J. (2013). To be or not to be green: Exploring individualism and collectivism as antecedents of environmental behavior. *Journal of Business Research*, *66*(8), 1052–1059. doi:10.1016/j.jbusres.2012.08.020

ADDITIONAL READING

He, Z., Zhou, Y., Wang, J., Li, C., Wang, M., & Li, W. (2021). The impact of motivation, intention, and contextual factors on green purchasing behavior: New energy vehicles as an example. *Business Strategy and the Environment*, *30*(2), 1249–1269. doi:10.1002/bse.2682

Lim, W. M., & Weissmann, M. A. (2021). Toward a theory of behavioral control. *Journal of Strategic Marketing*, 1–27.

Linder, N., Giusti, M., Samuelsson, K., & Barthel, S. (2022). Pro-environmental habits: An underexplored research agenda in sustainability science. *Ambio*, *51*(3), 546–556. doi:10.100713280-021-01619-6 PMID:34519955

Park, H. J., & Lin, L. M. (2020). Exploring attitude-behavior gap in sustainable consumption: Comparison of recycled and upcycled fashion products. *Journal of Business Research*, *117*, 623–628. doi:10.1016/j.jbusres.2018.08.025

Rausch, T. M., & Kopplin, C. S. (2021). Bridge the gap: Consumers' purchase intention and behavior regarding sustainable clothing. *Journal of Cleaner Production*, *278*, 123882. doi:10.1016/j.jclepro.2020.123882

Torma, G., Aschemann-Witzel, J., & Thøgersen, J. (2018). I nudge myself: Exploring 'self-nudging' strategies to drive sustainable consumption behavior. *International Journal of Consumer Studies*, *42*(1), 141–154. doi:10.1111/ijcs.12404

Wang, Y., Hao, F., & Liu, Y. (2021). Pro-environmental behavior in an aging world: Evidence from 31 countries. *International Journal of Environmental Research and Public Health*, *18*(4), 1748. doi:10.3390/ijerph18041748 PMID:33670167

Yang, X., & Zhang, L. (2021). Understanding residents' green purchasing behavior from a perspective of the ecological personality traits: The moderating role of gender. *The Social Science Journal*, 1–18. doi:10.1080/03623319.2020.1850121

KEY TERMS AND DEFINITIONS

Attitude-Behavior Gap: A notion which implies that consumers do not always do the things they think/say they would like to do.

Environmental Sustainability: Acting responsibly towards the environment so as to preserve its quality both for the prevailing and coming generations.

Green Consumer: An individual who is considerate of the environment in which he/she lives.

Green Consumption Behavior: Selecting, purchasing, using, and disposing of products/services in such a way so as to give the least amount of harm to the environment.

Pro-Environmental Behavior: All possible actions taken by individuals so as to protect the environment.

Sustainable Development: An approach to the process of growth and progress whereby societies meet their needs taking into consideration the coming generations, as well.

Sustainable Development Goal (SDG 12): One of the 17 sustainable development goals aimed at enhancing production and consumption practices that enable a move towards more sustainable patterns.

Sustainable Development Goals: Strategic aims set up in 2015 by the UN that are targeted at a better, healthier, and more prosperous future for us all.

Chapter 13
Green Innovation:
Balancing Economic Efficiency With Environmental Protection

Bartolomé Marco-Lajara
https://orcid.org/0000-0001-8811-9118
University of Alicante, Spain

Patrocinio Zaragoza-Saez
University of Alicante, Spain

Javier Martínez-Falcó
https://orcid.org/0000-0001-9004-5816
University of Alicante, Spain

ABSTRACT

Green innovation (GI) represents the voluntary commitment of companies to develop new environmentally friendly products and/or processes. This type of innovation represents a new business paradigm in which social, environmental, and societal issues are taken into consideration in a balanced way, satisfying the different types of demands of the organizations' stakeholders. GI is therefore a long-term commitment to balancing the economic needs of the organization and the environmental and social demands of customers. Given the relevance of the topic, this chapter aims to answer the following research questions: What are the characteristics that make up the concept of GI? Has there been any terminological evolution? and Under what theoretical approaches has the concept been addressed? Through a narrative review of the literature, the research addresses these research questions in order to bring clarity to the field of study, thus serving as a reference study for both neophyte and experienced researchers in the field.

INTRODUCTION

The global ecological crisis due to the different local and global environmental problems, such as overpopulation, pollution and the destruction of natural resources, which compromise the health of

DOI: 10.4018/978-1-6684-6750-3.ch013

ecosystems and the planet as a whole, is caused by the relationship that human beings have established with the environment throughout their history (Wang et al., 2021).

It is recognized that the clearest consequences of the ecological crisis, in the form of pollution, deforestation or depletion of resources and their harmful effects on human beings, began to be felt in the second half of the 20th century, which, together with the emergence of social movements, the energy crisis and the increasing media attention to ecological issues, are phenomena that lead to a clear concern for the environment and a widespread ecological awareness in broad sectors of society (Sun et al., 2019). Heberlein (1972) maintained that science and technology can also be considered as important contributors to the emergence and general increase of environmental concern. In particular, the discoveries of science about the harmful effects of environmental degradation have increased awareness of the negative consequences of environmental choices, and technology has generated alternatives to pollution, thereby triggering responsibility for the potential effects of the choice to pollute.

In this context, Green Innovation (GI) is a hot topic and of great relevance for society, as consumers themselves are increasingly demanding measures from companies and institutions to reconcile this balance between production and environmental sustainability (Marco-Lajara et al., 2022a; Marco-Lajara et al., 2022b; Marco-Lajara et al., 2022c; Marco-Lajara et al., 2022c, Marco-Lajara et al., 2022d). Indeed, intangible assets and organizational capabilities, such as the GI, have enabled companies to overcome the adversities resulting from COVID-19 (Marco-Lajara et al., 2021a; Marco-Lajara et al., 2021b). At the same time, there are a large number of national and international bodies dealing with issues related to GI.

The increasing demands of society force companies to integrate the maximization of their business activity with the achievement of social and environmental goals. There are two main forces promoting environmental management (Chen, 2008): (1) the international system of standards and regulations concerning environmental protection and (2) consumers' environmental awareness (Chen et al., 2006). The legitimate economic imperative of any business unit must be balanced with the moral imperative to act on climate change and promote sustainable development. Whatever the reasons for companies to become actively involved in environmental management - to comply with environmental laws and regulations, to become more competitive, to gain legitimacy, etc. - the integration of environmental sustainability issues into corporate strategy and the innovation process of companies is becoming a strategic opportunity for companies (Porter & Reinhardt, 2007).

Thus, since the introduction of the concept of GI, more and more managers are including social and environmental objectives in their decision-making process (Schiederig et al., 2012). The objective of GI is therefore to seek the well-being of society and the environment through organizational innovation. However, how has the concept evolved since its founding, what characteristics does this typology of innovations contain, under which theoretical approaches has the concept been studied, and under which theoretical approaches has the concept been studied? The research addresses these research questions in order to bring clarity to the field of study.

In order to achieve the proposed research objectives, the research is structured as follows. After this brief introduction, section two presents the methodology developed for the narrative literature review. Section three presents the results of the research in two sections: firstly, the concept of the GI and, secondly, the theoretical approaches. Section four presents the conclusions drawn from the study and, finally, section five shows the limitations and future lines of research.

METHODOLOGY

In the present research, a narrative literature review is conducted with the purpose of analyzing the conceptualization and theoretical perspectives under which GI has been studied. The literature review is considered a detailed study that aims to gather information on a given topic through the analysis of published literature (Oliver, 2012).

The objective of the narrative literature review is to synthesize the fragmented knowledge of previous research on GI. The research, therefore, presents a descriptive scope, given that there are no hypotheses to contrast, but rather to describe and make sense of the information collected. In addition, the present review follows more flexible and less restrictive procedures than systematic reviews (Ferrari, 2015). Therefore, the present review does not aim to generalize the results obtained to the population (Tranfield et al., 2003), but to offer an interpretation of the literature that allows a better understanding of the GI field of study. To conduct the literature review, the phases proposed by Wee & Banister (2016) were followed, which are: selection of the topic, selection and reading of sources, and writing of the topic. First, the selected topic is the conceptual evolution and the theories under which GI has been studied. Secondly, manuals, readings, books, chapters and articles focused on the evolution and conceptualization of the GI were included for the research, excluding colloquium reports, seminars, doctoral theses and working papers. The time period of the publications spans from the beginnings of the concept to the present. Likewise, the Scopus and Web of Science databases were used for the selection of publications, since they are prestigious databases containing articles published in high impact journals, which ensures that the information obtained is accurate and of high value, legitimizing reliable results. A total of 71 academic articles were reviewed and read in depth, this being the scientific production that allowed us to reflect on the conceptual evolution of GI, as well as the theories that have been used to analyze the concept. Thirdly, once the article and sources had been selected and the publications had been read, the bibliographic review was drafted.

RESULTS

GI Definitions and Characteristics

Human-induced ecological impact is a growing global concern for individuals, policy makers, countries and organizations. Governments have implemented corrective policies in recent years to reduce or mitigate environmental damage (Chen, 2008). Companies are not immune to this reality. On the contrary, they must successfully respond to a double dynamic of adjustment. On the one hand, they need to achieve a high level of efficiency in the market, which implies enhancing their resources and capabilities. On the other hand, the actions of organizations must be consistent with the society in which they operate (Albort-Morant et al., 2016).

In order to survive in the current dynamic environment, companies must foster their capacity for innovation. To do so, they must remain abreast of the multiple changes, fluctuations and market trends that persistently emerge. This objective implies a customer orientation and a green orientation strategy. Along these lines, the ultimate goal of developing a green product/service innovation strategy has to do with improving the company's survival and performance (Laforet, 2009).

GI is of vital importance to properly develop the environmental management of organizations (Chen, 2008; Arenhardt et al., 2016; Zhang et al., 2016), being a topic of great interest among academics in recent years (Takalo & Tooranloo, 2021). Such type of innovation brings together a number of practices with the ultimate goal of improving the environmental performance of organizations (Tseng et al., 2012; Cuerva et al., 2014; Li et al., 2017), as GI not only reduces production costs, but also improves the consistency and standards of products, as well as their productivity (Chen et al., 2006).

There are several reasons why an organization can develop GI within its organization. On the one hand, companies must act in an environmentally responsible manner to contribute to the well-being of the environment in which they operate (Bansal, 2005, Starik & Kanashiro, 2013). On the other hand, managers must increasingly consider environmental issues in their decisions, not only to promote ethical and social values in their companies, but also to ensure sustainable economic success (Molina-Azorín et al., 2009). Therefore, GI has been recognized as a key factor in the economic, social and environmental development of the organization (Bansal & Gao, 2006; Dangelico & Pujari, 2010).

GI involves energy conservation, pollution prevention, waste recycling, green product design and environmental management of companies, going beyond regulatory compliance (Aragón-Correa et al., 2013). Thus, companies that develop GIs engage in a process of continuous change and development that results in tangible green developments, i.e., green products and/or processes (Marcus & Fremeth, 2009). In the following section we attempt to address the definitions and characteristics existing in the academic literature around the GI construct.

Historically, companies have viewed investment in green behaviors as an over-investment, but today's stringent environmental standards and the prevalence of environmentalism are changing the strategies, policies and competitive patterns of companies (Porter et al., 2007), increasing interest in a type of innovation that improves the environmental management of organizations: GI. The "green" label is an incentive for continuous innovation, since it creates new market opportunities for companies to meet new consumer demands and, therefore, create value and improve their performance. Table 1 shows a selection of the most notable definitions over the last seven decades.

Table 1. Definitions of GI

Authors	Definition
Fussler & James (1996, p. 2)	"New products and processes that provide value to the customer and the company, while significantly reducing environmental impact."
Driessen & Hillebrand (2002, p. 344)	"New practices, systems and products that benefit the environment and thus contribute to environmental sustainability."
Beise & Rennings (2005)	New and improved practices, processes, techniques, systems and products aimed at preventing or minimizing environmental damage
Chen et al. (2006, p. 534)	"Hardware or software innovations related to green products or processes, including innovation in technologies related to energy saving, pollution prevention, waste recycling green product design or enterprise environmental management."
Kemp & Pearson (2007, p. 3)	"The production, assimilation or exploitation of a product, production process, service or management method that is novel to the organization (developing or adopting it) and that results, over its life cycle, in a reduction of environmental risk, pollution and other negative impacts of resource use (including energy use) compared to relevant alternatives."
Reid & Miedzinski (2008, p. 7)	"Creation of goods, processes, systems, services and procedures that can satisfy human needs and bring quality of life to all people with a minimum use of natural resources throughout the entire life cycle (material, energy carriers and surface area) per unit of production, and the minimum of toxic substances."
Andersen (2008, p. 5)	"Innovations that are able to attract green rents in the market. [...] The concept is closely related to competitiveness and the degree to which environmental issues are integrated into the economic process."
Chen (2008)	"Ability of the organization to generate products and services by saving energy and reducing air pollution."
OECD (2009, p. 19)	"Creation or implementation of products (goods and services), processes, marketing methods, organizational structures and institutional arrangements that, intentionally or unintentionally, lead to environmental improvements compared to relevant alternatives."
Arundel & Kemp (2009, p. 34)	"New concept of great importance for companies and policy makers. It is about innovations with lower environmental environmental impact than the relevant alternatives. Innovations can be technological or non-technological (organizational, institutional or marketing) and can be motivated by economic or environmental considerations."
Oltra & Saint Jean (2009, p. 567)	"Innovations consisting of new or modified processes, practices, systems and products that benefit the environment."
Jones et al. (2008)	It aims to systematically align and implement a sustainable strategy throughout the supply chain, from the development of new products and services to consumption.
Huang et al. (2009)	Techniques or new practices that improve an organization's environmental performance and competitive advantage.
Aguilera-Caracuel & Ortiz-de-Mandojana (2013)	Hardware or software innovation related to the use of environmentally friendly products or processes.
Wong et al. (2013)	It facilitates the reduction of the environmental impact of companies, enabling them to achieve ecological objectives and incorporate environmental benefits.
Woo et al. (2014)	Emphasizes manufacturing process and product design improvements that reduce pollution, save energy, minimize waste, and improve environmental conditions.
Weng, Chen & Chen (2015)	It offers companies the possibility to reduce emissions beyond regulatory requirements, thus reducing their production costs.
Albort-Morant et al. (2016)	It strives to develop environmentally friendly products and processes by adopting organizational practices, i.e. greener raw materials, eco-friendly design, reducing consumption of water, electricity and other raw materials, etc.
Li et al. (2017)	Invention of products, processes, technologies and management structures aimed at protecting the environment.

Continued on following page

Table 1. Continued

Authors	Definition
Albort-Morant et al. (2017)	"A type of innovation whose main objective is to mitigate or avoid environmental damage, protecting the environment and enabling companies to meet new consumer demands, create value and increase returns."
Tang et al. (2018)	"GI involves product and process innovation. It involves improvements in product design and manufacturing processes that save energy, reduce pollution, minimize waste and reduce the company's negative impact on the environment."
Galbreath (2019)	"An effort to reduce the impacts of business activity on the natural environment, in order to protect and preserve natural capital for current and future generations."
Xie et al. (2019)	Actions aimed at developing environmentally friendly products, so that the Sustainable Development Goals can be achieved.
Wang & Juo (2021)	Innovative environmental management capabilities that can enhance a company's ability to develop environmentally friendly products and processes.

Source: own elaboration

As can be seen, there is no single definition of the concept of GI. However, there are a number of ideas that converge in the definitions given. Six aspects that are reflected in the definitions are identified below:

1. Type of innovation: product, process, service, method.
2. Market orientation: To satisfy needs / to be competitive in the market.
3. Environmental aspect: Reducing the negative impact of the company's activity on the environment.
4. Motivation: Motivation can be economic or ecological.

The first two characteristics are of a general nature and are identified in most of the GI definitions selected, since the innovation can be a product, a process, a service or a method aimed at satisfying the needs of users, thereby improving the company's competitiveness in the market. With regard to the environmental aspect, all the definitions cited agree that GI should reduce the negative externalities generated by the organization's activity. Therefore, the optimal GI would be one with no negative impact on the environment. Fourthly, the definitions emphasize that the motives for developing GI can be both economic and environmental.

Theoretical Perspectives of GI

Theoretical perspectives on GI reflect how it has been interpreted by different scholars and practitioners over time. The three predominant theoretical approaches in the academic literature on GI are discussed below. These are: Institutional Theory, Stakeholder Theory, and Resource and Capability Theory.

Institutional Theory has been used to study the adoption and diffusion of organizational practices of various kinds among organizations (Meyer & Rowan, 1977; Scott, 2005). In particular, proponents of this theory argue that organizations that share the same environment will employ similar practices for legitimate reasons (DiMaggio & Powell, 1983) and will therefore be "isomorphic" to each other (Kostova et al., 2008). As Gooderham et al. (1999) note, "cross-national differences in institutional structures are likely to result in management practices that vary from country to country" (p. 508).

The institutional perspective on organizations suggests that "organizational practices are deeply embedded and reflect a generalized understanding of social reality, imposed by public opinion, by the views of important constituents, by knowledge legitimized through educational systems, by social prestige, and by laws" (Meyer & Rowan, 1977, p. 343). Thus, as practices become institutionalized, they come to be seen by society as legitimate and are adopted by organizations for reasons of legitimacy (Zucker, 1977).

According to the premises of this theory, it is important to consider two dimensions that determine how the institutions of different countries and their organizations deal with environmental issues: the regulatory and normative dimension. On the one hand, the regulatory dimension refers to "the laws and norms existing in a given national environment that promote certain types of behavior and restrict others" (Kostova, 1999, p. 314). The normative dimension, on the other hand, reflects the cultural values, beliefs and goals of society that determine the legitimacy of organizational behavior (Kostova & Roth, 2002).

Regulatory pressures have been identified as a primary determinant of organizations' environmental behavior (Henriques & Sadorsky, 1996; Christmann, 2004). Moreover, unlike the normative dimension, the regulatory dimension is the easiest to observe, understand and interpret correctly, as it is formalized through laws, rules, sanctions and regulations (Kostova & Roth, 2002). The main objective of environmental regulation is therefore to exert pressure on companies to make their processes and products more environmentally friendly. In this context, Porter & Van der Linde (1995) state that strict environmental regulations can force industries and firms to develop innovations, among which GI stands out (Aguilera-Caracuel & Ortiz-de-Mandojana, 2013).

The normative dimension includes the deeply rooted beliefs in a society, regardless of the legal structure of a country. Consequently, normative elements are the values and social norms that define the rules of the game, i.e., "what is right to do here" (Marquis et al., 2007, p. 934). Thus, the promotion of prominent environmental values throughout society should be considered as a precursor to GI (Aguilera-Caracuel & Ortiz-de-Mandojana, 2013). In fact, the cultural values of a society can be considered as an essential institutional requirement to develop advanced and proactive environmental management initiatives (Hoffman, 1999).

Since Freeman's (1984) pioneering work, it has become increasingly accepted that companies need to address the demands of their stakeholders, since their consideration can play a crucial role in improving organizational performance (Laplume et al., 2008). As Freeman (1984, p. 47) notes, "to be an effective strategist, you must deal with the groups that can affect you."

Stakeholder management is considered a fundamental element in the innovation process (Achterkamp & Vos, 2008; Assudani & Kloppenborg, 2010). In fact, several researchers have explored the effect of stakeholders on innovation, technology and R&D projects (Elias et al., 2002). Specifically, several studies have addressed the impact of stakeholders on GI (Fliaster & Kolloch, 2017). For example, Polonsky & Ottman (1998) argued for the need to involve a broad set of stakeholders in the process of developing new green products, as these groups may have information and knowledge that is determinant for their successful commercialization. Through a case study, Stafford et al. (2000) investigated how a partnership between a company and an environmental could foster the "green spirit" of companies. Tanimoto (2011) studied the start-up of the first community wind energy company in Japan, concluding that the GIs developed by the company were influenced by its different stakeholders.

To classify the most relevant stakeholders in the development of innovations, scholars have differentiated between primary and secondary stakeholders. According to Clarkson (1995), primary stakeholders are those that the company needs to survive. As far as innovation projects are concerned, this category consists mainly of the members of the value chain, especially suppliers, customers, employees and investors (Afuah & Bahram, 1995; Hall & Martin, 2005).

Secondary stakeholders, on the other hand, are not directly involved in economic transactions and value-creating relationships with the company. However, they can cause serious damage to the firm (Clarkson, 1995). As far as innovation is concerned, several empirical studies reveal the importance of environmental advocacy groups (Elias et al., 2002; Hall & Martin, 2005). In this regard, Henriques & Sadorsky (1999) identified four interest groups that exert pressure to address environmental claims: governments, customers, non-governmental organizations and the media. Therefore, it is essential to identify the environmental demands of these stakeholders, in order to, subsequently, meet them through GI strategies (Singh et al., 2020; Rehman et al., 2021).

RBV has been widely applied in the study of innovation (Verona, 1999; Kleinschmidt et al., 2007; Henard & McFadyen, 2012). From this approach, innovation is a capability that enables firms to differentiate their products from those of other competitors (Barney, 1991), thus achieving superior overall performance (Peteraf & Barney, 2003). Thus, the RBV allows us to explain the relationship between the ability to innovate and the attainment of competitive advantages.

In particular, the NRBV provides a framework conducive to analyzing the different GI strategies that firms can adopt to cope with environmental threats. This framework is proposed as an extension of the RBV (Barney, 1991; Wernerfelt, 1984), for while that approach stresses the importance of valuable, rare, inimitable and non-substitutable resources as preconditions for competitive advantage, the NRBV emphasizes the importance of the firm's relationship with its natural environment as the main source of competitive advantage (Hart, 1995). Thus, the NRBV provides a connection between the natural environment and a company's resources and capabilities. It proposes, fundamentally, three strategic capabilities to address threats to the natural environment: pollution prevention, product management and clean technology. These capabilities form the basis of the GIs, enabling companies to improve their environmental performance and, in turn, to obtain higher performance (Porter & Van-der-Linde, 1995; Russo & Fouts, 1997; King & Lenox, 2002).

To prevent pollution, it is necessary to develop new technologies and processes that reduce emissions and waste in all areas of production (Klassen & Whybark, 1999). Moreover, this innovative effort to obtain cleaner resources and greener capabilities allows companies to redesign processes to optimize their efficiency (Russo & Fouts, 1997). Along these lines, Christmann (2000) and Sharma & Vredenburg (1998) argue that combining efforts to reduce pollution with innovative capabilities can generate significant savings and improve competitiveness. Thus, GI can simultaneously improve productivity, reduce costs and satisfy environmentally conscious customers, strengthening business performance (Amores-Salvadó et al., 2014).

One of the intangible resources that conditions to a greater extent the success of GI is green knowledge, given that a greater knowledge of the organization about the environment increases its ability to detect and implement innovative environmental opportunities. Therefore, environmental training of workers to reduce the environmental impact of waste and improve product sustainability can lead towards GI improvement (Hart, 1995). This commitment to green ethical behavior can energize the company's culture and image, further motivating it to preserve its green reputation, since, by developing new skills to innovate in sustainable products and processes, companies acquire a green corporate image (Chen, 2008), which reinforces their legitimacy and operational performance.

CONCLUSION

The present research is of great relevance both for experienced scholars in the field of GI and for those who are new to its study, as it provides new insights through the collection and understanding of fragmented knowledge on the subject.

The results of the research show that there is no single definition of the concept of GI. However, there are a number of ideas that converge in the definitions given. In fact, four aspects are reflected in the definitions: (1) eco-innovations can be product, process, service, method, (2) this type of innovation is oriented towards satisfying needs, (3) they aim to reduce the negative impact of the company's activity on the environment and (4) the motivation for implementing eco-innovations can be economic or ecological. The first two characteristics are of a general nature and are identified in most of the selected GI definitions, since the innovation can be a product, a process, a service or a method aimed at satisfying the needs of users, thereby improving the company's competitiveness in the market. As far as the environmental aspect is concerned, all the definitions cited agree that GI must reduce the negative externalities generated by the organization's activity. Therefore, the optimum GI would be one with no negative impact on the environment. Fourth, the definitions emphasize that the motives for developing GI can be both economic and environmental.

Likewise, this research has made it possible to identify the theories under which GI has been studied: institutional theory, stakeholder theory, and human resources theory. Under the institutional theory, companies develop innovations of an ecological nature to comply with the legal system (law) and to comply with the values rooted in society (legitimacy). Under the stakeholder view, firms develop GIs to meet the environmental demands of stakeholders, under the resources and capabilities theory, the development of GIs allows to obtain competitive advantages, as well as to combat the dynamism of the environment.

The present research, therefore, is highly relevant as it presents different theoretical contributions. Firstly, through the research, it is possible to learn about the terminological evolution of the GI. Secondly, the study provides insight into the theories under which GI has been studied. Thirdly, the study serves as a guide both for those academics who are beginning to study ecological innovations and for those who are experts in the subject. Likewise, the study can be of use to quality and environmental managers in organizations, since the research offers a first approach to the different types of GIs, as well as to the motivations that can lead the organization to implement them.

LIMITATIONS AND FUTURE LINES OF RESEARCH

Despite the important contributions of the study, it is important to point out that the research suffers from certain limitations. The fundamental limitation of the study is methodological in nature, given that narrative reviews are dominated by the subjective criteria of the authors and do not quantitatively synthesize the data found in the different publications. To overcome these limitations of narrative reviews, a systematic review of the conceptual evolution of GI over time is proposed as a future line of research with the aim of increasing the reproducibility of the research and increasing the validity of the results obtained.

REFERENCES

Achterkamp, M., & Vos, J. (2008). Investigating theuse of the stakeholder notion in project management literature, a meta-analysis. *International Journal of Project Management, 26*(7), 749–757. doi:10.1016/j.ijproman.2007.10.001

Afuah, A., & Bahram, N. (1995). The hypercube of innovation. *Research Policy, 24*(1), 51–76. doi:10.1016/0048-7333(93)00749-J

Aguilera-Caracuel, J., & Ortiz-de-Mandojana, N. (2013). Green innovation and financial performance: An institutional approach. *Organization & Environment, 26*(4), 365–385. doi:10.1177/1086026613507931

Albort-Morant, G., Henseler, J., Leal-Millán, A., & Cepeda-Carrión, G. (2017). Mapping the field: A bibliometric analysis of green innovation. *Sustainability, 9*(6), 1011. doi:10.3390u9061011

Albort-Morant, G., Leal-Millán, A., & Cepeda-Carrión, G. (2016). The antecedents of green innovation performance: A model of learning and capabilities. *Journal of Business Research, 69*(11), 4912–4917. doi:10.1016/j.jbusres.2016.04.052

Amores-Salvadó, J., Martín-de Castro, G., & Navas-López, J. (2014). Green corporate image: Moderating the connection between environmental product innovation and firm performance. *Journal of Cleaner Production, 83*, 356–365. doi:10.1016/j.jclepro.2014.07.059

Andersen, M. (2008). *Eco innovation: towards a taxonomy and a theory. 25th Celebration DRUID Conference*, Copenhagen, Denmark.

Aragón-Correa, J. A., Martín-Tapia, I., & Hurtado-Torres, N. (2013). Proactive environmental strategies and employee inclusion: The positive effects of information sharing and promoting collaboration and the influence of uncertainty. *Organization & Environment, 26*(2), 139–161. doi:10.1177/1086026613489034

Arenhardt, D., Battistella, L., & Grohmann, M. (2016). The influence of the green innovation in the search of competitive advantage of enterprises of the electrical and electronic Brazilian sectors. *International Journal of Innovation Management, 20*(1), 1650004. doi:10.1142/S1363919616500043

Arundel, A., & Kemp, R. (2009). *Measuring Eco innovation. United Nations.* University – Maastricht Economic and Social Research and Training Centre on Innovation and Technology.

Assudani, R., & Kloppenborg, T. (2010). Managing stakeholders for project management success: An emergent model of stakeholders. *Journal of General Management, 35*(3), 67–80. doi:10.1177/030630701003500305

Bansal, P. (2005). Evolving sustainably: A longitudinal study of corporate sustainable development. *Strategic Management Journal, 26*(3), 197–218. doi:10.1002mj.441

Barney, J. (1991). Firm resources and sustained competitive advantage. *Journal of Management, 17*(1), 99–120. doi:10.1177/014920639101700108

Beise, M., & Rennings, K. (2005). Lead markets and regulation: A framework for analyzing the international diffusion of environmental innovations. *Ecological Economics, 52*(1), 5–17. doi:10.1016/j.ecolecon.2004.06.007

Chen, Y. (2008). The positive effect of green intellectual capital on competitive advantages of firms. *Journal of Business Ethics*, *77*(3), 271–286. doi:10.100710551-006-9349-1

Chen, Y., Lai, S., & Wen, C. (2006). The influence of green innovation performance on corporate advantage in Taiwan. *Journal of Business Ethics*, *67*(4), 331–339. doi:10.100710551-006-9025-5

Christmann, P. (2000). Effects of "best practices" of environmental management on cost advantage: The role of complementary assets. *Academy of Management Journal*, *43*(4), 663–680.

Christmann, P. (2004). Multinational companies and the natural environment: Determinants of global environmental policy standardization. *Academy of Management Journal*, *47*(5), 747–760. doi:10.2307/20159616

Clarkson, M. (1995). A stakeholder framework for analyzing and evaluating corporate social performance. *Academy of Management Review*, *20*(1), 92–117. doi:10.2307/258888

Cuerva, M. C., Triguero-Cano, Á., & Córcoles, D. (2014). Drivers of green and non-green innovation: Empirical evidence in Low-Tech SMEs. *Journal of Cleaner Production*, *68*, 104–113. doi:10.1016/j.jclepro.2013.10.049

Dangelico, R., & Pujari, D. (2010). Mainstreaming green product innovation: Why and how companies integrate environmental sustainability. *Journal of Business Ethics*, *95*(3), 471–486. doi:10.100710551-010-0434-0

DiMaggio, P., & Powell, W. (1983). The iron cage revisited: Institutional isomorphism and collective rationality in organizational fields. *American Sociological Review*, *48*(2), 147–160. doi:10.2307/2095101

Driessen, P. (2002). Hillebrand, B. Adoption and diffusion of green innovations. In *Marketing for Sustainability: Towards Transactional Policy-Making*. IOS Press.

Elias, A., Cavana, R., & Jackson, L. (2002). Stake-holder analysis for R&D project management. *R & D Management*, *32*(4), 301–310. doi:10.1111/1467-9310.00262

Fliaster, A., & Kolloch, M. (2017). Implementation of green innovations-The impact of stakeholders and their network relations. *R & D Management*, *47*(5), 689–700. doi:10.1111/radm.12257

Freeman, R. (1984). *Strategic Management - A Stakeholder Approach*. Pitman.

Freeman, R. (1994). The politics of stakeholder theory: Some future directions. *Business Ethics Quarterly*, *4*(4), 409–421. doi:10.2307/3857340

Fussler, C., & James, P. (1996). *Driving eco-innovation: a breakthrough discipline for innovation and sustainability*. Financial Times/Prentice Hall.

Galbreath, J. (2019). Drivers of green innovations: The impact of export intensity, women leaders, and absorptive capacity. *Journal of Business Ethics*, *158*(1), 47–61. doi:10.100710551-017-3715-z

Gooderham, P. N., Nordhaug, O., & Ringdal, K. (1999). Institutional and rational determinants of organizational practices: Human resource management in European firms. *Administrative Science Quarterly*, *44*(3), 507–531. doi:10.2307/2666960

Hall, J., & Martin, M. (2005). Disruptive technologies, stakeholders and the innovation value-added chain: A framework for evaluating radical technology development. *R & D Management, 35*(3), 273–284. doi:10.1111/j.1467-9310.2005.00389.x

Hart, S. (1995). A natural resource-based view of the firm. *Academy of Management Review, 20*(4), 986–1014. doi:10.5465/amr.1995.9512280033

Heberlein, T. (1972). The Land Ethic Realized: Some Social Psychological Explanations for Changing Environmental Attitudes 1. *The Journal of Social Issues, 28*(4), 79–87. doi:10.1111/j.1540-4560.1972.tb00047.x

Henard, D., & McFadyen, M. A. (2012). Resource dedication and new product performance: A resource-based view. *Journal of Product Innovation Management, 29*(2), 193–204. doi:10.1111/j.1540-5885.2011.00889.x

Henriques, I., & Sadorsky, P. (1996). The determinants of an environmentally responsive firm: An empirical approach. *Journal of Environmental Economics and Management, 30*(3), 381–396. doi:10.1006/jeem.1996.0026

Henriques, I., & Sadorsky, P. (1999). The relationship between environmental commitment and managerial perceptions of stakeholder importance. *Academy of Management Journal, 42*(1), 87–99.

Hoffman, A. (1999). Institutional evolution and change: Environmentalism and the US chemical industry. *Academy of Management Journal, 42*(4), 351–371.

Huang, Y., Ding, H., & Kao, M. (2009). Salient stakeholder voices: Family business and green innovation adoption. *Journal of Management & Organization, 15*(3), 309–326. doi:10.5172/jmo.2009.15.3.309

Jones, P., Clarke-Hill, C., Comfort, D., & Hillier, D. (2008). Marketing and sustainability. *Marketing Intelligence & Planning, 26*(2), 123–130. doi:10.1108/02634500810860584

Kemp, R., & Pearson, P. (2007). Final report MEI project about measuring eco-innovation. *UM Merit, Maastricht, 10*(2), 1–120.

King, A., & Lenox, M. (2002). Exploring the locus of profitable pollution reduction. *Management Science, 48*(2), 289–299. doi:10.1287/mnsc.48.2.289.258

Klassen, R., & Whybark, D. (1999). The impact of environmental technologies on manufacturing performance. *Academy of Management Journal, 42*(6), 599–615.

Kostova, T. (1999). Transnational transfer of strategic organizational practices: A contextual perspective. *Academy of Management Review, 24*(2), 308–324. doi:10.2307/259084

Kostova, T., & Roth, K. (2002). Adoption of an organizational practice by subsidiaries of multinational corporations: Institutional and relational effects. *Academy of Management Journal, 45*, 215–233.

Kostova, T., Roth, K., & Dacin, M. (2008). Institutional theory in the study of multinational corporations: A critique and new directions. *Academy of Management Review, 33*(4), 994–1006. doi:10.5465/amr.2008.34422026

Laforet, S. (2009). Effects of size, market and strategic orientation on innovation in non-high-tech manufacturing SMEs. *European Journal of Marketing*, *43*(1/2), 188–212. doi:10.1108/03090560910923292

Laplume, A., Sonpar, K., & Litz, R. (2008). Stakeholder theory: Reviewing a theory that moves us. *Journal of Management*, *34*(6), 1152–1189. doi:10.1177/0149206308324322

Li, D., Zhao, Y., Zhang, L., Chen, X., & Cao, C. (2018). Impact of quality management on green innovation. *Journal of Cleaner Production*, *170*, 462–470. doi:10.1016/j.jclepro.2017.09.158

Marco-Lajara, B., Seva-Larrosa, P., Martínez-Falcó, J., & Sánchez-García, E. (2021b). How Has COVID-19 Affected The Spanish Wine Industry? An Exploratory Analysis. *Natural Volatiles & Essential Oils*, *8*(6), 2722–2731.

Marco-Lajara, B., Seva-Larrosa, P., Ruiz-Fernández, L., & Martínez-Falcó, J. (2021a). The Effect of COVID-19 on the Spanish Wine Industry. In *Impact of Global Issues on International Trade* (pp. 211–232). IGI Global. doi:10.4018/978-1-7998-8314-2.ch012

Marco-Lajara, B., Zaragoza-Saez, P., Martínez-Falcó, J., & Sánchez-García, E. (2022c). COVID-19 and Wine Tourism: A Story of Heartbreak. In Handbook of Research on SDGs for Economic Development, Social Development, and Environmental Protection (pp. 90-112). IGI Global.

Marco-Lajara, B., Zaragoza-Saez, P., Martínez-Falcó, J., & Millan-Tudela, L. A. (2022b). Analysing the Relationship Between Green Intellectual Capital and the Achievement of the Sustainable Development Goals. In *Handbook of Research on Building Inclusive Global Knowledge Societies for Sustainable Development* (pp. 111–129). IGI Global. doi:10.4018/978-1-6684-5109-0.ch005

Marco-Lajara, B., Zaragoza-Sáez, P., Martínez-Falcó, J., & Sánchez-García, E. (2022a). Green Intellectual Capital in the Spanish Wine Industry. In Innovative Economic, Social, and Environmental Practices for Progressing Future Sustainability (pp. 102-120). IGI Global. doi:10.4018/978-1-7998-9590-9.ch006

Marco-Lajara, B., Zaragoza-Sáez, P., Martínez-Falcó, J., & Sánchez-García, E. (2022d). El capital intelectual verde como hoja de ruta para la sostenibilidad: el caso de bodegas Luzón [Green intellectual capital as a roadmap for sustainability: the case of Bodegas Luzón]. *GeoGraphos: Revista Digital para Estudiantes de Geografía y Ciencias Sociales*, *13*(147), 137–146.

Marcus, A., & Fremeth, A. (2009). Strategic direction and management. In *Business Management and Environmental Stewardship: Environmental Thinking as a Prelude to Management Action* (pp. 38–55). Palgrave McMillan. doi:10.1007/978-1-349-92307-6_3

Meyer, J., & Rowan, B. (1977). Institutionalized organizations: Formal structure as myth and ceremony. *American Journal of Sociology*, *83*(2), 340–363. doi:10.1086/226550

Molina-Azorín, J., Claver-Cortés, E., López-Gamero, M., & Tarí, J. (2009). Green management and financial performance: A literature review. *Management Decision*, *47*(7), 1080–1100. doi:10.1108/00251740910978313

OECD. (2009). *Eco-innovation in industry: enabling green growth*. OECD.

Polonsky, J., & Ottman, J. (1998). Stakeholders' contri-bution to the green new product development process. *Journal of Marketing Management*, *14*(6), 533–557. doi:10.1362/026725798784867707

Porter, M., & Reinhardt, F. (2007). A strategic approach to climate. *Harvard Business Review*, *85*(10), 22–39.

Porter, M., & Van der Linde, C. (1995). Toward a new conception of the environment-competitiveness relationship. *The Journal of Economic Perspectives*, *9*(4), 97–118. doi:10.1257/jep.9.4.97

Porter, M. E., Reinhardt, F. L., Schwartz, P., Esty, D. C., Hoffman, A. J., Schendler, A., & Rendlen, B. (2007). Climate businessl business climate. *Harvard Business Review*, *85*(10), 21–44.

Rehman, S., Kraus, S., Shah, S., Khanin, D., & Mahto, R. (2021). Analyzing the relationship between green innovation and environmental performance in large manufacturing firms. *Technological Forecasting and Social Change*, *163*, 120481. doi:10.1016/j.techfore.2020.120481

Reid, A., & Miedzinski, M. (2008). *Eco-innovation: final report for sectoral innovation watch*. Technopolis Group.

Schiederig, T., Tietze, F., & Herstatt, C. (2012). Green innovation in technology and innovation management–an exploratory literature review. *R & D Management*, *42*(2), 180–192. doi:10.1111/j.1467-9310.2011.00672.x

Scott, W. R. (2005). Institutional theory: Contributing to a theoretical research program. *Great Minds in Management: The Process of Theory Development*, *37*(2), 460–484.

Singh, S., Del Giudice, M., Chierici, R., & Graziano, D. (2020). Green innovation and environmental performance: The role of green transformational leadership and green human resource management. *Technological Forecasting and Social Change*, *150*, 119762. doi:10.1016/j.techfore.2019.119762

Stafford, E., Polonsky, M., & Hartman, C. (2000). Environmental NGO-business collaboration and strategicbridging: A case analysis of the Greenpeace-Foronalliance. *Business Strategy and the Environment*, *9*(2), 122–135. doi:10.1002/(SICI)1099-0836(200003/04)9:2<122::AID-BSE232>3.0.CO;2-C

Starik, M., & Kanashiro, P. (2013). Toward a theory of sustainability management: Uncovering and integrating the nearly obvious. *Organization & Environment*, *26*(1), 7–30. doi:10.1177/1086026612474958

Sun, H., Edziah, B., Sun, C., & Kporsu, A. (2019). Institutional quality, green innovation and energy efficiency. *Energy Policy*, *135*, 111002. doi:10.1016/j.enpol.2019.111002

Takalo, S., & Tooranloo, H. (2021). Green innovation: A systematic literature review. *Journal of Cleaner Production*, *279*, 122474. doi:10.1016/j.jclepro.2020.122474

Tang, K., Qiu, Y., & Zhou, D. (2020). Does command-and-control regulation promote green innovation performance? Evidence from China's industrial enterprises. *The Science of the Total Environment*, *712*, 136362. doi:10.1016/j.scitotenv.2019.136362 PMID:31935549

Tanimoto, K. (2011). The process of social innovation: multi-stakeholders perspective. In D. Chauvel (Ed.), *Leading Issues in Innovation Research* (pp. 172–186). Academic Publishing International Ltd.

Tseng, S. (2016). The effect of knowledge management capability and customer knowledge gaps on corporate performance. *Journal of Enterprise Information Management*, *29*(1), 51–71. doi:10.1108/JEIM-03-2015-0021

Verona, G. (1999). A resource-based view of product development. *Academy of Management Review, 24*(1), 132–142. doi:10.5465/amr.1999.1580445

Wang, C., & Juo, W. (2021). An environmental policy of green intellectual capital: Green innovation strategy for performance sustainability. *Business Strategy and the Environment, 30*(7), 1–14. doi:10.1002/bse.2800

Wang, G., Li, Y., Zuo, J., Hu, W., Nie, Q., & Lei, H. (2021). Who drives green innovations? Characteristics and policy implications for green building collaborative innovation networks in China. *Renewable & Sustainable Energy Reviews, 143*, 110875. doi:10.1016/j.rser.2021.110875

Weng, H., Chen, J., & Chen, P. (2015). Effects of green innovation on environmental and corporate performance: A stakeholder perspective. *Sustainability, 7*(5), 4997–5026. doi:10.3390u7054997

Wernerfelt, B. (1984). A resource-based view of the firm. *Strategic Management Journal, 5*(2), 171–180. doi:10.1002mj.4250050207

Wong, S. (2013). Environmental requirements, knowledge sharing and green innovation: Empirical evidence from the electronics industry in China. *Business Strategy and the Environment, 22*(5), 321–338. doi:10.1002/bse.1746

Woo, C., Chung, Y., Chun, D., Han, S., & Lee, D. (2014). Impact of green innovation on labor productivity and its determinants: An analysis of the Korean manufacturing industry. *Business Strategy and the Environment, 23*(8), 567–576. doi:10.1002/bse.1807

Xie, X., Huo, J., & Zou, H. (2019). Green process innovation, green product innovation, and corporate financial performance: A content analysis method. *Journal of Business Research, 101*, 697–706. doi:10.1016/j.jbusres.2019.01.010

Zhang, P., Wu, X., Needs, S., Liu, D., Fuentes, S., & Howell, K. (2016). The influence of apical and basal defoliation on the canopy structure and biochemical composition of Vitis vinifera cv. Shiraz grapes and wine. *Frontiers in Chemistry, 5*, 48. doi:10.3389/fchem.2017.00048 PMID:28736728

Zucker, L. (1977). The role of institutionalization in cultural persistence. *American Sociological Review, 42*(5), 726–743. doi:10.2307/2094862

ADDITIONAL READING

Amore, M., & Bennedsen, M. (2016). Corporate governance and green innovation. *Journal of Environmental Economics and Management, 75*, 54–72. doi:10.1016/j.jeem.2015.11.003

Arici, H., & Uysal, M. (2022). Leadership, green innovation, and green creativity: A systematic review. *Service Industries Journal, 42*(5-6), 280–320. doi:10.1080/02642069.2021.1964482

Chen, Y. (2008). The driver of green innovation and green image–green core competence. *Journal of Business Ethics, 81*(3), 531–543. doi:10.100710551-007-9522-1

Kapoor, K., Dwivedi, Y., & Williams, M. (2014). Examining consumer acceptance of green innovations using innovation characteristics: A conceptual approach. *International Journal of Technology Management & Sustainable Development, 13*(2), 135–160. doi:10.1386/tmsd.13.2.135_1

Kunapatarawong, R., & Martínez-Ros, E. (2016). Towards green growth: How does green innovation affect employment? *Research Policy, 45*(6), 1218–1232. doi:10.1016/j.respol.2016.03.013

Schiederig, T., Tietze, F., & Herstatt, C. (2012). Green innovation in technology and innovation management–an exploratory literature review. *R & D Management, 42*(2), 180–192. doi:10.1111/j.1467-9310.2011.00672.x

Song, W., & Yu, H. (2018). Green innovation strategy and green innovation: The roles of green creativity and green organizational identity. *Corporate Social Responsibility and Environmental Management, 25*(2), 135–150. doi:10.1002/csr.1445

KEY TERMS AND DEFINITIONS

Green Process Innovation: Incremental or radical improvement of a process aimed at environmental improvement.

Green Product Innovation: Incremental or radical improvement of a product aimed at environmental improvement.

Sustainability: It refers to the balance of a species with the resources of its environment.

Sustainable Development Goals: There are 17 interconnected global goals designed to be a blueprint for achieving a better and more sustainable future for all.

Compilation of References

Ablah, E., Oslon, C., Brown, J., Merriman, V., & Lee, C., Konda, Bronleewe, T., & Buzard, A. (2018). Need for Transparency and Ongoing Communication After Residents With Contaminated Water Wells Are Connected to City Water. *Journal of Environmental Health*, *81*(3), 26–31.

Achterkamp, M., & Vos, J. (2008). Investigating theuse of the stakeholder notion in project management literature, a meta-analysis. *International Journal of Project Management*, *26*(7), 749–757. doi:10.1016/j.ijproman.2007.10.001

Acosta, A. (2015). El Buen Vivir como alternativa al desarrollo. Algunas reflexiones económicas y no tan económicas [Good Living as an alternative to development. Some economic and not so economic reflections]. *Politica y Sociedad*, *52*(2), 301–305. doi:10.5209/rev_POSO.2015.v52.n2.45203

Afuah, A., & Bahram, N. (1995). The hypercube of innovation. *Research Policy*, *24*(1), 51–76. doi:10.1016/0048-7333(93)00749-J

Água, P. B., & Morgado, A. V. (2020a). Business Policy: A Systems Approach to Corporate Governing. In Dynamic Strategic Thinking for Improved Competitiveness and Performance (pp. 216-242). IGI Global. doi:10.4018/978-1-7998-4552-2.ch009

Água, P. B., & Morgado, A. V. (2020b). An essay on the business policy approach as applied to the governance of megaprojects. *The Journal of Modern Project Management*, *8*(2).

Água, P. B., & Correia, A. (2020). Innovation governance in practice: A business policy approach. *Corporate Board: Role. Duties and Composition*, *16*(2), 54–64.

Agudelo, M., Jóhannsdóttir, L., & Davídsdóttir, B. (2019). A literature review of the history and evolution of corporate social responsibility. *International Journal of Corporate Social Responsibility*, *4*(1), 1–23. doi:10.118640991-018-0039-y

Aguilera-Caracuel, J., & Ortiz-de-Mandojana, N. (2013). Green innovation and financial performance: An institutional approach. *Organization & Environment*, *26*(4), 365–385. doi:10.1177/1086026613507931

Aguinis, H., & Glavas, A. (2012). What we know and don't know about corporate social responsibility: A review and research agenda. *Journal of Management*, *38*(4), 932–968. doi:10.1177/0149206311436079

Ahaibwe, G., Mbowa, S., & Lwanga, M. M. (2013). Youth Engagement in Agriculture in Uganda : Challenges and Prospects. *Research Series*, *7*(106), 4–20.

Alberdi, O. (2011). La Separación de poderes en el Constitucionalismo Burgués [The separation of powers in bourgeois constitutionalism]. *Nómadas*, *32*(4), 32–45. doi:10.5209/rev_NOMA.2011.v32.n4.38083

Albort-Morant, G., Henseler, J., Leal-Millán, A., & Cepeda-Carrión, G. (2017). Mapping the field: A bibliometric analysis of green innovation. *Sustainability*, *9*(6), 1011. doi:10.3390u9061011

Albort-Morant, G., Leal-Millán, A., & Cepeda-Carrión, G. (2016). The antecedents of green innovation performance: A model of learning and capabilities. *Journal of Business Research*, *69*(11), 4912–4917. doi:10.1016/j.jbusres.2016.04.052

Alier, J. M. (2021). *El ecologismo de los pobres: conflictos ambientales y lenguajes de valoración* [The environmentalism of the poor: environmental conflicts and languages of valuation]. Icaria.

Altmann, P. (2016). Buen Vivir como propuesta política integral: Dimensiones del Sumak Kawsay [Good Living as a comprehensive political proposal: Dimensions of Sumak Kawsay]. *Mundosplurales*, *3*(1), 57–60. doi:10.17141/mundosplurales.1.2016.2318

Álvarez, S. (2017). Territorio comunal en la costa de Ecuador: Buscando caminos de entendimiento entre el Buen Vivir y el principio de bien común [Communal territory on the coast of Ecuador: looking for paths of understanding between Good Living and the principle of the common good]. *Revista de Antropología Social*, *26*(2), 355–378. doi:10.5209/RASO.57610

AMBRIZZI. (2017). *Tercio Ambrizzi, Cintia Barcellos Lacerda e Lívia Márcia Mosso Dutra. Construção de núcleo de pesquisa interdisciplinar em mudanças climáticas: o caso INCLINE da USP. Ensino e Pesquisa da Inovação Desenvolvendo a Interdisciplinaridade*. Manole.

Amores-Salvadó, J., Martín-de Castro, G., & Navas-López, J. (2014). Green corporate image: Moderating the connection between environmental product innovation and firm performance. *Journal of Cleaner Production*, *83*, 356–365. doi:10.1016/j.jclepro.2014.07.059

Andersen, M. (2008). *Eco innovation: towards a taxonomy and a theory. 25th Celebration DRUID Conference*, Copenhagen, Denmark.

Andrade, P. (2013). Sociological ontology of the Digital Public Sphere: The case of the Web 2.0/3.0. *Communicatio Socialis*, *23*, 186–201.

Aragón-Correa, J. A., Martín-Tapia, I., & Hurtado-Torres, N. (2013). Proactive environmental strategies and employee inclusion: The positive effects of information sharing and promoting collaboration and the influence of uncertainty. *Organization & Environment*, *26*(2), 139–161. doi:10.1177/1086026613489034

Arenhardt, D., Battistella, L., & Grohmann, M. (2016). The influence of the green innovation in the search of competitive advantage of enterprises of the electrical and electronic Brazilian sectors. *International Journal of Innovation Management*, *20*(1), 1650004. doi:10.1142/S1363919616500043

Arregui, A. (2020). Conectando con la Amazonia transparente. El cuerpo afroindígena y la comunicación más allá de las élites [Connecting with the transparent Amazon. The Afro-indigenous body and communication beyond the elites]. *Journal of American Anthropology*, *50*, 291-306. doi:10.5209/reaa.70442

Arundel, A., & Kemp, R. (2009). *Measuring Eco innovation. United Nations.* University – Maastricht Economic and Social Research and Training Centre on Innovation and Technology.

Asaoka, D. (2018). Collective intelligence or groupthink? Group decision making under the Japanese Companies Act. *Corporate Board: Role, Duties and Composition*, *14*(2), 27–37.

Assudani, R., & Kloppenborg, T. (2010). Managing stakeholders for project management success: An emergent model of stakeholders. *Journal of General Management*, *35*(3), 67–80. doi:10.1177/030630701003500305

Ayala del Pino, C. (2021). La responsabilidad social corporativa: Concepto, ámbito de aplicación, grupos de interés y objetivos. *Anuario Jurídico y Económico Escurialense*, *54*(54), 173–198. doi:10.54571/ajee.462

Ban, K. (2015). *Launch of new sustainable development agenda to guide development actions for the next 15 years.* Disponible en: https://sustainabledevelopment. un.org/?page=view&nr=1021&type=230&menu=2059

Bansal, P. (2005). Evolving sustainably: A longitudinal study of corporate sustainable development. *Strategic Management Journal, 26*(3), 197–218. doi:10.1002mj.441

Bărbuță-Mișu, N., Madaleno, M., & Ilie, V. (2019). Analysis of Risk Factors Affecting Firms' Financial Performance—Support for Managerial Decision-Making. *Sustainability, 11*(18), 4838. https://doi.org/10.3390/su11184838

Barney, J. (1991). Firm resources and sustained competitive advantage. *Journal of Management, 17*(1), 99–120. doi:10.1177/014920639101700108

Batista, M., Caiado, R. G. G., Yparraguirre, I. T. R., Filho, W. L., Lima, G. B. A., & Quelhas, O. L. G. (2021). A framework for sustainable and integrated municipal solid waste management: Barriers and critical factors to developing countries. *Journal of Cleaner Production, 312*, 127516. Advance online publication. doi:10.1016/j.jclepro.2021.127516

Battisti, L., Marcuello, C., & Messias, J. (2020). Las perspectivas Latinoamericana y Europea de la Economía Solidaria [The Latin American and European perspectives of the Solidarity Economy]. *Revista de estudios cooperativos, 134*, 1-10. doi:10.5209/reve.69171

Bauer, J. A., Devick, K. L., Bobb, J. F., Coull, B. A., Bellinger, D., Benedetti, C., Cagna, G., Fedrighi, C., Guazzetti, S., Oppini, M., Placidi, D., Webster, T. F., White, R. F., Yang, Q., Zoni, S., Wright, R. O., Smith, D. R., Lucchini, R. G., & Claus Henn, B. (2020). Associations of a Metal Mixture Measured in Multiple Biomarkers with IQ: Evidence from Italian Adolescents Living near Ferroalloy Industry. *Environmental Health Perspectives, 128*(9), 097002. https://doi.org/10.1289/EHP6803

Bay, A.-H., & Blekesaune, M. (2002). Youth, unemployment and political marginalisation. *International Journal of Social Welfare, 11*(2), 132–139. doi:10.1111/1468-2397.00207

BBC. (2012). *Former RBS boss Fred Goodwin stripped of knighthood.* https://www.bbc.com/news/uk-politics-16821650

Beise, M., & Rennings, K. (2005). Lead markets and regulation: A framework for analyzing the international diffusion of environmental innovations. *Ecological Economics, 52*(1), 5–17. doi:10.1016/j.ecolecon.2004.06.007

Belch, G. E., & Belch, M. A. (2021). *Advertising and Promotion: An Integrated Marketing Communications Perspective* (12th ed.). McGraw-Hill.

Bell, D. N. F., Blanchflower, D. G., Bell, D. N. F., & Blanchflower, D. G. (2010). *Youth Unemployment : Déjà Vu ?* Academic Press.

Benites-Lazaro, L., & Mello-Théry, N. (2017). CSR as a legitimatizing tool in carbon market: Evidence from Latin America's clean development mechanism. *Journal of Cleaner Production, 149*, 218–226. doi:10.1016/j.jclepro.2017.02.095

Bennett, G., & Williams, F. (2011). Mainstream green: Moving sustainability from niche to normal. The Red Papers: Issue 4. Ogilvy & Mather.

Bercovici, Costa. (2021). Nacionalização: Necessidade e Possibilidade. Academic Press.

Berkeley Library, University of California. (2022). *Non-governmental organizations.* Retrieved June 15, 2022, from https://guides.lib.berkeley.edu/c.php?g=496970&p=3427176

Biavaschi, C., Eichhorst, W., Giulietti, C., Kendzia, M. J., Muravyev, A., Pieters, J., Schmidl, R., & Zimmermann, K. F. (2013). *World Development Report on Youth Unemployment and Vocational Training.* Academic Press.

Biavaschi, C., Facchini, G., Mayda, A. M., & Mendola, M. (2018). South-South migration and the labor market: Evidence from South Africa. *Journal of Economic Geography, 18*(4), 823–853. doi:10.1093/jeg/lby010

Bilan, Y., Nitsenko, V., Ushkarenko, I., Chmut, A., & Sharapa, O. (2017). Outsourcing in international economic relations. *Montenegrin Journal of Economics, 13*(3), 175–185. doi:10.14254/1800-5845/2017.13-3.14

Borau, S., Elgaaied-Gambier, L., & Barbarossa, C. (2021). The green mate appeal: Men's pro-environmental consumption is an honest signal of commitment to their partner. *Psychology and Marketing, 38*(2), 266–285. doi:10.1002/mar.21321

Boswell, C., & Smith, K. (2017). Rethinking policy 'impact': Four models of research-policy relations. *Palgrave Communications, 3*(1), 44. Advance online publication. doi:10.105741599-017-0042-z

Bowen, H. (1953). *Social responsibilities of the businessman.* University of Iowa Press.

Bromiley, P., & Rau, D. (2016). Strategic risk management. A better way of managing major risks. *IESEInsight, 28.*

Brough, A. R., Wilkie, J. E. B., Ma, J., Isaac, M. S., & Gal, D. (2016). Is eco-friendly unmanly? The green-feminine stereotype and its effect on sustainable consumption. *The Journal of Consumer Research, 43*(4), 567–582. doi:10.1093/jcr/ucw044

Burrch, S. (2019). New directions in earth system governance research. *Earth Syst. Govern., 1,* 100006. Advance online publication. doi:10.1016/j.esg.2019.100006

Business for Goals Platform. (2020). https://www.business4goals.org/en/the-survey-results-on-the-impacts-of-the-covid-19-crisis-on-enterprises-are-published/

Business for Social Responsibility. (2000). *Introduction to Corporate Social Responsibility.* Disponible en: http://www.khbo.be/~lodew/Cursussen/4eingenieurCL/The%20Global%20Business%20Responsibility%20Resource%20Center.doc

Calderon-Monge, E., Sanz-Pastor, I., & Garcia, F. J. S. (2020). Analysis of sustainable consumer behavior as a business opportunity. *Journal of Business Research, 120,* 74–81. doi:10.1016/j.jbusres.2020.07.039

Calleja, R., & Melé, D. (2017). Valero's "Enterprise Politics": A model of humanistic management and corporate governance. *Journal of Management Development, 36*(5), 644–659. doi:10.1108/JMD-12-2015-0187

Canals, J. (2014). Renewing the board's mission. 6 Items for the top of every board's agenda. *IESEInsight, 21.*

Cao, Y., Chen, X., & Ma, Y. (2010). Urbanization, Urban-Rural Income Gap and Economic Growth—An Empirical Research Based on Provincial Panel Data in China. *Statistical Research*, 29–36. doi:10.19343/j.cnki.11-1302/c.2010.03.005

Capdevielle, M. (1993). *Economía de mercado y solidaridad* [Market economy and solidarity]. Política y Cultura.

Capes, C. de A. de P. de N. S. (2022, January 11). *Portal. periodicals.* CAPES - *Who we are.* https://www-periodicos-capes-gov-br.ezl.periodicos.capes.gov.br/index.php/sobre/quem-somos.html]

Card, D. (1990). The Impact of the Mariel Boatlift on the Miami Labor Market. *Industrial & Labor Relations Review, 43*(2), 245–257. doi:10.1177/001979399004300205

Card, D. (2001). Immigrant Inflows, Native Outflows, and the Local Labor Market Impacts of Higher Immigration. *Journal of Labor Economics, 19*(1), 22–64. doi:10.1086/209979

Carey, N., & Steitz. (2021, July 14). *UE proposes a ban on sales of combustion cars from 2035.* Agência Brazil. https://agenciabrasil.ebc.com.br/internacional/noticia/2021-07/ue-propoe-proibicao-de-vendas-de-carros-combustao-partir-de-2035]

Carroll, A. (1991). The Pyramid of CSR: Toward the Moral Management of Organizational Stakeholders. *Business Horizons*, *34*(4), 39–48. doi:10.1016/0007-6813(91)90005-G

Carroll, A. (1998). The four faces of corporate citizenship. *Business and Society Review*, *100*(1), 1–7. doi:10.1111/0045-3609.00008

Carroll, A. (1999). Corporate social responsibility. *Business & Society*, *38*(3), 268–295. doi:10.1177/000765039903800303

Carroll, A. (2008). A history of corporate social responsibility: concepts and practices. In A. M. Andrew Crane, D. Matten, J. Moon, & D. Siegel (Eds.), *The Oxford handbook of corporate social responsibility* (pp. 19–46). Oxford University Press.

Carroll, A. (2015). Corporate social responsibility: The centerpiece of competing and complementary frameworks. *Organizational Dynamics*, *44*(2), 87–96. doi:10.1016/j.orgdyn.2015.02.002

Carroll, A. B. (1979). A three-dimensional conceptual model of corporate performance. *Academy of Management Review*, *4*(4), 497–505. doi:10.2307/257850

Carroll, A., & Shabana, K. (2010). The business case for corporate social responsibility: A review of concepts, research and practice. *International Journal of Management Reviews*, *12*(1), 85–105. doi:10.1111/j.1468-2370.2009.00275.x

Casson, M. (1979). *Youth Unemployment*. The Macmillan Press Ltd. doi:10.1007/978-1-349-16120-1

Castillo, A. (2009). *Relaciones Públicas. Teoría e historia*. Editorial UOC.

Ceballos-Lascurain, H. (1987). The future of 'ecotourism. *Mexico Journal,* 13-14.

Cerf, C., & Navasky, V. (1984). *The Experts Speak*. Pantheon Books.

Cerrone, R. (2019). Risk management as increased corporate governance requirement in Italian banks and insurance companies. *Corporate Board: Role, Duties and Composition*, *15*(3), 58–69.

Cesaratto, S. (2020). *Heterodox Challenges in Economics: Theoretical Issues and the Crisis of the Eurozone*. Springer Nature. doi:10.1007/978-3-030-54448-5

Chaffey, D., & Ellis-Chadwick, F. (2019). *Digital Marketing* (7th ed.). Pearson Education.

Chalhoub, M. S. (2018). Public policy and technology choices for municipal solid waste management a recent case in Lebanon. *Cogent Environmental Science*, *4*(1), 1–18. doi:10.1080/23311843.2018.1529853

Charan, R. (2005). Boards that Deliver: Advancing Corporate Governance from Compliance to Competitive Advantage. Jossey-Bass Ed.

Chen, Q. (2013). Analysis on the Misunderstanding of Ecotourism from the Perspective of China's Practice. *Tourism Overview*, 36–37+40.

Chen, C. (2006). CiteSpace II: Detecting and visualizing emerging trends and transient patterns in scientific literature. *Journal of the American Society for Information Science and Technology*, *57*(3), 359–377. doi:10.1002/asi.20317

Chen, C. (2017). Science mapping: A systematic review of the literature. *Journal of Data and Information Science*, *2*(2), 1–40. doi:10.1515/jdis-2017-0006

Chen, Y. (2008). The positive effect of green intellectual capital on competitive advantages of firms. *Journal of Business Ethics*, *77*(3), 271–286. doi:10.100710551-006-9349-1

Chen, Y., Lai, S., & Wen, C. (2006). The influence of green innovation performance on corporate advantage in Taiwan. *Journal of Business Ethics*, *67*(4), 331–339. doi:10.100710551-006-9025-5

China Daily. (2018, March 13). *China plans to establish the Ministry of Natural Resources and the Ministry of Ecology and Environment.* Retrieved from https://baijiahao.baidu.com/s?id=1594805287518566570&wfr=spider&for=pc

Christensen, C. R., Andrews, K. R., & Bower, J. L. (1978). Business Policy: Text and Cases (4th ed.). R. D. Irwin Ed.

Christmann, P. (2000). Effects of "best practices" of environmental management on cost advantage: The role of complementary assets. *Academy of Management Journal, 43*(4), 663–680.

Christmann, P. (2004). Multinational companies and the natural environment: Determinants of global environmental policy standardization. *Academy of Management Journal, 47*(5), 747–760. doi:10.2307/20159616

Chuang, S., & Huang, S. (2016). The effect of environmental corporate social responsibility on environmental performance and business competitiveness: The mediation of green information technology capital. *Journal of Business Ethics, 150*(4), 991–1009. doi:10.100710551-016-3167-x

Clark, K., & Summers, L. (1982). The Dynamics of Youth Unemployment. In *The Youth Labour Market Problem* (Vol. I). Its Nature, Causes and Consequences., doi:10.3386/w0274

Clarkson, M. (1995). A stakeholder framework for analyzing and evaluating corporate social performance. *Academy of Management Review, 20*(1), 92–117. doi:10.2307/258888

Clow, K. E., & Baack, D. (2018). *Integrated Advertising, Promotion and Marketing Communications* (8th ed.). Pearson Education.

Cohen, M. J. (2020). Does the COVID-19 outbreak mark the onset of a sustainable consumption transition? *Sustainability: Science. Practice and Policy, 16*(1), 1–3.

Comisión Europea. (2001). *Libro Verde de la Comisión Europea para Fomentar un Marco Europeo para la Responsabilidad Social de las Empresas.*

Comisión Europea. (2011). Estrategia renovada de la UE para 2011-2014 sobre la responsabilidad social de las empresas. Brussels.

Coral, C. (2018). Emprendimiento indígena, ¿Una dimensión económica del Sumak? [Indigenous entrepreneurship, an economic dimension of Sumak? *Revesco: Revista de Estudios Cooperativos, 129*, 123–141. doi:10.5209/REVE.62849

Council of Europe (CE). (2022). *Goal 3 Ensure healthy lives and promote well-being for all at all ages.* https://www.coe.int/en/web/un-agenda-2030/goal-3

Covert, H. H., Sherman, M., Le, D., & Lichtveld, M. Y. (2020). Environmental health risk relationships, responsibility, and sources of information among Vietnamese Americans in coastal Mississippi. *Health Risk & Society, 22*(5–6), 362–376. https://doi.org/10.1080/13698575.2020.1840528

Creed, I. F., Duinker, P. N., Serran, J. N., & Steenberg, J. W. N. (2019). Managing risks to Canada's boreal zone: Transdisciplinary thinking in pursuit of sustainability [1]. *Environmental Reviews, 27*(3), 407–418. https://doi.org/10.1139/er-2018-0070

Crespo, G. G. (2019). La democracia del libre mercado. La intervención patronal en el sistema político de la transición [Free market democracy. Employer intervention in the political system of the transition]. *Centro de Estudios sobre Dictaduras y Democracias (CEDID)*, 299-300.

Cuerva, M. C., Triguero-Cano, Á., & Córcoles, D. (2014). Drivers of green and non-green innovation: Empirical evidence in Low-Tech SMEs. *Journal of Cleaner Production, 68*, 104–113. doi:10.1016/j.jclepro.2013.10.049

Cuervo, A. (2009). Corporate social responsibility, corporate governance and stakeholders (Corporate social responsibility, corporate governance and stakeholders.). In *Responsabilidad social: una reflexión global sobre la RSE* (pp. 51–61). Pretince Hall.

Cuesta, M., & Valor, C. (2003). Responsabilidad social de la empresa: concepto, medición y desarrollo en España (Corporate social responsibility: concept, measurement and development in Spain). *Boletín Económico De ICE. Información Comercial Española, 2755*, 7–20.

DALL'AGNOL. (2017). *Roberto, José Oswaldo Siqueira, Maria Cristina Maneschy, Pedro Walfir Martins e Souza Filho e Everaldo Barreiros de Souza. Interdisciplinaridade em instituto vinculado a empresa: experiências, desafios e perspectivas do Instituto Tecnológico Vale Desenvolvimento Sustentável. Ensino e Pesquisa da Inovação Desenvolvendo a Interdisciplinaridade.* Manole.

Dalmau, P. (2018). La reputación del notable. Escándalos y capital simbólico en la España Liberal [The reputation of the notable. Scandals and symbolic capital in Liberal Spain]. *Historia y Política, 39*(39), 79–107. doi:10.18042/hp.39.04

Dangelico, R., & Pujari, D. (2010). Mainstreaming green product innovation: Why and how companies integrate environmental sustainability. *Journal of Business Ethics, 95*(3), 471–486. doi:10.100710551-010-0434-0

Dávalos, P. (2008). Reflexiones sobre el sumak kawsay (buen vivir) y las teorías del desarrollo [Reflections on sumak kawsay (good living) and development theories]. *ALAI (Agencia Latino Americana Informaciones), Quito, Agosto 5.* Disponible en: http://alainet.org/ac-tive/25617

Davis, K. (1960). Can business afford to ignore social responsibilities? *California Management Review, 2*(3), 70–76. doi:10.2307/41166246

Davis, K. (1973). The case for and against business assumption of social responsibilities. *Academy of Management Journal, 16*(2), 312–322.

Davis, K., & Blomstrom, R. (1966). *Business and its environment.* McGraw-Hill.

De Göer, E. F. (2018). *Are immigrants responsible for France ' s low-skilled youth unemployment.* The Public Sphere.

de Magalhães, S. (2021). *Our Everyday Role: Recycle, Reuse and Learn—A Pedagogical and Environmental Proposal in a Carioca Public Extension School* [Dissertation]. West Zone State University Center Foundation – UEZO, Sectorial Center for Computing and Applied Mathematics.

Del Carpio, X. V., & Wagner, M. (2015). *The Impact of Syrian Refugees on the Turkish Labor Market.* Policy Research Working Paper 7402.

Del Carpio, X., Özden, Ç., Testaverde, M., & Wagner, M. (2015). Local labor supply responses to immigration. *The Scandinavian Journal of Economics, 117*(2), 493–521. doi:10.1111joe.12099

Dethlefs, J. C., & Chastain, B. (2012). Assessing Well-Integrity Risk: A Qualitative Model. *SPE Drill & Compl, 27*(2), 294–302. doi:10.2118/142854-PA

Di Giulio, Vasconcellos, & Ribeiro. (2017). Megacidades e mudanças climáticas: compreendendo problemas e desafios do município de São Paulo sob enfoque interdisciplinar. In *Ensino e Pesquisa da Inovação Desenvolvendo a Interdisciplinaridade.* Elsevier. https://hdl.handle.net/1884/66700

Di Noi, C., & Ciroth, A. (2018). Environmental and Social Pressures in Mining. Results from a Sustainability Hotspots Screening. *Resources, 7*(4), 80. https://doi.org/10.3390/resources7040080

Dietrich, H. (2012). Youth Unemployment in Europe: Theorical Considerations and Empirical Findings. *Friederich Ebert Stiftung,* 42. http://library.fes.de/pdf-files/id/ipa/09227.pdf

DiMaggio, P., & Powell, W. (1983). The iron cage revisited: Institutional isomorphism and collective rationality in organizational fields. *American Sociological Review*, *48*(2), 147–160. doi:10.2307/2095101

Ding, J., Chen, Y., Wang, X., & Cao, M. (2020). Land degradation sensitivity assessment and convergence analysis in Korla of Xinjiang, China. *Journal of Arid Land*, *12*(4), 594–608. https://doi.org/10.1007/s40333-020-0057-y

Do Paço, A. M. F., & Raposo, M. L. B. (2009). Green segmentation: An application to the Portuguese consumer market. *Marketing Intelligence & Planning*, *27*(3), 364–379. doi:10.1108/02634500910955245

Donkor, A. (2021). *Africa's Youth Unemployment Crisis Is a Global Problem. Foreign Policy*. https://foreignpolicy.com/2021/10/19/africa-youth-unemployment-crisis-global-problem/

Dorner, D. (1996). The Logic Of Failure: Recognizing And Avoiding Error. In *Complex Situations*. Metropolitan Books.

Drew, S. A., Kelley, P. C., & Kendrick, T. (2006). CLASS: Five elements of corporate governance to manage strategic risk. *Business Horizons*, *49*(2), 127–138. doi:10.1016/j.bushor.2005.07.001

Driessen, P. (2002). Hillebrand, B. Adoption and diffusion of green innovations. In *Marketing for Sustainability: Towards Transactional Policy-Making*. IOS Press.

Drucker, P. F. (1958). Business objectives and survival needs: Notes on a discipline of business-enterprise. *The Journal of Business*, *31*(2), 81–90. doi:10.1086/294178

Durif, F., Roy, J., & Boivin, C. (2012). Could perceived risks explain the 'green gap'in green product consumption? *Electronic Green Journal*, *1*(33). Advance online publication. doi:10.5070/G313310923

Dustmann, C., & Preston, I. A. N. P. (2013). The Effect of Immigration along the Distribution of Wages. *The Review of Economic Studies*, *80*(1), 145–173. doi:10.1093/restud/rds019

Economic Commission for Latin America and the Caribbean (ECLAC). (2020). *The 2030 Agenda for Sustainable Development in the New Global and Regional Context: Scenarios and Projections in the Current Crisis (LC/PUB.2020/5)*. https://repositorio.cepal.org/bitstream/handle/11362/45338/4/S2000207_en.pdf

Edmonds, E. V. (2008). Child Labor. Handbook of Development Economics, 4(9), 3607-3709. doi:10.1016/S1573-4471(07)04057-0

Edmonds, J., Nichols, C., Adamantiades, M., Bistline, J., Huster, J., Iyer, G., Johnson, N., Patel, P., Showalter, S., Victor, N., Waldhoff, S., Wise, M., & Wood, F. (2020). Could congressionally mandated incentives lead to deployment of large-scale CO2 capture, facilities for enhanced oil recovery CO2 markets and geologic CO2 storage? *Energy Policy*, *146*, 111775. doi:10.1016/j.enpol.2020.111775 PMID:35444362

Eells, R., & Walton, C. (1974). Conceptual Foundations of Business. Richard D. Irwin.

Eells, R. (1956). *Corporation giving in a free society*. Harper.

Eilbert, H., & Parket, I. R. (1973). The current status of corporate social responsibility. *Business Horizons*, *16*, 5–14.

Ekwurzel, B., Mann, M. E., Clement, J., Santer, B. D., Edwards, L., Zelikova, T. J., Frumhoff, P., Kapuscinski, A. R., Ehrlich, P. R., Kailath, T., Michaels, D. H., Lubensky, T., Dumas, M., Grey, D., Jacobs, N., Rector, T., Warwick, A., Crider, D. G., Kennedy, T., . . . Reardon, D. (2021). *Letter from Union of Concerned Scientists to Joseph R. Biden Jr.* https://ucsusa.org/sites/default/files/2021-04/scientist-biden-letter.pdf

ElHaffar, G., Durif, F., & Dube, L. (2020). Towards closing the attitude-intention-behavior gap in green consumption: A narrative review of the literature and an overview of future research directions. *Journal of Cleaner Production*, *275*(122556), 1–20. doi:10.1016/j.jclepro.2020.122556

Elias, A., Cavana, R., & Jackson, L. (2002). Stake-holder analysis for R&D project management. *R & D Management*, *32*(4), 301–310. doi:10.1111/1467-9310.00262

Elkington, J. (1998). Partnerships from cannibals with forks: The triple bottom line of 21st-century business. *Environmental Quality Management*, *8*(1), 37–51. doi:10.1002/tqem.3310080106

EpJafeta. (2019). *Orellana*. Retrieved from El Popular: https://www.elpopular.com.ec/orellana/

Ertz, M., & Sarıgöllü, E. (2019). The behavior-attitude relationship and satisfaction in pro-environmental behavior. *Environment and Behavior*, *51*(9-10), 1106–1132. doi:10.1177/0013916518783241

Essiz, O., & Mandrik, C. (2022). Intergenerational influence on sustainable consumer attitudes and behaviors: Roles of family communication and peer influence in environmental consumer socialization. *Psychology and Marketing*, *39*(1), 5–26.

Esty, B. C., Bitsch, F. (2013). *The Kashagan Production Sharing Agreement (PSA)*. Harvard Business School Case Study 9-213-082.

European Commission (EC). (2014). *Commission Regulation (EU) No 316/2014 of 21 March 2014 on the application of Article 101(3) of the Treaty on the Functioning of the European Union to categories of technology transfer agreements Text with EEA relevance*. https://ec.europa.eu/competition/antitrust/legislation/transfer.html

European Commission (EC). (2019). *Communication From The Commission To The European Parliament, The Council, The European Central Bank, The European Economic And Social Committee, The Committee Of The Regions And The European Investment Bank. Annual Sustainable Growth Strategy 2020*. https://eur-lex.europa.eu/legal-content/EN/TXT/?qid=1578392227719&uri=CELEX%3A52019DC0650

European Commission (EC). (2022a). *Commission (Eurostat) publishes 2022 report on Sustainable Development Goals in the European Union. Press release*. https://ec.europa.eu/commission/presscorner/detail/en/IP_22_3212

European Commission (EC). (2022a). *Sustainable Development Goals*. https://ec.europa.eu/info/strategy/international-strategies/sustainable-development-goals_en

European Commission (EC). (2022b). *EU holistic approach to sustainable development*. https://ec.europa.eu/info/strategy/international-strategies/sustainable-development-goals/eu-holistic-approach-sustainable-development_en

European Commission (EC). (2022b). *Research and Innovation*. https://ec.europa.eu/info/research-and-innovation_en

European Commission (EC). (2022c). *Remarks by Commissioner Gentiloni. Remarks by Commissioner Gentiloni at the Eurogroup press conference*. Speech. https://ec.europa.eu/commission/presscorner/detail/en/SPEECH_22_3804

European Commission. (n.d.). *International carbon market*. https://ec.europa.eu/clima/eu-action/eu-emissions-trading-system-eu-ets/international-carbon-market_en

European Union (EU) & European Institute for Innovation and Technology (EIT). (2022). *Knowledge and Innovation Communities*. https://eit.europa.eu/our-communities/eit-innovation-communities

European University Association (EUA). (2022). *EU Research & Innovation Programmes*. https://eua.eu/issues/16:eu-research-innovation-programmes.html

Eurostat. (2022). *Sustainable development in the European Union Monitoring report on progress towards the SDGs in an EU context 2022 edition* (6th ed.). https://ec.europa.eu/eurostat/web/products-statistical-books/-/KS-09-22-019 doi:10.2785/313289

Facchini, G., Mendola, M., Facchini, G., & Mayda, A. M. (2013). *South-South Migration and the Labor Market : Evidence from South Africa.* IZA Discussion Paper Series No:7362.

Fang, Y., Yin, J., & Wu, B. (2017). Climate change and tourism: A scientometric analysis using CiteSpace. *Journal of Sustainable Tourism, 26*(1), 108–126. doi:10.1080/09669582.2017.1329310

Fantke, P., Aylward, L., Bare, J., Chiu, W. A., Dodson, R., Dwyer, R., Ernstoff, A., Howard, B., Jantunen, M., Jolliet, O., Judson, R., Kirchhübel, N., Li, D., Miller, A., Paoli, G., Price, P., Rhomberg, L., Shen, B., Shin, H.-M., … McKone, T. E. (2018). Advancements in Life Cycle Human Exposure and Toxicity Characterization. *Environmental Health Perspectives, 126*(12), 125001. doi:10.1289/EHP3871

Feldstein, M. (2013). *The Reagan-Thatcher revolution.* Disponible en: https://www.dw.com/en/the-reagan-thatcher-revolution/a-16732731

Felix, R., & Braunsberger, K. (2016). I believe therefore I care. The relationship between religiosity, environmental attitudes, and green product purchase in Mexico. *International Marketing Review, 33*(1), 137–155. doi:10.1108/IMR-07-2014-0216

Ferrari, R. (2015). Writing narrative style literature reviews. *Medical Writing, 24*(4), 230–235. doi:10.1179/2047480615Z.000000000329

Filkelstein, S., Whitehead, J., & Campbell, A. (2009). *Think Again: Why Good Leaders Make Bad Decisions and How to Keep it From Happening to You.* Harvard Business Review Press.

Fitch, H. (1976). Achieving corporate social responsibility. *Academy of Management Review, 1*(1), 38–46. doi:10.5465/amr.1976.4408754

Fliaster, A., & Kolloch, M. (2017). Implementation of green innovations-The impact of stakeholders and their network relations. *R & D Management, 47*(5), 689–700. doi:10.1111/radm.12257

Flores, D., Guzmán, C., & Barroso, M. (2015). La formación en economía social. Análisis de la oferta universitaria de posgrado en España [Training in social economy. Analysis of the postgraduate university offer in Spain]. *Revesco, 121,* 89–113. doi:10.5209/rev_REVE.2016.v121.49703

Folk, H. (1968). *The Problem of Youth Unemployment.* Institute of Labor and Industrial Relations, University of Illinois. https://files.eric.ed.gov/fulltext/ED022048.pdf

Fontaine, M. (2013). Corporate social responsibility and sustainability: The new bottom line? *International Journal of Business and Social Science, 4*(4), 1–10.

Fontrodona, J., & Sanz, P. (2015). The value of values. The keys to a positive business culture. *IESEInsight, 27.*

Foro de Expertos en Responsabilidad Social de las Empresas. (2007). *Informe del foro de expertos en responsabilidad social de las empresas* [Report of the forum of experts in corporate social responsibility]. Constituido el 17 de marzo de 2005 por iniciativa del Ministerio de Trabajo y Asuntos Sociales [Established on March 17, 2005 at the initiative of the Ministry of Labor and Social Affairs].

Forrester, J. W. (1968). *Principles of Systems.* Pegasus Communications.

Fraser, J. (2021). Mining companies and communities: Collaborative approaches to reduce social risk and advance sustainable development. *Resources Policy, 74*, 101144. https://doi.org/10.1016/j.resourpol.2018.02.003

Frederick, W. (1960). The growing concern over business responsibility. *California Management Review, 2*(4), 54–61. doi:10.2307/41165405

Freeman, R. (1984). *Strategic Management - A Stakeholder Approach.* Pitman.

Freeman, R. (1994). The politics of stakeholder theory: Some future directions. *Business Ethics Quarterly, 4*(4), 409–421. doi:10.2307/3857340

Freeman, R. (2001). A stakeholder theory of the modern corporation. *Perspectives in Business Ethics, 3*, 144.

Friedman, M. (1970). The social responsibility of business is to increase its profits. *The New York Times Magazine.*

Friedman, A., & Miles, S. (2002). Developing stakeholder theory. *Journal of Management Studies, 39*(1), 1–21. doi:10.1111/1467-6486.00280

Friedman, M. (1962). *Capitalism and freedom.* University of Chicago Press.

Fullwood, R., Straker, E., & Aron, W. (1977). Preliminary risk analysis of transportation of nuclear waste. *Transactions of the American Nuclear Society, 26*, 271–272.

Fussler, C., & James, P. (1996). *Driving eco-innovation: a breakthrough discipline for innovation and sustainability.* Financial Times/Prentice Hall.

Galbreath, J. (2019). Drivers of green innovations: The impact of export intensity, women leaders, and absorptive capacity. *Journal of Business Ethics, 158*(1), 47–61. doi:10.100710551-017-3715-z

Galiano-Maritan, G., & Tamayo-Santana, G. (2018). Análisis constitucional de los derechos personalísimos y su relación con los derechos del buen vivir en la Constitución de Ecuador [Constitutional analysis of very personal rights and their relationship with the rights of good living in the Constitution of Ecuador]. *Revista de Derecho Privado*, (34), 123–156. doi:10.18601/01234366.n34.05

García-Albán, F., González-Astudillo, M., & Vera-Avellán, C. (2021). Good policy or good luck? Analyzing the effects of fiscal policy and oil revenue shocks in Ecuador. *Energy Economics, 100*, 105321. doi:10.1016/j.eneco.2021.105321

Garcia, G. (2019). La democracia del libre mercado. La intervención patronal en el sistema político de la transición [Free market democracy. Employer intervention in the political system of the transition]. *Historia y Política, 42*(42), 297–330. doi:10.18042/hp.42.11

García-Marzá, D. (2004). *Ética empresarial. Del diálogo a la confianza [Business ethics. From dialogue to trust].* Trotta.

Garrison, R. (1996). Central Banking, Free Banking, and Financial Crises. *The Review of Austrian Economics, 9*(2), 109–112. doi:10.1007/BF01103332

General Office of the Central Committee of the Communist Party of China & General Office of the State Council, Guiding Opinions on Establishing a Natural Reserve System with National Parks as the Main Body. (2019). The State Council of The people's Republic of China.

Ghazali, E. M., Mutum, D. S., & Ariswibowo, N. (2018). Impact of religious values and habit on an extended green purchase behaviour model. *International Journal of Consumer Studies, 42*(6), 639–654. doi:10.1111/ijcs.12472

Gindling, T. H. (2009). South-South Migration: The Impact of Nicaraguan Immigrants on Earnings, Inequality and Poverty in Costa Rica. *World Development, 37*(1), 116–126. doi:10.1016/j.worlddev.2008.01.013

Global Footprint Network. (2022). Retrieved February 15, 2022, from https://www.footprintnetwork. org

Global Sustainable Tourism Council. (n.d.). *GSTC criteria*. Retrieved from https://www.gstcouncil.org/gstc-criteria/

Glotz, G. (2013). *Ancient Greece at work*. Routledge. doi:10.4324/9781315005348

González de Molina, M., & Toledo, V. M. (2014). *The Social Metabolism. A Socio-Ecological Theory of Historical Change*. Springer.

González, E., & Ramiro, P. (2022). *Smurfit Kappa en Colombia: impactos socioecológicos y violaciones de derechos humanos.* Omal. Retrieved from https://omal.info/spip.php?article9737

Gooderham, P. N., Nordhaug, O., & Ringdal, K. (1999). Institutional and rational determinants of organizational practices: Human resource management in European firms. *Administrative Science Quarterly, 44*(3), 507–531. doi:10.2307/2666960

Goolsbee, A., & Syverson, C. (2021). Fear, lockdown, and diversion: Comparing drivers of pandemic economic decline 2020. *Journal of Public Economics, 193*(C). doi:10.1016/j.jpubeco.2020.104311

Gössling, S. (1999). Ecotourism: A means to safeguard biodiversity and ecosystem functions? *Ecological Economics, 29*(2), 303–320. doi:10.1016/S0921-8009(99)00012-9

Govindarajan, V. (2016). A Estratégia das 3 Caixas. Academic Press.

Green, D. A., & Riddell, W. C. (2001). *Literacy, numeracy and labour market outcomes in Canada*. http://en.copian.ca/library/research/nls/ials/numeracy/english/numeracy.pdf

Gudynas, E., & Acosta, A. (2011). El buen vivir más allá del desarrollo [Good living beyond development]. *Revista Quehacer*, (181), 70–83.

Gumiran, B. A., & Daag, A. (2021). Negotiated participatory action research for multi-stakeholder implementation of early warning systems for landslides. *International Journal of Disaster Risk Reduction, 58*, 102184. https://doi.org/10.1016/j.ijdrr.2021.102184

Gunasekaran, A. (1999). Agile manufacturing: A framework for research and development. *International Journal of Production Economics, 62*(1-2), 87–105. doi:10.1016/S0925-5273(98)00222-9

Guzmán, M. (2015). *Del concepto a la medicion: Propuesta metodologica para medir el Buen Vivir en Ecuador* [From concept to measurement: Methodological proposal to measure Good Living in Ecuador]. Instituto Nacional de Estadisticas y Censos.

Haberl, H., Fischer-Kowalski, M., Krausmann, F., & Winiwarter, V. (2016). *Social Ecology. Society-Nature relations across Time and Space*. Springer.

Hall, J., & Martin, M. (2005). Disruptive technologies, stakeholders and the innovation value-added chain: A framework for evaluating radical technology development. *R & D Management, 35*(3), 273–284. doi:10.1111/j.1467-9310.2005.00389.x

Hammarström, A. (1994). Health consequences of youth unemployment-review from a gender perspective. *Social Science & Medicine, 38*(5), 699–709. doi:10.1016/0277-9536(94)90460-X PMID:8171348

Hao, Y., Gai, Z., Yan, G., Wu, H., & Irfan, M. (2021). The spatial spillover effect and nonlinear relationship analysis between Environmental Decentralization, government corruption and air pollution: Evidence from China. *The Science of the Total Environment, 763*, 144183. doi:10.1016/j.scitotenv.2020.144183 PMID:33383516

Hart, S. (1995). A natural resource-based view of the firm. *Academy of Management Review, 20*(4), 986–1014. doi:10.5465/amr.1995.9512280033

Heberlein, T. (1972). The Land Ethic Realized: Some Social Psychological Explanations for Changing Environmental Attitudes 1. *The Journal of Social Issues*, *28*(4), 79–87. doi:10.1111/j.1540-4560.1972.tb00047.x

Hediger, W. (2010). Welfare and capital-theoretic foundations of corporate social responsibility and corporate sustainability. *Journal of Socio-Economics*, *39*(4), 518–526. doi:10.1016/j.socec.2010.02.001

Henard, D., & McFadyen, M. A. (2012). Resource dedication and new product performance: A resource-based view. *Journal of Product Innovation Management*, *29*(2), 193–204. doi:10.1111/j.1540-5885.2011.00889.x

Henriques, I., & Sadorsky, P. (1996). The determinants of an environmentally responsive firm: An empirical approach. *Journal of Environmental Economics and Management*, *30*(3), 381–396. doi:10.1006/jeem.1996.0026

Henriques, I., & Sadorsky, P. (1999). The relationship between environmental commitment and managerial perceptions of stakeholder importance. *Academy of Management Journal*, *42*(1), 87–99.

Hernández Zubizarreta, J., & Ramiro, P. (2022). *Declaración universal de los derechos del poder corporativo* [Universal declaration of the rights of corporate power]. Ctxt. Retrieved from https://ctxt.es/es/20220501/Firmas/39628/poder-corporativo-derechos-humanos-necropolitica-derecho-internacional.htm

Hernández Zubizarreta, J., & Ramiro, P. (2016). *Contra la lex mercatoria* [Against the lex mercatoria]. Ed. Icaria.

Hoffman, A. (1999). Institutional evolution and change: Environmentalism and the US chemical industry. *Academy of Management Journal*, *42*(4), 351–371.

Hopkins, M. (1998). *The Planetary Bargain: Corporate Social Responsibility Comes of Age*. Macmillan.

Hopkins, M. (2004). *The Planetary Bargain. Corporate Social Responsibility Matters*. Routledge.

Hou, L. (2018, July 18). *River chiefs keep water bodies clean*. The State Council of The People's Republic of China. Retrieved from http://english.www.gov.cn/state_council/ministries/2018/07/18/content_281476226902566.htm

Huang, B., Ma, Y., Huang, K., Su, L., Zhang, C., Cheng, D., & Wang, Y. (2018). Strategic Approach on Promoting Reform of China's Natural Protected Areas System with National Parks as Backbone. *Bulletin of Chinese Academy of Sciences*, 1342–1351. doi:10.16418/j.issn.1000-3045.2018.12.007

Huang, Q. (2014). *The special function of ecological civilization construction in the "five-in-one" overall layout*. Guangming Daily.

Huang, Y., Ding, H., & Kao, M. (2009). Salient stakeholder voices: Family business and green innovation adoption. *Journal of Management & Organization*, *15*(3), 309–326. doi:10.5172/jmo.2009.15.3.309

Hubbard, D. W. (2009). *The failure of risk management. Why it's broken and how to fix it*. John Wiley & Sons, Inc.

Humphrey, C., & Hugh-Jones, S. (Eds.). (1992). *Barter, exchange and value: an anthropological approach*. Cambridge University Press. doi:10.1017/CBO9780511607677

Iacobucci, D., Gabriel, M. L. D. S., Schneider, M. J., & Hamza, K. M. (2020). Marketing research on environmental sustainability. *Review of Marketing Research*, *17*, 261–292. doi:10.1108/S1548-643520200000017019

ILO. (2019). *World Employment Outlook Social Trends 2019*. ILO. https://www.ilo.org/wcmsp5/groups/public/---dgreports/---dcomm/---publ/documents/publication/wcms_670542.pdf

International Labour Organization. (2017). *Profiling youth labour market disadvantage: A review of approaches in Europe*. https://www.ilo.org/wcmsp5/groups/public/---ed_emp/documents/publication/wcms_613361.pdf

IOM & AU. (2020). *Africa Migration Report 2020.* https://reliefweb.int/sites/reliefweb.int/files/resources/africa-migration-report.pdf

IPCC (Intergovernmental Panel on Climate Change). (2022). *Climate change 2022: Impacts, adaptation, and vulnerability.* Retrieved June 15, 2022, from https://www.ipcc.ch/report/ ar6/wg2/downloads/report/IPCC_AR6_WGII_Final-Draft_FullReport.pdf

IPCC. (2022). AR6 Synthesis Report. Ginebra: ONU. Retrieved from https://www.ipcc.ch/report/sixth-assessment-report-cycle/

Ipiranga, A. S. R., Godoy, A. S., & Brunstein, J. (2011). Introdução. *RAM. Revista de Administração Mackenzie*, *12*(3), 13–20. https://doi.org/10.1590/S1678-69712011000300002

Ismail, M. (2009). Corporate social responsibility and its role in community development: An international perspective. *Journal of International Social Research*, *2*(9), 1–12.

Iza, M., & Heredia, D. (2011). *Sumak Kawsay? Los derechos humanos al agua y al trabajo en la provincia de Orellana* [Sumak kawsay? The human rights to water and work in the province of Orellana]. INREDH.

Johnstone, M.-L., & Tan, L. P. (2015). Exploring the gap between consumers' green rhetoric and purchasing behavior. *Journal of Business Ethics*, *132*(2), 311–328. doi:10.100710551-014-2316-3

Jones, P., Clarke-Hill, C., Comfort, D., & Hillier, D. (2008). Marketing and sustainability. *Marketing Intelligence & Planning*, *26*(2), 123–130. doi:10.1108/02634500810860584

Jones, T. (1980). Corporate social responsibility revisited, redefined. *California Management Review*, *22*(3), 59–67. doi:10.2307/41164877

Joshi, Y., & Rahman, Z. (2015). Factors affecting green purchase behavior and future research directions. *International Strategic Management Review*, *3*(1-2), 128–143. doi:10.1016/j.ism.2015.04.001

Kahneman, D. (2011). Think fast and slow. New York: Farrar, Straus & Giroux Ed.

Kalamas, M., Cleveland, M., & Laroche, M. (2014). Pro-environmental behaviors for thee but not for me: Green giants, green Gods, and external environmental locus of control. *Journal of Business Research*, *67*(2), 12–22. doi:10.1016/j.jbusres.2013.03.007

Kao, E., Yeh, C., Wang, L., & Fung, H. (2018). The relationship between CSR and performance: Evidence in China. *Pacific-Basin Finance Journal*, *51*, 155–170. doi:10.1016/j.pacfin.2018.04.006

Karapınar Kocağ, E., & Kambhampati, U. (2020). Impact of Immigration on Employment: The Case of Turkey. *Empirical Economics Review*, *10*(4), 291–312.

Kardash, W. J. (1974). Corporate responsibility and the quality of life: Developing the ecologically concerned consumer. In Ecological Marketing. AMA.

Keller, K. L., Parameswaran, M. G., & Jacob, I. (2020). *Strategic Brand Management: Building, Measuring, and Managing Brand Equity* (5th ed.). Pearson Education.

Kemp, R., & Pearson, P. (2007). Final report MEI project about measuring eco-innovation. *UM Merit, Maastricht*, *10*(2), 1–120.

Khoury, G., Rostami, J., & Turnbull, J. (1999). *Corporate Social Responsibility: Turning Words into Action.* Conference Board of Canada.

Kilbourne, W. E., Beckmann, S. C., & Thelen, E. (2002). The role of the dominant social paradigm in environmental attitudes: A multinational examination. *Journal of Business Research*, *55*(3), 193–204. doi:10.1016/S0148-2963(00)00141-7

King, A., & Lenox, M. (2002). Exploring the locus of profitable pollution reduction. *Management Science*, *48*(2), 289–299. doi:10.1287/mnsc.48.2.289.258

Klassen, R., & Whybark, D. (1999). The impact of environmental technologies on manufacturing performance. *Academy of Management Journal*, *42*(6), 599–615.

Klöckner, C. A. (2013). A comprehensive model of the psychology of environmental behaviour – a metaanalysis. *Global Environmental Change*, *23*(5), 1028–1038. doi:10.1016/j.gloenvcha.2013.05.014

Koiffmann, B. (2019). Geopolítica de la Amazonía [Geopolitics of the Amazon]. *Revista de estudios sobre espacio y poder, 10*(1), 135-151. Doi:10.5209/GEOP.63836

Kolahi, J., Khazaei, S., Bidram, E., Kelishadi, R., Iranmanesh, P., Nekoofar, M. H., & Dummer, P. M. (2020). Science Map of Cochrane Systematic Reviews Receiving the Most Altmetric Attention Score: A Network Analysis. *Journal of Scientometric Research*, *9*(3), 293–299. https://doi.org/10.5530/jscires.9.3.36

Kollmuss, A., & Agyeman, J. (2002). Mind the gap: Why do people act environmentally and what are the barriers to pro-environmental behavior. *Environmental Education Research*, *8*(3), 239–260. doi:10.1080/13504620220145401

Komljenovic, D., Groves, W. A., & Kecojevic, V. J. (2008). Injuries in U.S. mining operations – A preliminary risk analysis. *Safety Science*, *46*(5), 792–801. https://doi.org/10.1016/j.ssci.2007.01.012

Kostova, T. (1999). Transnational transfer of strategic organizational practices: A contextual perspective. *Academy of Management Review*, *24*(2), 308–324. doi:10.2307/259084

Kostova, T., & Roth, K. (2002). Adoption of an organizational practice by subsidiaries of multinational corporations: Institutional and relational effects. *Academy of Management Journal*, *45*, 215–233.

Kostova, T., Roth, K., & Dacin, M. (2008). Institutional theory in the study of multinational corporations: A critique and new directions. *Academy of Management Review*, *33*(4), 994–1006. doi:10.5465/amr.2008.34422026

Kotler, P., & Armstrong, G. (2020). *Principles of Marketing* (18th ed.). Pearson Education.

Kotler, P., & Lee, N. (2007). *Corporate Social Responsibility: doing the most good for your company and your case*. John Wiley & Sons.

Laforet, S. (2009). Effects of size, market and strategic orientation on innovation in non-high-tech manufacturing SMEs. *European Journal of Marketing*, *43*(1/2), 188–212. doi:10.1108/03090560910923292

Lakuma, C. P., Marty, R., & Kuteesa, A. (2016). Survival Analysis of Regional Unemployment in Uganda: Evidence from the Uganda National Panel Survey (UNPS). *African Development Review*, *28*(1), 140–154. doi:10.1111/1467-8268.12173

Langenbach, B. P., Berger, S., Baumgartner, T., & Knoch, D. (2020). Cognitive resources moderate the relationship between pro-environmental attitudes and green behavior. *Environment and Behavior*, *52*(9), 979–995. doi:10.1177/0013916519843127

Lantos, G. (2001). The boundaries of strategic corporate social responsibility. *Journal of Consumer Marketing*, *18*(7), 595–632. doi:10.1108/07363760110410281

Laplume, A., Sonpar, K., & Litz, R. (2008). Stakeholder theory: Reviewing a theory that moves us. *Journal of Management*, *34*(6), 1152–1189. doi:10.1177/0149206308324322

Laroche, M., Bergeron, J., & Barbaro-Forleo, G. (2001). Targeting consumers who are willing to pay more for environmentally friendly products. *Journal of Consumer Marketing*, *18*(6), 503–520. doi:10.1108/EUM0000000006155

Larrouy, D. (2022). *La gran banca pide menos obligaciones para la transición ecológica y no tener que ejercer como "policía del clima"* [The banking sector asks for fewer obligations for the ecological transition and not having to act as "climate police"]. Retrieved from https://www.eldiario.es/economia/gran-banca-pide-obligaciones-transicion-ecologica-no-ejercer-policia-clima_1_8983575.html

Laskaris, Z., Milando, C., Batterman, S., Mukherjee, B., Basu, N., O'neill, M. S., Robins, T. G., & Fobil, J. N. (2019). Derivation of Time-Activity Data Using Wearable Cameras and Measures of Personal Inhalation Exposure among Workers at an Informal Electronic-Waste Recovery Site in Ghana. *Annals of Work Exposures and Health*, *63*(8), 829–841. https://doi.org/10.1093/annweh/wxz056

Laval, C., & Dardot, P. (2017). *La pesadilla que no se acaba nunca: El neoliberalismo contra la democracia* [The nightmare that never ends: Neoliberalism against democracy]. 360º Claves contemporáneas.

Lee, L. M. (2017). A Bridge Back to the Future: Public Health Ethics, Bioethics, and Environmental Ethics. *The American Journal of Bioethics*, *17*(9), 5–12. https://doi.org/10.1080/15265161.2017.1353164

Lee, M. (2008). A review of the theories of corporate social responsibility: Its evolutionary path and the road ahead. *International Journal of Management Reviews*, *10*(1), 53–73. doi:10.1111/j.1468-2370.2007.00226.x

Lee, P.-S., Sung, Y.-H., Wu, C.-C., Ho, L.-C., & Chiou, W.-B. (2020). Using episodic future thinking to pre-experience climate change increases pro-environmental behavior. *Environment and Behavior*, *52*(1), 60–81. doi:10.1177/0013916518790590

Leonidou, C. N., Leonidou, L. C., & Kvasova, O. (2010). Antecedents and outcomes of consumer environmentally friendly attitudes and behavior. *Journal of Marketing Management*, *26*(13-14), 1319–1344. doi:10.1080/0267257X.2010.523710

Li, Z. (2021). Research on Ecotourism Positioning and Effect in Chinese National Park System. *Tourism and Photography*, 82–83.

Li, D., Zhao, Y., Zhang, L., Chen, X., & Cao, C. (2018). Impact of quality management on green innovation. *Journal of Cleaner Production*, *170*, 462–470. doi:10.1016/j.jclepro.2017.09.158

Lin, J. Y. (1989). An economic theory of institutional change: induced and imposed change. *Cato Journal*, *9*(1), 1-33. https://www.cato.org/sites/cato.org/files/serials/fl/1989/5/cj9n1-1.pdf

Lin, S.-T., & Niu, H.-J. (2018). Green consumption: Environmental knowledge, environmental consciousness, social norms, and purchasing behavior. *Business Strategy and the Environment*, *27*(8), 1679–1688. doi:10.1002/bse.2233

Liu, T., & Cai, J. (2009). Public participation in Community Tourism Planning. *Tourism Research*, 55–61.

Liu, Y., Shi, D., & Li, X. (2009). A research on phenomena, causes and countermeasures of expansion of eco-tourism in China. *Resources & Industries*, 131–134.

Liu, X., Fu, Z., Wen, R., Jin, C., Wang, X., Wang, C., Xiao, R., & Hou, P. (2020). Characteristics of human activities and the spatio-temporal changes of national nature reserves in China. *Geographical Research*, 2391–2402.

Li, W. (2004). Environmental management indicators for ecotourism in China's nature reserves: A case study in Tianmushan Nature Reserve. *Tourism Management*, *25*(5), 559–564. doi:10.1016/j.tourman.2003.06.001

Li, Y., Zhang, L., Gao, Y., Huang, Z., Cui, L., Liu, S., Fang, Y., Ren, G., Fornacca, D., & Xiao, W. (2019). Ecotourism in China, misuse or genuine development? an analysis based on map browser results. *Sustainability*, *11*(18), 4997. doi:10.3390u11184997

Lopera, J., Ramírez, C., Zuluaga, M., & Ortíz, J. (2010). El Método Analítico como método natural [The analytical method as a natural method]. *Nómadas*, *1*, 25–30. doi:10.5209/NOMA.27128

Lorsch, J. W. (2012). *The Future of Boards*. Harvard Business Review Press.

Luque & Casado. (2020a). Procesos de Covid-19 en Ecuador: cuando la distopía se convierte en realidad [Covid-19 processes in Ecuador: when dystopia becomes reality"]. Revista Venezolana de Gerencia, 25(92), 1271-1281. Doi:10.37960/rvg.v25i92

Luque & Casado. (2020b). Public Strategy and Eco-Social Engagement in Latin American States: An Analysis of Complex Networks Arising from Their Constitutions. *MDPI Sustainability, 12*(20), 1-29. doi:10.3390/su12208558

Luque, A. (2017). Promoción del hiperconsumo textil transnacional: la moda y el exceso como leit motiv [Promotion of transnational textile hyperconsumption: fashion and excess as leitmotiv]. *Revista Chasqui, 134*, 83-104. doi:10.16921/chasqui.v0i134.3016

Luque, A. (2021). Fallacies of Consumerism: An Analysis of Its Impact and Depth in Today's Society. In Handbook of Research on Changing Dynamics in Responsible and Sustainable Business in the Post-COVID-19 Era. IGI Global. doi:10.4018/978-1-6684-2523-7.ch004

Luque, A., & Álvarez, J. (2021). How the social and solidarity economy is defined: an analysis of 100 concepts. In P. Baisotti & H. López (Eds.), The Social and Solidarity Economy in Latin America. The development of the common good (pp. 1-47). Cambridge Scholars Publishing.

Luque, A., & Jiménez, A. (2019). Procesos de sostenibilidad textil: éxito, o nueva forma de contaminar bajo un paradigma amable. *Revista Inclusiones, 6*, 259-288.

Luque, A., Bengoetxea, A., & Ordoñez, J. L. (2021) The Social and Solidarity Economics, Public Policies, and Non-Monetary Economic Practices: The Case of Associative Firms in Loja, Ecuador. In Handbook of Research on Emerging Business Models and the New World Economic Order. IGI Global. doi:10.4018/978-1-7998-7689-2.ch012

Luque, A. (2018). Transnational Systemic Corruption: Exceptionality or Norm? *Revista Empresa y Humanismo*, *21*(2), 123–184. doi:10.15581/015.XXI.2.123-184

Luque, A. (2021). Implications and Asymmetries of the Knowledge Society: An Analysis of 82 Constructs. In C. Popescu (Ed.), *COVID-19 Pandemic Impact on New Economy Development and Societal Change* (pp. 154–176). IGI Global. doi:10.4018/978-1-6684-3374-4.ch008

Luque, A. (2022). Analysis of the concept of informal economy through 102 definitions: Legality or necessity. *Open Research Europe*, *2022*, 1–134. doi:10.12688/openreseurope.13990.2

Luque, A., & Herrero-García, N. (2019). How corporate social (ir)responsibility in the textile sector is defined, and its impact on ethical sustainability: An analysis of 133 concepts. *Corporate Social Responsibility and Environmental Management*, *26*(6), 1–22. doi:10.1002/csr.1747

Lustgarten, A. (2012). *Run to Failure: BP and the Making of the Deepwater Horizon Disaster*. W. W. Norton & Company.

Maignan, I., & Ferrell, O. (2004). Corporate social responsibility and marketing: An integrative framework. *Journal of the Academy of Marketing Science*, *32*(1), 3–19. doi:10.1177/0092070303258971

Mainieri, T., Barnett, E. G., Valdero, T. R., Unipan, J. B., & Oskamp, S. (1997). Green buying: The influence of environmental concern on consumer behavior. *The Journal of Social Psychology*, *137*(2), 189–204. doi:10.1080/00224549709595430

Majid, K. A., & Russell, C. A. (2015). Giving green a second thought: Modeling the value retention of green products in the secondary market. *Journal of Business Research, 68*(5), 994–1002. doi:10.1016/j.jbusres.2014.10.001

Maldonado, W. P., Bastidas Aráuz, M., & Durán Pinos, A. (2017). Propuesta metodológica de evaluacion del balance social en asociaciones de economía popular solidaria del Ecuador [Methodological proposal for the evaluation of the social balance in associations of popular solidarity economy of Ecuador]. *CIRIEC-España, Revista de Economía Pública. Social y Cooperativa, 90*(90), 123–157. doi:10.7203/CIRIEC-E.90.9240

Malik, F. (2012). *The right corporate governance. Effective Top management for mastering complexity*. Campus Verlag.

Malik, M. (2015). Value-enhancing capabilities of CSR: A brief review of contemporary literature. *Journal of Business Ethics, 127*(2), 419–438. doi:10.100710551-014-2051-9

Malloy, T. F., Zaunbrecher, V. M., Batteate, C. M., Blake, A., Carroll, W. F., Corbett, C. J., Hansen, S. F., Lempert, R. J., Linkov, I., McFadden, R., Moran, K. D., Olivetti, E., Ostrom, N. K., Romero, M., Schoenung, J. M., Seager, T. P., Sinsheimer, P., & Thayer, K. A. (2017). Advancing Alternative Analysis: Integration of Decision Science. *Environmental Health Perspectives, 125*(6), 066001. https://doi.org/10.1289/EHP483

Mandato, J, & Devine, W. (2020). Why the CEO shouldn't also be the board chair. *Harvard Business Review*.

Manne, H., & Wallich, H. (1972). *The Modern Corporation and Social Responsibility*. American Enterprise Institute for Public Policy Research.

Marafa, L. M. (2018). Leisure in nature: The advent of eco-leisure in academic discourse. *World Leisure Journal, 60*(3), 178–180. doi:10.1080/16078055.2018.1496526

Marco-Lajara, B., Zaragoza-Saez, P., Falcó, J. M., & Millan-Tudela, L. A. (2022). Analysing the Relationship Between Green Intellectual Capital and the Achievement of the Sustainable Development Goals. In Handbook of Research on Building Inclusive Global Knowledge Societies for Sustainable Development (pp. 111-129). IGI Global.

Marco-Lajara, B., Zaragoza-Saez, P., Falcó, J. M., & Sánchez-García, E. (2022c). COVID-19 and Wine Tourism: A Story of Heartbreak. In Handbook of Research on SDGs for Economic Development, Social Development, and Environmental Protection (pp. 90-112). IGI Global.

Marco-Lajara, B., Zaragoza-Sáez, P., Martínez-Falcó, J., & Sánchez-García, E. (2022a). Green Intellectual Capital in the Spanish Wine Industry. In Innovative Economic, Social, and Environmental Practices for Progressing Future Sustainability (pp. 102-120). IGI Global. doi:10.4018/978-1-7998-9590-9.ch006

Marco-Lajara, B., Zaragoza-Saez, P., Martínez-Falcó, J., & Sánchez-García, E. (2022c). COVID-19 and Wine Tourism: A Story of Heartbreak. In Handbook of Research on SDGs for Economic Development, Social Development, and Environmental Protection (pp. 90-112). IGI Global.

Marco-Lajara, B., Seva-Larrosa, P., Martínez-Falcó, J., & Sánchez-García, E. (2021b). How Has COVID-19 Affected The Spanish Wine Industry? An Exploratory Analysis. *Natural Volatiles & Essential Oils Journal, 8*(6), 2722–2731.

Marco-Lajara, B., Seva-Larrosa, P., Martínez-Falcó, J., & Sánchez-García, E. (2021b). How Has COVID-19 Affected The Spanish Wine Industry? An Exploratory Analysis. *Natural Volatiles & Essential Oils, 8*(6), 2722–2731.

Marco-Lajara, B., Seva-Larrosa, P., Ruiz-Fernández, L., & Martínez-Falcó, J. (2021a). The Effect of COVID-19 on the Spanish Wine Industry. In *Impact of Global Issues on International Trade* (pp. 211–232). IGI Global. doi:10.4018/978-1-7998-8314-2.ch012

Marco-Lajara, B., Zaragoza-Saez, P., Falcó, J. M., & Millan-Tudela, L. A. (2022b). Analysing the Relationship Between Green Intellectual Capital and the Achievement of the Sustainable Development Goals. In *Handbook of Research on Building Inclusive Global Knowledge Societies for Sustainable Development* (pp. 111–129). IGI Global. doi:10.4018/978-1-6684-5109-0.ch005

Marco-Lajara, B., Zaragoza-Sáez, P., Martínez-Falcó, J., & Sánchez-García, E. (2022d). El capital intelectual verde como hoja de ruta para la sostenibilidad: el caso de bodegas Luzón [Green intellectual capital as a roadmap for sustainability: the case of Bodegas Luzón]. *GeoGraphos: Revista Digital para Estudiantes de Geografía y Ciencias Sociales, 13*(147), 137–146.

Marco-Lajara, B., Zaragoza-Sáez, P., Martínez-Falcó, J., & Sánchez-García, E. (2022d). El capital intelectual verde como hoja de ruta para la sostenibilidad: El caso de bodegas Luzón. GeoGraphos. *Revista Digital para Estudiantes de Geografía y Ciencias Sociales, 13*(147), 137–146.

Marcoulaki, E., López de Ipiña, J. M., Vercauteren, S., Bouillard, J., Himly, M., Lynch, I., Witters, H., Shandilya, N., van Duuren-Stuurman, B., Kunz, V., Unger, W. E. S., Hodoroaba, V.-D., Bard, D., Evans, G., Jensen, K. A., Pilou, M., Viitanen, A.-K., Bochon, A., Duschl, A., … Dulio, V. (2021). Blueprint for a self-sustained European Centre for service provision in safe and sustainable innovation for nanotechnology. *NanoImpact, 23*, 100337. doi:10.1016/j.impact.2021.100337

Marcus, A., & Fremeth, A. (2009). Strategic direction and management. In *Business Management and Environmental Stewardship: Environmental Thinking as a Prelude to Management Action* (pp. 38–55). Palgrave McMillan. doi:10.1007/978-1-349-92307-6_3

Marsden, C. (2001). *The Role of Public Authorities in Corporate Social Responsibility*. http://www.alter.be/socialresponsibility/ people/marchri/en/displayPerson

Massaro, M., Dumay, J., & Guthrie, J. (2016). On the shoulders of giants: Undertaking a structured literature review in accounting. *Accounting, Auditing & Accountability Journal, 29*(5), 767–801. doi:10.1108/AAAJ-01-2015-1939

Ma, T., Lü, C., & Lei, G. (2019). The spatial overlapping analysis for China's natural protected area and countermeasures for the optimization and integration of Protected Area System. *Shengwu Duoyangxing, 27*(7), 758–771. doi:10.17520/biods.2019087

Matthews, E. N. (1937). Unemployed Youth of New York City. *Monthly Labor Review, 44*(2), 267–284. https://www.jstor.org/stable/41815043

Mazzucato, M. (2016). *O Estado Empreendedor: desmascarando o mito do setor público vs. setor privado*. Portfolio-Penguin.

Mc Donald, S., & Oates, C. J. (2006). Sustainability: Consumer perceptions and marketing strategies. *Business Strategy and the Environment, 15*(3), 157–170. doi:10.1002/bse.524

Mc Donald, S., Oates, C. J., Thyne, M., Timmis, A. J., & Carlile, C. (2015). Flying in the face of environmental concern: Why green consumers continue to fly. *Journal of Marketing Management, 31*(13-14), 1503–1528. doi:10.1080/0267257X.2015.1059352

McGuire, J. (1963). *Business and society*. McGraw-Hill.

McWilliams, A., Siegel, D., & Wright, P. (2006). Corporate social responsibility: Strategic implications. *Journal of Management Studies, 43*(1), 1–18. doi:10.1111/j.1467-6486.2006.00580.x

Meyer, J., & Rowan, B. (1977). Institutionalized organizations: Formal structure as myth and ceremony. *American Journal of Sociology, 83*(2), 340–363. doi:10.1086/226550

Miller, D. C. (1941). Youth and National Morale. *Journal of Educational Sociology*, *15*(1), 17–28. doi:10.2307/2262093

Ministerio de Agricultura Pesca y Alimentación & Ministerio para la Transición Ecológica y el Reto Demográfico. (2022). *GeoPortal*. https://sig.mapama.gob.es/geoportal/

Ministry of Tourism. (2020). *Orellana un destino para conocer la cultura amazónica* [Orellana a destination to learn about the Amazonian culture]. Retrieved from https://www.turismo.gob.ec/orellana-un-destino-para-conocer-la-cultura-amazonica/

Mohr, L., Webb, D., & Harris, K. (2001). Do consumers expect companies to be socially responsible? The impact of corporate social responsibility on buying behavior. *The Journal of Consumer Affairs*, *35*(1), 45–72. doi:10.1111/j.1745-6606.2001.tb00102.x

Molina-Azorín, J., Claver-Cortés, E., López-Gamero, M., & Tarí, J. (2009). Green management and financial performance: A literature review. *Management Decision*, *47*(7), 1080–1100. doi:10.1108/00251740910978313

Monfort, A., & Villagra, N. (2016). Corporate Social Responsibility and Corporate Foundations in Building Responsible Brands. *El Profesional de la Información*, *25*(5), 767–777. doi:10.3145/epi.2016.sep.07

Montgomery, C. A., & Wernerfelt, B. (1992). Risk reduction and umbrella branding. *The Journal of Business*, *65*(1), 31–50. doi:10.1086/296556

Mortimer, J. T. (2006). *Youth Unemployment and Society* (A. C. Petersen & J. T. Mortimer, Eds.). Cambridge University Press. https://books.google.com.tr/books?id=_UwF3QsAuG4C&dq=youth+unemployment&lr=&source=gbs_navlinks_s

Moser, A. K. (2015). Thinking green, buying green? Drivers of pro-environmental purchasing behavior. *Journal of Consumer Marketing*, *32*(3), 167–175. doi:10.1108/JCM-10-2014-1179

Muñoz, F. (2008). El debate de la nueva Constitución [The debate on the new Constitution]. *La Tendencia. Revista de analisis politico, 16*, 7-8. Doi:10.4067/S0718-52002018000200527

Naredo, J. M. (2010). *Raíces económicas del deterioro ecológico y social* [Economic roots of ecological and social deterioration]. Siglo XXI de España Editores.

National Constituent Assembly. (2008). *Constitución de la Republica del Ecuador* [Constitution of the Republic of Ecuador]. https://www.asambleanacional.gob.ec/sites/default/files/documents/old/constitucion_de_bolsillo.pdf

National Development and Reform Commission (NDRC), the People´s Republic of China. (2016). *Notice on Issuing the "Green Development Index System" and "Ecological Civilization Construction Assessment Target System"*. Author.

National Institute of Statistics and Censuses. (2021). *Estadísticas - Diciembre 2021*. Retrieved from https://www.ecuadorencifras.gob.ec/estadisticas-diciembre-2021/

National Institute of Statistics and Censuses. (2021). *INEC*. Retrieved from Demografia: https://www.ecuadorencifras.gob.ec/censo-de-poblacion-y-vivienda/

National Ocean Service. (n.d.). *A brief history of pollution.* https://oceanservice.noaa.gov/education/tutorial_pollution/02history.html#:~:text=Pollution%20is%20not%20a%20new,broke%20out%20all%20across%20Europe

National Secretariat of Planning and Development. (2015). *Provincias de Pichincha, Napo y Orellana. Quito* [Pichincha, Napo and Orellana provinces. Quito]. Senplades.

NBR ISO 31000: Risk Management—Guidelines, no. NBR ISO 31000 Second Edition. (2018).

Nguyen, H. V., Nguyen, C. H., & Hoang, T. T. B. (2019). Green consumption: Closing the intention-behavior gap. *Sustainable Development, 27*(1), 118–129. doi:10.1002d.1875

Nhamo, L., Ndlela, B., Mpandeli, S., & Mabhaudhi, T. (2020a). The water-energy-food nexus as an adaptation strategy for achieving sustainable livelihoods at a local level. *Sustainability (Switzerland), 12*(20), 1–16. doi:10.3390u12208582

Nishi, D., Ishikawa, H., & Kawakami, N. (2019). Prevalence of mental disorders and mental health service use in Japan. *Psychiatry and Clinical Neurosciences, 73*(8), 458–465. doi:10.1111/pcn.12894 PMID:31141260

Nittala, R. (2014). Green consumer behavior of the educated segment in India. *Journal of International Consumer Marketing, 26*(2), 138–152. doi:10.1080/08961530.2014.878205

North, D. C. (1990). *Institutions, institutional change, and Economic Performance*. Cambridge University Press. doi:10.1017/CBO9780511808678

Nueno, P. (2016). *The 2020 Board: The Future of Company Boards*. LID Publishing.

O'Higgins, N. (2001). *Youth unemployment and employment policy*. Academic Press.

O'higgins, N. (1997). The challenge of youth unemployment. *International Social Security Review, 50*(4), 63–93. doi:10.1111/j.1468-246X.1997.tb01084.x

O'Regan, K. M. (1993). The effect of social networks and concentrated poverty on black and hispanic youth unemployment. *The Annals of Regional Science, 27*(4), 327–342. doi:10.1007/BF01583572

Observatorio de RSC. (2014). *Introducción a la Responsabilidad Social Corporativa [Introduction to Corporate Social Responsibility]*. Observatorio de RSC.

OECD. (2009). *Eco-innovation in industry: enabling green growth*. OECD.

Oliveira, W.K. de, Rohlfs, D.B., & Garcia, L.P. (2019). The Brumadinho disaster and the role of Health Surveillance. *Epidemiology and Health Services, 28*(1). https://doi.org/10.5123/S1679-49742019000100025

Oliver, P. (2012). *Succeeding with your literature review. A handbook for students*. McGraw-Hill, Open University Press.

Orellana. (2022). *Gobierno de Orellana* [Government of Orellana]. Retrieved from https://www.orellana.gob.ec/es/canton/datos-del-canton.html

Organization for Economic Co-operation and Development (OECD). (2016). *Better Policies for 2030. An OECD Action Plan on the Sustainable Development Goals*. https://www.oecd.org/dac/sustainable-development-goals.htm

Organization for Economic Co-operation and Development (OECD). (2019). *Beyond Growth: Towards A New Economic Approach*. Report of the Secretary General's Advisory Group on a New Growth Narrative. OECD Conference Centre. SG/NAEC(2019)3. https://www.oecd.org/naec/averting-systemic-collapse/SG-NAEC(2019)3_Beyond%20Growth.pdf

Organization for Economic Co-operation and Development (OECD). (2021). *Meeting of the Members of the Council on the 2030 Agenda for Sustainable Development 1 March 2021*. Draft Agenda. https://www.oecd.org/sdgs/

Organization for Economic Co-operation and Development (OECD). (2022a). *OECD and the Sustainable Development Goals: Delivering on Universal Goals and Targets*. https://www.oecd.org/dac/sustainable-development-goals.htm

Organization for Economic Co-operation and Development (OECD). (2022b). *The Sustainable Development Goals: An overview of relevant OECD analysis, tools and approaches*. https://www.oecd.org/dac/sustainable-development-goals.htm. https://www.oecd.org/dac/The%20Sustainable%20Development%20Goals%20An%20overview%20of%20relevant%20OECD%20analysis.pdf

Ormazabal, G. (2016). Risk oversight: What every director should know. *IESEInsight, 28.*

Orquin, J. L., Bagger, M. P., Lahm, E. S., Grunert, K. G., & Scholderer, J. (2020). The visual ecology of product packaging and its effects on consumer attention. *Journal of Business Research, 111*, 187–195. doi:10.1016/j.jbusres.2019.01.043

Pang, J., Li, N., Mu, H., & Zhang, M. (2021). Empirical analysis of the interplay between shadow economy and pollution: With panel data across the provinces of China. *Journal of Cleaner Production, 285*, 124864. doi:10.1016/j.jclepro.2020.124864

Passet, R. (2012). *Las grandes representaciones del mundo y la economía a lo largo de la historia: del universo mágico al torbellino creador* [The great representations of the world and the economy throughout history: from the magical universe to the creative whirlwind]. Clave Intelectual.

Peattie, K., & Charter, M. (2003). Green marketing. In M. J. Baker (Ed.), *The Marketing Book* (5th ed., pp. 726–755). Butterworth Heinemann.

Peng, S. (2004). Some Environmental Problems and Countermeasures in Developing Ecotourism in China. *Environmental Protection*, 25–30.

Peralta, B. I., & Roldán Monsalve, D. (2019). La importancia de la evaluación como paso previo a la implementación de una moneda complementaria. Un estudio de caso rural en Ecuador, la parroquia Sinincay [The importance of evaluation as a preliminary step to the implementation of a complementary currency. A rural case study in Ecuador, the Sinincay parish]. *CIRIEC-España, Revista de Economía Pública, Social y Cooperativa,* 283-284.

Pereira. (2021). *Marcio Batista. Análise de modelos e práticas de gestão de resíduos sólidos: o caso do aproveitamento energético do lixo urbano no Brasil. Pag. 69.* Editora Dialética.

Philippi, Fernandes, Pacheco, & Roberto. (2017). *Ensino, pesquisa e inovação: Desenvolvendo a interdisciplinaridade.* Editora Manole.

Pischke, J.-S., & Velling, J. (1997). Employment effects of immigration to Germany. *The Review of Economics and Statistics, 79*(4), 594–604. doi:10.1162/003465397557178

PNUMA/ILRI. (2020). *Preventing the Next Pandemic: Zoonotic Diseases and How to Break the Chain of Transmission.* Author.

Polanyi, K., & MacIver, R. M. (1944). *The great transformation, 2.* Beacon press.

Polonsky, J., & Ottman, J. (1998). Stakeholders' contri-bution to the green new product development process. *Journal of Marketing Management, 14*(6), 533–557. doi:10.1362/026725798784867707

Polonsky, M. J. (2011). Transformative green marketing: Impediments and opportunities. *Journal of Business Research, 64*(12), 1311–1319. doi:10.1016/j.jbusres.2011.01.016

Popescu, C. R. G., Popescu, G. N., & Popescu, V. A. (2015a). Corporate Governance in Romania: Theories and Practices. In *Corporate Governance And Corporate Social Responsibility: Emerging Markets Focus* (pp. 375-401). World Scientific Publ. https://www.worldscientific.com/doi/abs/10.1142/9789814520386_0014 doi:10.1142/9789814520386_0014

Popescu, C. R. G., Popescu, V. A., & Popescu, G. N. (2015b). The Entrepreneur's Role In The Performance Growth Of The Financial Audit Activity In Romania. *Amfiteatru Economic, 17*(38), 228-246.

Popescu, C. R. (2021). Impact of Innovative Capital on the Global Performance of the European Union: Implications on Sustainability Assessment. In C. Popescu (Ed.), *Handbook of Research on Novel Practices and Current Successes in Achieving the Sustainable Development Goals* (pp. 90–124). IGI Global. doi:10.4018/978-1-7998-8426-2.ch005

Popescu, C. R. (2022). Mindfulness at Work, a Sound Business Investment: Focusing on the Employee Well-Being While Increasing Creativity and Innovation. In C. Popescu (Ed.), *Handbook of Research on Changing Dynamics in Responsible and Sustainable Business in the Post-COVID-19 Era* (pp. 1–34). IGI Global. doi:10.4018/978-1-6684-2523-7.ch001

Popescu, C. R. G. (2021). Sustainable and Responsible Entrepreneurship for Value-Based Cultures, Economies, and Societies: Increasing Performance Through Intellectual Capital in Challenging Times. In C. Popescu & R. Verma (Eds.), *Sustainable and Responsible Entrepreneurship and Key Drivers of Performance* (pp. 33–58). IGI Global. doi:10.4018/978-1-7998-7951-0.ch002

Popescu, C. R. G. (2022b). Mindfulness Business Principles: Producing Outstanding Value and Encouraging Community Connections. In C. Popescu (Ed.), *COVID-19 Pandemic Impact on New Economy Development and Societal Change* (pp. 196–228). IGI Global. doi:10.4018/978-1-6684-3374-4.ch010

Popescu, C. R. G. (2022c). Impressive, Inspiring, and Profound Mindfulness Movement in Organizations: Boosting Productivity, Cultivating Joy, and Sharping Awareness. In C. Popescu (Ed.), *Handbook of Research on Building Inclusive Global Knowledge Societies for Sustainable Development* (pp. 60–96). IGI Global. doi:10.4018/978-1-6684-5109-0.ch003

Portelinha, M. K., Almeida, C., Vargas, N. R. C., & Lopes, C. V. (2021). Interlaces among health, sustainability and environment: An integrative review. *Research Journal Care is Fundamental Online, 13*, 1001–1006. doi:10.9789/2175-5361.rpcfo.v13.9767

Porter, M. E., Reinhardt, F. L., Schwartz, P., Esty, D. C., Hoffman, A. J., Schendler, A., & Rendlen, B. (2007). Climate businessl business climate. *Harvard Business Review, 85*(10), 21–44.

Porter, M., & Kramer, M. (2006). Strategy & Society. *Harvard Business Review, 84*(12), 1–16. PMID:17183795

Porter, M., & Reinhardt, F. (2007). A strategic approach to climate. *Harvard Business Review, 85*(10), 22–39.

Porter, M., & Van der Linde, C. (1995). Toward a new conception of the environment-competitiveness relationship. *The Journal of Economic Perspectives, 9*(4), 97–118. doi:10.1257/jep.9.4.97

Pour, B. S., Nazari, K., & Emami, M. (2014). Corporate social responsibility: A literature review. *African Journal of Business Management, 8*(7), 228–234. doi:10.5897/AJBM12.106

Prieto, W., & Tejedor, J. (2017). La ciencia económica en tiempos de crisis [Economic science in times of crisis. *Cenes, 38*(64), 47–78. doi:10.19053/01203053.v36.n64.2017.5937

Program Development and Cultural Diversity for Poverty Reduction and Social Inclusion. (2004). *Nacionalidades y Pueblos Indígenas, y Políticas Interculturales en Ecuador.* Manthra Editores.

Prothero, A., Dobscha, S., Freund, J., Kilbourne, W. E., Luchs, M. G., Ozanne, L. K., & Thogersen, J. (2011, Spring). Sustainable consumption: Opportunities for consumer research and public policy. *Journal of Public Policy & Marketing, 30*(1), 31–38. doi:10.1509/jppm.30.1.31

Qin, H., Wan, Y., & Xia, Y. (2006). A Study on Over-cxtending Ecotourism and the Construction of Its Concept Model. *Huanjing Kexue Yu Guanli*, 146–140.

Qiu, S., & Tang, X. (2020). Effect of Ecotourism Development on Precision Poverty Alleviation of Farmers in Ethnic Minority Areas. *Ecological Economy.*

Quadagno, J. (1987). Theories of the welfare state. *Annual Review of Sociology, 13*(1), 109–128. doi:10.1146/annurev.so.13.080187.000545

Rahimah, A., Khalil, S., Ming-Sung, J., Tran, M. D., & Panwar, V. (2018). Understanding green purchase behavior through death anxiety and individual social responsibility: Mastery as a moderator. *Journal of Consumer Behaviour*, *17*(5), 477–490. doi:10.1002/cb.1733

Ramírez, R. (2008). *Igualmente pobres, desigualmente ricos* [Equally poor, equally rich]. Ariel-PNUD.

Rampasso, I. S., Quelhas, O. L. G., Anholon, R., Pereira, M. B., Miranda, J. D. A., & Alvarenga, W. S. (2020). Engineering Education for Sustainable Development: Evaluation Criteria for Brazilian Context. *Sustainability*, *12*(10), 3947. https://doi.org/10.3390/su12103947

Rehman, S., Kraus, S., Shah, S., Khanin, D., & Mahto, R. (2021). Analyzing the relationship between green innovation and environmental performance in large manufacturing firms. *Technological Forecasting and Social Change*, *163*, 120481. doi:10.1016/j.techfore.2020.120481

Reid, A., & Miedzinski, M. (2008). *Eco-innovation: final report for sectoral innovation watch.* Technopolis Group.

Ren, L., Li, J., Li, C., & Dang, P. (2021). Can ecotourism contribute to ecosystem? Evidence from local residents' ecological behaviors. *The Science of the Total Environment*, *757*, 143814. doi:10.1016/j.scitotenv.2020.143814 PMID:33248787

Resico, M. (2011). *Introducción a la Economía de Mercado* [Introduction to the Market Economy]. Konrad Adanauer Stifung.

Rettie, R., Burchell, K., & Barnham, C. (2014). Social normalisation: Using marketing to make green normal. *Journal of Consumer Behaviour*, *13*(1), 9–17. doi:10.1002/cb.1439

Rettie, R., Burchell, K., & Riley, D. (2012). Normalising green behaviours: A new approach to sustainability marketing. *Journal of Marketing Management*, *28*(3-4), 420–444. doi:10.1080/0267257X.2012.658840

Rex, E., & Baumann, H. (2007). Beyond ecolabels: What green marketing can learn from conventional marketing. *Journal of Cleaner Production*, *15*(6), 567–576. doi:10.1016/j.jclepro.2006.05.013

Rhou, Y., & Singal, M. (2020). A review of the business case for CSR in the hospitality industry. *International Journal of Hospitality Management*, *84*, 102330. doi:10.1016/j.ijhm.2019.102330

Riskos, K., Paraskevi, D., Mylonas, N., & Tsourvakas, G. (2021). Ecolabels and the attitude-behavior relationship towards green product purchase: A multiple mediation model. *Sustainability*, *13*(12), 6867. doi:10.3390u13126867

Roberts, J. A. (1996). Green consumers in the 1990's: Profile and implications for advertising. *Journal of Business Research*, *36*(3), 217–231. doi:10.1016/0148-2963(95)00150-6

Roberts, J. A., & Bacon, D. R. (1997). Exploring the subtle relationships between environmental concern and ecologically conscious consumer behavior. *Journal of Business Research*, *40*(1), 79–89. doi:10.1016/S0148-2963(96)00280-9

Robinson, D. (2022). *Twelve biggest environmental problems of 2022.* Retrieved April 27, 2022, from https://earth.org/the-biggest-environmental-problems-of-our-lifetime/

Roden, J. (2021). Exploring the Perceived Health, Community, and Employment Impacts of an Announced Closure of a Coal-Fired Power Station in Upper Hunter Valley, Australia. *Journal of Environmental Health*, *83*(7), 26–35.

Rojas, C. (2015). Tipos de Investigación científica: Una simplificación de la complicada incoherente nomenclatura y clasificación [Scientific Research Types: A Simplification of Complicated Incoherent Nomenclature and Classification]. *Redvet*, *16*, 6–9.

Romero, C. B. A., Golam, M. L., Aurup, M., & Ferraz, S. B. (2018). Ethnicity and acculturation of environmental attitudes and behaviors: A cross-cultural study with Brazilians in Canada. *Journal of Business Research*, *82*, 300–309. doi:10.1016/j.jbusres.2017.09.009

Rotondaro, R. G. (2002). SFMEA: Analysis of the effect and mode of failure in services – applying prevention techniques to improve services. *Production*, *12*(2), 54–62. https://doi.org/10.1590/S0103-65132002000200006

Royal Government of Bhutan. (2012). *The Report of the High-Level Meeting on Wellbeing and Happiness: Defining a New Economic Paradigm*. New York: The Permanent Mission of the Kingdom of Bhutan to the United Nations. https://sustainabledevelopment.un.org/content/documents/617BhutanReport_WEB_F.pdf

Ruíz, C., René, P., Fernández, G., Luz del Carmen, Lecuona, M., & Gómez, N. (2015). Elementos para el debate e interpretación del Buen Vivir/Sumak Kawsay [Elements for the debate and interpretation of Good Living/Sumak Kawsay]. *Contribuciones desde Coatepec*, 6-7.

Russo, J. E., & Schoemaker, P. J. H. (1990). Decision Traps. The Ten barriers To Brilliant Decision-Making and how to Overcome Them. New York: Fireside Ed.

Santos, C. M. da C., Pimenta, C. A. de M., & Nobre, M. R. C. (2007). The PICO strategy for the research question construction and evidence search. *Revista Latino-Americana de Enfermagem*, *15*(3), 508–511. https://doi.org/10.1590/S0104-11692007000300023

Sarkar, S., & Searcy, C. (2016). Zeitgeist or chameleon? A quantitative analysis of CSR definitions. *Journal of Cleaner Production*, *135*, 1423–1435. doi:10.1016/j.jclepro.2016.06.157

Schiederig, T., Tietze, F., & Herstatt, C. (2012). Green innovation in technology and innovation management–an exploratory literature review. *R & D Management*, *42*(2), 180–192. doi:10.1111/j.1467-9310.2011.00672.x

Scott, W. R. (2005). Institutional theory: Contributing to a theoretical research program. *Great Minds in Management: The Process of Theory Development*, *37*(2), 460–484.

SDG Progress Report. (2022). *Advanced Unedited Version. Progress towards the Sustainable Development Goal: Report of the Secretary-General*. https://digitallibrary.un.org/record/1627573. https://digitallibrary.un.org/record/3930067

Secretariat of Hydrocarbons. (2022). *Mapa de bloques petroleros* [Oil block map]. Retrieved from http://www.historico.secretariahidrocarburos.gob.ec/mapa-de-bloques-petroleros/

Selau, C. C. (2018). Gestão E Gerenciamento De Resíduos Sólidos No Município de Criciúma/Sc [Solid Waste Management in the Municipality of Criciúma/Sc. Academic Press.

Selekman, B. (1959). *A moral philosophy for management*. McGraw-Hill.

Senge, P. (1990). *The fifth discipline*. Doubleday.

Sethi, S. (1975). Dimensions of corporate social performance: An analytical framework. *California Management Review*, *17*(3), 58–64. doi:10.2307/41162149

Shaffer, R. M., Sellers, S. P., Baker, M. G., de Buen Kalman, R., Frostad, J., Suter, M. K., Anenberg, S. C., Balbus, J., Basu, N., Bellinger, D. C., Birnbaum, L., Brauer, M., Cohen, A., Ebi, K. L., Fuller, R., Grandjean, P., Hess, J. J., Kogevinas, M., Kumar, P., … Hu, H. (2019). Improving and Expanding Estimates of the Global Burden of Disease Due to Environmental Health Risk Factors. *Environmental Health Perspectives, 127*(10), 105001. doi:10.1289/EHP5496

Shao, J. (2019). Sustainable consumption in China: New trends and research interests. *Business Strategy and the Environment*, *28*(8), 1507–1517. doi:10.1002/bse.2327

Sharma, A. P. (2021). Consumers' purchase behavior and green marketing: A synthesis, review, and agenda. *International Journal of Consumer Studies*, *45*(6), 1217–1238. doi:10.1111/ijcs.12722

Sheehy, B. (2015). Defining CSR: Problems and solutions. *Journal of Business Ethics*, *131*(3), 625–648. doi:10.100710551-014-2281-x

Shell, M. (1993). *The economy of literature*. JHU Press.

Shi, J., & Shen, G. (2002). On the classification criteria between institutional change theory and institutional change mode. *Economist*, 41–46.

Shi, K. (2006). *China's ten five-year plans*. Macroeconomic Management. doi:10.19709/j.cnki.11-3199/f.2006.12.023

Shim, D., Shin, J., & Kwak, S.-Y. (2018). Modelling the consumer decision-making process to identify key drivers and bottlenecks in the adoption of environmentally friendly products. *Business Strategy and the Environment*, *27*(8), 1409–1421. doi:10.1002/bse.2192

Shi, Y., & Liu, X. (2019). Research on the literature of Green Building based on The web of science: A scientometric analysis in CITESPACE (2002–2018). *Sustainability*, *11*(13), 3716. doi:10.3390u11133716

Silva Portero, C. (2008). *Qué es el buen vivir en la Constitución? Constitución del 2008 en el contexto andino: análisis de la doctrina y el derecho comparado* [What is good living in the Constitution? Constitution of 2008 in the Andean context: analysis of the doctrine and comparative law] (R. Á. Santamaría, Ed.). Ministerio de Justicia y Derechos Humanos.

Simon, H. A. (1957). *Models of man, social and rational*. Wiley.

Singh, S., Del Giudice, M., Chierici, R., & Graziano, D. (2020). Green innovation and environmental performance: The role of green transformational leadership and green human resource management. *Technological Forecasting and Social Change*, *150*, 119762. doi:10.1016/j.techfore.2019.119762

Smith, N. (2001). Changes in corporate practices in response to public interest advocacy and actions. Handbook of Marketing and Society.

Smith, N. (2003). Corporate social responsibility: Whether or how? *California Management Review*, *45*(4), 52–76. doi:10.2307/41166188

Song, W., Li, G., & Yang, Y.-L. (2018). Analysis of residents' willingness to accept compensation of ecological protection and its influencing factors——Based on the research data of 660 households in Shaanxi National Nature Reserve. *Ganhanqu Ziyuan Yu Huanjing*, 63–69. doi:10.13448/j.cnki.jalre.2018.074

Stafford, E., Polonsky, M., & Hartman, C. (2000). Environmental NGO-business collaboration and strategicbridging: A case analysis of the Greenpeace-Foronalliance. *Business Strategy and the Environment*, *9*(2), 122–135. doi:10.1002/(SICI)1099-0836(200003/04)9:2<122::AID-BSE232>3.0.CO;2-C

Starik, M., & Kanashiro, P. (2013). Toward a theory of sustainability management: Uncovering and integrating the nearly obvious. *Organization & Environment*, *26*(1), 7–30. doi:10.1177/1086026612474958

Sterman, J. (2000). *Business dynamics: Systems thinking and modeling for a complex world*. Irwin McGraw-Hill.

Stratford, B. (2020). The threat of rent extraction in a resource-constrained future. *Ecological Economics*, *169*, 106524. doi:10.1016/j.ecolecon.2019.106524

Stumpf, A. M., Erlandson, G., Ruths, J., Meinke, D. K., Newman, L. S., Krisher, L., Pilloni, D., Cruz, A., & Asensio, C. (2020). Noise exposures of sugar cane mill workers in Guatemala. *International Journal of Audiology*, *59*(Suplemento), S48–S53.

Sugiyama, M., Asayama, S., Kosugi, T., Ishii, A., Emori, S., Adachi, J., Akimoto, K., Fujiwara, M., Hasegawa, T., Hibi, Y., Hirata, K., Ishii, T., Kaburagi, T., Kita, Y., Kobayashi, S., Kurosawa, A., Kuwata, M., Masuda, K., Mitsui, M., … Yoshizawa, G. (2017). Transdisciplinary co-design of scientific research agendas: 40 research questions for socially relevant climate engineering research. *Sustainability Science, 12*(1), 31–44. doi:10.1007/s11625-016-0376-2

Sun, H., Edziah, B., Sun, C., & Kporsu, A. (2019). Institutional quality, green innovation and energy efficiency. *Energy Policy, 135*, 111002. doi:10.1016/j.enpol.2019.111002

Sun, M., Li, X., Yang, R., Zhang, Y., Zhang, L., Song, Z., Liu, Q., & Zhao, D. (2020). Comprehensive partitions and different strategies based on ecological security and economic development in Guizhou Province, China. *Journal of Cleaner Production, 274*, 122794. https://doi.org/10.1016/j.jclepro.2020.122794

Sunyer & Dadvand. (2021). Environment and the COVID-19 pandemic. *Environmental Research, 195*(1). doi:10.1016/j.envres.2021.110819

Sustainable Development Solutions Network (SDSN). (n.d.). *A Global Imitative for the United Nations (UN).* https://www.unsdsn.org/

Sustainable Development Solutions Network (SDSN). A Global Imitative for the United Nations (UN). (n.d.). *The 2022 Sustainable Development Report (SDR): From Crisis to Sustainable Development, the SDGs as Roadmap to 2030 and Beyond.* https://www.sdgindex.org/reports/sustainable-development-report-2022/

Swanson, D. (1995). Addressing a theoretical problem by reorienting the corporate social performance model. *Academy of Management Review, 20*(1), 43–64. doi:10.2307/258886

Takalo, S., & Tooranloo, H. (2021). Green innovation: A systematic literature review. *Journal of Cleaner Production, 279*, 122474. doi:10.1016/j.jclepro.2020.122474

Taleb, N. (2010). *The black swan. The impact of the highly improbable.* Penguin Books.

Tang, K., Qiu, Y., & Zhou, D. (2020). Does command-and-control regulation promote green innovation performance? Evidence from China's industrial enterprises. *The Science of the Total Environment, 712*, 136362. doi:10.1016/j.scitotenv.2019.136362 PMID:31935549

Tanimoto, K. (2011). The process of social innovation: multi-stakeholders perspective. In D. Chauvel (Ed.), *Leading Issues in Innovation Research* (pp. 172–186). Academic Publishing International Ltd.

Tapies, J., & Toninato, F. (2005). Milking Money out of Parmalat. IESE Business School Case Study IES119-PDF-ENG.

Tariq, M. A. U. R., Wangchuk, K., & Muttil, N. (2021). A Critical Review of Water Resources and Their Management in Bhutan. *Hydrology, 8*(1), 31. https://doi.org/10.3390/hydrology8010031

Taylor, B. M., & Harman, B. P. (2016). Governing urban development for climate risk: What role for public-private partnerships? *Environment and Planning. C, Government & Policy, 34*(5), 927–944. https://doi.org/10.1177/0263774X15614692

Testa, F., Pretner, G., Iovino, R., Bianchi, G., Tessitore, S., & Iraldo, F. (2021). Drivers to green consumption: A systematic review. *Environment, Development and Sustainability, 23*(4), 4826–4880. doi:10.100710668-020-00844-5

Tetteh, M. O., Chan, A. P. C., Darko, A., Yevu, S. K., Boateng, E. B., & Nwaogu, J. M. (2021). Key drivers for implementing international construction joint ventures (ICJVs): Global insights for sustainable growth. *Engineering, Construction and Architectural Management.* doi:10.1108/ECAM-07-2020-0512

Tezer, A., & Bodur, O. (2020). The green consumption effect: How using green products improves consumption experience. *The Journal of Consumer Research, 47*(1), 25–39. doi:10.1093/jcr/ucz045

The International Ecotourism Society. (n.d.). *What is ecotourism*. Retrieved from https://ecotourism.org/what-is-ecotourism/

The National People's Congress, the People´s Republic of China. (2016). *Outline of the 13th Five-Year Plan for the National Economic and Social Development of the People's Republic of China*. Author.

The State Council. the People's Republic of China. (1993). Circular on the Outline of Regional Planning for Some Provinces and Regions in Southwest and Southern China. Author.

The State Environmental Protection Administration. the People's Republic of China. (2002). Notice on Printing and Distributing the Tenth Five-Year Plan for National Ecological Environmental Protection. Author.

Themelis, N. J., Barriga, M. E. D., Estevez, P., & Valesco, M. G. (2016). *Guia Para Recuperar Energia E Materiais (Rem) de Resíduos Sólidos* [Guide to Recovering Energy and Materials (Rem) from Solid Waste]. Vitória: Wtert-brasil. Available in: http://www.wtert.com.br

Tranfield, D., Denyer, D., & Smart, P. (2003). Towards a methodology for developing evidence-informed management knowledge by means of systematic review. *British Journal of Management*, *14*(3), 207–222. doi:10.1111/1467-8551.00375

Trapp, N. (2012). Corporation as climate ambassador: Transcending business sector boundaries in a Swedish CSR campaign. *Public Relations Review*, *38*(3), 458–465. doi:10.1016/j.pubrev.2012.03.004

Tseng, S. (2016). The effect of knowledge management capability and customer knowledge gaps on corporate performance. *Journal of Enterprise Information Management*, *29*(1), 51–71. doi:10.1108/JEIM-03-2015-0021

TUDOKSAD. (2020). *Covid - 19 Pandemisinin Türk Döküm Sektöründe Çalışma Hayatına Etkileri* [Effects of the Covid - 19 Pandemic on Working Life in Turkish Foundry Industry]. https://tudoksad.org.tr/upload/files/T%C3%BCrkd%C3%B6k%C3%BCm_56-s%C4%B1k%C4%B1%C5%9Ft%C4%B1r%C4%B1ld%C4%B1%20%281%29.pdf

TUDOKSAD. (2020). *Türkiye Döküm Sektörü* [Foundry Sector in Turkey]. https://tudoksad.org.tr/turkiye-dokum-sektoru

TUDOKSAD. (2020). *Türkiye Dünya Döküm Üretiminde 9. Avrupa'da İse 2. Sıraya Çıktı* [Turkey Ranks 9th in Casting Production in the World and 2nd in Europe]. https://tudoksad.org.tr/turkiye-dunya-dokum-uretiminde-9-avrupa-da-ise-2-siraya-cikti

Tukker, A., & Jansen, B. (2006). Environmental impacts of products - a detailed review of studies. *Journal of Industrial Ecology*, *10*(3), 159–182. doi:10.1162/jiec.2006.10.3.159

Uccelli, R., Mastrantonio, M., Altavista, P., Caiaffa, E., Cattani, G., Belli, S., & Comba, P. (2016). Female lung cancer mortality and long-term exposure to particulate matter in Italy. *The European Journal of Public Health*. doi:10.1093/eurpub/ckw203

UN (United Nations). (2022). *Population*. Retrieved June 15, 2022, from https://www.un.org/en/ global-issues/population

UNDESA. (2020). Inequality in a Rapidly Changing World. In *World Social Report 2020*. https://www.un.org/development/desa/dspd/wp-content/uploads/sites/22/2020/02/World-Social-Report2020-FullReport.pdf

UNDP (United Nations Development Program). (2022a). *Sustainable development goals*. Retrieved May 26, 2022, from https://www.undp.org/sustainable-development-goals

UNDP (United Nations Development Program). (2022b). *Sustainable development goals*. Retrieved May 26, 2022, from https://www.undp.org/sustainable-development-goals#responsible-consumption-and-production

UNEP (United Nations Environment Program). (2017). *Consuming differently, consuming sustainably: Behavioral insights for policymaking*. Retrieved May 26, 2022 from, https://sustainabledevelopment. un.org/content/documents/2404Behavioral%20Insights.pdf

UNFPA (United Nations Population Fund). (2022). *World population*. Retrieved June 15, 2022, from https://www.unfpa.org/ data/world-population-dashboard

United Nations (UN). (2015). *What are the Sustainable Development Goals?* https://www.undp.org/sustainable-development-goals

United Nations (UN). (2021). *The Sustainable Development Goals Report 2021*. https://unstats.un.org/sdgs/report/2021/The-Sustainable-Development-Goals-Report-2021.pdf

United Nations (UN). (2022). *Department of Economic and Social Affairs. Sustainable Development. The 2030 Agenda for Sustainable Development. Transforming our world: the 2030 Agenda for Sustainable Development*. https://sdgs.un.org/goals

United Nations (UN). (2022). *SDG-contracts – EU budget support to partner countries to meet their financing needs*. European Commission (Intergovernmental organization). https://sdgs.un.org/partnerships/sdg-contracts-eu-budget-support-partner-countries-meet-their-financing-needs

United Nations (UN). (2022a). *Goal 7: Affordable and Clean Energy*. https://www.jointsdgfund.org/sustainable-development-goals/goal-7-affordable-and-clean-energy

United Nations (UN). (2022b). *Meetings Coverage and Press Releases. Secretary-General Warns of Climate Emergency, Calling Intergovernmental Panel's Report 'a File of Shame', While Saying Leaders 'Are Lying', Fuelling Flames. The 4th of April 2022*. Author.

United Nations (UN). (2022c). *Secretary-General. Secretary-General's video message to the Press Conference Launch of IPCC Report*. https://www.un.org/sg/en/content/sg/statement/2022-02-28/secretary-generals-video-message-the-press-conference-launch-of-ipcc-report-scroll-down-for-languages

United Nations (UN). (2022d). *Department of Economic and Social Affairs. Sustainable Development (SD). Make The SDGs A Reality*. https://sdgs.un.org/

United Nations Development Program (UNDP). (2022). *Sustainable Development Goals (SDGs). The SDGs in action. What are the Sustainable Development Goals?* https://www.undp.org/sustainable-development-goals

United Nations Economic Commission for Europe (UNECE). (2022). *Halfway to 2030: UNECE report shows we must accelerate progress to achieve SDGs in the region*. https://unece.org/media/press/366086

United Nations. (1987). *Report of the World Commission on Environment and Development: Our common future*. http://www.un-documents.net/our-common-future.pdf

United Nations. (1990). *Human Development Report 1990*. https://hdr.undp.org/sites/default/files/reports/219/hdr_1990_en_complete_nostats.pdf

United Nations. (2015a). *Paris agreement*. https://unfccc.int/sites/default/files/english_paris_agreement.pdf

United Nations. (2015b). *Transforming our world: The 2030 Agenda for Sustainable Development*. https://sdgs.un.org/2030agenda

United Nations. (2020). *The next frontier. Human development and the Anthropocene*. https://hdr.undp.org/sites/default/files/hdr2020.pdf

United Nations. (2021). *Glasgow Climate Pact*. https://unfccc.int/sites/default/files/resource/cop26_auv_2f_cover_decision.pdf

Universidad de San Martín de Porres. (2017). *Manual de Introducción a la Economía* [Manual of Introduction to Economics]. Author.

Universidade de Leiden. (2022). *VOSviewer—Visualizing scientific landscapes* (1.6.15) [Computer software]. https://www.vosviewer.com/

Valerdi, R., & Rouse, W. B. (2010). When systems thinking is not a natural act. *IEEE International Systems Conference*, 184-189.

Valero, A., & Figueroa, E. T. (2011). La empresa de negocios y la alta dirección: Procedimientos políticos de gobierno (3rd ed.). Pamplona: Eunsa.

Valero, A., & Lucas, J. L. (2018). Business Policy. Sevilla: San Telmo Eds.

Van Marrewijk, M. (2003). Concepts and definitions of CSR and corporate sustainability: Between agency and communion. *Journal of Business Ethics*, *44*(2), 95–105. doi:10.1023/A:1023331212247

Velte, P. (2021). Meta-analyses on corporate social responsibility (CSR): a literature review. *Management Review Quarterly*, 1-49.

Verona, G. (1999). A resource-based view of product development. *Academy of Management Review*, *24*(1), 132–142. doi:10.5465/amr.1999.1580445

Votaw, D. (1973). Genius becomes rare: A comment on the doctrine of social responsibility Pt. II. *California Management Review*, *15*(3), 5–19. doi:10.2307/41164435

Waldamn & Dalpia. (2017). *A Universidade e a construção da interdisciplinaridade. Ensino, pesquisa e inovação: Desenvolvendo a interdisciplinaridade*. Editora Manole.

Waldman, D., Luque, M., Washburn, N., & House, R. (2006). Cultural and leadership predictors of corporate social responsibility values of top management: A GLOBE study of 15 countries. *Journal of International Business Studies*, *37*(6), 823–837. doi:10.1057/palgrave.jibs.8400230

Walton, C. (1967). *Corporate social responsibilities*. Wadsworth Publishing Company.

Wang, Z., & Wang, L. (2007). North's Theory of Institutional Change and Its Implications for Chinese Reform. *Forward Position*, 45–47.

Wang, C., & Juo, W. (2021). An environmental policy of green intellectual capital: Green innovation strategy for performance sustainability. *Business Strategy and the Environment*, *30*(7), 1–14. doi:10.1002/bse.2800

Wang, G., Li, Y., Zuo, J., Hu, W., Nie, Q., & Lei, H. (2021). Who drives green innovations? Characteristics and policy implications for green building collaborative innovation networks in China. *Renewable & Sustainable Energy Reviews*, *143*, 110875. doi:10.1016/j.rser.2021.110875

Wang, K.-L., Zhao, B., Ding, L.-L., & Miao, Z. (2021). Government intervention, market development, and pollution emission efficiency: Evidence from China. *The Science of the Total Environment*, *757*, 143738. doi:10.1016/j.scitotenv.2020.143738 PMID:33223188

Wang, L., Zhong, L., Zhang, Y., & Zhou, B. (2014). Ecotourism Environmental Protection measures and their effects on protected areas in China. *Sustainability*, *6*(10), 6781–6798. doi:10.3390u6106781

Wang, S., & Ouyang, Z. (2007). The Rural-urban Income Disparity and Its Effects to Economic Growth in the Case of China. *Economic Research Journal*, 44–55.

Wankel, C. (2008). *21st century management: A reference handbook*. SAGE Publications. doi:10.4135/9781412954006

WBCSD (World Business Council for Sustainable Development). (2015). *Sustainable consumption facts and trends-from a business perspective*. Retrieved January 5, 2017, from http://www.wbcsd.org/ Clusters/Sustainable-Lifestyles/Resources/Sustainable-Consumption-Fact-and-Trends-From-a-Business-Perspective

Wee, B. V., & Banister, D. (2016). How to write a literature review paper? *Transport Reviews*, *36*(2), 278–288. doi:10.1080/01441647.2015.1065456

Weng, H., Chen, J., & Chen, P. (2015). Effects of green innovation on environmental and corporate performance: A stakeholder perspective. *Sustainability*, *7*(5), 4997–5026. doi:10.3390u7054997

Wernerfelt, B. (1984). A resource-based view of the firm. *Strategic Management Journal*, *5*(2), 171–180. doi:10.1002mj.4250050207

Wernerfelt, B. (1988). Umbrella branding as a signal of new product quality: An example of signalling by posting a bond. *The RAND Journal of Economics*, *19*(3), 458–466. doi:10.2307/2555667

Werther, W. Jr, & Chandler, D. (2005). Strategic corporate social responsibility as global brand insurance. *Business Horizons*, *48*(4), 317–324. doi:10.1016/j.bushor.2004.11.009

White, K., Habib, R., & Hardisty, D. J. (2019). How to SHIFT consumer behaviors to be more sustainable: A literature review and guiding framework. *Journal of Marketing*, *83*(3), 22–49. doi:10.1177/0022242919825649

Whyte, J. (2019). *The morals of the market: Human rights and the rise of neoliberalism*. Verso Books.

Wijekoon, R., & Sabri, M. F. (2021). Determinants that influence green product purchase intention and behavior: A literature review and guiding framework. *Sustainability*, *13*(11), 6219. doi:10.3390u13116219

Winegarden, C. R., & Khor, L. B. (1991). Undocumented Immigration and Unemployment of U.S. Youth and Minority Workers: Econometric Evidence. *The Review of Economics and Statistics*, *73*(1), 105–112. doi:10.2307/2109692

Wolhuter, S. (2021). *How VR is transforming customer experience*. Retrieved February 7, 2022, from https://wearebrain.com

Wong, S. (2013). Environmental requirements, knowledge sharing and green innovation: Empirical evidence from the electronics industry in China. *Business Strategy and the Environment*, *22*(5), 321–338. doi:10.1002/bse.1746

Woo, C., Chung, Y., Chun, D., Han, S., & Lee, D. (2014). Impact of green innovation on labor productivity and its determinants: An analysis of the Korean manufacturing industry. *Business Strategy and the Environment*, *23*(8), 567–576. doi:10.1002/bse.1807

World Bank (WB). (2021). *Vietnam COVID-19 High Frequency Phone Survey of Households (HFPS-R4) 2021, Round 4*. Ref. VNM_2021_HFPS_v01_M. www.microdata.worldbank.org

World Business Council for Sustainable Development. (2022). *Achieving the Sustainable Development Goals can unlock trillions in new market value*. https://www.wbcsd.org/Overview/News-Insights/General/News/Achieving-the-Sustainable-Development-Goals-can-unlock-trillions-in-new-market-value

World Economic Forum (WEF). (2019). *Sustainable Development Impact Summit. Article on Sustainable Development entitled "We need an economic model that works for people and the planet"*. https://www.weforum.org/agenda/2019/09/how-to-make-markets-more-sustainable/

World Economic Forum. (2021). *The Davos Agenda*. https://www.weforum.org/events/the-davos-agenda-2021

World Health Organization (WHO). (2022a). *Coronavirus Disease (COVID-19). Overview*. https://www.who.int/health-topics/coronavirus#tab=tab_1

World Health Organization (WHO). (2022b). *Coronavirus disease (COVID-19): Vaccines*. https://www.who.int/news-room/questions-and-answers/item/coronavirus-disease-(COVID-19)-vaccines

World Tourism Organization. (n.d.). *Ecotourism and Protected Areas*. Retrieved from https://www.unwto.org/sustainable-development/ecotourism-and-protected-areas

Worley, J. M., & Doolen, T. L. (2006). The role of communication and management support in a lean manufacturing implementation. *Management Decision*, *44*(2), 228–245. doi:10.1108/00251740610650210

Wymer, W., & Polonsky, M. J. (2015). The limitations and potentialities of green marketing. *Journal of Nonprofit & Public Sector Marketing*, *27*(3), 239–262. doi:10.1080/10495142.2015.1053341

Xi, J. (2017, October 10). *Xi Jinping: Decisive Victory to Build a Well-off Society in an All-round Way and Win the Great Victory of Socialism with Chinese Characteristics in the New Era* [Poster presentation]. The 19th National Congress of the Communist Party of China, Beijing, China.

Xia, X., Wang, Z., Xu, W., Zhang, H., Zhou, D., & Jiang, M. (2016). Problems in Construction of Management System of Nature Reserves in China and Countermeasures. *Journal of Ecology and Rural Environment*, 30–34.

Xiao, F., Li, C., Sun, J., & Zhang, L. (2017). Knowledge domain and emerging trends in Organic Photovoltaic Technology: A Scientometric Review based on CITESPACE analysis. *Frontiers in Chemistry*, *5*, 67. Advance online publication. doi:10.3389/fchem.2017.00067 PMID:28966923

Xiao, L., & Zhong, L. (2017). Quantitative study on the evolution of Ecotourism Policy Development in China. *Journal of Resources and Ecology*, *8*(5), 460–469. doi:10.5814/j.issn.1674-764x.2017.05.003

Xie, X., Huo, J., & Zou, H. (2019). Green process innovation, green product innovation, and corporate financial performance: A content analysis method. *Journal of Business Research*, *101*, 697–706. doi:10.1016/j.jbusres.2019.01.010

Xinhua News Agency. (2015). *Opinions of the State Council of the People's Republic of China on Accelerating the Construction of Ecological Civilization*. The State Council. Retrieved from http://www.gov.cn/gongbao/content/2015/content_2864050.htm

Xinhua News Agency. (2018). *The Institutional Reform Program of the State Council*. The State Council of the People's Republic of China. Retrieved from http://www.gov.cn/xinwen/2018-03/17/content_5275116.htm

Xu, W., Gao, J., Xia, X., Zhou, D., Li, Z., & Jiang, M. (2016). Distribution of Community Residents in Nature Reserves and Its Impacts on the Reserves in China. *Journal of Ecology and Rural Environment*, 19–23.

Xue, B., Zhang, Z., & Li, P. (2020). Desempenho ambiental corporativo, gestão ambiental e risco firme. Estratégia Empresarial e Meio Ambiente, 29(3), 1074-1096. doi:10.1002/bse.2418

Xu, S., Mingzhu, L., Bu, N., & Pan, S. (2017). Regulatory frameworks for ecotourism: An application of total relationship flow management theorems. *Tourism Management*, *61*, 321–330. doi:10.1016/j.tourman.2017.02.012

Yan, Y., Hu, A., & Wang, S. (2012). The evolution of the Chinese government's decision-making model: taking the five-year plan as an example. *National Report*.

Yang, F., Yang, M., & Xu, J. (2018). The Productivity Dynamics of China's Environmentally Friendly Production Technologies in terms of Wastewater Treatment Techniques. *BioMed Research International, 2018*, 1–10. https://doi.org/10.1155/2018/6878741

Yan, L., Keh, H. T., & Wang, X. (2021). Powering sustainable consumption: The roles of green consumption values and power distance belief. *Journal of Business Ethics, 169*(3), 499–516. doi:10.100710551-019-04295-5

Yoon-Na, C., Thyroff, A., Rapert, M. I., Park, S.-Y., & Lee, H. J. (2013). To be or not to be green: Exploring individualism and collectivism as antecedents of environmental behavior. *Journal of Business Research, 66*(8), 1052–1059. doi:10.1016/j.jbusres.2012.08.020

Zhang, H., Qin, W., Zhou, D., Fan, L., Li, Z., & Jiang, M. (2016). Status Quo of Ecological Tourism in Nature Reserves in China. *Journal of Ecology and Rural Environment*, 24–29.

Zhang, P., Wu, X., Needs, S., Liu, D., Fuentes, S., & Howell, K. (2016). The influence of apical and basal defoliation on the canopy structure and biochemical composition of Vitis vinifera cv. Shiraz grapes and wine. *Frontiers in Chemistry, 5*, 48. doi:10.3389/fchem.2017.00048 PMID:28736728

Zhang, T., Wu, Q., & Zhang, Z. (2020). Probable Pangolin Origin of SARS-CoV-2 Associated with the COVID-19 Outbreak. *Current Biology, 30*(7), 1346–1351. doi:10.1016/j.cub.2020.03.022 PMID:32197085

Zhang, X., & Wang, Z. (2019). How Does Paired Assistance to Disaster-Affected Areas (PADAA) Contribute to Economic Sustainability? A Qualitative Analysis of Wenchuan County. *Sustainability, 11*(14), 3915. https://doi.org/10.3390/su11143915

Zhao, Y., & Jiao, L. (2019). Resources development and tourism environmental carrying capacity of ecotourism industry in Pingdingshan City, China. *Ecological Processes, 8*(1), 7. Advance online publication. doi:10.118613717-019-0161-0

Zhou, Y., Buesching, C. D., Newman, C., Kaneko, Y., Xie, Z., & Macdonald, D. W. (2013). Balancing the benefits of ecotourism and development: The effects of visitor trail-use on mammals in a protected area in rapidly developing China. *Biological Conservation, 165*, 18–24. doi:10.1016/j.biocon.2013.05.007

Ziegler, J. (2013). Destrucción Masiva: Geopolítica del hambre [Mass Destruction: Geopolitics of Hunger]. Barcelona: Booket (Península).

Zucker, L. (1977). The role of institutionalization in cultural persistence. *American Sociological Review, 42*(5), 726–743. doi:10.2307/2094862

Zulfiqar, K., & Akhtar, S. (2016). *Youth Unemployment and Immigration : A Case Study of Ontario, Canada.* doi:10.3968/8413

About the Contributors

Cristina Raluca Gh. Popescu is Full-Professor Habil. at the University of Bucharest, Bucharest, Romania and PhD. Supervisor and Doctoral School Member at The Bucharest University of Economic Studies, Bucharest, Romania. Having more than 21 years of experience, focuses on helping students learn and apply the subjects more effectively, and centers on improving scientific research excellence. Values a special environment where her in-depth knowledge of creative thinking and academic writing can help deliver accurate research results. She is skilled in Business Administration, Economics, Management, Accounting, and Audit. Collaborations: The National Institute for Research and Development in Environmental Protection (I.N.C.D.P.M.), Romania; National Research and Development Institute for Gas Turbines COMOTI, Romania; University of Craiova, Romania; Ministry of Research and Innovation, Romania. She is Member of Chamber of Financial Auditors of Romania (CAFR), Romania as Financial Auditor, and Member of Authority for the Public Oversight of the Statutory Audit Activity (ASPAAS), Ministry of Public Finance, Romania as Financial auditor. Single author and coauthor of more than 289 scientific works, with national and international publishers, having national and international coauthors: books, book chapters, articles, conference papers. She has more than 1047 citations in national and international publications. Member of Scientific Committee (SC): International Congress of Management, Economy and Policy (ICOMEP), Turkey; Symposium on Migration and Asylum in Turkey, Tekirdağ Namık Kemal Üniversitesi (Tekirdag Namık Kemal University), Turkey; International Congress "Multidimensional Sustainability: Transitions and Convergences", Instituto Superior Politécnico Gaya (ISPGAYA), Portugal. Editor and Editorial Advisory Board (EAB) member: IGI Global – Publishing House (Pennsylvania, USA). Guest Editor and Academic Editor for Multidisciplinary Digital Publishing Institute (MDPI, Basel, Switzerland): Mathematics, Journal of Risk and Financial Management (JRFM), Businesses. Topic Editor for Multidisciplinary Digital Publishing Institute (MDPI, Basel, Switzerland): Mathematics, Businesses. Associate Editor for The International Academy of Organizational Behavior Management (IAOBM): International Journal of the Academy of Organizational Behavior Management (IJAOBM); The International Journal of Management Science and Information Technology (IJMSIT). Editorial Advisory Board (EAB) Member for North American Institute of Science and Information Technology (NAISIT) (The International Journal of Management Science and Information Technology (IJMSIT)); Journal of Emerging Economies and Policy (JOEEP). Review Board member: IBIMA Conferences and IBIMA Publishing, USA (Journal of E-Government Studies and Best Practices, The MENA Journal of Business Case Studies); International Conference on Decision Making for Small and Medium-Sized Enterprises (DEMSME 2021); IGI Global – Publishing House (Pennsylvania, USA); University of Bucharest (International Journal of Health Economics (IJHE)); Multidisciplinary Digital Publishing Institute (MDPI, Basel, Switzerland) (Sustainability, Symmetry, Journal of Risk and Financial Management (JRFM), Mathematics, Economies, Risks, Journal of Open Innovation: Technology, Market, and Complexity (JOItmC), Journal of Administrative Sciences, World, Informatics, Water, Agriculture, Businesses, Microorganisms, Energies, Agronomy, Urban Science, Businesses). Invited reviewer: Management Decision (MD), Sustainable Development (SD), Corporate Social Responsibility & Environmental Management (CSREM), Journal of Business Economics and Management (JBEM), Engineering Economics (Inzinerine Ekonomika), International Journal of Sustainable Development and Planning (IJSDP), Transformations in Business & Economics (TIBE), Open Research Europe (ORE), Coffee Science (CS).

* * *

Pedro B. Água is a Professor of General Management at the Portuguese Naval Academy. He has authored several articles and book chapters, while continuing his research in the field of cutting-edge technology, industrialization, innovation and business policy. Professor Água has over twenty-five years of experience across high technology endeavours, from defence to telecommunications and oil and gas industry, combining his extensive professional and business background with teaching. Professor Água holds an MBA from IESE Business School and a Ph.D. in Management and Engineering awarded by the University of Lisbon.

Wenderson Alvarenga is a PhD student in Sustainable Management Systems at Universidade Federal Fluminense (UFF), Master in Management System at Universidade Federal Fluminense (UFF), graduated in Production Engineering at Universidade Católica de Petrópolis (UCP) and graduated in Oil and Gas Technology by the Capixaba College of Nova Venécia (UNIVEN). He has experience in administrative management, sales, costs, production, and process improvement. He currently holds a leadership position in the packaging industry, implementing industrial projects and process improvement.

F. Gül Aygen-Ispahi is an independent researcher. She worked at Istanbul Bilgi University as an assistant professor of marketing from 1998 to 2000. She later worked at Telsim (former Vodafone), a mobile telecommunications company, as a marketing researcher for three and a half years. In 2003, she began working at Doğuş University, Istanbul, Turkey, both as the Dean of Students and an assistant professor, till the second half of 2014. She taught at Boğaziçi University as a part time lecturer in the second half of 2014. She presently concentrates on conducting research with regard to consumers. Her research interests are in the fields of consumer behavior, food safety, green marketing, sustainable development, and environmental sustainability.

Sergio Ricardo Barros is Associate Professor at the Fluminense Federal University in the Geoenvironmental Analysis Department of the Geosciences Institute. He has a Post-Doctorate from the Laboratory of Technology, Business Management and the Environment - LATEC, a PhD in Geography from the UFF in the area of Territorial and Environmental Planning, and is Coordinator of the REMADS UFF Network for the Environment and Sustainable Development.

Marcio Batista Pereira is a doctoral student in Sustainable Management System - Universidade Federal Fluminense, Professional Master in Social Responsibility and Sustainability Management System - UFF. MBA in Business Law, Distribution of Fuels, Biofuels and Petroleum Derivatives – FGV, Specialist in Oil, Gas and Energy Law – UCAM, Specialist in Public Law.

Nilşah Cavdar Aksoy, Ph.D., received her Ph.D. in Marketing from Gebze Technical University in 2021. Her research interests include consumer behavior, digital marketing, and tourism marketing. Her researches have been published in The Service Industries Journal, Journal of Marketing Management, Appetite, Tourism Economics, and in numerous Turkish-language scholarly journals.

Anacleto Correia (M) is an Associate Professor and lecturer of Management and Information Systems at the Portuguese Navy Academy. He holds a Ph.D. in Computer Science, an M.Sc. in Statistics and Information Management, a B.Sc. degree in Management, and also a B.Sc. at Portuguese Naval Academy. His research interests are focused on requirements engineering, software engineering, process modeling, data mining, machine learning, and business engineering. He has also more than 20 years of experience in industry-leading projects and architecting large software development projects and is the author of several scientific papers in journals and conference proceedings.

Sérgio Luiz França is a Doctor in Civil Engineering (UFF), emphasis on Management, Production, Quality, and Sustainable Development. Graduated in Civil Engineering (UFF). Specialist in Occupational Safety Engineering (UFF). Professor at the Department of Civil Engineering (UFF). Coordinator of the Center for Innovation and Technology for Sustainability (NITS/UFF). Accredited professor at the Postgraduate Program in Management Systems (LATEC/UFF). Member of the Organizing Committee of the National Congress of Excellence in Management (CNEG). Reviewer of national and international scientific journals. Since 2004, he has been working on R&D projects in the areas of Sustainability, Quality, Environment, Social Responsibility, and Occupational Safety.

Arturo Luque Gonzalez is full professor at the Technical University of Manabí, Ecuador, and member of Euro-Mediterranean Observatory on Public Policies and Democratic Quality at the University King Juan Carlos (Spain). He holds a Ph.D. in Social Sciences and Law and a Master of two years about Labor Relations. He supervises several doctoral theses (Ph.D.) in Córdoba (Spain) and in the Basque Country (GEZKI Institute) like a director and co-director. It has 74 indexed articles and his latest publications includes topics about corporate social (Ir)responsibility (How corporate social (ir)responsibility in the textile sector is defined, and its impact on ethical sustainability: An analysis of 133 concepts), transnational companies (The transnational textile companies relationship with environment: a Delphi analysis approach) and their relations with ethics (Corruption in the transnational textile industry: an exception or the rule?), social economy and cooperative system like economic alternative (Socially responsible public management: case spinning development in Ecuador), media analysis and social conflicts (Analysis of the indigenous uprising of Ecuador, 2019).

Leonor Karina Guamán is a professor and junior researcher at the Technical University of Manabí, in addition to being a teaching assistant.

Emanuela Hanes is an independent researcher. Her cooperations include the Vienna University FH BFI Campus Wien, University of Graz and University of Salzburg. Her research interests include China-EU business strategies, RegTech, FinTech, Cryptocurrencies, Geopolitics, Chinese Strategic Planning and Development Policies.

Keyi He is an independent researcher. Her research interests include Truism Economy, FinTech and Chinese business.

Alev Kocak Alan, Ph.D., is an associate professor of Marketing. She received her PhD degree at Gebze Technical University. Her studies focus on consumer behavior, retailing, digital marketing and experiential marketing. Her researches have been published in several scholarly journals including in Journal of Marketing Management, Appetite, Service Business, The Service Industries Journal, Entertainment Computing and in numerous Turkish-language scholarly journals.

Arturo Luque is full professor at the Technical University of Manabí, Ecuador, and member of Euro-Mediterranean Observatory on Public Policies and Democratic Quality at the University King Juan Carlos (Spain). He holds a Ph.D. in Social Sciences and Law and a Master of two years about Labor Relations. He supervises several doctoral theses (Ph.D.) in Córdoba (Spain) and in the Basque Country (GEZKI Institute) like a director and co-director. It has 74 indexed articles and his latest publications includes topics about corporate social (Ir)responsibility (How corporate social (ir)responsibility in the textile sector is defined, and its impact on ethical sustainability: An analysis of 133 concepts), transnational companies (The transnational textile companies relationship with environment: a Delphi analysis approach) and their relations with ethics (Corruption in the transnational textile industry: an exception or the rule?), social economy and cooperative system like economic alternative (Socially responsible public management: case spinning development in Ecuador), media analysis and social conflicts (Analysis of the indigenous uprising of Ecuador, 2019).

Bartolomé Marco-Lajara is Professor of Business Organization at the University of Alicante (Spain). He holds a PhD in Economics and his doctoral dissertation focused in strategic alliances management. His research interests are on Strategic Management and Tourism Management. He is author of several books, book chapters and international articles related to teaching methodology and the areas above mentioned. On the other hand, he is member of the Tourism Research Institute at the University of Alicante since its foundation. He has participated in many public- and private-funded projects, being the main researcher in many of them. He was assistant dean of the Economics Faculty at the University of Alicante during eight years, holding now the position of Head of the Department of Business Organization at this University.

Javier Martínez Falcó is Assistant Professor in the Department of Management at the University of Alicante. In the field of research, he focuses his interest on issues related to the Strategic Management of the Company, specifically in the areas of Knowledge Management and Corporate Sustainability of wine companies, on which he has written several publications in the form of articles, book chapters and contributions to conferences. He has also participated in several national research projects and teaches Strategic Management on the ADE, TADE and DADE degree courses.

Luis Antonio Millán-Tudela is Assistant Professor in the Department of Management at University of Alicante. MBA and Bachelor of Mechanical Engineering, his research focuses on business longevity, and more specifically on the factors that influence the survival of companies. This activity is developed within the research group "Dirección estratégica, conocimiento e innovación en una economía global (DECI-GLOBAL)". He also teaches strategic management in the Degree of Business Administration.

Julio Neto is a PhD in Civil Engineering from Fluminense Federal University (UFF), Master's in Management System (UFF), Postgraduate with MBA in Organization and Strategy, an MBA in Business Management and Graduate in Business Administration. He is currently an Associate Professor at the Fluminense Federal University in the Department of Actuarial Sciences and Finance where he teaches the following subjects: Demographic Dynamics and Quantitative Methods. In the Stricto Sensu Courses, he teaches the following subjects: Life Cycle Analysis, Integrated Reporting, Bibliometrics and Quali-quantitative Methodology. Researcher of the Doctoral Program in Sustainable Management Systems and the Professional Master's Degree in Management Systems, both at UFF, in the areas of Product Life Cycle Management, Product Life Cycle Cost (CCVP), Intangible Assets and Integrated Reporting, topics related to Organizational Sustainability. He serves as Editor-in-Chief of the Brazilian Journal of Operations & Production Management (BJO&PM - ISSN (Online): 2237-8960).

Eduardo Sánchez-García (PhD) is an assistant professor in the Department of Business Organization at the University of Alicante (Spain). His research is in the field of strategic management of the company. Specifically, he focuses on the study of the territorial agglomeration of companies in clusters and the absorptive capacity, and its influence on the innovative performance and entrepreneurial orientation of companies. He is co-author of several papers presented at conferences, both national and international, as well as several articles and book chapters related to his field of research.

Poshan (Sam) Yu is a Lecturer in Accounting and Finance in the International Cooperative Education Program of Soochow University (China). He is also an External Professor of FinTech and Finance at SKEMA Business School (China), a Visiting Professor at Krirk University (Thailand) and a Visiting Researcher at the Australian Studies Centre of Shanghai University (China). Sam leads FasterCapital (Dubai, UAE) as a Regional Partner (China) and serves as a Startup Mentor for AIC RAISE (Coimbatore, India). His research interests include financial technology, regulatory technology, public-private partnerships, mergers and acquisitions, private equity, venture capital, start-ups, intellectual property, art finance, and China's "One Belt One Road" policy.

Patrocinio Zaragoza-Sáez (PhD) is Professor at the University of Alicante (Spain). Her research interests are focused on knowledge management, intellectual capital, sustainable intangible capital and tourism management. She has taken part in several public and private research projects and has published research papers in international journals including Journal of Business Research, Personnel Review, Journal of Knowledge Management, Journal of Intellectual Capital, Knowledge Management Research & Practice, Regional Studies, Current Issues in Tourism, Cornell Hospitality Quarterly, Tourism Management, or International Journal of Contemporary Hospitality Management, among others.

Luiz Zotes graduated in Civil Engineering from the Pontifical Catholic University of Rio de Janeiro (1973), with a master's degree in Civil Engineering from the Fluminense Federal University (1992), and a Ph.D. in Production Engineering from the Federal University of Rio de Janeiro (1994). He is currently a Full Professor at the Fluminense Federal University. He has experience in the areas of General Administration, with an emphasis on Financial Administration, Strategic Management, and Project Management, as well as in the areas of Civil Engineering and Security Engineering.

Index

H

I

K

L

M

N

O

P

R

S

U

V

W

Y

www.ingramcontent.com/pod-product-compliance
Lightning Source LLC
LaVergne TN
LVHW062144300926
849161LV00010B/2618
9781668467503